THE MASCOT

THE MASCOT

The extraordinary story of a young
Jewish boy and an SS extermination squad

MARK KURZEM

RIDER

LONDON · SYDNEY · AUCKLAND · JOHANNESBURG

1 3 5 7 9 10 8 6 4 2

Published in 2007 by Rider, an imprint of Ebury Publishing
A Random House Group Company

Copyright © Mark Kurzem 2007

Mark Kurzem has asserted his right to be identified as the author of this
Work in accordance with the Copyright, Designs and Patents Act 1988

The Random House Group Limited Reg. No. 954009

Addresses for companies within the Random House Group can be found at
www.randomhouse.co.uk

A CIP catalogue record for this book is available from the British Library

The Random House Group Limited makes every effort to ensure that the
papers used in our books are made from trees that have been legally sourced
from well-managed and credibly certified forests. Our paper procurement
policy can be found on www.randomhouse.co.uk

Printed and bound in Great Britain by Clays Ltd, St Ives plc

ISBN 978-1-84-604036-8

To buy books by your favourite authors and register for offers visit
www.rbooks.co.uk

In memory of my mother,
Patricia Kurzem (1937–2003).

CONTENTS

PART II

PART III

ACKNOWLEDGEMENTS

This journey has been a long and difficult one. Without the support, advice, assistance and, above all, the friendship of many, my father and I may not have reached this point.

Sarah Blair has supported me enormously throughout the writing of the book – typing and proof-reading, and offering general advice and encouragement. I am forever grateful to Sarah, and also to Jane Enright, who was similarly unstinting in her help. Thanks also to Luke Mason, who also pitched in with valued work on the manuscript early on in the process.

Robert Guinsler, my agent, has been very generous with his time. His sound advice and good-humour have kept my spirits up during the darker moments of writing. The commitment of the editorial team at Ebury, in particular Judith Kendra, Martin Bryant and Sue Lascelles, was thorough, solid and always very reassuring. Thanks to Caspian Dennis for his words of support and efforts on behalf of the book. I am also especially grateful to Bernard Nyman for protecting the integrity of my work.

At the outset, I had little knowledge of the time and space of the world in which my father lived and moved. I listened to the stories and anecdotes of many who did share his world and my gratitude to them is immense – I am humbled by their lives. The research of countless historians also informed my general understanding of Europe at that time. Special note must be made of the scholarship of Professor Andrew Ezergailis in his book *The Holocaust in Latvia*, which later helped me piece together some of the movements and identities of Latvian troops.

During the actual journeys to Belarus and Latvia I received invaluable support from many individuals and organisations. In particular I want to acknowledge the support of the World Jewish Relief, London; Frank and Galina Schwarz of the Eastern European Jewish Heritage Project in Minsk, who became generous friends and hosts to my mother and father during our time there; Frida Reizman from The Gilf Society in Belarus; The Latvia State Archive for Audiovisual Document in Riga; and Ryuta Akamatsu of Telesis Inc.

In a project such as this, with its inevitably disheartening setbacks and periods of isolation, it is frequently the face of a friend, a kind word now and then, or a laugh that make the world of difference. There are many dear people who did so for me:

Gro Ween, wonderful Daphne Lennie, kind and generous Audrey and Michael Phillips, Jeffery Lies, Rachel Moseley and John Turner, Andrew Woodgate, Uma Battachyra, Jane Enright, Alan Russell, Lee Parsons and Gordon Hickson. Distant friends, too, seemed close at hand and ever present in their support: dear Anne Rahilly, Janet Westwood, Peter Westwood, Lisa Reichenbach, Irene Kuipjers, William J. Holmes, Margaret Chu, Maria Norris, Mary Ida Bagus and family. And then there is Sim Tan, a great friend, who lightened my load considerably.

Special thanks to Eiko and Takaaki (deceased) Hosokawa for their considerable support and friendship during the past years and, similarly, the three branches of my family spread around the globe – the Kurzems in Australia, the Galperin family in Belarus and the Krupitsky family in the US.

Other kinds of help and care bestowed on me must be acknowledged. Thanks to Helen Beer for her information on Yiddish culture, and to Heathcote Williams, a man of erudition and immense talent, who took a strong interest in my father's story, and his partner Diana, who opened her home to me.

Mention must also be made of every staff member at the Oxford Eye Hospital, where I received excellent and compassionate care from all quarters as they struggled to save my eyesight. They did! In particular, I wish to thank Miss Susan Downes, Mr Paul Rosen and Mr John Salmon and their respective teams for holding back that dark prospect.

There are only two people remaining to thank. Firstly, my very dear friend Alastair Phillips, who has shown faith in my ability to tell this story, even when I faltered. His support, encouragement, compassion and care have greatly guided me.

And then last but of course not least, there is my father, who entrusted me with his voice.

AUTHOR'S NOTE

The story of my father, the mascot, is a true one. In order to protect the privacy of some of the individuals and organisations that I have encountered during my research over the years, I have altered various names, titles and details. I have also condensed the time frame of much of the chronology of my research in order to protect the narrative flow of the book, but the actual sequence of events remains true and accurate. I beg your indulgence with these alterations, since they were done with readability in mind. The story therefore remains, in essence, true to all the events and characters it portrays and I take full responsibility for any editorial decisions. In addition, historians' accounts of the Second World War vary. Almost inevitably perhaps, there are discrepancies on such matters as the dates, locations and troop movements involved in certain incidents. An important case in hand would be the precise date of the Slonim Massacre, which still remains unclear and which my father may or may not have witnessed, as reflected in this book. I have also encountered inconsistencies in the recollections of some individuals who were direct witnesses to the times, and have done my best to navigate these discrepancies.

LIST OF ILLUSTRATIONS

Black and white plates

1   Alex in the second of his uniforms, that of the *Wehrmacht*, circa 1943.
2   The Latvian commander, Colonel Karlis Lobe. (*Sourced in* The SS: Hitler's Instrument of Terror *by Gordon Williamson, Spellmount Publishers, 2006*)
3   Alex as a little boy, with Wilma Kulis.
4   Alex with his rifle slung over his shoulder, in the company of officers including Captain Erzum.
5   Alex and officers standing next to the flowers arranged to depict the emblem of the Latvian SS.
6   Alex sitting on his 'rescuer' Sergeant Kulis's knee, next to the floral insignia of the Latvian SS at Volhov, near the Russian Front.
7   Alex standing next to the finished insignia.
8   The newspaper cutting showing Alex in full military uniform, sitting on Lobe's knee and posing among bandaged soldiers and other dignitaries and officials during a hospital tour.
9   A film still showing Alex playing with Aryan children at either Carnikava or Dzintari, the other location where the film was shot.
10 Alex and Auntie in the garden at Carnikava.
11 The Dzenis' holiday home at Carnikava, near Riga.
12 Alex, about nine years old, dressed in a cap, quasi-military jacket and trousers, standing by the steps of Moritzburg Castle outside Dresden.
13 A newspaper cutting showing a still from the Latvian propaganda newsreel in which Alex appeared in 1943.
14 An article about Alex, with a still from the same propaganda film in which he featured.
15 The Latvian certificate from the Orphan's Court of Riga which gave Jekab Dzenis guardianship of Alex, alongside its English translation.
16 The photograph of Alex at the age of nine or ten in 1944, sitting alone at a table decorated with flowers.

Maps   Page

PART I

Map 1: The Baltic States and Belarus

1

THIS IS ALL THAT I KNOW

IF I'm ever asked, 'What's your father like?' a simple answer always escapes me. Even though I can look back on a lifetime spent in his company, I have never been able to take his measure; one part of him is a shy, brooding Russian peasant, who shows a certain air of naivety, if not gullibility, with strangers. Then there is another side: alert, highly gregarious, and astonishingly worldly.

His unexpected appearance on my doorstep in Oxford one May afternoon in 1997 left me more mystified than ever. I was walking back to my digs, weighed down by books that I'd just bought at Blackwell's bookshop. I was looking forward to getting home, already picturing myself there in an armchair by the window, immersed in a new purchase, the door of my study closed to the world for several hours.

As I let myself in I noticed that a scrap of paper had been slipped under the door. It was the stub of a boarding pass for a flight from Melbourne. Written on its margin was 'OVER AT DAPHNES DAD'.

I immediately recognised my father's handwriting. He wrote only in capital letters and without any punctuation. He had always formed his sentences like this; he'd grown up in Eastern Europe during the Second World War and had no formal schooling.

I was taken aback. I had spoken to my father on the phone only a couple of days earlier. He had been at home in Melbourne, watching television with my mother, and when I had asked how their week had been, all he would say was, 'Oh, it's been the same as usual here, son. Nothing much happens in this neck of the woods.'

His tone had not altered in the slightest nor had his voice missed a beat when I asked what they were planning for the coming week: 'No plans really.'

At that moment a slight clicking sound indicated that he had just turned on the speaker-phone so that my mother could join in the conversation. He did this every time I called.

'Winter's really here now,' she had called across the room towards the phone.

'It's freezing, luv. I've already got my dressing gown on.'

I could hear my mother's words above the noise from the television set and could picture her in the chair by the fire. My father would have returned to the living room and more than likely would be lying on the floor in front of her, his feet resting on the hearth to keep them warm. It was a position he'd taken up every winter's evening for as long as I could remember.

'I'm toasting my foots,' he would always joke when we were little.

'Feet, Dad, feet,' my brothers, Martin and Andrew, and I would all chorus.

'Yes, Alex, speak proper English. You've been here long enough now!' my mother would add teasingly. As with much of their banter there was always a playful element that reflected the deep and lasting affection between them.

The three of us chatted on the phone for some time about things that had happened during the past week in Oxford where I was a research student. We touched upon my plans to visit Tokyo – where I'd be for about a month, conducting research on a *matsuri* or ritual festival – in about ten days' time.

My father didn't have much to say about this so the conversation drifted into silence. While he and my mother were always supportive about my path in life, the intense connection I'd always felt towards the culture and history of Japan slightly baffled them. It had become something of a family legend that as a child I would insist on dressing up as a miniature samurai, before going to the corner shop to buy the milk and bread.

'Take care of yourself, Mark,' my mother called across the room. I detected just the slightest note of anxiety in her voice.

'Don't worry, Mum. I'll be fine,' I laughed into the mouthpiece. 'I know Tokyo like the back of my hand.'

I promised to call my parents again before my departure. Then, just as I was hanging up, I heard my father give a nervous little cough. This was often a sign that something was troubling him. I hesitated but before I could ask him if all was well he had put the phone back on the hook. Throughout our conversation he'd given no other indication of the dramatic scenario that was forming in his mind.

My eyes fixed on the note again: 'OVER AT DAPHNES DAD'. Although it had to be true I still couldn't quite believe that my father was here and I felt a rising unease. What was he doing here? Ever since I'd been a student at Oxford I'd wanted him and my mother to visit me. My mother had been keen to do so, but had always been held back by my father's reluctance; he hadn't been back to Europe since leaving in 1949 and was adamant that he hadn't the slightest interest in returning.

'That's the past,' he'd insist fiercely, 'there's nothing there for me. Australia's my home now.'

As I was growing up he often made such assertions, but none of us, family or friends, ever gave them much thought. We had never asked him why he felt this way, and he never volunteered any particular explanation. Just like him, we were absorbed in the business of living in the bright and healthy sunshine of the 'lucky country' as it was so often called.

I made my way over to Daphne's. Daphne was my elderly neighbour from the other side of the street, and she must have been peeping through the curtains in her front room, because the door opened gently before I'd even knocked on it. She stood wide-eyed on her front step, and pointed excitedly towards the back of her house. 'It's your father!' she said, seemingly as astonished as I was. 'But he seems to be nodding off,' she whispered. 'Come in quietly.'

Daphne led me down the narrow hallway and opened the door into her living room. From the doorway I could see my father, his legs stretched out in front of him and his head resting against the wing of the chair so that his eyes were concealed from view. His arms were folded across the small brown case sitting on his lap.

I tiptoed further into the room and whispered a thank you to Daphne for taking my father in and for looking after him. We'd been facing away from my father to avoid disturbing him. But from behind me I heard him stir, and I felt his eyes on me. I turned round. He had raised his head slightly and fixed his strong blue eyes on me with curiosity. I took in his familiar impish features: his arched eyebrows and his high and rosy cheeks that gave him a permanently mischievous air. But I was struck by something else – it was as if I'd captured his image in a photograph and glimpsed an aura of sadness. But this quickly sank beneath the surface of his mobile features.

I can't pretend I wasn't alarmed by his impetuousness, but his presence didn't entirely surprise me. Over the years, I'd become accustomed to his highly impulsive and quixotic nature. He often made decisions on the spur of the moment without much regard for our likes or dislikes.

'Marky!' my father exclaimed warmly.

'Dad?'

'Open your ears. Daphne offered you a drink.'

I wanted to start questioning my father there and then. But I didn't want to make a fuss in front of Daphne, who seemed to have sensed that I was thrown by my father's appearance. She cut in with her own effort to keep the atmosphere calm. 'Let's have a beer. A Foster's,' she said cheerfully, then added that ubiquitous Aussie term of affection 'mate!', which made my father and I both smile despite the fact that I rarely thought of myself as an Aussie.

Not only was I not a blond, blue-eyed surfer boy, or a footy player, but my years in schools away from the sunburnt country had left my body with an academic pallor.

'To Melbourne!' Daphne toasted.

'To Melbourne,' my father responded with a sheepish grin in my direction.

It was early evening before we finally made our way back across the street. In the half-light I fumbled with the door key while my father waited patiently behind me, coughing nervously.

The door open, I turned to help him. I reached down to the small battered brown case beside him, but his hand shot out immediately, snatching the case from my grasp. 'Let me take that,' he said emphatically.

He had always been protective of his case – in fact it was an unstated rule that nobody apart from him should ever lay hands upon it. The case was everything to him. He took it with him everywhere, clasping it so closely under his arm it might have been grafted on to his ribcage.

It was all he'd brought with him from Europe at the end of the Second World War. In it he carried his few meagre belongings: mementoes from his childhood in Russia and Latvia. For as long as I could remember the case had been a feature of our family life. Although we knew that it contained photographs, documents and other remnants of his past, none of us had ever been allowed to see inside it. Instead we'd have to wait until he decided to display its contents to us. My mother would sometimes chide him for his secretiveness, exclaiming, 'For God's sake, Alex, you guard it as if it's Fort Knox! What have you got in there, the Crown Jewels?'

When he was at home, my father invariably kept the case in the bottom of his wardrobe. It was always locked and, to give it extra and somewhat superstitious security, it was hidden beneath my Catholic mother's family Bible. He kept the keys to the case in his pocket and out of our reach at all times. This of course gave the case an almost totemic power over our imaginations and this was never more strongly felt than when my father decided to tell us a story from his past, using the case as a prop.

This usually took place once or twice a month, after my mother had done the dinner dishes, and we had all settled down in front of the 'telly', absorbed in some police drama or thriller. My father would take up his position on the floor in front of the fireplace – regardless of the season – and my mother would sit in her armchair close to the hearth.

It always seemed as if the deepening silence amongst us as we became absorbed in the 'idiot box', as my mother liked to call it, created in my father the urge to assert himself as the centre of the household. He seemed to be saying tacitly: 'I have a much better story to tell than the one you're watching now.'

He would become visibly restless, raising his head slightly as if he were straining to hear something. Then his eyes would begin to dart about the room, unfocused, as if he were staring into another world and quite spellbound by what he saw there. Above all else, it was his slight, barely audible clearing of the throat, as if he were struggling to release his trapped voice, that would alert us all to what was coming.

He would rise from the floor and disappear from the room while we silently prepared ourselves for his return. With a nod from our mother someone would turn off the television. Even if we'd been on the point of learning who the villain was in *Homicide* or *Consider Your Verdict* – our favourites – we never uttered a word of protest. We were all much more riveted by what was coming.

If we were lucky my mother would even pass us each a small bar of chocolate. We would wait impatiently, my brothers and I fidgeting and wiggling about on the couch, for our father's return some moments later, case in hand. He would place it gently on the floor in the centre of the room and prepare himself for his performance.

With a small flourish he would draw out a photograph or document, creased and frayed around the edges and yellow with age. Then he would abruptly close the lid on the case, placing the selected item on top.

Whatever he chose was used as a prop around which he would weave a tale, sometimes no more than a series of fragments, about his life during the war, and more frequently, about his adventures on the freight trains in the Australian outback or with a travelling circus in the 1950s. As the story unfolded, we would sit in rapt attention, licking our chocolate bars. From time to time he would reach back into the case to fetch another memento and would slowly turn it over as if doing a conjuring trick. In fact, my father did have the aura of a magician, the case being a magician's hat from which he'd pluck one rabbit after another in quick precisely timed succession. My father never had to lower his eyes to locate his next prop. He would draw out each one as if by divination. We were always enchanted by his stories and by the artful way he related to his battered old case.

Apart from his love for Eastern European foods, the case seemed to provide my father with his only connection to his past – the only one he seemed to want. From the moment he'd set foot on Australian soil in December 1949, my father had embarked with unabashed enthusiasm on his journey toward becoming an authentic Aussie – 'dinkydi' – through and through. Quickly he came to believe he was one. When out driving, for example, he would curse a bad manoeuvre from another car as the work of a 'bloody new Australian!' driver, forgetting that he himself – cursing in broken English with his thick Russian accent – was pretty far removed from being 'true blue' – in the minds of many Anglos.

Though he cut a very different figure from the brawny, rough-and-ready Australian men who followed the game, it was, above all, his love for 'footy' – Australian Rules football – that in his mind admitted him to the world of 'being an Aussie'. On Saturday afternoons he'd wash the family car in the driveway of our house, wearing headphones so he could tune into the match of the day. He'd listen in rapt attention to the radio commentary, especially if his beloved team, 'The Magpies', were playing. It was the only time my brothers and I weren't allowed to bother him, and it was the only time he displayed any impatience, if we tried to interrupt.

My father's love for Australia extended far beyond the 'footy' and it was rare that anything ever compared favourably to the place he had called 'home' since he'd arrived there as a refugee on board a ship called *Nelly*. He even carried a photo of the *Nelly* in his wallet as a measure of his attachment, five decades later, to the vessel that had ferried him away from war-torn Europe to the haven of Australia.

'From the moment they set foot in Australia,' he would say, 'people are free to be who they are, without persecution, and to make something of themselves.' Then he'd exclaim, raising his eyes to the heavens theatrically, 'Why on earth would I want to go back to Russia? The poverty, the weather. God forbid! You'd have to be crazy!'

He would put himself forward as an example. 'Look at me,' he would say, 'if I'd not come to Australia I'd be stuck in a freezing field, somewhere in the middle of nowhere in Russia, looking after sheep. Here, I've built up my own business.'

The tone was not one of boastful pride, but rather of modest gratitude. To him, his adopted country was the 'best little place on earth'.

I'd always admired my father's attitude, but it set him apart from the immigrant parents of many of my friends who would often complain about how much better life had been back in the mother country.

The outer western suburbs of Melbourne where I grew up was a predominantly immigrant area populated by, among others, Italians, Maltese and Greek families, and many of them seemed dominated by a longing to return to their homeland. They would cling tenaciously to their own language, even as it began to atrophy, and use just enough English to make themselves understood. They would surround themselves with clothing, foods, religions and customs which helped keep their pre-émigré world alive.

Not so my father. He never showed any interest at all in his Russian origins, and because he didn't, we didn't either.

Despite his determination to be an 'Aussie' in every sense of the word, it would also be true to say that my father and I didn't bond over the 'footy' or any other sport or 'mateship' rituals which would have been typical of a father–son relationship in Australia in the 1970s. Rather, it was the image of my father with his case indelibly stamped on my imagination that created a bond between us. Whenever I picture my father in my mind's eye, he is invariably holding the case. Yet I still hadn't seen inside it.

I reached across and picked up, instead of his case, the small travel bag at his feet, the type that you would take for a weekend break, not a trek halfway around the world. We made our way down the dark corridor and into my tiny living room. My father remained standing, taking in his surroundings.

'So this is where you live,' he declared rhetorically. 'Small,' he added, raising his eyebrows melodramatically, 'like a cave or a bunker.' Then he declared, glowing at the thought, 'Not sunny like Australia.'

I observed him as he stood there in the half-light of my living room. His features had suddenly crumpled, and he seemed tired from the long flight.

'Dad,' I said as gently as I could, 'do you feel like talking about this at all?'

'About what?'

The question provoked him to shift away from me to the other end of the room, where he began to examine the prints on the walls, and the Japanese porcelain arranged on the mantelpiece.

'What do you think, Dad?' I said, baffled. 'Why you're here, of course.'

'What's the matter with you?' he retorted innocently, 'I told you I would visit you one day. To see what kind of life my number one son has made for himself.'

He stopped at the window, peering out at the small rear courtyard. Mollified a fraction, all I could manage was, 'A bit of advance warning would have been nice, Dad.'

'How much notice do you need?' he said lightly. 'I won't take up much space.'

Space wasn't the issue, of course, but it was clear he wouldn't entertain any further discussion about his sudden appearance. He turned towards me, and, for the first time, I noticed a gaping hole where his front tooth should have been.

'Your tooth!' I said, pointing to the gap.

'It fell out on the way here. Somewhere over India I think,' he said, 'but the rest of me got here OK.'

Despite his glib remark, the gap made him seem vulnerable, wounded even, and prevented me from pursuing him any further.

Over supper in the kitchen he suddenly confessed to me that my mother had no idea that he was with me in Oxford and that he had told her a 'fib'. He had said to her that he needed to go to Sydney to see Otto, an old friend from the circus who was in poor health. This elderly friend, another émigré, had taken my father under his wing when he first arrived in Australia and now that Otto was all alone, it was natural that my father should go up to Sydney to help him.

My father said that he had promised to call my mother every day and he was ready to do so now. I led him to the phone in the study but then immediately returned to the kitchen, afraid that listening in would make me a collaborator in this unfathomable charade.

But of course my collusion was inevitable. Even as I waited in the other room I tried to avoid making noises that might betray my father's odd scheme to my mother.

Through the partly opened door I could hear him chatting amiably with her and I tried to keep track of their conversation.

'Yes, I'm OK, luv. The doctor said Otto will be fine. He just needs rest,' I heard him say, 'I think it would be better if I stayed here a few more days to keep him company, to get things organised for him.'

The tone of my father's voice as he explained his plan to my mother sounded just as convincing as his words. In fact I was sure my mother would have no doubts about the situation in Sydney; extending his visit to Otto would have seemed to her to be perfectly natural behaviour for her husband. He was a caring person and over the years had always gone to great lengths to help his friends, often putting their needs before his own. Sensing this, my mother often complained that people were taking advantage of him, but he would always just shrug and say gently, 'That might be so, luv, but don't be hard on them. Anyway I'd rather be kind to someone, even if they don't deserve it, than turn my back on them.'

I peeped into the room to see if my father was showing any unease about having to lie in this way. It was not obvious to me that he was. He was moving around the study casually, still holding the handset and pretending to my mother to be in Otto's home.

'Naah, between you and me,' he whispered into the mouthpiece, 'it's not much of a place, luv. Dark and dingy. Poor chap.'

He broke off the conversation to put on his reading glasses and then began to examine the contents of my bookshelf, now and then removing a book, perusing its cover and then replacing it. I watched him do this a number of times, before he noticed me in the doorway. He nodded at me, indicating that I should leave the room, but I remained leaning against the frame of the door, slightly vexed at the way he'd described my study – dark and dingy – and passed it off as Otto's place. I watched him as he signed off:

'Bye bye then, luv. I'll call you tomorrow. Around the same time.'

He put the receiver down.

'Poor chap?' I repeated, jumping in immediately, 'do you mean Otto or me?'

'What are you talking about? Otto, of course.' He gave me an impish grin.

In the days that followed my father seemed reluctant to move, as if, having reached Oxford, he was seeking refuge there, and was content to lie low. We made occasional trips into town, wandering from college to college, as I pointed out places and objects of interest. My father was attentive to my words yet someone who knew him well, as I believed I did, would have noticed that he still seemed distracted as if something was bothering him. He seemed to have some unfinished business to address just as he had when he arrived.

One evening towards the end of that week, we sat in silence over dinner. We had run out of small talk, and it was becoming increasingly difficult to skirt around the larger question of his entirely unexplained appearance in Oxford. The evasive dance we'd been doing all week was proving more and more difficult to sustain.

As he sat opposite me, he began to play with his spoon, running it around the edge of his empty bowl while at the same time shifting his gaze from object to object around the room.

Then out of the blue he announced that he had decided to return to Australia the following evening. I was dumbfounded and found it hard to believe that the visit might now come to an end without my having the slightest understanding as to what had instigated it.

'So that's it then, Dad?'

'What?' he looked up at me, perplexed.

'You've made up your mind to go home? Just like that?'

'Well I've got to go home sometime,' he laughed, 'Mum will be wondering what I'm up to in Sydney. That reminds me, I'd better check the weather there in case she asks me.'

He clicked his fingers at me. 'Check in the newspaper for me, luv,' he demanded.

I grunted in a half-hearted way, unsure whether even doing this for my father was tantamount to some form of complicity with him.

He always had affectionate names for me – 'number one son' and 'Marky' were his favourites, but often he would use the endearment 'luv' quite casually, and without any of its usual cloying overtones. Despite these surface intimacies, however, I never felt that I was being taken into his confidence. He was a man who kept his own counsel.

'Go on,' he pressed me.

I gave in, reaching for the newspaper.

Mystified, it crossed my mind that a change of scenery might have a salutary effect on us both, and perhaps even help to break our odd impasse. Still partly hidden behind the broadsheet, I suggested we spend his final day in London. He had never visited and readily agreed.

Despite my perplexity about his visit, and the awkward and frustrating silences that had punctuated our week together I still wanted to please my father and leave him with some happy memories of his time in England.

We began to make a plan for how we would spend the day in London, at the end of which I would put him on the Underground to Heathrow in time for his departure to Melbourne. But before that, we would have lunch at the Cafe Daquise, an old Polish restaurant in South Kensington.

The Daquise was known for its traditional Eastern European food, always my father's favourite. Sometimes during my childhood as we sat down to our Australian meals of roast lamb or fish and chips, my father would decline to join us, preferring instead dill pickles, rye bread and – even now I shudder at its sight and smell – raw herring.

I hoped that the Daquise might remind him of the cafes and deli-catessens of Acland Street, one of the few places in Melbourne in the 1960s and 1970s where he could indulge in these delicacies, and that he would find himself back in the kind of world where he could relax.

As a child I used to love going to Acland Street with my father to buy cheesecake from one of its Eastern European bakeries. I would stand next to him, holding his hand, as he stared into the front windows laden with pastries stacked high on display trays.

Thinking about Acland Street now, one recollection came unexpectedly to mind. I had forgotten it completely so I was a little perplexed at its sudden appearance. The memory seemed to have forced itself to the surface in order to point me toward an explanation for my father's visit.

On the occasion in question I had noticed him staring intently between gaps in the trays into the darker recesses of a pastry shop. I followed his gaze and saw that he was peering into a world I had never seen before: an exotic scene of somewhat alien-looking women, dressed up to the nines, with vividly painted lips and exaggerated eyebrows. My father seemed captivated by their mask-like faces, and the studied and individual way in which they ate – their hands delicately poised, their fingers, laden with gold rings and bracelets, lightly touching their cheeks as they brought forks laden with moist cheesecake to their lips. Looking back on it now it was as if these women were in some way or other after-images of an arcane world that my father somehow recognised and was enchanted with.

I suddenly remembered another incident from one of those visits to Acland Street. One day, as we stood before the window of a cake shop, I noticed that my father had become distracted by something reflected in the window. It was the image of a man behind us, leaning on the bonnet of a car parked directly opposite. The man's arms were folded across his chest, and he gazed frankly, and with a friendly smile, at my father. I noticed that when his eyes met this man's my father seemed to freeze to the spot, even though this man continued to smile broadly, even giving my father a gentle wave. My father gripped my hand tightly and abruptly moved on, as if eager to escape from something. In retrospect, it seemed that even though the man did not know my father, he recognised something about him.

While my father was clearly attracted to these denizens of Acland Street sometimes I saw him cock his ear too, sparrow-like, as if to listen for something. He also seemed slightly afraid of them. It was as if what he saw through the shop windows was the landscape of another life, part of a web that threatened to ensnare him, as if he belonged to them and they to him.

2

THE HAEMORRHAGE

THE train into London was almost empty, and we found ourselves alone in our carriage. My father sipped his coffee and stared out at the measured English landscape. For a second I caught sight of his reflection in the carriage window and saw that he'd been staring at me, evaluating me. His expression softened when my eyes met his.

'You've done well, son. You're an educated man,' he said. I felt a little embarrassed to see him beaming with such pride. It was not his habit to praise me or my brothers.

I turned my head to look out the window, mumbling 'Thanks, Dad.'

'I've never been to school, what with the war and things,' he continued.

'But you told me you were at school in the displaced persons camp outside Hamburg.'

'Yeah, just for about a year. But I didn't learn one single thing. None of the teachers could control me – I was a little devil. I just wouldn't settle. I must have been restless from the war.'

These comments had come out of the blue and without any apparent or obvious connection to our trip to London. I was intrigued because he had never been willing to discuss his schooling before, cursorily dismissing any questions we posed. But before I could engage him any further, he abruptly raised his newspaper, hiding behind it and lowering it only when we had safely reached Paddington Station.

The sunlight was almost blinding, as we emerged from the Underground at South Kensington. It was not yet 11 a.m. and I hoped that the émigrés who usually settled themselves at the Daquise mid-mornings would by now be there in full force: drinking coffee, eating cheesecake and chatting volubly. If we got there any later the cacophony of Eastern European languages, especially Polish and Russian, would be supplanted by the lunchtime rush of local office workers and I wanted everything to be undilutedly nostalgic.

We made our way to the cafe. I stood back as I watched my father peer through the Daquise's front window. He put on his glasses, perusing the menu posted in the window.

'Look, Marky, they've got latkes as well!' He gripped me by the elbow, trying to hasten me inside. 'I'm starving. Let's eat,' he declared as if he couldn't wait another moment. 'Open sesame,' he chuckled with relish as he pushed through the door. We stepped across the threshold.

From her stool behind the cash register the matronly owner, precisely coiffed, cast a disdainful look at us and raised her bulk from the stool just enough to pass menus across the counter in a desultory fashion. With a barely detectable nod she indicated that we should sit wherever we could find a table. It was what I imagined to be a typical Eastern European welcome, a sour melancholy passing for enthusiasm.

We settled in a corner at the rear of the cafe. My father looked around the room, taking in his surroundings. Customers sat huddled at tables, drinking coffee, gesticulating, seemingly engaged in debate. At other tables, men or women sat alone, smoking, staring into space, or immersed in foreign newspapers.

'God forbid. Where have you brought me, son?' he joked somewhat edgily.

'I thought you'd like it here, Dad. Just like Acland Street.'

He smiled at me, seemingly touched by my consideration, then visibly relaxed.

'Anyway, it's the food you come here for. What'll you have, Dad?'

'Cabbage rolls of course.'

'Not the latkes?' I exclaimed.

'You think latkes?'

'Why not both? Remember, you've a long journey ahead of you tonight. You need to keep your strength up!'

'But I don't have to flap my arms all the way back to Melbourne, I hope,' he joked.

He nodded, leaning back in his seat. As he did so I noticed that as ever he was guarding his battered case closely, nursing it like a ventriloquist's dummy on his knee. I offered to take it.

'Give it over here, Dad. I'll put it against the wall behind me. Next to your weekend bag.'

'It's fine here, son,' he said, gently dismissing my fussing.

'C'mon, I'm not going to steal it or anything.'

He shook his head emphatically.

'It's more than my life is worth, your life too,' he declared, 'it's your inheritance.'

We both laughed, knowing that it was true: he really did have little else but his case to leave me.

'Is that all I'll get?' I shot back, with mock disappointment.

'Be grateful for whatever comes your way,' he grinned at me.

I signalled to the elderly waitress, who waddled over to take our order and gave a contemptuous snort in response to our indecisiveness. For an instant I feared that this unfriendly reception would dampen my father's interest in the surroundings, but I needn't have worried. He found her behaviour amusing and stared after her, making light of her moodiness. 'We must have got her on a good day,' he whispered, a twinkle in his eyes.

Just as on our visits to Acland Street years ago, my father was alert to the sounds of the various Eastern European languages he could hear around him – Polish, Russian and even a smattering of Yiddish. He glanced over his shoulder, stretching to see who owned the voices. Clearing his throat, he turned back to me. The sounds seemed to have triggered something within.

'You know before I went to Riga when I was a child . . .' he started.

'You mean when you were lost in the forest?'

'No. Even earlier than that,' he said quietly.

'I thought you couldn't remember anything from that time?'

'There is something I remember,' he said and paused for what seemed an inordinate amount of time. Then he leant forward to confide in me. 'I have these two words locked away inside of me. I've never forgotten them.' Then he was silent. I waited.

'One is Koidanov,' he said finally, 'and the other is Panok.' He repeated the words, 'Panok. And Koidanov.' Immediately after the words left his lips, he seemed distracted by them.

'Are they the names of people? Places? What do they mean?'

He leant even closer across the table towards me. Then he shook his head, grim-faced, and shrugged: 'No idea.' Then, just as suddenly, he was energised by a thought. 'But you know what I think, son? Those words are the key to who I was before the forest, before the Latvian soldiers . . .'

'When you were with your Russian parents?'

That was all that I could ask because that was the extent of what any of us knew of my father's pre-war life.

He fell silent, again seemingly lost in his thoughts. Then he said quietly, 'If that's who I am.'

'If that's who you are?' I blurted out sharply. 'What on earth do you mean, Dad?'

I shot him a questioning look but his eyes darted around, avoiding mine. I tried another tack.

'You've remembered these words all your life?' I asked more gently. 'Have you told anybody about them?'

He shook his head. He stared at his hands which rested on the table.

'I can't understand that, Dad.'

His head was slightly bowed, perhaps under the burden of what he had just revealed or in a vain attempt to deflect my line of questioning.

But I persisted: 'Why did you keep them secret?'

He gave a shrug then abruptly pulled away from me, back to his side of the table.

'It wasn't a secret,' he said, 'I just thought that there was nothing to say about them. I didn't know what they meant and I didn't know how I could find out what they were.'

He seemed exasperated by my puzzlement. 'And besides,' he smirked, 'Mum and I were busy raising you three boys. I didn't have time to think about anything else.'

I suddenly pictured my mother sitting alone in the living room in Melbourne.

'Does Mum know about this?' I asked.

'I don't want her to know,' my father said, 'for the time being. I just don't want to worry her.'

'Why tell me then? And why now?'

'I want you to do something for me, son,' Though he tried to seem off-hand there was an underlying note of urgency in his voice. 'I want you to find out what these words mean.'

He leant further back in his chair, folding his arms in a gesture of finality as if all he wanted me to do was to discover the significance of these words and not trouble myself with his reasons for keeping them secret.

'I want to know who I am. I want to know who my people are before I die,' my father said, and then leaning forward across the table again, he added pensively, 'I want to place a flower on my mother's grave. Wherever that might be.'

I fell silent. I was shocked.

'Please, son,' he said as if he needed to convince me.

While I was thrown by his request, never being able to recall a time when he'd asked me so directly for my help, it went without saying that I

would help him, even if what he wanted still seemed so vague and tenuous.
I pulled out a piece of paper.

'Tell me how to spell the words . . .'

We were interrupted by the waitress who now arrived with our meals,
and slapped the plates down on the table. We ate in silence, my father bent
forward, as was his habit, with one arm curled around his plate, protecting
the steaming cabbage rolls as he devoured them greedily.

I had lost my appetite, however. I thought about his brown case again. It
was true that I saw the case and all the stories it contained as my inheritance. Despite its battered exterior I saw it as something laden with riches,
especially all the tales of my father's life since his arrival in Australia. They
were the kind of enchanting stories of human bravado that would make any
child proud of his father.

By contrast I felt more ambivalent about the stories of his childhood in
Europe during the war. I could never get a clear picture of what had gone
on. My father painted that time in the broadest of brushstrokes as if his
memories of the period were no more than a skeletal blur.

There was one particular story that my father told us often that we
enjoyed more than the others. It was the story of the time he spent wandering alone in a dark, overgrown forest at the age of five or six, when he had
become separated from his parents, two Russian pigherders. He could
never remember how this had actually occurred, he said, but he always
believed that the trauma of it, together with his time spent alone in the forest – for weeks and perhaps even months, he was never sure – caused him
to forget both his name and his origins.

My father told us that he'd wandered alone in freezing winter conditions. At night he would tie himself inside the forks of trees to survive the
wolves whose howling he could hear in the distance. As he sat high above
the ground, shaking with cold, swinging his tiny legs, waiting for the first
light of dawn, he imagined sometimes that he could hear his mother's voice
calling out to him. But he could never remember her words. This part of
the story prompted our avid enquiries.

'Weren't you afraid, Daddy?' we would ask. 'Could you see the wolves'
eyes glowing in the dark?'

He would be dismissive of any questions that ever suggested that
he'd been at all vulnerable, always responding as if he'd been brave and
confident, and readily equipped for any contingency. 'Naah, boys,' he'd say,
'I'd just make sure that I'd tied the knot tight enough.'

As he told us all this, as if by an agreed upon formula, one of us would usually exclaim insistently: 'But, Daddy, you must know where you come from. Everyone does!'

When he would deny that he did, it only made us more insistent: 'You must know, Daddy!'

My mother, always very protective of my father, would usually step in at moments like these when our naivety made us ruthless, pressing him too much. 'Boys! Leave your father alone,' she would insist gently. 'Settle down now, and let him get on with his story.'

As the years passed and he retold this story, my mother, brothers and I all came to accept the ground rules he set: sit in silence and ask nothing. But in my imagination I would create my own child-like images of my father as a little boy, a Mowgli-like creature wide-eyed with fear, despite what he'd said about his courage, being chased, as I imagined, down dark twisting forest trails by some large shadowy figure, possibly half-human half-beast.

My father told us that the turning point in his life came when he was found by Latvian soldiers in a forest on the outskirts of a deserted village somewhere near the Russian border in 1942. They had fed him and tidied him up. It was then that two figures surfaced who would play important roles in his future. The first was Kārlis Lobe, the commander of the Latvian Police Brigade whose soldiers had discovered him, and taken it upon themselves to give the boy a new name. They called him Uldis Kurzemnieks. (Later on my father would abbreviate Uldis Kurzemnieks to Alex Kurzem to spare his fellow Australians the unpronounceable foreign name.) Lobe later gave my father a false birthday, chosen for him because it commemorated Latvian National day, the 18th of November, and he had then made another key decision about my father's life. He had eventually arranged for him to be removed from the potential dangers of armed conflict at the front and be taken to the safety of Riga and to the home of a Latvian family called Dzenis, who ran a chocolate factory.

I looked around at the other tables in the Daquise, and the sight of many elderly European gentlemen of a certain bearing led me to reflect on my father's account of his life with Lobe. My father was always circumspect, even evasive whenever I asked him about Lobe. His response never varied: 'He was a good soldier. He was firm with me, but always fair.'

When I would try to draw him out further on Lobe's appearance in those days, he was always dismissive: 'He looked like a soldier. That's all. Nothing special.' I could never get my father to say anything more than that, so that over the years in my imagination I came to picture Lobe as tall and upright, and with an aristocratic, almost Prussian, manner. In the mental snapshot I had formed, Lobe was holding my wildly laughing father, at that time a boy, aloft in the air. Somehow this image became my own private expression of gratitude to the man who had 'rescued' my father from the wolves.

Now, having just learnt of a new element to my father's past, I began to wonder what other revelations would follow.

After we left the Daquise we wandered the streets of South Kensington, slightly disorientated. It was just as well that we had no special plans for the remainder of the afternoon. It seemed as if the little crack that had appeared in the surface of my father's demeanour less than an hour ago had now somehow resealed itself. He was content to walk in silence, as was I.

Eventually we came to the underground tunnel that took us beneath Exhibition Road. Its tiles provided cool relief from the unusually stifling humidity of the late May afternoon. The tunnel was deserted, and as we moved into its deepest section, the sound of the overhead traffic became muted. In the stillness our footsteps echoed back at us. This had a disquieting effect on my father. The rat-a-tat-tat of our steps made his body stiffen as if he'd heard something I could not.

Suddenly he stopped and stared at me.

'Something terrible happened,' he said. I waited for what he was going to say next. He studied my face, but then turned away from me facing the wall. 'No. Forget it,' he said. 'It's nothing really.'

'What do you mean nothing? You just said something terrible happened. What was terrible, Dad?'

He turned to face me again. 'Forget it, son. You wouldn't understand.'

I could only see his silhouette against the light from the other end of the tunnel. I moved closer towards him. His face was pale and his features had become inexplicably gaunt. He breathed more heavily than usual as if trying to expel some inner tension.

'It was terrible what they asked me to do!'

'Who are they? What did they make you do?'

He was distracted again this time by the sound of someone else entering the tunnel, and stiffened again at the echo of approaching steps. I was baffled by his response to these innocuous sounds and instinctively reached out to him and grasped his arm in an attempt to soothe his nerves. I was surprised by my own gesture as neither my father nor I were physically demonstrative with each other.

A man in a suit hurried past us, head down. My father gave him an embarrassed smile. We must have made a strange scene – two men standing in silence in the dark centre of the tunnel.

By the time the figure had faded into the distance, my father seemed calmer. I could almost feel his heart slowing down. After some moments he had completely composed himself.

'Tell me, Dad,' I said gently, 'are you in trouble? Is there something the matter in Melbourne?'

He shook his head. 'Naah, son. It's not worth worrying about. Just something that came into my mind. Out of nowhere.'

He repeated the words 'Out of nowhere', and then seemed genuinely perturbed by what he'd just blurted out as if he'd given too much away. But in fact he hadn't given anything away at all.

'I won't force you, Dad,' I persisted, 'but if you feel like telling me . . .'

He stared at me with a blank face. Finally he spoke, 'C'mon, Marky, I feel like an ice cream. Where can we get one?'

He loved sweets and desserts, especially chocolate and ice cream, but I knew immediately that this abrupt change of topic was nothing more than a ploy to try to make light of what he had just said. Yet such was the force of his personality that I felt compelled to go along with it.

'Let's get out of here,' he said, taking charge, 'this place makes me feel . . .' He clicked his fingers as he habitually did when he was trying to search for a word in English, 'claustrophobic.' He chuckled lightly at finding the right word so quickly. He put his arm around my shoulder affectionately – again in an uncharacteristic gesture – and began to move us both towards the light at the far end of the tunnel.

We surfaced into the hubbub of the street above. My father, who had always had keen eyesight, spotted a gaudy pink-striped ice cream van further down the road, and after queuing for his favourite – 'Strawberry. I love strawberry' – we made our way to a park nearby. As we walked along I cast a furtive glance at him. His face was alight with a child-like pleasure.

A small crowd had gathered in the park, enjoying the late afternoon sun. We found a bench, and silently observed the children playing on the grass nearby. My father must have quietly drawn his case on to his lap. Suddenly out of the corner of my eye I noticed that he was fumbling in his pocket for something. He pulled out the well-worn key and inserted it into the case's lock. As always, he opened the case just wide enough for his hand to slip inside. He pulled out a flat envelope, carefully closing the lid of the case before passing the envelope to me.

'What's this?' I asked in a low voice.

'Something you should see, son.'

I felt a sense of trepidation and hesitated to open it. As I made a move to do so he suddenly snatched it back.

'On second thoughts let me do it!' He opened the envelope and slowly withdrew a small photograph. He gripped it firmly, grimacing as if in pain.

I drew closer to him and gazed down at the photo. Although it had discoloured with age, the image was relatively sharp. It was of a small boy no more than six or seven years old, posing in front of a gaily decorated Christmas tree. He was dressed in a military uniform, replete with knee-high marching boots that must have been made especially for him so that he resembled a miniaturised version of the stereotypical soldier one sees in war movies.

My eyes scanned the image of the boy more closely, and for a moment I caught my breath. It was my father, staring frankly at the camera.

What was my father doing dressed like this? What sort of people would let a child dress in this fashion? Who took this photograph? When was it taken? And why take a photograph like this? A myriad of questions ran through my mind at once. Where was it taken? In Russia? In Latvia? Was it connected to Koidanov or Panok?

It didn't make sense. My father had never mentioned being a soldier, only a boy scout of sorts.

I began to move even closer to my father in order to scrutinise the details. But before I could he abruptly shoved the photo back into its innocent white envelope. He slid the envelope back into the brown case. 'It's awful, son,' was all he managed to say.

'Is this why you're here?' I asked. 'Is that what you've been hedging around all week?'

He avoided my eyes. 'It's a complicated story. We'll talk another time.'

'Where did it come from, Dad?'

'It's from the war.' He said nothing else.

At that moment my feelings about the case, my so-called inheritance shifted. I resented it and felt an inexplicable disgust towards it and even towards my father. I shrank away, wanting to escape both. I wondered what else the case might contain. Was there something even darker, if that was possible, than what I had just seen? I found myself questioning how much he'd left out of the stories he'd been telling us all our lives. What hadn't he told me, or my mother or my brothers about his childhood? I began to see the battered case as a Pandora's box, which now it had been truly opened, might never be shut again. I couldn't help wondering whether he'd be quite as protective of it now that he had intimated the secrets it might contain.

It seems absurd now but instead of pressing him further I looked around me, worried that someone nearby might have caught sight of the photograph and could have identified my father as the boy in it. Or indeed observed any resemblance to me. Nobody had noticed anything. The family on the neighbouring bench were chatting happily amongst themselves. I began to act as if nothing had happened. I glanced at my watch. The afternoon was almost gone. 'C'mon, Dad, you've got a plane to catch. I'll take you to the Underground.'

I grasped his free hand and rose, barely giving him time to secure his case, and headed off in the direction of South Kensington station.

The platform was crowded with commuters. The train appeared suddenly.

The doors opened directly where we were standing and passengers began to pile out. I eased my father out of their way and to one side of the carriage doors. By now, his head had dropped forward, making him seem even more dispirited than before, almost lifeless.

I feared saying anything at all to him, even a simple goodbye or a bland 'Safe journey, Dad.'

In a flash, however his listlessness evaporated just as if he'd been struck by a bolt of lightning. Above the din of the platform he shouted at me breathlessly:

'It was Lobe and Dzenis – something they wanted me to do years ago – Dzenis made me do it – Dzenis said tell everyone you saw nothing – that Lobe did nothing. But it's not true! It's not true! I did see things.'

The words spilled out of him in an uncontrollable torrent, as if some old scar tissue had burst open to reveal a festering wound.

'Dzenis told me that they had saved my life and now it was my turn to repay them. I didn't want to, but I felt that I had no choice. Dzenis had already written it so I just signed it. I did wrong.'

He was beside himself and in a paroxysm of fear, anxiety and shame, and yet he seemed driven by the need to speak.

A voice over the loudspeaker warned us to mind the closing doors.

'Dad, step back!' I shouted. But before I fully realised what was happening, he had grabbed his bags and squeezed through the doors as they slammed shut. We stood facing each other, separated by glass. My father's eyes were wide open, almost bulbous as if he were starved of oxygen. He seemed to be in shock, astonished by his own involuntary outburst. I was appalled by his transformation but could do nothing. A railway guard's whistle warned me to back off for safety.

The train began to move away. I followed the carriage, breaking into a jog to keep pace with it. Through its window I saw my father find a seat and settle down, delicately nursing his case. As the train gathered speed, his carriage moved away from me. He raised his hand in a tentative farewell. For just an instant I glimpsed in him the boy in the uniform. Then the train was gone, swallowed up by the tunnel, leaving only the rattling of the tracks.

I remember very little of my return journey to Oxford. The train soon left behind the outer suburbs of London, and began to weave its way through the countryside that I normally found so comforting. Now as the certainties of my life fell by the wayside, it seemed quite alien.

What had my father seen that he had not mentioned to our family before? What had the chocolate-factory manager Dzenis wanted my father to lie about? He had mentioned Lobe but what was the lie about Lobe? It seemed from his sudden emotional convulsion that the roles Dzenis and Lobe had played in my father's life were far more complex than I'd been led to believe. And, as much as I tried, I could not erase the image of that photograph from my mind's eye. I regretted that I hadn't had the presence of mind either to pull him back out of the carriage, or to jump on to the train with him. And now, of course, there was no way that I could persuade my father to explain himself.

When I reached home, I headed straight to bed, curling up, foetus-like, under the covers, feeling vulnerable and exposed by the bewildering events of the afternoon. Yet sleep eluded me as I imagined my father at this moment. He would be airborne by now. I pictured him perched upright in his cramped aeroplane seat, still nursing his case, many of whose secrets I now suspected had tormented him for most of his life.

It dawned on me that I was losing my father and would never have him back again in the same way that I had always known him. As my father. As Dad. The comfort and safety that these terms of affection had supplied throughout my life had suddenly been undermined as if the family nest with its familiar twigs and eggs had been scattered to the four winds.

3

EARTH TREMORS

Aﬀter my father had returned to Australia I prepared for Tokyo and tried to bury the concerns that he'd aroused on his visit.

Nonetheless I found that I had been mentally tracking every single stage of my father's journey back to Melbourne, subconsciously calculating how much time I imagined he would need to recover from the long flight after he got home. Still I held back from calling him until he'd been home for nearly a week.

As I dialled my parents' number, I wondered if by now he would have confessed to my mother where he'd really been and imagined he might now explain to me his cryptic outbursts. I couldn't have been more wrong.

When he answered the phone my father greeted me in his usual fashion, almost immediately turning on the speaker-phone so that my mother could listen in. Jovial and relaxed, he asked me what I had been up to and how my week had been, careful not to indicate that he had been with me only days earlier. Clearly he'd been maintaining the charade with my mother.

Hearing his voice for the first time since his outburst on the London Underground I realised that the bond between my father and I had strengthened; even if he hadn't told me very much, it was me in whom he'd chosen to confide.

'Make sure that you call us when you get to Tokyo,' he said at the end of the conversation, adding that I should let them know my address. When I put the phone down I realised that he hadn't imparted a single piece of information, certainly nothing that related to the dramatic climax of his visit.

By the end of the following week, I had spoken with my father two or three times. He never missed a beat during these calls, still acting as if nothing had happened.

On one occasion he even echoed my mother's oft-repeated question:

'When are you coming home for a visit, Marky?' he asked affectionately. 'It's been ages since we've seen you.'

'Soon I hope,' I said non-committally, feeling more and more complicit in my father's fiction. I decided to broach the subject with him and it occurred to me that if I could catch my father alone at home I might be able to get him to speak. I called him on a Friday afternoon, Melbourne time, when my mother routinely lunched with her close friend Marie and had her hair done at the local beauty salon.

The phone rang only once before my father picked up the receiver.

'Hello, son. Mum's not home,' he said.

'I know. That's why I called,' I responded quickly.

There was silence at the other end of the line.

'You there, Dad?'

'Of course!'

'What's up?'

'What do you mean? Nothing's up.'

'I thought we could have a chat . . .'

The words bounced back and forth between us.

'About what?'

'About what you started to tell me in London . . .'

'Hang on, son,' he cut in, 'there's someone at the door.'

It was such an obvious ploy that I was immediately suspicious, especially since I couldn't hear anyone knocking in the background. But before I could challenge him about this, there was a clunking sound as he put the handset down. Then another long silence ensued before my father returned to the phone.

'Sorry, Mark,' he said, 'I'll have to call you back later. There's someone here with a TV to be fixed.'

'OK. What time will that be?'

'Not sure.'

'Half an hour from now?' I pressed him. 'Tonight?'

'I don't know. Whenever I can,' he said in a rushed tone.

My father didn't return my call that day nor over the weekend so that I felt returning the same sense of exasperation he'd caused me in Oxford.

Over the next week I waited for his call, but it didn't come. I imagined him going about his business – driving my mother to the shops, picking up spare parts for the TV repairs he had to do, chatting with the neighbours – but I was sure that all the time he was aware of me, waiting in Oxford for his call and some further revelation.

I decided to take matters into my own hands. I called a travel agent and booked a flight for the following evening to Melbourne. My research would have to wait.

My father was waiting for me in the Arrivals terminal at Melbourne airport. We were both bleary-eyed – me from the journey which had taken nearly twenty-four hours and my father from having to rise so early to meet my 5 a.m. flight. But he bore no other sign on his face that showed the slightest surprise at my unexpected arrival. I suspected that he knew why I was there.

I hadn't seen him in nearly a month, since his brief visit to Oxford. I felt very strange to be in his actual physical presence, self-conscious and even a little ashamed, as if my arrival was tantamount to a demand for access to his secrets. But I also felt that what had transpired in Oxford and London had been a tentative invitation to be his companion. To the outsider my father may have seemed to be an emotionally 'intense' person – paradoxically making him appear 'gruff' rather than sensitive at times – but I had got used to it. He did want to express his emotions but they seemed trapped. He said 'What are you doing here, son?' then stretched out his hand to shake mine while I opened my arms to embrace him, bungling our greeting.

'What are you doing?' my father exclaimed, attempting to smooth over the awkwardness. 'Trying to push me over or something?'

With that, he grabbed my luggage and headed for the car park, with me following behind, benumbed and disorientated. It took me several moments to notice the familiar scent of the pungent eucalyptus trees, the dawn chorus of birds – kookaburras, rosellas, wild parrots, the slightly ungainly pink and grey galahs that often thumped into trees for no reason and the vast high Australian sky. I gave an involuntary shiver.

After the unusual humidity of the Oxford summer, it was a relief to feel the chill of an early morning Melbourne winter. At this hour of the morning, a frost still carpeted the ground and my father misinterpreted my reaction.

'You should've dressed warmly, son,' he scolded me lightly, and then drew the collar of his overcoat around his neck. 'Did you forget it's still winter here?'

It was now the start of the early rush hour and traffic was building up on the freeway as we sped towards Melbourne.

We drove home in silence. Somehow the incident on the tube in London had become the lodestone of our relationship and until it was mentioned, we wouldn't have much to say to each other.

I wound down the window and stared out at the passing landscape of the sprawling suburbs, built when the Australian dream – the triple-fronted brick house nestled on a quarter-acre plot of land – was in full bloom. The 'brick veneers', as they were called, dominated either side of the freeway. Even as a child I knew I didn't ever want to live in one, though I had envied their atmosphere of proper Englishness. They all seemed so quiet and ordered compared to the chaos of my own arid, desolate childhood suburb, Altona, in the outer west. Altona was in essence a vast open volcanic plain, full of dry scrub and tiger snakes, on which were dotted little pockets of newly built homes, some still incomplete, with dry weedy gardens. When I was growing up, the roads were largely unmade and the sewage was not yet connected so that inhabitants would have to wait for the 'dunny man' who came weekly to change over the smelly metal toilet tanks.

Altona was the site of the city's petroleum industry and had been named after a sister oil town in Germany. The town surrounding the industrial complexes had been built to support the factories.

As we drove, my father drew my attention to some new buildings under construction.

'Melbourne's really coming on, isn't it?' he said, obviously searching for a neutral topic. I didn't respond but instead gazed at his profile, reflected next to me in the passenger window. I saw him turn his head briefly in my direction before facing the road again.

As he turned into the main arterial road leading into Altona, and then into a smaller road which took us directly to our street, a familiar sight came into view – the oil refinery complex with its spidery web of pipes rising high into the sky. A single flame burned continuously from the top of a slender pipe at its upper end and cast a thin glow over the houses that otherwise lay within the refinery's shadow. When I was a child, this flame had always comforted me – like an Olympic torch or the eternal candle on a church altar, sending me off to sleep, safe in the knowledge that it was giving off its protective light. Sometimes, when I awoke during the night I would raise my blind and peer out of the window, just to make sure that it was still burning.

At the other end of our street lay the abattoirs whose smell of freshly slaughtered carcasses added to the acidic taste of petroleum that regularly coated the inside of our mouths. Always upwind of our neighbourhood, the stench would blow down and settle over the street by mid-morning.

Sometimes it was so bad you would have to cover your mouth and nose with a handkerchief.

As a child I spent the long hot Australian summers sitting in the dusty gutter of our then unpaved street. On some days, the heat was so stultifying that I rarely did more than play with a stick, slowly carving my name into the dirt, waiting for the cool air the weatherman had promised.

Throughout the morning I would watch the trucks as they arrived, carrying sheep, cattle and pigs to their final destination. Sometimes, if traffic was heavy, there would be a tailback along our street so that I would find myself looking up from the gutter into the blank gaze of a cow or pig whose head was wedged between the slats of its mobile pen. They jostled and bucked against one other, restless and apprehensive as if able to detect the scent of their imminent death.

This was what I had grown up with. This was the world I knew, but now returned home to, unknowing and trepidatious.

We turned into the driveway and came to a halt. My mother was already standing on the front porch.

'Go and say hello to Mum,' my father said, unlocking the boot of the car. 'I'll look after your bags.'

'You didn't feel well enough to come to the airport, Mum?' I asked as I kissed her.

'Sorry, luv,' was all my mother replied.

She was not averse to complaining of her various aches and pains – her Irish stock was not a sturdy one – but now her stoic response made me think that something more serious may have been affecting her.

The house was full of familiar smells.

'I've got your breakfast on,' she called across to me from the stove. 'A full Aussie fry-up. How many snags do you want?'

'Two sausages are fine, Mum,' I answered.

'Oh, you call them sausages now, do you?' she said teasing me. 'That's your posh Oxford way of talking, is it?'

I sat down at the kitchen table. After my father had taken my luggage through to my old bedroom at the back of the house, he joined us. He poured himself some coffee and sat down opposite me, pretending to immerse himself in reading the morning paper. My mother served my breakfast and sat down beside me.

Just as she sat, my father rose, gulping down the remains of his coffee.

'Well,' he announced gruffly, 'some of us have work to do. I'll be in the workshop if you need me.'

'Workshop?' my mother snorted, winking at me conspiratorially. 'Is that what you call it? It's a junk heap. He hasn't tidied it since the day we moved here in 1963.'

He pretended not to have heard her, and turned his back on us. 'He's never gonna do it!' she silently mouthed across the table, shaking her head in a gesture of mock disgust. I laughed, suddenly pleased to be home.

A short while later I took my breakfast dishes over to the sink where my mother was standing. I came up next to her, gazing with her into the back-yard. We could see my father tinkering in his workshop, an old ramshackle garage that was literally falling down around him.

She began to wash my breakfast dishes.

'It's a bit of a surprise,' she said, 'you coming home like this . . .'

My mother expressed herself in her typical low key fashion but I felt her eyes intently examining me for any clue as to why I was here.

I tried to shrug her off.

'Things seem to be a bit slow in Tokyo. My research won't begin for some time yet,' I said, being deliberately vague. 'So I thought I'd come and see how me old Mum and Dad are.'

My mother laughed lightly before her expression became serious.

'Just as well you did,' she murmured, looking down into the sink.

I shot my mother a questioning look which she must have sensed.

'It's your father,' she said. 'I can't explain it at all. He's been in a strange mood the last few weeks. Ever since he went to see an old friend in Sydney.'

'Any idea why?' I asked. I hated lying to my mother like this.

My mother shook her head.

'He's not said a word,' she answered. 'In fact, it almost seems like he doesn't want me here. He doesn't want to do anything, not even go out on Sundays.'

Sundays had always been their day together.

'Perhaps he'll talk to me,' I said. 'After all I've come halfway across the world to visit.'

My mother stopped what she was doing, and seemed to reflect on my answer for some moments before responding.

'Give him time, luv. You've just got here,' she said in a way which conveyed the modest wisdom I always associated with her. 'In good time, we'll learn what this is all about.'

Then she changed the subject. 'You must be wrecked,' she said. 'Why don't you have a nap?'

When I awoke it was just before lunchtime. I lay on the bed staring at the ceiling. Everything was just as I had left it years earlier when I had left home for the first time. I sensed that my mother had never given up the hope that I would return permanently, and on every visit home she would always find an opportune moment to ask me at least once, 'Do you ever think you'll come back home to live?'

I usually took this line of questioning as her test of my attachment to family life with them, but I wondered now if instead it betrayed a fear of being left alone with something she was as yet unable to put her finger on. My mother was a highly intuitive woman – she knew something was wrong.

A light tap on the door roused me from my thoughts. My father poked his head around the door.

'Lunch, son,' he said and went away again.

I was acutely conscious of the fact that my father had avoided me all day. I wondered how I was going to broach the topic when he seemed so determined to remain silent.

Dinner came and went. I retreated again to my room to unpack. When the last of my luggage had been put away I looked at my watch. It was after one in the morning, and I was still sleepless. Without thinking, I drew aside the curtain to check if the flame was still alight at the end of the street. It was.

Almost a week had passed since my return to Melbourne. During that time my father and I had resumed the bizarre *pas de deux* of our time together in Oxford and London. But this time the dynamics of our choreography had subtly altered. He still set its terms but now that we were under the same roof he could escape only as far as his workshop and he couldn't stay there for ever.

Twice I approached him with a cup of tea as he pottered there. He would thank me awkwardly and then delve back into the guts of the machine he was working on. I decided to bide my time and wait until he was ready to speak. He knew I wasn't going anywhere.

In the meantime I spent my time catching up with my brothers, aunts and old friends. Everybody was surprised by my unexpected visit, but I would just shrug in response to their probings.

It was as if a bomb had been dropped into the midst of my family that had yet to explode. Only I knew about it and I couldn't warn them.

Pulling into the driveway late one night toward the end of that first week, I noticed a faint light coming from the kitchen of the dark house. I let myself in quietly. I could hear my mother snoring gently along with her radio in the front bedroom.

I was tiptoeing across the living room towards the kitchen to get a glass of water, when I heard my father's nervous cough. I opened the door a fraction to see what he was up to. My father was seated at the kitchen table. The room was dark apart from the light cast by a reading lamp. His reading glasses were perched on the end of his nose, and his head was bent down over his case. He was rummaging through it with the lid wide open, but from where I was standing I could not get a clear view of its contents.

For several moments I remained at the door, but he must have sensed my presence. He turned abruptly and caught me hovering there. He snapped the suitcase shut and laid his arms across its lid protectively.

For a moment I was offended. It was as if I were an enemy theatening to intrude on his territory.

'How long have you been there?' he asked suspiciously.

'Only a moment,' I replied.

He chose to accept my response, though I sensed that he suspected otherwise.

'I didn't hear you come in,' he said.

I walked over to the sink and poured myself a glass of water.

'What are you still doing up at this hour?' I asked. 'It's nearly one in the morning.'

'Can't sleep,' he said wearily.

I sat down opposite him.

'You're late in tonight,' he said. He sat his case casually on the floor next to him, trying to make it as inconspicuous as possible.

'Been out with Annie,' I said. Annie was one of my dearest friends, whom I'd known from primary school. She was an extremely compassionate person, in whom I could have easily confided my situation. Yet I'd refrained. There seemed as yet no words to speak of 'it'. Perhaps, I told myself, after my father spoke to me, the 'it' would become something that could be rendered into language.

My father leant back in silence.

'What were you looking for just now?' I said, nodding in the direction of the case on the floor.

My father stretched his arms above his head, feigning nonchalance as if the case was of little significance to him.

'Nothing,' he answered casually, but his nervous cough betrayed him.

'Nothing?' I said evenly. 'Always the same thing. Nothing!'

My father looked at me with sharp appraising interest but he didn't say a word. I was too tired to pursue a game of cat and mouse at this hour. I rose and walked over to the sink to deposit my empty glass. My back was still to him when I heard him mumble something. I turned around and saw that he had again brought his case to the table and was opening its lid.

'Sorry, Dad, I missed that,' I said, approaching him as he began to rummage in the case.

'My identity paper,' he said, looking up briefly.

'What do you want them for at this hour?' I asked.

He shrugged and began unfolding a piece of yellowing paper.

'Uldis Kurzemnieks,' he read.

'Don't forget Alex Kurzem,' I added.

He gave a bitter laugh.

'I've got more names than most people but I don't know my real name.'

I nodded my head grimly. I decided to grasp the opportunity.

'But you know who you were at least – a little pigherd,' I said, suspecting since his outburst in London that this was unlikely to be the case.

He shook his head. 'Not at all, son,' he said. 'Not at all.'

'Tell me, Dad,' I prodded gently.

'I wouldn't know where to begin,' he said.

'Start anywhere,' I almost pleaded. 'I promised you in London that I would help you find out the significance of those words. But I need more to go on.'

He looked up from the identity paper he still held. His face suddenly looked drawn.

'But they are only pieces . . .'

'Don't worry, Dad,' I urged him.

'It was terrible . . .'

He paused, reflecting, and then began in earnest. 'It started during the night. We were in the kitchen. I was playing on the floor with my little brother. I can see my mother now. She was sitting in the candlelight, nursing my baby sister and quietly watching us. Suddenly the door flew open and two soldiers stormed in, shouting crazily. They had truncheons. They began smashing up the place. My mother didn't make a sound, but my brother screamed. She must have been quick-witted because somehow she scooped us all up in her arms and dashed to a stool and sat down. She pushed my brother under her skirt and then I saw her thrust the baby under there as well. She tried to cover me with what was left of her skirt but there wasn't much space. Then things went quiet. They must have stopped smashing up the place. From where I was I heard the soldiers' footsteps coming closer and felt my mother freeze. I heard this thudding sound and every time I heard it, I felt my mother's body shake. They must have been hitting her over and over with their truncheons. She took all the blows. I just gripped the two little ones tightly, praying that they wouldn't make a sound.

'I must have blocked the rest out because the next thing I remember it was quiet again. Not a single sound. The soldiers had gone.

'At first I was too scared to come out. I just waited there holding my brother and sister and gripping my mother's leg. Then I heard my mother whimpering softly.

'Slowly I put my head out from underneath her skirt. I put my head in her lap and gripped her tightly around the waist. I felt something strange on my forehead. It was wet. It ran down my cheek and trickled on to my lips. It was warm but I had no idea what it was.

'Then my mother moved. She got up from the stool, and I saw that her face was covered in blood. Then I understood what the sweet taste in my mouth had been. My mother's blood. I had tasted my mother's blood. But she seemed oblivious to her injury. The little ones were now screaming in fear and panic and she took them both in her arms and tried to calm them. She began to sing to them.

'Suddenly I heard screams coming from our neighbours' homes and I ran to the door to see what was going on. But my mother called to me to stop and close the door. I tried to, but the door had been half torn from its hinges by the soldiers. Looking back now, I remember that rain was pouring in through the doorway and the wind was bitter.'

I was struggling to grasp what my father was describing but didn't dare interrupt him. I knew that soon enough I would find my way through the words that tumbled out of him.

He went on: 'Later that night I was sitting in the kitchen alone. I remember looking at my feet swinging backwards and forwards. My mother was in the next room – just a small space divided off by a curtain – still singing to my little brother and baby sister. Try as she might, she couldn't calm them after what had happened; they hadn't eaten all day and were hungry. I remember that empty feeling too, like rats gnawing at your insides.'

'When did this happen to you?' I asked.

'I'm not sure,' he replied. 'I guess I was about five, possibly going on six.'

'Have you any idea what year it might've been?'

He shook his head.

'Think, Dad,' I urged him. 'Do you remember what time of the year it was?'

'Autumn? Perhaps it was early autumn. I have this vivid memory of leaves all over the ground.

'Finally,' my father continued, 'my brother and sister must have gone to sleep. I must have dozed off as well, right where I was, in the kitchen chair. When I opened my eyes my mother was sitting opposite me in the dark. She was very quiet. I could only see her silhouette, but I felt her looking at me. She beckoned me over gently. She pulled me on to her lap, hugging me. She stroked my hair, over and over. I remember the rhythm of it, her fingers moving gently. Then she said, "We are all going to die tomorrow." '

He fell silent. A moment or two later, he raised his eyes toward me, looking mystified.

'You know . . .' my father said slowly, 'my mother called me by my name, she must have done, but, for the life of me, I can't remember it. I can hear her voice speaking to me but I just can't hear my name.'

'Do you remember any names at all? What about your family name?'

My father shook his head despondently.

'Can you remember what your brother or sister were called?'

'No names. Nothing at all.'

'Do you remember them at all, Dad?' I asked.

'They were younger than me. My little brother was just beginning to walk – he would toddle about. My sister was still a baby in my mother's arms.' My father paused and a slight smile crossed his lips at the memory.

'My mother told me that I was the head of the house because my father had gone . . .'

'Where was your father?'

'He was dead.'

'Do you know how he died?' I asked gently.

'I don't know. My mother told me one day that he was dead. That's all I remember. I just have this vague impression of him not being there.'

'When was this, Dad?'

'I'm not sure, Marky.'

I was growing slightly impatient with my father's inability to recollect all the detail. I felt as if I was becoming an interrogator. I didn't like this role but my father didn't object to my tone. He also seemed frustrated by the gaps in his memory.

'Do you feel all right to continue?' I asked, and when he nodded I reminded him, 'You were in the kitchen with your mother . . .'

My father began to speak, slowly and meticulously.

'My mother said to me that we would all die tomorrow.'

'How did she know?' I asked, unnerved by the harshness of my tone.

'I have no idea. I only remember what she said to me. But I don't see why it's important how my mother knew.'

At this he seemed to retreat into his shell. Then after some moments he went on . . . 'She said that I mustn't be afraid . . .'

'But you must've been, Dad. You were just a boy.'

'I don't know how I felt. I suppose I didn't want to die. Of course I didn't really know what death was. But I knew it was something bad. I'd seen my father kill chickens and things like that . . .

'My mother said that I must stay with her. She said I should help her with my little brother. She said that the soldiers would take us down the hill and not to be afraid. "I will have the baby with me," she said, "so I want you to take your brother's hand and not let go. No matter what happens, stay beside me with your brother so he isn't frightened. Then when I tell you, just close your eyes and hold on to me. Don't be afraid."

'My mother helped me into bed then. My brother was already asleep in the same bed. She sat on the edge of the bed and put a blanket over me. She bent down, kissed me on the cheek, and then, whispering gently, urged me to go to sleep. I watched her climb into her own bed with my baby sister. I think it must have been the moonlight coming through the window because I could see her silhouette cuddling the baby. I can see it now. I must have dropped off to sleep after that because the next thing I remember was waking up. I opened my eyes. It was still dark outside. I could hear my mother's breathing across the room. I lay there and suddenly this thought came into my head "I don't want to die" as if someone was whispering it into my ear. I just didn't want to die like the chickens in the back garden. I didn't want anyone to wring my neck. And then I couldn't get rid of that thought until I did something about it.'

My father's voice dropped now to a whisper. 'I got up as quietly as I could and got dressed. I walked across to my mother's bed. I looked down at her face. She was asleep. I didn't want to wake her. But I bent down and I kissed her goodbye.' My father could now barely get the words out.

'I kissed my mother goodbye,' my father said again, falling completely silent.

After a moment or two he continued, 'I went through the dark house and out of the door. I stood on the doorstep. It was raining. I remember the rain falling on top of me. There were big drops coming off the edge of the roof. It was dark. The moon must have gone behind the clouds because there was no light at all.'

'Nothing was moving. It was so quiet. I went down the back garden, past the apple tree that I always played in with my friend . . .'

'Do you remember his name, Dad?' I asked softly, as if I was in the back garden with him.

He shook his head.

'I came to a fence at the back of the garden. I knew a way out. There was a loose plank that I would sneak through when no one was looking. I used to do this all the time. Coming and going from our house secretly. I began to climb through but suddenly I was trapped. Something was holding me back. I panicked. I thought that one of the soldiers had sneaked up behind me and grabbed me by the trousers. I struggled alone, lashing out in the dark and somehow I got myself free. When I was through on to the path on the other side I could tell that there had been no soldier there, only my fear. My trousers had been caught in the fence.

'I was frightened. But then suddenly something came into my mind – a safe place at the edge of the village, a field where I used to play with my friend. If I could get there first of all, then from there I could go on further to the hill behind it where there were lots of trees. It must have been in my mind that I could hide there. I must have had my wits about me. And at that age! Hardly born!'

My father shook his head in a mixture of pride and disbelief.

'By day I knew all the pathways. But now I was like a blind man. I couldn't see anything. But somehow or other I got to the village hall. I remember seeing a movie there, a silent one. It might've been Charlie Chaplin, or the other person, Buster Keaton.' He smiled nostalgically. 'I remember being there with my friend, having an ice cream. My father must have given us some coins. They used to have dances there too. All us kids would be there laughing at our parents dancing!'

I was torn. This was likely the first time my father had ever shared these memories with anyone and I wanted to hear more. But first I wanted to know what happened that night.

My father seemed to have read my mind. 'After that I kept walking. It was only a couple of minutes from the village hall to the edge of the field. I knew I had to cross it to get to the hill and the trees. I was frightened then. It was the noise this time, not just the dark. I could hear someone crying.

'It was a woman. But I couldn't see where she was. I waited until she quietened. Then when I thought it was safe to do so I started to walk across the field. It was tough because the rain was almost torrential. A couple of times I got stuck. I couldn't lift my feet and kept falling over in the mud. Then the rain stopped. I wasn't sure how far I'd got but I mustn't have been as quiet as I thought I'd been, because suddenly I heard a groan as if I'd woken someone up. I froze to the spot. After some time – I am not sure how long I stood there – the groaning stopped. Slowly I took a step, there was no sound, so I began to take another one when all of a sudden, a voice called out to me – "You!" It was a woman's voice. I just stood there unable to move, like a statue.

'I was petrified. Then the woman spoke again. This time her voice was softer, "Help me! I am over here!" I don't know why but I trusted the voice. I took a step to where it was coming from. And then I saw it. I could just make it out. An arm. Coming out of the ground. It was waving to me. I couldn't understand. How could an arm rise up out of the earth?

' "Can you see my hand, boy? I can see you! Don't be frightened," she said to me gently, just like my mother would. "Come here!"

'I took another step towards the arm. And then another. I could hear her breathing heavily now. In and out. I kept my eyes on the arm. I put one foot in front of the other when suddenly the arm disappeared as if it had been sucked back into the earth. I went closer to where I thought it had gone. Then you know what happened? It shot out of nowhere. It grabbed me by the wrist and yanked me forwards. I was tumbling over, dragged down, sucked into the earth.'

My father began to breathe heavily, slightly out of control as if his memory had taken over and was forcing the words out of him.

I made a move to help him but he waved his hand to stop me.

'I was struggling, kicking and fighting,' he said. 'Suddenly I stopped falling. I was lying on top of someone. The lady.'

'Terrifying,' I said gently. My father shifted his gaze slightly to look at me. 'No. It wasn't. It was beautiful. I was lying against her. She had her arm across me. She was so soft and warm. I could feel her breathing, her chest was rising and falling. She was like my mother. I don't know how long I lay there like that.

'I know that sounds strange. Now I understand what was really going on. I was in a sort of big hole in the ground. And it wasn't only this lady and me. There were lots of other people there. Now that I was nearer to them I could also hear their groans and other squeaking, wheezing noises.

'I must have fallen asleep because the next thing I remember was her arm shaking me. She was crying, "Wake up! Wake up!" She told me that I had to help her out of the hole. She told me to climb out first. I don't know how long it took me, but I got out in the end. Then she told me what to do.

'I lay on my stomach at the edge of the pit and stretched my arms out to her. I could just make out her hand in the darkness. I clasped it in my two hands, and when she told me to, I pulled as hard as I could. She tried to raise herself up as I tugged. But in vain. I wasn't strong enough.

'Then without warning the lady's arm went limp. She whispered to me in a weak voice, "Leave me!" But I didn't want to. I had to help her.

'I don't know, perhaps I went crazy, I was tugging at her arm over and over, but it was limp. I realised much later that she had died there and then with me yanking stupidly at her. But then at that time I just didn't understand. I felt that I let her down, I didn't want to leave her alone but in the end I did. I just got up and ran. I didn't stop. I didn't look back.'

Even now, my father looked distressed by his inability to help this woman. I wanted to offer him words to ease his guilt. All I managed was a limp 'What else could you have done, Dad?' before urging him to continue with his recollections.

'Where did you run to?' I asked.

'There was a thin light now so it must have been around dawn. I could see the hill and the trees ahead. I ran up the hill and into the trees. I didn't know what to do. I just wandered among the clump of trees for some time. Eventually, I found one that looked comfortable and I curled up in a hollow in its roots.

'I must have fallen asleep because a terrifying noise woke me up. It was like a crack of thunder. Then I heard the sound of people screaming, shouting, crying out, women and children's voices. I knew something dreadful was going on but I had no idea what.

'I was very quiet. I didn't want anyone to find me. I moved from tree to tree until I was near to the top of the hill and could see down to where I'd been with the lady and where the noises were coming from. I peeked around a tree trunk.'

My father lowered his head, shaking it repeatedly. He seemed disconsolate and his voice got very quiet.

'If only I hadn't looked.'

He let out a deep sigh and shrugged. Finally he looked up. He screwed up his eyes as if squinting at images of the past he could not bring into focus. His words came out steadily, carefully.

'Blood was everywhere. And mud. And people, naked, in a big pit. Most were dead. But some of them must have still been alive, because the whole pit seemed to be moving; it was rising and falling like a wave.

'Then it dawned on me that's where I had been the night before. In the pit. Where I had slept with the lady. They must have killed some people the day before.

'There were soldiers everywhere with guns. They were making women and children stand in front of the pit. Then I heard the cracking noise again and all the people fell forward into the pit.

'The soldiers were killing them with their rifles, with their pistols. Later I understood what was going on but I didn't get it at that time. All I knew beyond doubt that what was happening was terrible. I must have been able to sense fear and terror.'

'Do you know who these people were?'

The expression on my father's face tightened as he tried to remember.

'People from the village. Some faces I knew. There was one man. I'm sure that he had come to our house. I remember sitting on his knee. He had this very long beard. His clothes had smelt musty. Then I saw this other lady, one of our neighbours. She would march up and down the street with her umbrella rain or shine. She was always telling me and my friend off but she was nice really. Sometimes she gave me a plum from her tree.'

For just an instant my father seemed to recollect a happy moment from his childhood.

'I remember,' he said gently, as if caressing the pleasurable memory itself.

But the reverie dissolved in the next instant.

'They just looked like ordinary people to me. But now I am sure they were Jewish.'

At this point my father tensed his shoulders, as if bracing himself for an even more shocking revelation. His voice came out in a hoarse whisper.

'I could see the soldiers forcing more people down the hill using bayonets on the tips of their rifles. Then I saw that my mother, brother and sister were among them, and other members of my family. I can't remember who they were but I know I belonged to them somehow.'

My father looked ahead, transfixed by the memory.

'I wanted to call out to my mother, I wanted her to know where I was. I wanted to show her I was OK. But I was too far away from her. I wanted to go to her but somehow I knew that I couldn't. If I'd joined them the same thing would happen to me, as what was happening down the hill.'

He spoke these words as if he was hoping for some sort of absolution, a comforting word that might tell him that it was all right, that the situation would have made it impossible for him to do so. But I was mute with shock.

My father's face became pale.

'I have this terrible impression from those moments. I don't know if it is memory but what else could it be?' He hesitated, now seemingly reluctant to expose this memory.

'Go on,' I urged him.

My father cleared his throat.

'Well, while all this was going on I noticed other people from the village in the distance. I can see them now just as they were then. They were standing on the balconies of their houses. They seemed light-hearted, smoking and talking, some even laughing. I wanted to get them to do something to stop this. They just stood there, watching.

'I couldn't understand why they didn't help my mother, my brother, sister and all the other ones. I felt like I was burning up inside . . .'

My father's face reddened now, as he seemed to relive his hopeless frustration.

'I saw my mother again. By then she was at the bottom of the hill. I could see her struggling to hold on to my brother. Then I remembered I'd promised to take my brother's hand. I felt guilty that I'd let my mother down.'

In spite of the horror of what he was describing my father maintained a matter-of-fact tone.

'The soldiers shot my mother. They put the bayonet into my brother and sister. I cried out, and then bit my hand to stop myself. So that no one could hear my scream. I kept thinking, "Don't let anyone hear you, or they'll do the same to you."

'I saw it all,' he said evenly. 'All day. The shooting went on all day. I covered my ears to block out the noise. The horror went on and on. I believe I must have gone mad, coming in and out of consciousness.'

An eerie stillness descended on my father and he stared blankly into space for several moments. I realised that he'd never spoken about what he'd seen, and that while his manner seemed composed he was struggling to find the right words to describe the extermination of his family.

Then he leant forward in my direction. 'Sometimes I wished I'd died with them that day,' he said. 'Held my brother's hand like I'd promised my mother. Gone into the pit and died with them. Even now.'

The remorse and despondency in my father's voice shocked me, as did the revelation that he had lived with this guilt throughout his life. His face now betrayed his turmoil and finally he asked, almost pleading, to stop for a moment.

I felt the same way. It was as if I had been transported from the safety of the family kitchen to a cold autumn morning in Russia, more than fifty years before. For a moment it was as if I had begun to inhabit my father's body, and point of view.

I rose and crossed to the sink, where I filled the kettle and then put it on the stove. I remained standing where I was, wanting to separate and reclaim myself from my father whose figure seemed frozen in space on the other side of the room.

I placed a mug of tea on the table before him. He gulped from it so greedily that for a moment I was alarmed that he might burn his throat but the hot liquid revived him almost immediately. He stared at me resolutely and began to speak again.

'I can see that my memories are frustrating for you,' he said, 'but I don't have any choice about what I can remember and when. My memories are here inside me like vipers inside my bones, gnawing their way out.'

My father had accurately read my concerns. Some of his memories were unnervingly acute while others were no more than vague impressions containing many gaps.

Still, he was only a child at that time.

I worried whether I had sounded too harsh in my responses. But he showed no signs of resentment. I looked at him now, suddenly shocked by the coolness of my appraisal: I still recognised him as my father even if I had never seen him in this state before. It was as if the face I had known all my life had been peeled back to reveal the unadorned man, the raw human being.

I glanced at the clock on the wall. It was after 2 a.m. but my father showed no signs of flagging. I waited for him to continue.

4

INTERROGATED

'WHEN I woke up among the roots of the tree it was dark. I crawled back to the edge of the wood. The moon was out so I could see back down to where . . .' he paused, lowering his voice, '. . . where it had all gone on.'

'That place,' he added pointedly, 'was all covered up now and I couldn't hear any sound. I didn't know what to do. I simply stood there. Then suddenly I heard a twig snap. It brought me to my senses – whatever senses I still had – and I turned and ran back through the trees. On and on, away from my village – my home – I kept on running, too frightened to look back.

'It got colder and a heavy mist had descended to the level of my neck. I didn't want to be caught, so you know what I did? I crawled along under the mist. I couldn't see much, but I knew nobody would be able to see me either.'

My father seemed pleased by the recollection of his ingenuity.

'I was freezing. That's what I remember more than anything in those first days. I'd run away from home with only what I had on – short trousers and a jumper. I couldn't stop my entire body from shivering. Sometimes I had to grip my jaw to stop my teeth from chattering. My feet were really burning as if the ice was eating into them.'

I thought of my father's feet now. He was in his mid-sixties and ever since I could remember his feet were gnarled and badly swollen, which doctors later attributed to the cold and damp of the forest penetrating his delicate child's bones.

'How long were you there, Dad?'

'I have no idea. I was lost. I just wandered. Then I would fall asleep, wake up, scavenge for food, and go to sleep again.'

'What kind of food did you eat?'

'Plums. Wild plums. Berries. I didn't know which ones were suitable. I ate them to fill the hole in my belly. Once or twice I ate poisonous ones and got so sick I thought I would die. I just lay on the ground, throwing up, and at those moments I couldn't have cared less who or what found me – bears, wolves, monsters. Then I would have to force myself to get up and keep walking.

'Not that the berries or the plums were ever enough. There were days when I couldn't find anything at all to eat and I would chew on the sleeve of my jumper. That made me feel safe and helped me get off to sleep.

'It was not long before the first snow appeared. From then on I had to be careful about leaving trails of footprints. As the snow became heavier, I left the small paths that I had been following and I went deeper into the forest where nobody would be able to spot my tracks so easily.

'I had to keep walking to stay as warm as I could but I soon realised that I was going in circles. I came to the same cottage in a clearing more than once. I would peek at it from behind a tree. But I never approached it.

'Anyway, it turned out to be a good move to go deeper among the trees, because one day I had a great stroke of luck which saved my life.

'I was crawling on all-fours through some undergrowth. I put my hand forward and it suddenly touched something: I immediately knew it was human. I jumped backwards. I was petrified and panting with fear. I expected that whoever it was would grab me and that would be the end of me.

'But nothing happened. I waited for some time and I found a stick nearby. I crawled back through the bushes. I could see a man lying there. I wasn't sure if he was dead or alive.

'I reached out and poked him gently with the stick. He didn't move. I jabbed him again, harder this time and on his chest, but he didn't stir at all. That restored my courage. I stood above him. I could see he'd been a soldier. He was still in his uniform. There was a stream of blood coming out of his body. It was brown and congealed on top of the snow.

'I crouched down next to him. His eyes were closed. Then suddenly it crossed my mind that he might be like that lady stuck in the pit. You know, everyone must've thought she was dead, but she was alive.

'I commanded him in a loud voice "Wake up, mister, wake up!" so that I could be sure that he would hear me. When he didn't answer I was a hundred per cent certain that he was dead.

'I sat down next to him. Despite the fact he was dead, I started talking to him. I hadn't spoken to anyone for a long time, and well, he was better than nobody. I wanted to tell him what had happened to me. I told him those words I remembered, the ones that I told you: Koidanov and Panok. Even then they were already fixed in my mind. Perhaps my mother had drummed them into me, told me not to forget them . . .'

'Why would your mother say that to you?' I cut in, mystified. 'If she thought that you were going to die, then why would she tell you to remember something?'

My father paused, looking puzzled. 'I don't know,' he said, and then went quiet as if something was dawning on him for the first time.

'What's wrong?' I probed.

'Well,' my father said, 'what if somehow or other, my mother knew that I was going to escape?'

My father stared at me.

'You know,' he continued slowly, 'she might've put me up to it.'

'What do you mean?' I asked. 'That's not how you described it before.'

'No, that's true,' my father admitted, 'I can't remember every detail of that night. But perhaps somehow because she knew what was going to happen the next day, she hoped that one of us – me – might stand some chance of getting away. It would have been impossible for her to escape with the two little ones. Perhaps she did say something to me like 'Get away, son' or 'Go now while you can!' – something like that . . .'

We sat in silence. Then my father seemed to set aside the thought, and sipping on the dregs of his cold tea, returned to what he had just been describing.

'I started to examine the dead soldier more closely. I noticed his overcoat, and then I thought to myself, "Take it! He doesn't need it!" I tugged away at it for ages. His arms were so heavy but somehow or other I managed to get them out of the sleeves.

'The hardest part was getting the back of the coat from underneath him. He was a big man and I had to keep pushing at him, trying to get him over on to his side and then to flip him over completely. But I had no luck since I kept falling over in the snow. I hunted around for a bigger stick and soon found one that I used like a lever. I pushed it under the soldier, and with all my might I managed to raise his body on to one side. And when it was raised high enough, I pushed my whole body against the soldier's back. Quick as a flash he'd rolled over face down and I'd freed the coat. I was exhausted and sat down, leaning against his side for quite a while.

'Then the real problem began,' he went on, 'I had to get the coat on. But it was so enormous that I could hardly lift it off the ground. Somehow I managed to get my arms into the sleeves. Of course I couldn't see my hands and most of the coat was in the snow, rather than on me. It was like a wedding dress where the back of it drags behind. But I didn't care. I eventually tied most of it round me with the belt it had. I was warm for the very first time.

'Then I thought, "His boots! Take his boots!" The soldier had tied them up in such knots that my icy fingers couldn't get them undone. But finally I tugged them off and I took his socks too. It was heaven having them on. They went up beyond my knees. The boots were far too big for me too but that didn't matter either. The shoes I had left home in had almost fallen apart by then. I put my new boots on and wound the laces round and round my skinny ankles. I remember thinking that I looked like a clown with such big feet stretching out in front of me.

'There was one last thing. The soldier's cap to keep my ears warm. Lifting it off was the worst thing of all: I had to touch his face. When I put the cap on it sank down over my eyes so that everything went black for a moment. I pushed it back off my face and for the first time my head wasn't freezing cold.'

My father gave a slight chuckle.

'God knows what I looked like, wading through the snow, half-buried in all that stuff. I was always tripping up on the hem or getting the sleeves snagged on bushes. But I am certain of one thing: that dead soldier saved my life.'

'How could anyone survive this?' I wondered aloud, aghast at the picture my father was painting.

My father leant forward. 'I can tell you about that,' he said. 'Don't think about survival, just survive. That's the answer. Once you start thinking, that's when the trouble starts.'

'You were a very resourceful boy,' I said.

My father nodded, grateful for my admiration.

'I was always alert to a noise, even the slightest one – the break of a twig, the rustle of some leaves. Anything could indicate danger. I had to be on guard every moment. It was when the sun started to go down that I would become most frightened. All sorts of sounds would start up in the forest. Things rustling in the undergrowth nearby. Wolves in the distance. A sound that still give me goosebumps.

'I had to be quick-thinking. You know how I'd escape from them?' he asked me. Without waiting for a response, he said, 'I would climb as high up as I could in a tree, and wedge myself into the fork of one of the branches. I had learnt to climb our apple tree when I was little. Now I could climb any tree I wanted and the wolves were never able to get me, even if I fell asleep!

'Again I owed it all to that dead soldier. I'd use the belt from his overcoat – I'd wind it around my waist and then round and round the branch – so that I didn't fall down. I'd wake with a start if I slumped forward too far or when the flaps of the coat had fallen open and I was too cold. Then I'd pull the coat around me, and tighten the belt again to make sure that I didn't lose my balance. Sometimes I couldn't sleep at all. I could hear noises below me in the darkness. I'd wait patiently until the sun came up. It seemed as if daylight would never come.'

As he spoke of being frightened, I formed a different picture of my father. This version had none of the bravado of his fireside tales.

'Those long nights would eventually turn into day when I could walk and scavenge, walk and scavenge, but then the dark would come back again.' My father paused. 'So that was my life and I owed it to that soldier.' He hesitated a moment, and then added, 'And the other dead people I came across.'

'There were others?' I cut in, appalled.

My father nodded. 'Quite a few. Whenever I came across one – they were mostly men – there was always something good growing around them. Much later, when I was with the soldiers and the weather was warmer I'd often find wild strawberries growing around or underneath the bodies. And they were the biggest juiciest strawberries you would ever see! I guess the bodies fertilised the soil as they decomposed.'

'Did you ever come across any living people?' I asked.

'Sometimes I did,' my father replied, 'there were occasions when I heard voices in the distance, or the sound of footsteps on one of the paths nearby, but I'd move away as quickly and quietly as possible and hide in the undergrowth. They must've been peasants or woodsmen I suppose.

'But I did meet someone once. Properly. And that day my life was to change for ever. I can't imagine how my life would've turned out otherwise. I told you before that I was wandering in circles and that I kept coming across the same isolated cottage which I would watch from the safety of the trees. Well, one time I saw this old woman come out. She was a *babushka* all rigged out with her coloured headscarf. I watched her as she gathered up some logs from a woodpile. Then she went back inside with them. I crept over to the window of her cottage. I was just tall enough to peep in. I could see that she was alone, cooking something in a big pot on the fire.

'I moved across to the door and I knocked. I was nearly mad from cold and hunger. Her face appeared at the window and she rushed to open the door immediately. I remember her words exactly.

' "What in God's name?" she said. I stood there, shivering. But then she bent down and took my face in her hands. I hadn't felt anything like the touch of another human being in a long time. Certainly not one who was alive. Her hands were covered with hard callouses, but they were so warm.

' "You're freezing!" she exclaimed. "Come." I allowed her to usher me in. She sat me down by the fire and began to rub me up and down vigorously.

' "Whatever were you doing out there?" she asked. "You must be starving." She prepared me some soup from the pot. I don't know how many bowls I ate. I just ate and ate. At one point she took the bowl away from me. "That's enough," she said. "You'll be sick." My reaction was terrible. I was like a wild animal. I growled at her and made a dive for the bowl, trying to snatch it back. I must have frightened her, because she took a few steps back. "Have it your own way," she said. Then she went to the other side of the room and sat down there, watching me. I calmed down eventually, and she slowly edged the stool closer to me until finally she was next to me again. I must have looked and smelt disgusting because I saw her flinch. She reached out her hand and touched my hair. She said that she would give me a wash. She took off my clothes and gave me a thorough washdown. I didn't mind. I can't tell you how happy I was at that moment.

'She put some old clothing on me and threw my rags into the fire. She made such a face as they burnt. We had a struggle though about the overcoat and boots. She wanted to toss them into the flames. She didn't understand what they meant to me – they were my survival. She chased me round the cottage for them, that poor old *babushka*. I wasn't ever letting go of them.'

My father chuckled. 'I wish I could see her again,' he said. For the first time my father's eyes moistened slightly.

'So how long did you stay with her?' I asked.

'Only that one night. She'd settled me down on the floor near the fire, wrapped up in a thick woollen blanket. It was the first time I had felt this degree of warmth in such a long time. I felt myself nodding off, exhausted profoundly by the months spent tied to trees. And then something happened that changed everything in a flash. The door flew open, and this enormous hulk of a man stormed in. I thought he was an ogre from a fairytale that my mother had told me. He was filthy and smelly.

'He threw down the basket he was carrying and made a beeline for me. Before I knew what was happening he'd grabbed me by both my ears and dragged me out of the blanket. He lifted me off the floor so that my feet were dangling in mid-air. The pain in my ears was excruciating. I must have looked like a rag doll or a dead puppet.

'The *babushka* tried to intervene: she seized his arm, pleading with him to put me down, but he shouted at her violently. She retreated to the far corner of the room, looking worried and frightened. I heard him call her mother, and then I understood why he'd barged in – it was his home and he was in charge of it.

'Finally he released his grip on my ears but I was still immobilised by his enormous hand tightly grasping me by the scruff of my neck. I was petrified and moved as far away from him as possible, despite his grip on me. He yanked me closer. "So what have we got here? Let's get a good look at you!" He laughed out loud, looking me up and down very slowly and coldly, like a wild beast, evaluating its prey. "A little forest creature? No. We've got ourselves a little Jew here."

'I knew I was in danger because his tone was so threatening. The *babushka* must have sensed it too because she chose that moment to put a big bowl of soup down on the table for her son. He grunted and for a split second, he was distracted.

'I knew I had to get out of there. I made a dash for the door. But he just reached out and grabbed me around the neck, and then savagely kicked me across the room, like I was a football. I lost consciousness.

'When I came to, the pain was so bad. There was this terrible ache in my hand. While I was out of it he'd tied my hands together with rope and then tied the rope to the leg of the table. His feet, in big heavy boots were resting on my back, pinning me to the floor. I tried to move to relieve the pressure but he dug his heels into my back. "Stay there," he warned me. I did as I was told while he went on eating his soup.

'When he'd finished he undid the ropes and yanked me up by the arm. Then he lifted me into the air as if I was a rag doll and put me into his wooden basket. He tied me tightly in. I couldn't believe it. I struggled to free myself but it was pointless.

'He sat down by the fire, and glared at me with a hideous smile. "Tomorrow," he said in a whisper, and then he indicated his throat being cut. I understood his meaning.

'When I woke before dawn I was still tied into the basket. I remained there silently, listening to the ogre's snores. I dozed on and off. The *babushka* was pottering by the fire. I saw her look furtively at her son. Reassured that he was still sleeping, she then moved nearer to me, and slipped me a piece of bread. But he stirred at the next moment, and fearful of him, she snatched the bread away and retreated to her corner of the room.

'The son rose and then slung the basket with me still in it on to his back and set off from the cottage. As we moved away I saw the *babushka*'s face at the cottage window. She waved to me, and then with a sombre expression, she made the sign of the cross. I had no idea where we were going.

'By this time I'd been in the basket for hours. The pain was excruciating. I again struggled to free myself. He stopped, looked over his shoulder and raised his hand, saying "Do you want this again?" I held my breath, even though I wanted to groan from the pain.

'After quite some time he stopped abruptly at a gate. We'd come to a small yard next to a tiny schoolhouse. It was dusty but there was a smattering of snow on the ground as well. He slung the basket down and untied me. The next thing I saw were people slumped against the rear wall. They were mainly men. Of all ages.

'A moment later I was able to take in the entire situation. On the opposite side of the yard there were about a dozen soldiers. Some were squatted down on the ground, smoking, laughing and joking among themselves and swigging something from a big flagon.

'Another soldier appeared. His face was grim. He said something to the soldiers but it was in a language I'd never heard before. The soldiers slowly got up. They all had rifles with bayonets. They began to line up. Two of them prodded the people by the wall with the tips of their bayonets, shouting and kicking at them. At that moment the *babushka*'s son seized me around the waist, strode across the yard and tossed me down in front of the soldiers. He laughed and said, "Another one for you! From the forest."

'I cowered before them. All I could see were the soldiers' boots. I waited, unsure what would happen to me and then I decided – I don't know why – to raise my head up so I could get a clearer view of their faces.

'I was surrounded by them. They all stared down at me, smiling, but not in a friendly way. One of them started to kick me, forcing me to crawl towards the wall to join the others. I sat beside an old man. I felt his arm go around my shoulder. He spoke the same language as me and told me not to be frightened.

'I held on to him. One of the soldiers ordered us all to stand up straight. Then another shouted an instruction and the other soldiers raised their guns. I knew what was to come next. I'd seen this before, in my village.'

My father paused and then said, 'I thought, "I'm hungry. If I am about to die then I want something to eat before that. I want to taste bread."

'At that moment my eyes met the eyes of one of the soldiers, the one who appeared to be in charge. I broke away from the old man and I ran towards him, exclaiming defiantly "Bread! Give me bread!" I don't know what prompted me to do it – something much more than hunger I suspect.

'One soldier hurtled towards me and roughly propelled me back into the line. The old man tried to pacify me but something got into me. I dashed forward again. This time another soldier came at me, pointing a pistol at my head. Even now I'm sure he was going to shoot me but before he could pull the trigger I heard the lead soldier shout out, so that he lowered his weapon and the soldiers all lowered their rifles too.

'A few of them began muttering amongst themselves, seemingly resentful because the lead soldier had intervened and they couldn't get on with the shooting. Instinctively I knew that I had to do something at that moment to make the atmosphere less tense. I stepped forward, and thrust out my distended stomach to emphasise how hungry I was. To make sure they all understood, I started to mime eating a piece of bread, all the while chanting "Bread! Bread! Give me bread!"

'It must have looked comical because I saw the glimmer of a smile cross the lead soldier's face. I was scared but I trusted him. He had warm eyes. I started to think of him as the good soldier. Then some of the other soldiers burst out laughing. They were distracted by my jigging about. Out of the corner of my eye I noticed that some of the prisoners had begun to sidle away. I hoped they'd escape. But just then the good soldier noticed them too. Immediately he fired his pistol in the air and everything went deadly quiet. The other soldiers rounded up the escapees.

'At that point, the good soldier took me by the wrist and led me across to the building. Even though I felt I would be safe in his hands, I still struggled against him, digging my heels into the ground. He yanked me even harder until we reached the entrance. Then he turned back to the soldiers and indicated that they should hurry up with their task.

'The good soldier pulled me further into the schoolhouse and threw me down on the floor. I kicked out at him wildly and he tried to slap me but I ducked. The soldier chuckled and then I began to laugh as well and this broke the tension. "So, you want bread?" he asked me. He spoke to me in my language. I nodded.

'He pulled out a dirty cloth from his pocket and unwrapped it. It contained a piece of bread. He held it out to me. At that moment it was more precious than gold! I made a lunge for it and scampered away with it to the corner of the room, where I gnawed away at the rock-hard lump like a rat.

'The soldier tried to cajole me into parting with the bread. He stretched out his open hand to me, all the time staring me in the eye. I gripped it close to my chest. But one part of me trusted this soldier, so that eventually I passed him the bread. The soldier pretended to eat it which drove me to spring up at him, trying desperately to rip it out of his hand but he held me back at arm's length, dangling the bread in his other. Then the sound of his laughter made me realise that it was nothing more than a game and my rage gave way to pleasure. I was giggling in a way that I had not done since I was with friends back in my village.

'The soldier tore the bread into morsels, and passed them to me one by one indicating that I should chew them more slowly. Then he passed me his flask and I took a big swig, thinking it was water. But it was alcoholic. It burnt me inside and I nearly passed out.

'Then all of a sudden there was a sound like a cracking of thunder. I'd heard this sound before: the day my family died. I was petrified and ran to the schoolhouse window, hoping to escape that way but he dragged me firmly back across the room. "Stay!" he barked angrily. I did as instructed and watched as he paced back and forth: something else was clearly bothering him. Suddenly he stopped and stared at me. I thought I was done for and that he had decided to take me outside to be shot.

'He came closer and grasped me by the shoulders, telling me to stand up straight. He crouched down beside me and slowly began to remove the rags which I had on. I flinched.'

My father suddenly seemed shy and embarrassed.

'The soldier looked reluctant but he indicated that I had to lower my pants. I did what I was told. He inspected me, only for a moment, then he turned away. I hastily covered myself. He kept his back to me but was shaking his head, saying, "No good, no good, no good!" I looked inside my pants. "What was no good?" I wondered.

'I knew something was seriously wrong so I tried to copy the soldier's stern expression, just to make him laugh, but he wouldn't. My childish antics only seemed to fuel his annoyance so that he began shaking me and whispering harshly, "No good. Stupid."

'Slowly he calmed down. He sat down on an empty crate and lit up a cigarette. Then he pulled me on to his lap. He seemed to be considering something. This time I waited quietly.

'After several minutes he stood me up in front of him. He was grim-faced. "Never let anyone look at you!" he warned me. He nodded his head in the direction of – you know – what's down below, and then shook his head sternly. Again he said, "No good", and then he held his pistol to his head, pressing the business end of it several times against his temple in order to rub in the point.

'I mimed holding a pistol to my head, with my other hand pointing at my groin, again wanting to believe it was all a game. The soldier finally had

had enough of me and jerked me across to the window. He lifted me up so that I could see that the prisoners were now all lying on the ground.

'None of them moved and the soldiers were stumbling about amongst them, checking them for valuables. Then the good soldier turned his head and looked at me in this very forbidding way. It was then that I understood the seriousness of what he was warning me about – that this could be my fate too if anybody saw what was "no good" about me.

'He told me to wait in the schoolhouse. When he left I heard him bar the door behind him. I dragged a stool to the window and watched as he rejoined the other soldiers who quickly formed a circle around him. The good soldier seemed to be trying to convince the others about something. I saw him point to the schoolhouse. It dawned on me that he was talking about me.

'The soldiers were not happy and from where I was I could hear raised voices. They shook their heads vehemently and kicked at the ground, raising dust everywhere. The horrible soldier, the one who'd wanted to shoot me, broke away from the circle, spitting on the ground. Then another soldier joined him. I saw the good soldier quieten everyone down with his hand. He spoke again and this time some of the soldiers nodded. They seemed to be coming round to whatever the good soldier was suggesting.

'I jumped to the floor and moved about the room which was piled up with furniture. That's when I noticed something in the corner: an enormous crate. I could see that its lid was not sealed so I decided to look inside. The lid was hard to lift but I managed to shift it just enough to get a look inside. It was full of rifles. Without a moment's pause, I said to myself, "I'll shoot them all. I'll work out how to use the guns and then I'll shoot them all from the window!"'

My father seemed astonished even now by what had come into his mind at that time.

'I dragged one of the guns out of the crate and across to the window. It weighed almost as much as me. I couldn't work out how to use it and quickly gave up on the plan. I decided to snatch another peek from the window. It was lucky I did because at that exact moment I saw the soldiers nodding and then the good soldier suddenly turn and head back towards the schoolhouse. I ducked quickly before anybody saw me at the window and hurried to hide the gun behind the crate, but I wasn't quick enough because just then the soldier came in. Fortunately, he had no inkling of what I'd been planning, and instead he told me that soon he'd teach me how to take aim and shoot.

'With that, he lifted me up on to his shoulders, and off we marched, back into the sunlight. We joined the other soldiers who were now swaggering about aimlessly. I was frightened by their drunkenness and even though I was now safely on the good soldier's shoulders I sensed that some of the soldiers were uneasy about my presence.

'The horrible soldier scowled in my direction. Suddenly, he began howling like a wolf, obviously to frighten me, which it did. A few of the others joined in. It must have been the alcohol that turned them into beasts.

'I was still perched on the good soldier's shoulders, and I could sense that he was nervous. He took a stronger grip of my legs. He used his free hand to reach for his pistol and suddenly fired a shot in the air. Everybody went quiet. We were all motionless for what seemed like an eternity.

'Then the good soldier looked around the circle of men, still brandishing his pistol. Nobody made a move against him so that he eventually lowered it.

'The matter of my presence had been settled for the time being, but I had no idea how long I would remain protected by the good soldier. I must have come that close to death and knew I would have to be cautious in the future. But for the moment I felt as if the good soldier had become my guardian.'

'Why do you think he did this?' I asked.

'Who knows. Perhaps I reminded him of another boy he knew. Perhaps he pitied me. After all, what decent person would let harm come to a child? He saw that I was a human being, even though I looked feral after all those months in the forest.

'Mind you,' he added, 'the soldiers weren't much different. They looked like they hadn't washed in ages. Some of them, their teeth were green, like moss was growing on them. But that was more than I had. Most of mine had dropped out by then.'

My father returned to the scene in the schoolyard.

'After that the soldiers gathered up their weapons and packs, and we set off in silence. As we did so, I glanced back at the prisoners lying dead. What was strange were the butterflies that had suddenly descended out of the sky in a swarm. I was hypnotised by how beautiful it all was.'

'Beautiful?'

I must have sounded shocked, because my father quickly added, 'Of course I was sorry for them, especially the old man who'd tried to protect. me, but they were dead. What could I do? I had to think about myself. For the first time I felt safe. No, that is not the right word. I also knew I had to be very, very careful, as the good soldier had warned me. I felt I had a chance to survive if it wasn't found out that I was circumcised. In those days it indicated you were Jewish.'

My father blushed.

'So you believe you are Jewish?' I asked.

My father nodded.

Inside I wondered what that made my brothers and me. To what extent and in what way were we Jewish?

'Do you have any other memories of Jewishness?'

'I have one memory of a man, you know, like a priest with a long beard, coming to our house . . .'

'A rabbi?'

'Yes, that's it, a rabbi. He came for a ceremony that had something to do with my little brother.'

'Perhaps a circumcision.'

'Do you ever consider yourself to be Jewish?' I asked.

My father shrugged and looked slightly bewildered.

'In truth I've never known what to call myself,' he said, raising his eyes to the ceiling, 'I was born Jewish. What happened to me happened because I was Jewish so I think that might make me Jewish. But then the Latvians had me baptised a Lutheran. I am Russian but all my life everybody has believed I'm a Latvian. God forbid!'

'So what happened after you went with the soldiers?' I asked, steering my father back to his memories even though I sensed his interest in the question of his Jewishness. There would be time enough to return to that. At this moment I did not want to surrender the intimacy of the darkened room which now more than ever had become a confessional.

'I was soon back in the forest,' my father said. 'I was still scared but not in the way I was before. Of course I was now worried that what was "no good" about me would be discovered. All my old fears in the forest about wolves and things had been swept aside for a new and much darker one.

'That first night the soldiers made a camp with a fire. They sat around it, drinking. All the soldiers seemed hypnotised by the flames and the crackling of the fire. I sat quietly next to the good soldier, in fact I was almost cuddling him: I was hungry for human warmth. At one point I noticed the horrible soldier staring at me from the other side of the fire. He was smiling at me, but his eyes were hard. I looked away, pretending that our eyes hadn't met.

'But in truth I was quivering inside. I was desperate to stay alive and suddenly feared that now that the soldiers, even the good one, had time to think about their decision to take me with them, the more uncomfortable they might begin to feel about it.

'My body must have been shaking as well because I then felt the good soldier's arm tighten around my shoulder. He hadn't noticed the stare of the horrible soldier and didn't understand what I feared. "Cold," he said, taking off his scarf and wrapping it around me.

'Some time later as I was nodding off I heard the bad soldier call out. "Hey, boy," he said. I roused myself and looked across at him. He was now sitting upright and looked alert. He called out to me again and this time beckoned me over.

'I had no idea what he would do to me but I didn't want to make him angry in any way. I went over to him. I half-expected a slap from him since just the sight of me seemed to aggravate him. Instead, he pointed at his chest. "Vezis," he said and then repeated it. At first I didn't understand. Then it dawned on me; he was telling me his name. The bad soldier was called Vezis.

'Then the good soldier beckoned me back over to him. He pointed to himself and said "Kulis." I immediately tried to pronounce it. "Kulis. Kulis. Kulis," I said, savouring it a bit. "That's right!" he said pleased. I felt as if I had done something wonderful. Then the others joined in. I went around the circle learning all their names. There was, let me see, Rozes; Upe; Ozols; and Dzintars.

'There were about three or four more soldiers whose names I can't recall. Kulis called for bread and alcohol which they made me drink. It nearly knocked me out. "Samagonka" they called it: if you had just the right amount it was like an anaesthetic.'

'Did you tell them your name?'

'They kept pointing at me showing me that they wanted to know who I was, but there was nothing that I could tell them. I couldn't remember my name.

'The soldiers talked amongst themselves for quite a while and then finally they seemed to agree on something. Sergeant Kulis stood me up before him and pointed to my chest saying, "Uldis Kurzemnieks." He ordered me to repeat it, but I found it hard to pronounce. Every time I tried to say it they'd boisterously push at each other and slap each other on the back laughing. That set me off. I did a little jig around the fire while chanting the words to a tune I made up as I went along. That's how I became Uldis Kurzemnieks.

'Exhausted, I flopped down next to the sergeant.'

'Where on earth did they cook up this name for you?' I asked.'That's simple. "Uldis" is like John, it's a common first name for Latvian men, and Kurzemnieks, you see, was because many of the troop came from the

Kurzeme region. In Latvia. "Nieks" just meant "one of" so I was one of Kurzeme – just like them in fact.

'Not literally one of them . . . I wasn't any kind of volunteer,' my father immediately corrected himself, aware of how what he said had sounded.

'Inside I stood my ground on that. I was starving and lonely. I was a frightened little boy. That's all. There was no choice involved. I would have gone with the devil if he had offered me food and warmth.

'Anyway, I dropped off to sleep next to Sergeant Kulis and I woke up before dawn. The others were still asleep except for the sergeant. "Hurry, get up," he said to me. He had a small bucket in one hand and led me by the other into the surrounding woods. We came to a stream and he showed me how to collect water which we took back to the camp. He showed me how to stoke the fire and prepare tea. By that time the others had stirred. I went around pouring tea into their mugs. One or two of them even tousled my hair and smiled at me. I realised I had a job and I could make myself useful.

'Later that morning, I learnt how to collect kindling wood for the fire in the evening. The sergeant gave me a forage-bag that I wore over my shoulder so that whenever I came across some wood I could collect it. I was a quick learner. I started to make myself more and more useful to the soldiers in those early days with them. After the sergeant had taught me about the water and the fire I could do it all alone. I would be up and about before all of them preparing their tea. And I'd learnt so much from my time alone in the forest, that I would pick berries for them that they could eat safely. They were impressed with me. I became more certain that I had found my place in the group.

'I also picked up Latvian quickly. Whenever a soldier handled an object, or saw me doing something, he would call across to me, naming it in Latvian, and I would repeat it until I remembered it perfectly.

'During daylight we moved through the forest. The soldiers were always on the hunt for *partizani*, they called them. I heard that word constantly but for some time I had no idea what *partizani* was. We never seemed to see any.

'I remember one time they heard a noise behind a tree very close by and they all sprang into action. I was at the front of the group with Sergeant Kulis, and the first thing he did, even before raising his rifle, was to push me behind him so that I was safe. On that occasion it turned out that there was nothing behind the tree.

'Then no more than a few days after I'd been taken, Sergeant Kulis told me the troop was returning to base camp. "S" they all called it. Even though the *babushka* had tried to clean me up, I was still dirty and smelly when they captured me but they hadn't paid much attention to that. Now suddenly Sergeant Kulis was obsessed with cleaning me up. He scrubbed my face and hands, and combed my matted hair.

'Then he and the others tried to teach me how to march like a soldier, but of course I couldn't master that. I still had my clown boots on. They taught me how to salute and click my heels together at the same time shouting my name, "Uldis Kurzemnieks". It felt silly but I knew that they were deadly serious about all this. In the end they were satisfied with my performance. One of the soldiers hoisted me on to his shoulders – they all took turns carrying me now and would even bicker with each other about whose turn it was – and off we went.

'We passed through a village en route to the base camp. There were a few people going about their business but when we marched by they became very quiet. One man took a furtive look at us, and I could see that he was shocked by the sight of me, this little boy marching along with the soldiers.

'Finally we reached base camp in a school on the outskirts of a village.'

'Its name?' I asked.

'I remember "S", that's all,' my father answered.

'You've forgotten it?'

'No. The soldiers only ever referred to it as "S" as if they were talking in code.'

'Why would that have been?'

My father shrugged. 'The base was where I met the commander of the unit for the first time. Sergeant Kulis took me to his office, set up in a schoolroom in the main building. We stood outside the door for a moment. He leant down and tidied my hair, made me practise my salute and greeting one more time. Then he told me to wait there on the doorstep until I was summoned.

'As I stood there a few soldiers spotted me and called out "Hey! Kurzemnieks!" I had never seen them before, but obviously they'd already heard about the new member of their troop.

'Just then the door opened and Sergeant Kulis ordered me inside. Once I'd entered I immediately clicked my boots together, saluted and stated my name proudly. I stood at attention waiting to hear a return greeting, and to be dismissed. Instead I heard a roar of laughter. I dropped my pose and stared across the room. A man was seated behind a desk. As he stood up I could see that he was a short man and a bit plump. He was wearing a uniform – it looked brand new; sharply creased with shiny buttons and a high collar. But it was its colour that hypnotised me. It was a gorgeous light blue like the colour of the sky.

'The commander came around to my side of the desk. I saw that he wore black boots up to his knees. They shone like a mirror so that I could see myself reflected in them. He saluted me. Then he leant against the edge of the desk and lit himself a cigarette. He smoked the cigarette slowly, and sized me up through half-closed eyes. He was formidable. I could tell that he was important. There was an atmosphere about him. "Just be still and don't stare back," I told myself. I wondered what he would do next. It was an instinctive reaction but I felt that I didn't like him.

'After several moments he beckoned me closer. I flinched slightly.

'Sergeant Kulis must have sensed my hesitation. "Hurry up!" he whispered in my ear, giving me a quick shove from behind. Now that I was closer the commander made a grab for me and hoisted me up midair so that I hovered above him. I stared straight ahead, still not meeting his gaze.

' "Little man," he said directly to me, so that I had to look down and meet his gaze. His eyes were like steel, even though he was smiling up at me. "Do you know who I am?" he asked. I was surprised because he spoke my language perfectly. I shook my head. "I am your commanding officer," he said, "Commander Lobe. Can you say that?" I remained hovering in mid-air, as he made me repeat his name several times until I had mastered it perfectly.

'Then finally he put me down on his couch in the corner of the room and sat down next to me. He produced a pencil from somewhere and twirled it around between two fingers before making it disappear. I was mesmerised by his magic trick. I lost all my reserve with him and tugged at his jacket, trying to find the missing pencil. "Show me. Show me, Commander Lobe," I pleaded with him, hoping that if I pronounced his name perfectly again, he would let me in on his secret. And he did. Slowly the pencil edged its way out of the sleeve of his jacket as if it were alive. And I laughed at how I'd been fooled.

'My attitude to him changed for a moment. I was captivated as if we shared a special bond. It felt nice. I can't find another word for it, just nice to be there on his lap feeling the warmth of his hug.

'Then he reached across for a piece of paper and wrote something down on it. Still cradling me on his lap, he pointed at what he'd written and said "Kurzemnieks". He put the pencil into my hand, but I didn't know how to hold it. I'd never been to school, never learnt to read or write.

Commander Lobe was surprisingly gentle with me: he positioned the pencil in my hand and wrapped his hand around mine, trying to guide it to copy my name. He was patient with my clumsiness as I slowly began to master the first few letters.

'Then he indicated that I should try it by myself. I occupied myself with this – full of a desire to see both men pleased with my efforts and mastery – while they talked across me.

'As their conversation continued I could tell that it had become serious and urgent in tone. I kept my ears pricked, and even though it was in Latvian I got the gist of it; the sergeant was trying to convince Commander Lobe that I should stay with his troop.

'The commander listened closely to Sergeant Kulis's words. Sometimes his face looked doubtful, and at other times he smiled, giving a nod in agreement. Occasionally I could feel him staring into the back of my head, again coldly appraising me.

'Then the sergeant seemed to run out of words. The commander also remained silent, considering what Sergeant Kulis had just said.

'Suddenly the commander slapped his thighs and gave me a tight squeeze around the waist. I sensed the sergeant's relief. Then the commander got up and Sergeant Kulis indicated that I should salute again. I jumped to attention, determined to be the perfect soldier.

'The commander dismissed us from the room and in my last glimpse of him that day, I saw him reaching for the telephone on his desk with an absorbed look on his face.

'When we got outside, the sergeant lifted me on to his shoulders and galloped around the yard like a horse, so that the other soldiers there also joined in making whooping noises until it reached a crescendo.

'I laughed out loud. I knew that something momentous had been decided – they were not going to line me up and shoot me, that Sergeant Kulis had been planning something for me and Commander Lobe had agreed to it. But at that stage I had no idea what it was that lay in store for me.'

It was strange hearing about Commander Lobe. I had gone in search of him in the early 1980s and had located him in Stockholm. I wanted to meet him and thank him in person for caring for my father during the war. However my encounter with Lobe and his wife had gone awry, leaving me bewildered and disturbed. I had never told my father of what had transpired during that visit but in light of what my father had now revealed of his own past, the reason for Lobe's terrifying behaviour began to fall into place. It was too late in the evening to start then, but I resolved that I should find a time to finally tell my father what had happened in Stockholm.

5

THE SEDUCTION

'I SCREAMED the place down. The corporal – he was called Rozes – had lifted me into a metal tub full of icy cold water and was trying to get my underpants off. I gripped them for dear life and firmly stood my ground, fending him off. I couldn't get Sergeant Kulis's warning out of my head. I went wild so that there was water splashed everywhere. I hated water. In the months in the forest I'd got used to living in my own filth. It made me feel secure,' he chuckled to himself, 'and there was no way I was going to give up that little comfort. Eventually he got fed up with my antics. "Very well," he said. "Have it your way. Leave them on!"'

My father was explaining an incident that had happened after Commander Lobe had decided to let him stay with the soldiers. His story had begun to take on a momentum of its own and I remained largely silent.

'I was covered in soap, and shivering,' he continued. 'The corporal knelt beside the tub with his shirtsleeves rolled up and attempted to scrub me.

'Suddenly the door to the washroom flew open and Sergeant Kulis stormed in. "Quieten down!" he snapped at me. "The entire barracks can hear you." Sergeant Kulis then dismissed Corporal Rozes, who seemed pleased not to be responsible for me any more, and drew up a stool next to the washtub.

'I was still grimly gripping my wet underpants. He gave me a broad smile and then said "Good." He lifted me out of the tub and began to dry me vigorously with a towel. I liked that. My body felt alive and tingling, just as when my mother dried me. For a moment I forgot everything, all the misery I'd experienced.

'Sergeant Kulis was happy and laughing too as he rubbed me down. Then he wrapped the towel around me.

'At that precise moment Commander Lobe entered. I hadn't seen him since the day he'd agreed to let me stay with the soldiers. He instantly noted my wet underpants. For a moment he seemed perplexed by the sight of me:

he looked me up and down and was on the point of saying something when Sergeant Kulis suddenly leaped to attention in a very exaggerated way.

'I knew that the sergeant was trying to distract him and it did the trick because Commander Lobe seemed to have a change of heart about me: he gave the sergeant a curious look, telling him to relax, and then turned to me. He gave me a broad smile and looked genuinely pleased to see me.

'The commander had a parcel under his arm. He told me that it was a gift for me. I followed him into the next room where he set the package down.

'I removed the wrapping then the lid. It was a pale blue jacket. Then it dawned on me that it was a uniform just like the soldiers' ones but in miniature. It was in the same colour blue as theirs, with all the same flashes, buttons and badges. Underneath it were shiny black boots and jodhpurs as well.

'The commander ordered me to put on the outfit. It had been made especially for me, and fitted perfectly. We struggled a little to get my swollen feet into the shiny black boots but eventually we succeeded. I looked sleek and elegant. I was no longer a clown in my oversized boots and my overcoat. I had become a miniature version of Commander Lobe.

'Then the commander produced something else for me. It was a thick leather belt. He buckled it around my waist, and from his jacket he drew out a small glistening pistol. He made a great show of placing it in a holster that was attached to my new belt. Then he stepped back from me, appraising me. I had mixed feelings. On the one hand I felt proud, but I was also uneasy inside about what he had turned me into. Deep down, I knew this was not me. The commander was pleased with what he saw and saluted me formally. When I tried to return the salute I stumbled in the heavy uniform, belt and pistol which all together probably weighed more than I did. I felt like the awkward clumsy boy I was and not the strong soldier I was pretending to be.

'Sergeant Kulis watched us from the doorway as the commander led me over to a full-length mirror. I barely recognised myself. In fact I had no memory of ever having seen my reflection before. And now, the very first time was as a Jewish boy dressed in a police brigade uniform.

'The commander took a box camera from his military hold-all and positioned me against the opposite wall. He made me pull my shoulders back and thrust my jaw forward into the air. I had to hold the pose while the camera clicked over and over. There was no satisfying him. "Turn this way," he told me, "now turn that way." The camera clicked some more.

"Take the gun out!" he ordered. "Point it there! Stand nice and still!" More clicks! I was exhausted after all this.

'That night the soldiers took over a small cafe in a town nearby for a celebration. I was the guest of honour. I sat at the head of a long table on Sergeant Kulis's knee. The table was overflowing with food and drink and the soldiers made sure that I had enough of everything I desired. Needless to say they all got drunk and high-spirited very quickly. They were singing patriotic songs – some nonsense about wild eagles flying over Latvia and the bears in the forest – and clapping and cheering loudly, disturbing the other customers.'

'You thought it was nonsense?' I asked.

'Of course,' my father answered. 'They behaved like fools. Well, not fools then, just very strange. They weren't like any people I'd known before. They were . . .' My father raised his eyes to the ceiling as he sought out the word that would satisfy him. Then his face brightened. 'Oafs. That's it! They were clumsy oafs.

'I didn't enjoy being with them at all but I had to be sure that they believed I was grateful to them. I laughed and clapped along with them.

'Commander Lobe arrived later and immediately snatched me off the sergeant and stood me up on the table. He made a toast to me, and the soldiers raised their glasses. They all looked up at me as if I was the most important person in their lives.'

My father broke into a smile.

'So I did a little jig there and then on the table top, to please them. They clapped me wildly as if I was a star. Then the commander must have noticed that a customer at a neighbouring table was watching me out of the corner of his eye. Not surprising if you picture me there on the table dancing in my blue uniform. The commander said something harsh to the man, and the man quickly got up to leave. As he passed our table the commander ordered him to stop and bow to me before letting the frightened man scurry away. I felt terrible – the commander's attitude was wrong. I knew that. But of course I couldn't utter a single word of protest.

'I clambered down off the table. The soldiers had been feeding me capfuls of vodka and I must've fallen asleep because the next thing I recalled was the sergeant tucking me, still in uniform, into my bunk in the barracks.

'I woke early the next morning with a terrible hangover. I wanted to stay in my bunk and not move a muscle but one of the soldiers came to drag me out of my bunk. On the way to the mess hall he joked that I'd have to learn to take my liquor if I was going to be a soldier. Fortunately the tasteless breakfast gruel and the strong black tea fortified me.

'Later that morning we set off on patrol. We trudged on and on in the forest without a break. It was tough going and gradually I lagged behind. At one point the sergeant dropped back next to me and took me by the hand. "Keep up," he told me, "behave like a proper little soldier. Look at the special uniform you've been given."

'I nodded enthusiastically. I didn't want to make any of the soldiers fly off the handle with me. In the short time I'd been with them I'd quickly learnt not to do anything that would make them irate.'

'What sort of things made them angry?' I asked.

'I couldn't predict. More often than not they lashed out when they were drunk, but I had to be on the alert always. "Stay out of their way" I was forever telling myself.

'By the middle of the day we'd reached a railway siding. A goods train with supplies bound for the frontline was gearing up to go. Sergeant Kulis explained that our job was to keep a lookout for *partizani* and stop them blowing up the train. I was immediately anxious. I didn't know what a *partizani* looked like. They could have been anybody.

'There were about ten of us soldiers, and most of them had already perched themselves on the roofs of carriages. Sergeant Kulis hoisted me on to his shoulders and then into the grasp of another soldier who was up there. The soldier tied me to his waist with a rope, so I wouldn't fall. Then he thrust a rifle towards me – it was almost larger and heavier than me – and told me to take charge of it. It was ridiculous: how on earth could a child hold it up, let alone fire it? Besides I didn't have any idea how to use it. When he realised this the soldier positioned me between his knees and holding the rifle up for me, showed me how to take aim. Then he pulled the trigger himself. The force of the shot was like somebody had kicked me in the shoulder. I panicked at the explosive sound – it reminded me of that day in my village. For an instant I had the strength of Samson. I broke the soldier's grip and still on my leash I tried to scramble away on all fours. If I hadn't been tied to him I would've jumped off the roof – I wouldn't have cared whether I broke every bone in my body – and then escaped into the forest. They wouldn't have caught me there. I knew the forest better than they did – it had been my home. But I couldn't. I was trapped, tied to the soldier like a dog on a leash and there was nothing I could do. The soldier reined me in, laughing derisively and mocking the terrified expression on my face. When I was back wedged between his knees he gave me a clip across my ear for good measure. He had no inkling whatsoever of what had unnerved me.

'The train gathered speed and I held on for dear life, as they say. We must have been travelling like that for at least two hours or so, and we never came across a single partisan. Then the train came to a halt in another town.'

'Do you recall the name of the town?'

My father shook his head briefly.

'My first impression was that it was larger than "S". There were many more soldiers milling around the station. Some of them noticed me and gathered just below my carriage; they were curious about me, and when they caught sight of the rope still tied around me they fell about laughing. I was humiliated and tried desperately to release myself, but to no avail. I had to wait until my captor untied the rope. When I was on the ground I heard somebody call out "What's your name, soldier?" For a moment I was stumped. Perhaps because of shock. I looked across at Sergeant Kulis who called back to the crowd: "Private Uldis Kurzemnieks. Latvian Police Brigade."

'At that, many of the soldiers surrounded me, wanting to shake my hand or take their pictures with me. You see, there was a man there with a tripod and a large camera for some reason. Perhaps he was an official army photographer. In any case, he set up the camera and then positioned me in front of it. Somebody slung a rifle over my shoulder. Things became a bit unruly as the soldiers scrapped with each other to pose with me. At one stage a group of soldiers formed a half-circle around me, posing proudly. I remember that one of them thrust his pistol into my belt and put his arm around me. Once a photo had been taken, they were ordered into town and another group took their place. This went on for quite a while. I didn't mind. In fact I enjoyed being the centre of attention.

'Eventually Kulis called a halt to the photos. He crouched down to my level, staring into my face with a serious expression. He said *partizani* again. Then he took me by the hand and we started to march into the town. Other soldiers were also heading in the same direction. I knew something was up because they were passing flasks between each other, gulping down samagonka as they swaggered along. There was no discipline.

'It was eerie because the soldiers were noisy, yet underneath this noise it seemed to be deadly quiet. There wasn't a single soul about. The towns-people had retreated inside their homes. I saw curtains in windows twitch slightly as we passed by.

'I was frightened by then and didn't want to be at the front with Sergeant

Kulis. I let go of his hand. He didn't seem to notice. He was so intent on what lay ahead. I let myself fall behind until I found myself at the rear of the troops.

'Eventually we reached a crossroads. I peered through the forest of soldiers' legs. On the opposite side there was a building set back a little from the road. It was taller and wider than any building I'd ever seen before – it may have been two or even three storeys high. There were hundreds of people waiting outside – old people, women and children, huddled together. I could just make out some of their faces. They reminded me of people I'd known in my own village. Worse than that, they wore the same expression of fear that I'd seen on the day of the killings. That petrified me even more but I was confused too because the sergeant had called them *partizani*.

'I edged away slowly and was about to turn on my heels and flee when a soldier guarding the rear caught sight of me. He called me over and when I reached him he gripped me by the shoulders and spun me around in front of him so that I was facing forward again. I was too frightened to close my eyes in case I would get in trouble again. I tried as much as I could not to see anything, pretending that the sun was blinding me and squinting my eyes. I couldn't avoid glimpses of what was going on. Soldiers were prodding people into the building while others were hammering big planks of wood across the windows.

'Then I heard the outside doors being bolted. Soldiers put bunches of burning sticks and dead tree branches up against the building. In a flash it caught fire. For a minute or so it was deadly quiet apart from the crackling of the fire as it took hold. The flames spread quickly and then terrible screams and wails began. And the louder the screams became the more silent the soldiers were. Nobody laughed. They were hypnotised by the flames that rose higher and higher into the sky. Even the soldier I was with had forgotten about me. He too was frozen to the spot and entranced by the flames.'

My father paused again and took several steadying breaths.

'Maybe they saw their own souls burning at that moment,' he said in a low voice.

My father hesitated and then he continued. 'Then something snapped me out of it.' His voice was barely audible. For a moment he seemed to panic and gasped in air as if he was about to suffocate.

I gently encouraged my father. 'Go on Dad,' I said, 'tell me what you saw.'

'Suddenly there was a movement from the building. It was a woman . . . my God!'

My father let out a muted cry as if he were seeing her at this moment.

'She was on fire. She dashed out from the huge wall of flame. Two children ran behind her. They were also on fire. They didn't make a sound, as if I were watching a silent film.

'Then, before I knew what was happening I heard cracking sounds and the woman and the children fell to the ground. They didn't move. I knew they were dead. But the flames still rose from their bodies. I looked to where the noise had come from. I saw Sergeant Kulis and two other soldiers lowering their rifles.

'Kulis turned in the direction of the watching soldiers. Even though I was at the rear of the crowd, his eyes found me. He smiled and waved to me, shouting *partizani*, as if to explain his actions.

'Without any thought, I turned and fled. I heard the sergeant call after me but I ignored him. I didn't dare look back. I ran through the streets until I reached the outskirts of the town where I came across a small farmyard. I saw a shed there and crouched down behind it and covered both my ears with my hands. I didn't want to hear the screams which had reached a crescendo and could be heard even where I was now hiding.

'At that moment I hated the sergeant and all of the soldiers. I wanted to be free of them. Then in the next moment I felt defeated. Where could I go? I slumped down wishing death would take me too. I wanted to be free from this misery.

'I looked up into a man's face that was full of rage and hatred. It must have been the farmer who owned the shed. Before I could make a move to escape, he kicked me so hard that I went flying across the yard. But I didn't feel any pain. I was numb inside and felt like I deserved his kick. For being with the soldiers, and for being in uniform.'

My father paused briefly and then went on.

'I had no choice but to return to the soldiers,' he said. 'I know I said that I would have preferred to be alone in the forest, but deep down this was not true. I was a frightened little boy.

'I made my way back along the road into town. The troops were where I'd last seen them – in front of the remains of the building. The screams had ceased. There was only the crackling and hissing of the wood as it smouldered and then collapsed. I can still hear the screams of those poor people as they clawed at the burning doors trying to get out.'

My father was again silent for several moments.

'Sergeant Kulis spotted me and came over. He put his hand on my shoulder. I froze inside. I didn't want him to touch me. I hated him. He'd done what other soldiers had done to my family. He was no different from them.

'Slowly the soldiers headed back to the station. Corporal Vezis, who always seemed firm, went crazy, chasing some farmer's chickens that had strayed on to the road and kicking at them like they were footballs.'

'Where did this happen?' I asked, half-regretting that I'd urged my father to tell me the story.

'The soldiers never mentioned any names in front of me. We could've been anywhere. It was more than likely somewhere in Russia given that later the soldiers told me I was picked up in Russia but I have no idea how far I had wandered in the forest before I was handed over to the soldiers. And how far did they take me in order to reach their makeshift barracks and then later their main camp? How far did we go on the train that day? No idea.'

'What time of the year was it?'

'Not long after I was picked up by the soldiers,' my father replied. 'They told me later that they had found me in late May 1942, so it must have been early June the same year.'

'But that would have made it summer time.'

'Exactly and that's where I'm confused, because my impression is that it was cold, and that there was snow on the ground.'

'If they lied about the conditions under which they picked you up, they might've lied also about when they did so,' I suggested.

'But why would they?' my father said, genuinely mystified.

'Perhaps to hide their involvement in this massacre,' I mused. 'If only there were some way to find out more about the movement of Latvian troops.'

'Perhaps Koidanov or Panok is the key to where I was born. If that were the case, we could learn a lot about my movements and the soldiers as well . . .'

'What about this building?' I asked, 'what was it?'

My father shrugged.

'At that time I didn't recognise the building as anything in particular. But I wonder now if it was a synagogue.'

'That's what I was thinking,' I replied. From my limited knowledge of the Holocaust, I knew that it had been a commonplace occurrence.

'The people were very likely Jewish,' I added.

My father looked momentarily bewildered. 'Sergeant Kulis used the word *partizani*.'

'The Nazis often used that term for the Jews they hunted in the forests. They also called them Bolsheviks.'

'I didn't know,' my father said, visibly shocked. 'To be honest, I wouldn't have had the slightest idea who was Jewish and who wasn't even if they were my people. I was only five.' Then he added: 'All I thought was that they looked like people from my village. Certainly now, looking back, I am sure that they were Jewish.'

I was curious about the photographs and asked my father if he had any in his case.

'No, not a single one. The soldiers must've kept them as souvenirs for themselves. But nobody thought to give me one.'

'I have another photograph,' my father said, eager to please.

He reached across for his case. I heard the familiar clicks of the case's locks before he began to rummage inside it. After a few moments he held up a photograph. This one was a head and shoulders shot of my father in a military uniform I'd never seen before. 'Good God!' I heard myself say.

'You can't tell because the photo's in black and white,' he said, 'but the uniform is blue – a pretty blue colour like the sky. My first uniform. I loved it more than the other ones with their drab colours.'

'There were other uniforms? Other colours? How many uniforms did you have?'

'Three altogether. First of all the blue one, then we changed to a light brown one . . .'

'When was this?'

'I can't give you dates,' my father answered, 'but the first change must've been about six months after I got the blue one. Each time, a new miniature uniform was prepared for me. I remember being told that we were no longer "policemen" and that we'd become members of the Latvian army and part of the *Wehrmacht*.'

'And that one was light brown, you said?'

My father nodded.

'How long were you in that?'

'Until . . .' my father squinted, trying to recall. 'It must have been in the summer of 1943, when Commander Lobe decided to take me north with his new brigade. That's when I had to change to a green one, like khaki green only lighter.'

'How long were you in the green uniform?'

'Until I left Latvia in 1944. You have to remember, son, it was confusing at times. We had summer uniforms as well,' my father added.

'Just a moment,' I said, raising my hand. I repeated the details of uniform changes to myself, committing them to memory. It occurred to me then that much like a detective I was in dire need of a notebook to record the minutiae of my father's story.

After a short silence my father spoke. I could sense his unease.

'There were other times . . .' my father hesitated, 'when I saw things . . . other atrocities committed by the soldiers. Sometimes when I was shunted to the rear of the troops I could only hear things. That was bad enough, but I guess they thought they were protecting me.

'As if I could be protected in any way from their brutality.'

My father fell silent. I could see that he had again become despondent.

'I knew that the soldiers were doing wrong. If only I'd done more . . .'

I cut my father off.

'What could you have done?'

'I should've tried to stop them.'

'What? You were a child.'

My father didn't respond. I could tell that he was not convinced by my words.

'Dad,' I said, 'your life must have been hell with the soldiers.'

'I got used to it.'

I wondered silently how one got used to hell. Was it any easier for a child who had little memory or experience of anything better?

My father's voice interrupted my train of thought.

'They used me to get girls from the local villages when they wanted to have a party. They thought that because I was a small boy and so cute that the girls would be more willing to join them.

'One time we stopped for the night in a barn. The soldiers were already pretty drunk and unruly. They'd made this primitive distillery which they carried about with them on patrol in order to make samagonka. That evening they set up the contraption and had me watch over it until the bootleg was ready. Then it was my job to keep the soldiers' tin cups topped up. Some of them forced me to swig the stuff so that before long I was as unsteady on my feet as the rest of them.

'A young girl, no more than fourteen or fifteen years old – she must have been the farmer's daughter – came in with food for all of us. As she was passing it around, Corporal Vezis tried to kiss her. She laughed and pushed him away playfully but I could tell she was frightened. She got out of there quickly. The other soldiers joked amongst themselves, saying that that was exactly what they needed – some girls.

'I kept on pouring the samagonka, but as much as possible stayed out of the way. At one point I felt Corporal Vezis's eyes settle on me. He called me over and straightened my uniform. Then he got up and told me to follow him. I didn't want to. I wanted to sleep. But he and another soldier pushed me out of the barn and down the path towards the village. On the way he made me pick some wild flowers – pretty ones.

'When we got to the village square we hid behind a cart. Corporal Vezis and the other soldier quietly watched the comings and goings of people in their houses. Then a young woman appeared on the doorstep of one cottage. That's when Vezis pushed me out into the open. In a whisper he ordered me to present the flowers to the young lady. I didn't want to, but I didn't dare disobey him, what with his violent temper.

'The girl was so surprised to see me, a boy in a uniform, swaying drunkenly at her door. I held out the flowers and she seemed touched. Then I nodded my head in the direction of Corporal Vezis.

'From a distance, the two soldiers must have looked harmless enough – just like any country boys courting girls – despite their uniforms. They waved at her in a friendly way and she took me by the hand and went over. For a short while they talked and laughed amongst themselves forgetting all about me. I was still drunk, and was silently willing myself to stay upright.

'Then the girl disappeared back across the square. Soon she returned with three other young women in tow. Together we all headed back to the barn.

'The party got into full swing very quickly. The women sipped on samagonka and, before long, they were a little drunk as well. They began to dance for the soldiers. A few of the soldiers got up and were staggering around trying to join in with the women while other soldiers clapped and laughed at the way their comrades made fools of themselves.

'It had been more or less good-humoured when suddenly the atmosphere turned nasty. Corporal Vezis tried to force one of the girls to sit on his knee and she resisted. Instead she gave a breathless laugh and pulled me on to her lap and gave me a big cuddle. In a jealous rage, the corporal yanked me off the girl's knee, almost ripping my arm off and tossed me violently across the room.

'He then made a lunge for the girl, attempting to kiss her. She struggled with him and when she broke free he made a grab at one of the other girls. All the while, the other soldiers looked on, clapping and cheering.

'You can imagine what happened after that,' my father said quietly, shaking his head in disgust. 'I hid in a corner. I didn't want to see what was going on but I couldn't block out the panting and the screaming which seemed to come from all corners of the barn.

'My memories of what happened next are vague.'

My father seemed to be in pain and screwed up his eyes as if torn between his duty to visualise something more clearly and the desire to forget whatever it was he had witnessed.

'I must have fainted,' he said. 'When I came round I could only hear the soldiers' snoring. I peeped out and they were asleep scattered all around the barn, wherever they'd collapsed in their drunken stupor.

'Then I saw that the girls were still in the far corner of the barn trying to clean themselves up. Their clothes were torn and they had been badly beaten.

'I wanted to help them. All I could think of was to offer them water. I tiptoed over to them. They backed away from me as if I was one of the soldiers, and then, without a word, they all slipped out of the barn.

'I stood there for a moment. I was bereft. They were repelled by me even though I felt I was on their side. I wondered if I should follow them and find refuge with them. I imagined I'd be able to tell them who I was: that I wasn't one of these men, that I wasn't anything like them. But then I thought: "Who would want me after I'd been with these devils?"

'Now of course, I understand that the soldiers had been using me to lure the girls to the barn. I feel responsible for what had happened to them, even now.'

My father stared bleakly into space.

My body shuddered. I was unnerved by what I had just heard. I pictured my father moving amiably from one drunken soldier to the next, smiling as, solicitous, he poured the anaesthetising samagonka. I saw him on the doorstep of the young woman's cottage holding the bunch of wild flowers. I was overwhelmed by the vulnerability of this child immersed in a world of arbitrary and deliberate brutality. How had he managed to steer himself through it? He said himself that he tried not to stand out or attract any attention, never daring to disagree with the soldiers or recoiling from their sexual forays, which must have been unfathomable to a child of six or seven. I wanted to know more about these men, these soldier-puppeteers, who controlled and exploited my father.

Yet it was not only the horror of my father's experiences that had overtaken me; it was anxiety for my father and the possibly incredible

dimensions of his story. Would people be able to accept the predicament
of a child's memory, lacking comprehensive details of names, dates and
locations? Could I? Thus far my father had revealed a handful of names and
the letter 'S' to add to the mystery of Panok and Koidanov. The remainder
were impressions and sensations about incidents seen through the eyes of a
child, shaded by bloody violence and an all-consuming fear of being discovered. I looked at the clock on the wall. It was nearly 4 a.m. The house was
silent. Even my mother's snoring had ceased. It felt as if the very walls of
the house were listening to my father's story in rapt silence. And now like
me they waited to see if my father would continue.

I rose and stretched my tired body, catching a glimpse of my face reflected in the darkened kitchen window. Opposite me, my father also stood to
stretch. He smiled shyly at me, and his eyes betrayed no sign of fatigue.
Instead their usual intense vivid blue shone as if he'd just risen from a long
sleep.

'Tell me, Dad, do you want to continue?' I asked.

My father nodded.

6

THE DZENIS FAMILY

M Y father and I sat down at the table again, as if recommencing a formal interview.

'How long were you with the soldiers on patrol?' I asked.

'From when they picked me up, which they later told me was in May 1942, until towards the end of 1943,' he replied. 'I wasn't on duty all the time. Sergeant Kulis sometimes took me to visit Riga, the capital of Latvia.'

'How often?'

'At least twice, perhaps even three times; whenever he was given leave.'

'Does the length of time the soldiers claim you were with them make sense to you?'

'It does,' my father said, 'because I spent one winter alone in the forest before the soldiers captured me and then I was on patrol with them for a second freezing winter before I was taken to Riga for a short time in the summer of 1943.'

'Do you remember much of 1943?'

'I do,' my father answered, 'especially after reaching Riga where life was more stable. When I was with the soldiers on patrol nobody paid any attention to dates and times as far as I could tell. It was chaos. And I was older in Riga. I remembered when people mentioned dates, and I was learning to read, so I could follow details in newspapers and magazines.'

'If these dates are correct then the extermination of your village, wherever it was, must have taken place in 1941.'

'Late in 1941,' my father said.

'Why late '41?' I asked.

'It was getting cold and the nights were drawing in when it happened in my village.'

'I am trying to picture where your village might have been in Russia,' I said.

'The soldiers never mentioned where we were, apart from insults . . .'

'Insults?'

'Yes, you know, curses and swearing. Incessant.'

'Such as what, Dad?'

My father's face turned red with embarrassment. He coughed and looked around.

'If you'd rather not say,' I said.

My father nodded gratefully. I realised that I had rarely, if ever, heard him swear. Perhaps his aversion stemmed from his being forced to listen to the soldiers' abuse.

I changed the subject.

'How far was camp "S" from Riga?'

'I couldn't say, but the train journey to Riga with Sergeant Kulis seemed to take for ever. But then everything does for a child. We would have to change trains at least once and also spend one night on board – it was always uncomfortable, and I would cuddle up to the sergeant who'd wrap me inside his big army coat.'

'What did you do in Riga?'

'It was a real treat for me.'

My father's face lit up.

'Even though things must have been scarce during wartime they treated me very well. I did all the usual things that kids like doing. Sergeant Kulis would take me to stay with his mother and father, and we'd spend lots of time with his fiancée, Wilma, as well. We'd go to one of the parks if the weather was fine. That always attracted a lot of attention, especially from other children. Boys in particular were envious of my uniform. "How can we join the army?" they used to ask me.

'Once the Kulis family took me to see a movie and before it there was a newsreel about the war. Believe it or not I didn't like it: it was just propaganda. I'd been at the front. I knew the difference between what really went on and what was on the screen, which was just fantasy. I was a real soldier.

'The more time I spent in Riga, the more well known I became. One day Sergeant Kulis and Wilma took me to a cafe for ice cream. When I entered holding Wilma's hand the entire cafe seemed to recognise me and several people rose from their seats and applauded.

'I can taste it now, that ice cream. Strawberry, it was.'

My father smiled nostalgically.

'I hadn't had ice cream since I was a child in my village.'

'It sounds as if you no longer hated Sergeant Kulis.'

'I'm not sure what I felt. I never forgot or forgave what he'd done that day when the building was burnt down. But Commander Lobe had put him in charge of me, and I just made the best of it, trying to get along with him and everybody for that matter. I was a quick learner too, so it wasn't long before I was chattering away in Latvian with the soldiers and people I met in Riga.'

'You were turning into quite the little Latvian,' I joked.

My father gave an uneasy laugh.

'No,' he said. 'I wasn't one of them. I could feel them loving me but I didn't want any part of it. Deep inside me I wanted to be free of them. Always.'

My father paused.

'Anyway, it was in the late spring of 1943 when Sergeant Kulis told me that he and I would be making another journey to Riga. I imagined that it was going to be one of our typical visits together and began to anticipate the many treats that I knew would be coming my way.

'But as soon as the train pulled in to the main station in Riga, I had an inkling that something was up. Wilma was not there to greet us as she'd been on other occasions. Instead an enormous black and shiny limousine waited at the kerb outside the station exit. The sergeant gathered my knapsack and ushered me towards the car. A chauffeur, dressed in a soldier's uniform, stood to attention and held the door open for me. I couldn't believe the luxury inside the car; the seats were covered in leather and there was even a small cocktail bar. The engine was almost inaudible as we wound our way smoothly through the streets of Riga. I gazed out from the passenger window but I didn't recognise anything I saw – we were in a different part of Riga.

'I stared across at Sergeant Kulis who was still gripping my hand. "Where are we?" I demanded with a growing sense of panic. "We'll be there soon," he said, and I could tell that he too was uneasy about something. This visit seemed to be going very differently from other visits when he took me by bus to his family home.

'Then the car took a side turning, and moments later we pulled up outside a building that seemed to tower above the street. I was a village boy and I'd never seen anything like it before. I peered up at it through the car window. I was enchanted: I thought that it was a magical palace with all its coloured lights and its pretty lit sign above the entrance. The sign said "Laima Chocolates".

'It was then that I noticed a man was standing in the shadow of the building near the entrance. I stared intently at him but I couldn't quite make him out.

'The chauffeur came around and opened the door on my side, at which point the mysterious man stepped forward into the bright morning light. He wasn't a soldier. Instead he was wearing a well-cut suit of a fine shiny material. He seemed very formal: he stood very erect and rigid with his hands held behind his back, and I thought that he must be a well-bred sort of person. "Who is this strange man," I asked myself.

'He came towards the car, and stretched out his hand to shake mine but I held back. I waited for Sergeant Kulis to join me and, when he did, I instinctively tried to take his hand. But he shrugged me off and instead shook hands with this superior man. Then he turned to me. "This is Mr Dzenis," he said, "say hello."

'I hid behind Sergeant Kulis's leg. He tried to nudge me out to the front but I had frozen to the spot. Then the sergeant said, "Mr Dzenis is going to look after you." My heart sank. My intuition that something was wrong had been right but I had never imagined that I was going to be given away.

'Sergeant Kulis nudged me again, trying to get me to greet this forbidding man but I remained mute.

'Mr Dzenis tried to be friendly towards me. He leaned forward and smiled at me. "Don't worry," he said, "we'll soon get you out of that uncomfortable uniform." That only sent me into a rage. In desperation I gave a salute and barked, "I'm not surrendering my uniform." Then clicking my heels as if this would somehow save me, I shouted out: "I am a soldier!"

' "All right," he said, trying to placate me. "All right, little soldier, you may stay as you are." I could see that he was trying to contain his laughter which only incensed me more. Before I could gain control of myself, I shouted at Mr Dzenis: "I am not staying here with you! I want my battalion."

'I had lost my soldier's discipline and forgotten the promise of good behaviour I had made to the sergeant. I felt downcast and just stared at the ground. I could tell that Sergeant Kulis was annoyed with me for the resistance I was putting up at that moment, but I was sure that he didn't want to part from me as much as I was reluctant to leave him or any of the soldiers.

'Suddenly before I even understood what was happening the sergeant lifted me off the ground and gave me a hug, as if I were a child and not a soldier. "Farewell, my little friend," he said. With that he put me down and strode away. I lost control, again forgetting that I was a soldier, and began stamping my foot. I set my jaw stubbornly. I wanted Sergeant Kulis and not this Mr Dzenis even if he did live in a beautiful palace. I have always remembered that moment and the sergeant's parting words to me.

'Mr Dzenis literally began to drag me back towards the limousine. I was kicking and screaming but then I got hold of myself. I told myself not to make any trouble. I'd learnt better than that. For a moment we paused on the pavement, and I got one last chance to search the street with my eyes. By then there was no sign of the sergeant. At that moment I didn't think I would ever forgive him for deserting me.'

'Why were you reluctant to leave the soldiers?' I asked.

'I'd got used to them and the way they cared for me,' my father replied. Then with a shrug of his shoulders he added, 'Besides, I had nobody else.

'The limousine set off again. This time I was in the company of Mr Dzenis. Like Mr Dzenis himself, the part of the city we passed through somehow seemed more well off than where I usually went with Sergeant Kulis. There were shops with bright and colourful displays in their windows, and the ladies walking on the pavement appeared happy and fine looking.

'Eventually we turned off a main road and into a narrow street. There was a sign that said "Valdemara Street". Shortly after that, we came to a halt outside a well-kept apartment block. It was as impressive as the palace I'd just seen. There was a long path leading from the kerb up to the front door. On one side of the entrance the Nazi flag – a giant swastika – was flying, and on the other, the Latvian flag.

'I climbed out of the car and waited for Mr Dzenis to join me. He took my hand as we headed up the path and entered the building. We were in an elegant foyer and for a moment I was transfixed by a chandelier that hung from the ceiling and sparkled like a jewel. Then I was seduced by the over-powering scent of a spray of beautiful flowers that sat on a side table.

'Mr Dzenis told me that we should hurry. "Everybody is waiting for you," he said. I was curious – who was everybody and why were they waiting for me? But another part of me was confused and angry – I was still thinking about my duties and my comrades in the troop. "What could be more important than that?" I thought to myself.

'We climbed the stairs to the top floor and outside the door to the apartment Mr Dzenis smoothed my uniform and hair.

'The door opened and we stepped inside. The entrance hall was softly lit by lamps that seemed to flicker – like the Aladdin's cave of my imagination – and the moments after that were equally dream-like. Out of nowhere a beautiful made-up face bent down to my level and smothered me in kisses.

There was the scent of perfume; I can't describe it apart from saying that it was like I was falling down a deep well lined with cotton wool. In the next moment I was being hugged by another beautiful lady, who made cooing sounds and smiled at me with moistened eyes.

'Suddenly it was all too much for me. I squirmed free of her arms and stood to attention, saluting wildly at her. Mr Dzenis gave me a stern look and warned me to behave with proper manners. When I had calmed down, he introduced me to the first lady who had kissed me so much. She was Emily, his wife. "Call me Auntie," she said and then she made way for the other woman who'd fussed over me already. She was tall and glamorous looking, perhaps about eighteen years old. Her name was Zirdra and she was Mr Dzenis's eldest daughter. She had a beautiful laugh that tinkled like water in a stream. I felt instantly that she had a gentle nature.

'Another girl hovered in the background. She must have been about five years older than me. Immediately I could tell that she was a completely different kettle of fish from Zirdra. She had no intention of welcoming me in any way, and instead frowned down at me contemptuously. She turned out to be Ausma, Mr Dzenis's youngest daughter.

'Auntie told me that Zirdra and Ausma were going to be my big sisters and that I had another sister, the middle one, called Mirdza, who was unwell and confined to her room for the evening. Later I learnt that Mirdza had suffered from polio when she was younger and, though not disabled in any obvious way, her body was wracked with inexplicable pains and aches. I also learnt later that the three girls were all from Mr Dzenis's first marriage, which had ended in divorce, and that he and Auntie had no children from their own marriage.

'That first night the Dzenis' gave a lavish party in their apartment. I was the guest of honour. But it was not without drama beforehand. Zirdra had tried to give me a bath and, of course, I'd not forgotten Sergeant Kulis's warning. It was mayhem. Zirdra chased me around the room, wanting to undress me for the bath, and I was ducking behind chairs, under the table, wherever I could wriggle into. In the end she gave up, but only because the guests were due to arrive.

'The party was a great success for the Dzenis family. When I entered the room for the first time, yet again everybody stood and applauded me. I knew what was expected of me: I stood as erect as I could and proudly saluted in all directions. Everybody seemed very amused by this.

'Many of the guests were in uniform: there were Latvian and German officers with their wives. One of the German officers stepped forward and made a great show of giving me the Nazi salute. It was then that Mr Dzenis whispered in my ear how much I should appreciate such an important soldier taking an interest in me. He told me to return the special salute, which I did. This caused another round of applause.

'Later Commander Lobe appeared . . .'

'So you were reunited with Lobe at the Dzenis party?'

'Yes,' my father answered. 'He was in a jolly mood and seemed pleased to see me. He pulled me on to his knee and chatted to me in Latvian. He was impressed that I had mastered the language so quickly. At one point in the celebrations two men arrived. They hovered by the door and Commander Lobe went over to join them. One turned out to be a journalist called Arnold Smits, and a photographer whose name I didn't hear. They wanted to take some shots of me at the party and they got Zirdra to crouch down to my level and hug me for the camera, but I squirmed shyly. All the guests thought that this was hilarious except for me – I still wasn't relaxed in the company of women. The commander told me that I'd better get used to being photographed with glamorous women because he had great plans to make me into a star. I didn't understand what he meant but thought to myself "I don't want to be a star if it means being kissed by women all the time."

'That's all I can remember about the commander that night but, in the coming months, I was to spend a lot more time with him and got to know him much better.' My father's words sounded ominous but instead of telling me more he lapsed into a lengthy and impenetrable silence. I had no idea what my father might have been thinking.

Suddenly I heard the sound of his voice.

'Anyway,' he suddenly said, 'you know what kids are like at parties. I got bored and I was curious too about where I was to live. I decided to explore the apartment, leaving the adults to their merriment. The main hallway had doors leading off in all directions. The first door led into a study. I had never seen anything like it. It was full of books, and there was a large desk by the window. It smelt of leather and polish. It seemed so rich.

'After that I returned to the party. Zirdra spotted me slipping quietly back into the room and gave a little wave. I joined her on the sofa, and she immediately began tickling and cuddling me. After the long journey to Riga and meeting so many new people I actually fell asleep on her lap. Later when I awoke the guests had gone and the maid was cleaning up. But I was still on the sofa, nestled in Zirdra's arms.

'For a moment I remained hypnotised by the warmth of Zirdra's body but then, as I came to, I sprang to my feet. I was angry with myself and everybody around me. "I must return to my comrades!" I shouted. I'd become obsessed with the idea of being a soldier. Zirdra reached out to calm me down but I pushed her aside and dashed across the room. I wanted to escape, no matter where I ended up. I struggled to open the heavy door.

'Mr Dzenis must have heard the ruckus because at that moment he opened the door from the other side. His body blocked my way. "Wait. You live here now. With us," he said firmly. This only threw me into a deeper panic. I burst into tears.

'Zirdra hurried over to me and tried to comfort me again. "Don't worry I'll look after you," she whispered gently. "I'm your sister now." There was kindness in her voice and instinctively I trusted her but at the same time the word "sister" must have triggered something in me. I sobbed uncontrollably, "I want my own sister. My brother. Not you!" I wailed.

'Suddenly there was a stony silence in the room.

'Zirdra looked into my face. "You have a family?" She was astonished. "Where are they? Do you know?"

'You could have cut the tension in the air with a knife. Then, unimaginably, things took another turn for the worse. Ausma was fed up with my tears. "Why do we have to have him here?" she complained. Then she added: "Let's send him back to his real family, if he has one." Then something else occurred to her. "Besides," she said petulantly, "he's probably a little Yid . . ."

'Mr Dzenis sprang across the room and slapped her hard. She fell back into the sofa, holding her cheek and shrieking. Mr Dzenis was shaking with rage. "Stupid!" he spat at her so violently that both Ausma and I stopped crying, and the entire room fell into shocked silence.

'It was Zirdra who broke the spell. "Time for bed," she said, wiping my eyes with her scented handkerchief. Then taking my hand, she led me to my room and sat me down on the bed. "Don't you worry," she said, "we're just looking after you until your family comes back. We'll find them for you." I was forlorn at the thought. I had witnessed what had happened to my family. They were all gone. I knew that there was not one single person who would come back to me.'

I saw grief flash across my father's face but in the next instant his face contorted as he endeavoured to mask his pain with a bright smile. Quickly he dived back into his story.

'Zirdra reached under the pillow and pulled out a small blue bundle. "New pyjamas!" she smiled warmly, "let's put them on you."

'After all those months sleeping rough on patrol I couldn't have wished for more. Soft, warm and clean bedclothes. But of course I wouldn't let Zirdra near me. From what had just happened with Ausma unwittingly suspecting I was Jewish I knew with more certainty than ever that I would have to be on my guard. Always. Nobody would ever learn the truth about me no matter what happened in the future.

'Zirdra struggled to undress me for some time but in the end I was the stronger – I gripped my trousers with an incredible stubbornness – so that finally she gave up. I sat at one end of the bed and Zirdra at the other. "Very well then," she said, "tonight you'll sleep in your uniform." She folded back the bed cover and blankets and patted the sheet, indicating where I should climb in. I did so and she covered me. She took my face in her hands and gave me a goodnight kiss on my forehead. "Soon you'll get used to our ways," she told me. I closed my eyes and pretended to drop off to sleep.

Soon after that I heard her turn off the light and close the door gently. I was over-excited and my head was spinning with all my new experiences. There was no way I could sleep. I lay on my side with my head still resting on the pillow. My eyes moved around the room.

'I was just about to get up and examine the room more closely when I heard footsteps approach my door and then stop. The door latch clicked open. I pretended to be asleep for a second time but through my half-closed eyelids I could just make out Mr Dzenis peering into the room to make sure that I was fast asleep. I heard him close the door gently. Then there was the click of the key as it was turned quietly in the lock.

'I'd been shut in like a prisoner. Perhaps Mr Dzenis was still worried that I was going to escape and go in search of my real family. I sat on the edge of the bed for several minutes just staring into the darkened space. I couldn't resist the thought of the pyjamas and I decided that it would be safe enough for me to put them on. I told myself that I would have to wake up early the next morning, before the rest of the household, and change back into my uniform. I quietly slipped into them and folded my uniform neatly beside my pillow, within easy reach.

'I was still restless. My eyes scanned the room again. This time I noticed a sliver of light at the far end. It was coming from a tiny window. I went over and drew back the curtains.

'I don't know how long I stood there, mesmerised by the bright moonlight, but a scraping noise broke the spell. It was coming from the street below. I looked down and made out two figures cleaning the road. Their coats were tatty, even worse than mine from the forest. "If only I'd kept the dead soldier's coat," I thought to myself, "I could have tossed it down to them. It'd be better than what they've got now."

'Then something else caught my attention. It was like a jewel on the sleeves of their coats. A yellow star visible even at night and from this distance. "What are street cleaners doing with such pretty stars?" I asked myself. In truth I was envious because it was much more attractive than the red badge of Latvia that'd been sewn on the arm of my uniform.'

My father gave an ironic almost bitter laugh. 'Uncanny. My instinct was to prefer the yellow star to the symbol of Latvia.

'Soon enough I learnt the significance of that star. It wasn't remotely like a jewel. It was a curse on a people I knew I belonged with.'

My father gave a deep sigh. After a few moments he spoke again.

'I climbed back into the bed and drew the covers up so that even my face was hidden, and that was that,' my father said with finality. 'My first night with my new family.'

'Do you think any of them knew the truth about the fate of your family?' I asked.

'I can't see how they could have.'

'Did Uncle know you were Jewish?' I asked, referring to Mr Dzenis by the name I had used to address him when I was growing up.

'I'm sure he didn't . . .'

'Judging by his harsh reaction to Ausma, it's a possibility,' I suggested. 'He might have heard it from Kulis? Or perhaps Kulis had confided in Lobe who then told Dzenis?'

My father was clearly perplexed.

'Why would the sergeant have said anything when he'd warned me to be silent under threat of death? Besides, it would have been dangerous for him too if it'd been discovered that he was harbouring a Jew.'

My father shrugged.

'In any case I'm sure that Ausma didn't know about me. How on earth could she?' he asked. 'I think she was just using the worst insult of those times against me.'

'Or perhaps Ausma had overheard a comment made in a private conversation between Uncle and Auntie,' I said, 'or Uncle and Lobe. Who knows? It's all possible, Dad.'

I crossed to the sink and refilled the kettle for more tea.

'How about later in life?' I asked, resting against the row of cupboards, waiting for the kettle to boil. 'Did any of them ever give any indication that they knew you were Jewish?'

My father rose and joined me, leaning lightly against the refrigerator opposite, his hands behind his back.

'Never,' he said vehemently but the thought of it seemed to unsettle him. His eyes darted apprehensively, as if he still feared discovery.

After the war, in 1949, the Dzenis family had emigrated to Melbourne taking my father with them. My father had only just turned fourteen. Even though he was an independent lad, he was still grateful to have a family of sorts. Later, when he left the Bonegilla migrant camp in outback Victoria and went his own way – joining a travelling circus as elephant boy – my father had maintained contact with members of the family apart from Ausma, who had remained in Latvia with her mother, Dzenis's first wife, after the war.

Even in Latvia, he'd only ever had sporadic contact with her when she came to the apartment to visit. According to my father it was obvious that, like her sister Mirdza, Ausma resented his presence among them and the attention Uncle showered on him.

Auntie had passed away in 1970 and Uncle in 1979 in Melbourne but my father still saw Uncle's other two daughters, Zirdra and Mirdza, who had also made it to Australia. It was natural that my father gravitated towards Zirdra. She had been the only one who hadn't seemed to resent his presence in the Dzenis household. After divorcing her husband in Adelaide, she'd moved to Melbourne where my father got to see her more regularly. He had spoken on several occasions of his instinctive like and trust of her.

'Only once,' my father now explained to me, 'when I dropped by to say hello on the spur of the moment, did Zirdra mention the past. Uncannily, she reminisced about the pyjamas incident. "Why were you so terrified?" she asked me. I simply shrugged my shoulders non-committally. "You know what boys are like," I said. She held my gaze for several moments; there was a shrewd expression in her eyes. But then she let the matter drop.

'We never mentioned the past again – everything remained unstated between us – as if we'd agreed to be silent for ever. I was relieved. My secret had remained buried for many years and I was content for it to continue that way.'

My father seemed genuinely sad as he recalled her death many years ago.

'Later in life, long after she'd died,' he reflected, 'it occurred to me that

Zirdra understood my situation – what I felt inside – more than the others, perhaps even more than myself, without knowing that I was Jewish or any of the details of my story. Perhaps she even sensed that I had a history that might in some way shame Latvians if it ever became public.

'And then there is Mirdza,' my father said. Mirdza was the only one of the sisters still living. With her husband, Edgars, she had also settled in Melbourne and raised three children. They lived only a few miles from my parents and saw each other occasionally when my father was in Mirdza's good books.

There had always been tension between my father and Mirdza, he said: 'She'd always been the centre of attention, and then I was thrust into the limelight. I learnt later that Uncle had always wanted a son, and it was clear from the outset that he loved having me there.'

My father stood up straight and cupped his hands around the mug of tea I offered to him. Then he settled back in his chair.

'Will you tell Mirdza any of your story?' I asked, joining him at the table.

'God forbid! Could you imagine?' He looked daunted by the prospect of doing so.

Then he said, 'I'll have to. Just let me get over the shock I've caused to myself with all this . . .'

'What do you mean?' I asked. 'Do you regret speaking to me?'

'No,' my father said, 'but to be truthful I don't want to remember anything of what happened to me. Who in his right mind would? But the bigger truth is that I am more terrified to forget. I am trapped.'

THE VOLHOV SWAMPS

'I JUST couldn't settle at the Dzenis',' my father said. 'Firstly, Uncle and Auntie wanted me to give up my soldier's uniform, which I refused to do point-blank.

'Then there was the matter of school. I'd never attended school before, even in my village. I didn't want to go; I didn't see the point of it especially when I could've been out on patrol with the soldiers. While Uncle was willing to compromise on my uniform, he wouldn't tolerate any resistance about school. 'You have to learn to read and write', he said.

'From the outset school was disastrous. I was disruptive. I couldn't and wouldn't sit still at my desk like the other girls and boys whom I looked down upon as silly and spoilt. Worst of all was that I wouldn't obey my teacher – I still recall her name, Miss Eglits. As the days passed I became more unruly and more than once drove her to tears of exasperation.

'I'd been at school for just over a fortnight when Auntie and Uncle were called in by the headmaster. He made it clear that I was beyond redemption as a student, if not as a child as well. The headmaster told Uncle that it might be better if I had a private tutor or even returned to the soldiers. I'd been sitting there in his office perched between Auntie and Uncle bored and staring down at my boots. But that suggestion brought a smile to my face. I was going to be free of books and ink pens and the sour milky smell of the schoolroom. I looked up to share my pleasure with Auntie and Uncle but when I caught a glimpse of Uncle's reddened and angry face I quickly bowed my head again. Auntie must have sensed my sudden fear of Uncle because she secretly took my hand and gave it a gentle and reassuring squeeze.

'In all the time that I knew him Uncle never once laid a hand on me but that day he must have come close to doing so. As we left the schoolyard he said to me in a very hard voice that I'd brought shame on his name.

'Auntie and Uncle talked intently about my situation as our limousine made its way back to Valdemara Street. I knew better than to show how pleased I was at my escape from school so I sat quietly, staring out at the passing sights with a contrite expression on my face.

'At one point in the journey I heard Uncle say the name of Commander Lobe. From the tone of her voice I could tell that Auntie disagreed with whatever Uncle had said and was trying to reason with him. I sensed that she was springing to my defence. But by the time we reached Valdemara Street Auntie and Uncle had come to a decision,

'Once inside the apartment, Uncle sent me to my room, telling me that I would have to eat my lunch there alone as a punishment.

'After lunch, Auntie came to collect me from my room. She peeked around the door. "Uncle has returned to Laima," she said in an exaggerated whisper. "You can come out now."

'That afternoon we went into the centre of Riga. Auntie took me to my favourite cafe where she let me eat as much strawberry ice cream as I desired. I didn't get it – I'd been expelled from school, had caused Auntie and Uncle to argue – which was something I never saw them do – and I was being rewarded with ice cream.

'It became even more baffling because after I'd wolfed down a second mountain of ice cream Auntie took me to the cinema. It was a German film – a silly romance of some sort which didn't interest me at all, although I could understand the gist of what was going on because by then I'd picked up some German. You see out on patrol we'd cooperated with German soldiers, and quite a few of our commanding officers were German.'

Suddenly my father stopped speaking. His face bore a startled expression as if he'd just been slapped.

'Wait!' he exclaimed, raising his hand.

'It's on the tip of my tongue.'

His eyes darted about.

'Acun?' he said. 'No! Not Acun but something like that.'

'What on earth . . .' I began to say, but my father raised his hand again to silence me.

'Erzum!' my father said, excitedly. He repeated the name. 'Erzum.'

'Erzum?'

'It's just come to me out of nowhere,' my father said. 'He was one of the German officers. Erzum. He was with us on patrol. I remember being photographed with him.'

'On that day? The day of the massacre?'

My father shook his head.

'I can't say for sure. It might've been. He was standing next to me. I was waist-high to him. He may have even had his arm around me. I remember staring at the pistol he had in his belt. He noticed me admiring it. He took it out and tucked it into my belt. But for the life of me I can't remember when and where this was.'

My father gripped his head in both hands and stared down at the floor. Then he looked up.

'It may come to me later,' he said. His frustration was palpable.

My father took his time to return to events in the Dzenis household.

'Although the day had started out badly the afternoon with Auntie had been wonderful, and at dinner that evening Uncle seemed to be in a better mood. I awoke the following morning to find the maid in my room. The small khaki rucksack that Sergeant Kulis had given me was open in front of her and she was stuffing my meagre belongings into it. At that moment Uncle appeared and sat down beside me on the bed. He told me that Commander Lobe had been put in charge of a new brigade called the 2nd Latvian Division. Uncle explained to me that the 18th Kurzeme Battalion, my old battalion, had been incorporated with another battalion that had in turn been divided to form two new divisions.

'Then came the piece of news I'd only dreamed of. Commander Lobe wanted me to join the brigade and accompany them on a new mission. I was overjoyed and relieved too that my time as a "normal" child was over. I was going to be a soldier again.

'It occurred to me then that Uncle had had enough of me after just two weeks and didn't want responsibility for me any more. For a second I felt regretful about my unruly behaviour. Auntie and Uncle and Zirdra too had been kind to me. I even had a change of heart. While I'd been happy to put on a show of bravado about being a soldier now that the reality was upon me I wasn't quite so sure I wanted to give up the comfort of life in Riga.

' "All your old comrades will be with you," Uncle said, "so you'll be better off there. Of course you shall still come and stay with us when you're not on duty. Now hurry up and get dressed. It's time for breakfast and then we'll be on our way. We don't want to keep the commander waiting?" That convinced me. The decision had been made and I was capable of recognising that it was the best possible solution. I was getting into such trouble in Riga and it was better that I went back to a situation that I was used to, no matter how horrible it was.'

'What year was this?' I asked.

'Around the summer of 1943.'

'So you must have been seven, nearly eight years old by then.'

'That's right.'

My father returned to his story.

'I fastened the buttons on my uniform. I examined my reflection in the mirror and, content that I looked the part, I strode confidently into the entrance hall to wait for Uncle. Auntie, Zirdra and Mirdza were already there. I don't think that Ausma was visiting that day. Auntie took my face in both her hands and planted a kiss on my forehead. Then Zirdra did the same.

'Mirdza was standing to one side. To be honest, I don't think she cared less about leaving me – we'd bickered continually since the night I arrived. But I said to myself: "At least give her a smile." I did so and she begrudgingly smiled back but she refused to kiss me when Auntie told her to.

'Uncle appeared carrying my case. He was eager for us to be on our way. But then Auntie turned to Uncle. "He's too young, Jekabs," she said. At that Zirdra joined in, pleading with her father to reconsider. Both women were quite upset and, at that moment I too became sad. As I said before I'd miss Auntie and Zirdra more than I imagined.

'For a split second Uncle seemed to waver. But then he became resolute. "The commander can't be kept waiting," he said, as if that in itself explained everything.

'I straightened my uniform, put on my army cap and slung my rucksack on to my back. And for a show of bravery I gave them all one final salute.

'When we arrived at Laima Chocolates, Commander Lobe was already waiting in Uncle's office. I gave him a formal salute but he waved at me quite casually, the way he did with Uncle who was an old friend. The commander was in a good mood. He patted the spot next to him on the sofa so I sat down. He gave me a slap on my knee as if we were longtime friends too. Then he reached into the inner pocket of his jacket and pulled out a piece of paper. He unfolded it and spread it out on the low table in front of him. It was a military map.

' "See, here is Riga," he said, pointing, "and here is Leningrad. And this is where we'll be going – it's called Velikiye Luki. What do you think about that?" I grinned to show the commander that I was pleased but in reality I didn't have any particular opinion about it. I'd heard of Leningrad which I'd been told was in Russia. But I had no idea where it actually was.

'When I heard the next piece of news I was overjoyed. "I've decided to promote you from Private to Corporal. You are now Corporal

Kurzemnieks." I was so proud of myself. I thought, "Imagine! You are only a boy yet you are a corporal."'

My father beamed with pleasure as he recalled this moment.

'But I could sense that Uncle had had a change of heart and like Auntie and Zirdra was not entirely happy about my fate. "The boy is too young for this Kārlis," he said, but the commander was dismissive. "The boy won't be in any danger," he countered, "we'll keep him behind the frontline. His job will be to boost the morale of the troops. Like a puppy, that's all."

'The commander rose, telling Uncle that he was taking me to SS headquarters for a fitting of a new uniform – an SS one. I was to be SS Sturmann Kurzemnieks.'

I was appalled to hear what they had done to my father and my face must have betrayed my sense of horror. But my father must have misread its source, and he immediately sprang to his own defence. He appeared deeply bewildered.

'I did not volunteer or choose that,' he insisted, 'a decision was made to assign me to the brigade. There was no choice involved. I had no say in it.'

Yet even as he spoke his voice lost its usual melodic vigour, as if with my reaction I had accused him of complicity.

He sighed deeply. I watched as he struggled to take up where he had left off with his recollections.

'Uncle accompanied the commander and me as far as the foyer of Laima. As we were on the point of leaving, he pulled out a small parcel from his pocket. "Chocolate bars," he said, passing the package to me. "A gift from Laima. Don't eat them all at once. Ration them." Then he added, "And don't let your comrades steal them from you. They have their own supply of Laima chocolates."

'I shook Uncle's hand firmly. He told Commander Lobe to take good care of me. The commander reassured him casually and then looked at his watch. "We have to be off, Jekabs," he said. Taking me by the hand he ushered me briskly out onto the street so that I barely had time to turn and give Uncle a wave.

'The headquarters of the SS turned out to be quite close to the factory so we walked there. En route Lobe put his arm around my shoulder and smiled at me, saying, "One more thing, Corporal, you'll be with your comrade Sergeant Kulis in the Sapira Troop." Sapira means pioneer.

'Hearing this I forgot my anger towards Sergeant Kulis. I pictured myself alongside him on patrol as in the old days.

'When we reached Lobe's headquarters the commander took me directly to a small office where his secretary was waiting and passed me over to her care. She took me to a neighbouring room where I noticed a box down on a low table. It held my new SS uniform. Immediately she tried to remove my jacket. I adopted a no-nonsense and haughty attitude and turned my back on the secretary, dismissing her with the words "You may go now."

' "Very well," she said and then left me alone to put on the uniform. Several minutes later I returned to the office in my new uniform. The lady began to fuss over me – she said that I'd buttoned the jacket lopsidedly – but I backed away from her, making it clear that she was not to touch me.

'Unexpectedly in response she gave me a flirtatious pout and told me to wait for the commander who would be back shortly. When he did return Commander Lobe was carrying a full-length black leather overcoat that had been tailored especially for me. He held it open and I slipped my arms into the sleeves so that I was reminded for an instant of my dead soldier's overcoat: it was so heavy that I could barely move and its hem dragged slightly on the floor. But it felt so much more elegant.

'The uniform was light khaki but the design wasn't much different from the other ones I'd worn. And of course I still had my long riding boots which I wore over my jodhpurs.'

My father squinted. It was as if he was staring into his past, at an image of himself in Lobe's office. He then nodded his head.

'There were these – how do you call them? "Insignia" is it? – sewn on the jacket, on its arm and sleeve and the collar.'

My father raised his left arm slightly to demonstrate to me.

'Here,' he said, pointing first at his upper arm close to the shoulder, 'was one identical to the one on the *Wehrmacht* uniform. It was shaped like a shield and was red-coloured with a white band going across it at an angle. On it was written "Latvijas" which meant Latvia.'

'And the sleeve?'

'There was a stripe that showed my rank. On the other cuff was an eagle with its wings spread wide open which was pretty . . .'

'Pretty?' I cut in. I was dismayed by my father's choice of word. For just a moment I had forgotten again that my father was remembering through not only child's eyes but also the emotions he had felt at the time.

'Yes,' my father answered, fortunately seeming oblivious to my tone. 'But my favourite was the emblem on the collar of the jacket. There was a little black patch on either side of the neck. One had a stripe for my rank as Sturmann and the other one had a symbol on it – an outline of the sun with three stars inside it. The commander told me that it was the symbol of the

Latvian SS. I loved that one. Best of all though was the one Commander Lobe had. He'd been awarded one of the highest military medals of the German Army: the German Cross in gold, which he wore around his neck on a ribbon. He would let me play with that too for hours on end. It kept me entertained whenever I got bored.

'In fact Uncle told me that Commander Lobe had travelled to Berlin and received the medal from Hitler himself,' my father added, both ashamed of and visibly impressed by Lobe's achievement.

I was aghast at the predicament of the innocent boy-soldier, oblivious to the significance of the medal. The boy had treated as a toy a symbol that most probably had been awarded to Lobe for horrendous crimes against people.

'It was sometime in the early mid-summer of 1943 when we left Riga for the Russian front. Our first port of call in occupied Russia was Velikiye Luki. I travelled with the commander up until that point, but immediately after we reached Velikiye Luki, he was taken up with serious military business and I was handed back to Sergeant Kulis. I was certain that the sergeant would let no harm come to me.

'I'd become a bit of a celebrity by that stage – I think that an article about me had been published in a newspaper in Riga where I was pictured with Commander Lobe. So many of the soldiers knew about me. They were always wanting to play with me or simply have me around. Sometimes I'd get overwhelmed by it all. I'd be tired and grizzly and then Sergeant Kulis would keep the soldiers at bay.

'We must have stayed in Velikiye Luki for about a month. It was a base camp for our brigade and the troop spent time doing extra training for the frontline. During the day the sergeant was often involved in military activities away from base camp. When he returned in the evening we'd sit together on the steps outside the barrack entrance. He would quietly smoke a cigarette and I'd be by his side, scraping dried mud off his boots.

'I had my regular duties as well. The main one was to tidy our barracks once the soldiers had left for the day's training. But for most of the day I was left to my own devices. I'd chat to the soldiers who were off duty, and on rare occasions, if Commander Lobe allowed it, I would visit him in his makeshift office. He was always pleased to see me, and he'd sit me on his knee and ask me if I was being a good corporal. But when he was very busy and preoccupied I'd be told to sit quietly in the corner.

'There were so many visitors coming and going all day long. Some of them were clearly very important, German officers, for example, who arrived with entourages of assistants. But I can't remember any of their names. The commander didn't usually introduce me to them. I would simply salute them and after that he would dismiss me, telling me to return to my barracks.

'Eventually we were ordered to move further north into Novgorod. We stopped briefly in the occupied city where we then changed trains before heading north towards Volhov.

'In a matter of days we reached the Volhov area. There was no town or village that I can recall. Simply a train junction which was the end of the line for the type of train we were travelling on. We had to change over to funny little trains, more like toy trains, on narrow-gauge tracks. There were no carriages as such; only open wagons that we had to crouch in. These took us as far as possible into the swamps – the swamps of Volhov – and then we had to dismount again. From there we made our way deeper into the swamps on foot along narrow wooden planks that were elevated off the ground.

'It was eerie. We were surrounded by trees that had no branches or leaves. Just trunks standing upright, like skeletons stretching up into the sky. I remember one of the soldiers joked that we were on patrol for ghosts.

'The heart of the swamps was like nothing I'd ever experienced even during my time alone in the forest. It was hellish. Everywhere was covered in mud and the stifling humidity was unbearable. It didn't seem to drop at all, regardless of whether it was day or night. On the top of this the air was thick with clouds of mosquitoes and other bugs so that within hours of arriving every part of our bodies exposed to air were covered in bright red bites and swollen lumps, even on our faces. They itched like hell.

'By night we slept in dugouts in small groups of about four men. This was terrible too – the bottom of the dugouts often contained a few inches of water, which we had to scoop out. But the bottom always remained muddy.

'And then there were the rats that loved the dugouts. We could see their red eyes glowing up at us as we prepared to climb in for the night. We'd shoot at them, or if there were too many of them we'd simply toss down a hand grenade to kill them in one go. Then we'd have to fish them out before we could climb down to get some sleep. All this on top of the humidity and the mosquitoes. Sometimes the soldiers were too exhausted to care and just dropped down on the ground wherever they could and slept.'

My father shook his head in disbelief.

'In our crude camp there was an open kitchen that was equipped with an enormous cauldron for cooking. Three times a day, day in and day out, the same meal – a kind of soupy gruel – was cooked in it. It simmered away all day long. Before meals it was poured into a large trough at which the soldiers would line up, as if they were farm animals waiting for their turn at the watering hole. It tasted rancid, and the soldiers would constantly complain about it in low voices. The soldiers always put me at the head of the queue. "Watch out," they would shout. "Let the little mascot through." After my bowl had been filled I'd find a place to sit with the sergeant if he was around.

'The soldiers always passed me extra pieces of food from their kits. Our troop had received a small supply of Laima chocolate and the soldiers would always slip me a chunk from their rations. Later, I was to learn that Laima was the official sponsor of the 18th and the 2nd Division, and kept it supplied with chocolate.

'Unlike in Velikiye Luki things were now much less regulated and orderly. I would remain behind in the camp but there wasn't much to do apart from my few duties. I'd try to be of use fetching things for the soldiers or helping them with their laundry. Not that any of us were ever very clean. It was hard to keep your dignity.

'More often than not the soldiers wanted me to simply sit and talk with them. They'd tell me stories about the villages they came from, or they'd talk endlessly about their families or girlfriends or school. To tell the truth, behind their camaraderie many of them seemed very lonely and frightened by their situation. And some of them seemed almost as young and childish as me. I couldn't equate these young men who were my friends with their savagery as soldiers.

'Sometimes I would be left alone for hours. Nobody kept a watch on me and I'd venture outside the camp and often stray some distance away. But I always kept within earshot of the sound of gunfire and used that as a bearing to find my way back to camp.

'I often came across dead bodies as I had done in the forest. Some of the corpses were badly decomposed – they must have been there for months – and judging from the scraps of uniform that clung to their remains – some of them were soldiers. They'd been left where they had died, without even a burial in an unmarked grave. I'd become bigger and stronger by then so I had no difficulty in turning them face up in order to check their pockets.

'Then I'd sometimes come across a photograph of a loved one, or an ID card, which I'd gently place back on them. It felt wrong to take anything from them, now that I was being cared for. I'd put a twig or two over the body just to pretend that it was buried. I thought of it as my special secret duty. Nobody in my battalion needed to know about this, I thought. I performed this ritual on every single corpse I came across regardless of whether they were soldiers or not. I guessed that some of them might even have been the enemy *partizani* but I did the same for them. I always made my way back in camp before the light faded. I didn't want any trouble.

'One day when I'd ventured away from the camp, I was taken over by a sort of madness. "Here's your chance," I thought, "nobody will miss you. Just keep heading into the swamp and away from the brigade." I was sure that I could survive, since I'd done so before in the forest.

'The afternoon wore on and I trudged deeper and deeper into the swamps. It was hard going. I kept falling down in the mud and struggled to get myself up again. The sun was behind me so I knew that I was heading east. Gradually the sunlight grew thinner but I didn't stop nor did I look back once.

'When I'd been alone in the forest before I had grown used to it, despite my fear and desperation. But this was different and somehow unnerving with the strange skeletons of trees that rose out of the swirling mist and noises of a sort I'd not heard before – creaking and whooshing sounds. There wasn't even the noise of birds which spooked me. Perhaps the war had frightened them away. I started to think that my attempt to escape had not been such a good idea.

'I panicked. I turned and ran back in the direction of the setting sun, hoping that I would eventually reach the soldiers. I scrambled on and on through the swamp and the broken trees with their withered arms.

'It was almost twilight when I stopped for breath. There was still no sign of the camp, nor the sound of gunfire, and I hadn't been able to locate any of the markers that usually pointed me in the right direction. I realised then that I was completely lost.

'There was nothing to do but to keep on walking. To calm myself and keep myself company I chatted to myself in Latvian and sang songs that came to me.'

My father hummed a few words in a soft voice. The lyrics were in a language I did not recognise. Nor could I identify the melody.

'Where did you learn that?' I asked.

'I don't know. I just know it.'

I was intrigued by my father's recollection. Had it been something he had picked up from his mother? But my curiosity went unsatisfied as my father dived abruptly back into his story.

'Then I noticed something in the distance,' he said. 'At first I thought I was imagining it. In that grey wasteland of dead wood I saw what seemed to be a clump of green trees.'

My father gave a small laugh.

'As I made my way closer to it I realised that I hadn't gone mad after all. It was real. I was relieved. I knew how to take refuge safely in a forest.

'I plunged into the rich undergrowth. Then I stopped. Once again I panicked. "What if this forest is ruled by those ghostly trees outside? What if this is a trap?" I thought, "to catch me and devour me."

'By the time night had fallen I'd reverted to my old strategy. I'd climbed a tree and tied myself into a fork in the branches, this time with the leather belt from my uniform. Nothing came that night to frighten me – the trees did not come to life, nor were there any sounds of wolves or bears and other predators.

'In the morning I remained where I was, perched high up in the tree, and looked all around, trying to get my bearings. I was surprised because through the tops of the trees I could see the outline of a city in the far distance. I thought that it must've been Leningrad because Sergeant Kulis had spoken of how close we were to "the greatest of Russian cities".

'I decided to make my way out of the forest and head in the direction of Leningrad. "If I can see it," I thought, "then it cannot be too far away." I unbuckled my belt and clambered down the tree. I wanted to reach Leningrad as quickly as possible. I took my bearings from the rising sun and headed off in what I estimated was a northerly direction.

'I'd taken no more than a dozen steps when I heard voices and footsteps nearby. Whoever they were, they were almost upon me. I scrambled back up the tree and held my breath. Then almost directly below me I saw about six people come to a halt. They were carrying guns and packs too. There were men and women, all quite young and speaking in a language I recognised – Russian.'

'You knew that you were Russian?' I asked.

'I didn't think of myself as being any nationality but I recognised some of the words that Kulis had tested on me and that he'd told me were Russian. And the other soldiers had kept insisting that I was Russian.'

'What did you feel about your false identity?'

My father shrugged.

'What could I do? Even though I knew it wasn't the truth, part of me accepted it as such. I'd been warned by Sergeant Kulis to only repeat his version of events. In any case I had no clear idea who I really was so what was the point of protesting against the identity they'd given me?'

'But you knew at least what had happened to your family. You realised that you were Jewish. Wasn't there anybody you felt you could confide in?'

'Not a soul. That would've meant certain death. I was an enemy of the Nazis and the Latvian people.'

After several moments my father returned to his story.

'These people standing below my tree, I sensed that they were the *partizani* that the soldiers were always cursing. One tiny move and they might discover me and if they saw my SS uniform I would be shot on the spot.

'But then suddenly it also occurred to me that if they were the enemies of the Latvians, then perhaps I should be on their side. I sat there high up in the tree, both petrified and wondering what would be the right thing to do, when something very strange happened. I caught a glimpse of the face of one of the women. I recognised her. At first I didn't know who she was or where she was from but then it dawned on me that she was from my village. I had this vivid impression that she'd been in our house when I was playing in the yard, and that she'd smiled at me. I nearly fell out of the tree.

'I had an overwhelming urge to spring down from my hiding-spot and ask her outright, "Do you remember me?" But I didn't. I cannot describe clearly what happened to me. I must have become transfixed by my thought of home because the next thing I recall was coming to and realising that the group had picked up their packs and had moved quietly away. I felt defeated by their departure. But still I couldn't make up my mind what to do. Try to find them or stay hidden in the tree? I was tormented.

'If only I'd made myself known to them . . .' my father said.

Even now he appeared to be devastated by this lost chance.

'The forest was deadly silent. I rubbed my eyes. I must still have been half in a dream. "Did this happen?" I asked myself, "or was it as I had suspected all along – that the forest was some kind of evil magic? Had they been ghosts?" Had the woman I recognised from my village come back to punish me for deserting my family?

'Suddenly I didn't care whether that group of people was real or imagined. I scrambled down the tree and fled in the opposite direction. I ran without any concern about where I was going, and within moments I landed directly into the arms of two soldiers from the division who'd been sent out to search for me. I was hysterical and one soldier had to slap me hard to bring me to my senses.

'I learned that I'd been gone for nearly two days and how worried everybody had been. Many believed that I must have perished somewhere.

'The soldiers told me how ungrateful I was for all that had been done for me. But I was too overwhelmed by my experience to respond. They dragged me roughly back to camp. I feared what was in store for me.

'They took me directly to Sergeant Kulis, who was furious with me. One of the commanding German officers had ordered that I be sent back to Velikiye Luki immediately as punishment. The sergeant packed my stuff there and then and that evening I left in the company of a platoon that were being relieved from the frontline duty. I didn't even say farewell to Sergeant Kulis.

'The platoon reached Velikiye Luki a couple of days later. Even though I was famished I wasn't permitted to stop at the mess for breakfast. I was ordered directly to Commander Lobe's quarters.

'The soldier who took me there pushed me forward, telling me to knock on the door. I heard the commander call out "Enter". He was in his bathroom and standing, bare-chested, at the sink, shaving. The commander stared at my reflection in his mirror.

' "You," he said, looking down at me disdainfully. Then he went on shaving in silence. I remained standing at attention and he did not bother to put me at ease. I watched as he then washed and dried himself off. He turned and brushed past me as he went into the main room. It was as if I'd become invisible.

'I remained standing where I was but felt drowsy because of lack of food and sleep. Suddenly his face was inches from mine. His eyes were bulbous and bloodshot and his face was purple. He was like a vicious dog snarling and barking words at me, most of which I didn't hear because I was scared out of my wits, trembling and shaking uncontrollably.

'Then he stood upright and glared down at me with steely eyes. "I know what you were trying to do," he said. He realised that I had been trying to run away from the army. He brought his face close to mine again and raised his hand. I braced myself. But he didn't hit me – instead he tore off the corporal's insignia from the collar of my jacket. "You're no longer a corporal," he said sharply, "you are a private again. You're no longer on active duty. You're going back to Riga, to the Dzenis family."

'Then he dismissed me. As I left he called after me so that I had to stop and turn. "You try this again," he said, "and I'll kill you."

'I had been disgraced. I didn't feel like a soldier at all. I felt small, like a child, and was too ashamed of myself to be worried by his threat.

'I was sent back to Riga by train that same day in the company of a guard. All the way back to Riga he didn't utter a single word to me as if he distrusted me as a traitor.'

My father paused, seemingly exhausted by his recollection.

'I never saw Sergeant Kulis again,' he said reflectively. 'He never came for me as I thought he would and I never asked about him. I didn't want to be reminded of my failure. Or remind anybody about it.'

'Do you know what became of him?' I asked.

'For many years I assumed that he had died during the war. But then in the late 1950s, long after the Dzenis' took me with them to Australia, a letter arrived out of the blue. It was from Sergeant Kulis and had been sent from a suburb in New York City. He'd traced me through a network of Latvian soldiers – Daugavas Vanagi – he'd kept in touch with after the war. The envelope contained a short note and a photograph of Sergeant Kulis in the living room of his home with a boy of seven or eight sitting on his knee. I have the note here.'

My father reached into his case, and immediately produced a yellowed envelope. He perched his reading glasses on the end of his nose and began to read.

' "The seventh of June, Nineteen Fifty Eight. Dear Uldis. It's been years since I last saw you. But I have often thought about you. Many times my wife Wilma and I have talked about you and wondered if you would remember us. We spent some nice days in Riga, do you remember? Then came the day you were sent back to Riga. It's been fifteen long years since then. God gave me luck and I survived the war. Now I live in America and work in the building industry. I have a son who is the same age as you when we parted. It would make me very happy if you were interested to be in contact with me. I want to hear about you and your life in Australia. I still think of you as my son. I always regret that I never adopted you. With kind regards, Jekabs Kulis." '

'Amazing. Did you reply to the letter, Dad?'

'No.'

'Did you ever try to make contact with him?'

'Never.'

'Why?'

'I wanted to look to the future. Not rake up the past. I locked the letter away in my case and for a very long time, decades in fact, I forgot that I'd ever received it or that Kulis existed. That case is a bit of a curse, isn't it? You never know what you might find in it.'

I needed to clear my head. I got up and without thinking went to the back door. I opened it a fraction and was assaulted by a violent gust of icy wind.

'For God's sake!' my father exclaimed. I immediately slammed the door shut.

I was disturbed, perhaps even slightly annoyed, that my father had kept so many things from me – more facts about Lobe, his initiation into the Latvian SS, the letter from Kulis, a fuller picture of his life in the Volhov swamps – and the truth was that I needed also to take stock of my father. I was baffled by the fact that my father had remained silent for more than fifty years. What almost superhuman strength had this required? What toll had silence taken on his inner life? He seemed to inhabit two separate worlds. In one, he was my father with an 'official' history, an authorised and edited version of the past. But in the other world he was still largely a stranger to me: a boy-soldier, origins unknown, who was shunted about, wide-eyed, in one of the worst bloodbaths in history.

One world was inexorably unravelling while a new, unpredictable one emerged.

8

THE CHOCOLATE SOLDIER

'I T was early October 1943 when I arrived back in Riga. By my calculation I'd been away at the front for about four months. Uncle was waiting for me at the main station. All the way back to the flat in Valdemara Street, he remained silent next to me in the limousine.

'The atmosphere in the flat was subdued when we went in. In the entrance hall I heard only the ticking of the ornate grandfather clock in the corner.

'Then I heard Auntie's footsteps in the hallway. She came into the foyer, and greeted me much more formally than she had ever done before – she shook my hand. It dawned on me that the commander's suspicions about my attempted escape had been passed on to Uncle and Auntie and that they too felt betrayed by me.

'That afternoon Uncle had to go back to work at Laima and he left Auntie and me alone. No sooner had he closed the door behind him than Auntie swept me up into her arms and planted kisses on both my cheeks. She told me how much she'd missed me. I was overjoyed: Auntie had been pleased to see me after all, and she still cared for me. She scrutinised my face and a look of concern crossed her features. She told me that I had become much too frail and that I needed fattening up, and lots of fresh air.

'That night I overheard her discussing a holiday with Uncle and shortly after that Auntie took me to a country house the family kept in a place called Carnikava on the Riga coast, some miles west of the city.

'We stayed there for about a week.' My father's face beamed at the memory so that I could almost see the little boy in him.

'On the day of our arrival, Auntie took me down to the sea which was only a few minutes away. I'd never laid eyes upon the sea before and, that first time, I was shocked. I stood on the shoreline for ages, entranced by the waves as they flowed into shore. Even though it was the Baltic and had nothing of the wildness I later saw in the Australian oceans, I remember how impressed I was by its immensity and power. For a moment I recollected when I was a child in the village and I'd pretend to be the ship's captain scanning the sea for pirates. Now here was the real sea before me, but I had no interest in playing pirates. I had become a real soldier.

'The following morning we headed down to the shore again. The weather was still mild and Auntie wanted me to go into the water with her. She did all she could to coax me in, but I wouldn't have a bit of it. I couldn't quite believe it. I wasn't ready to enter this unknown just yet.

'Auntie prepared delicacies for me every evening, especially my favourites, lamprey and smoked eel. At night together we'd build a fire to ward off the damp early autumn chill in the air. I'd lie on the sofa with my head on her lap and she would read to me from a book of Latvian fairy tales. It was full of stories about ogres and mischievous spirits and other evil beings in the forests. I'd experienced enough of that already, but I didn't mind listening as it gave me an excuse to nestle close to Auntie. The sound of her gentle voice would lull me into a light slumber, so that later Auntie would have to rouse me, take me upstairs and tuck me in bed.

'I always dropped off to sleep easily, but later I'd wake up screaming, haunted by nightmares I couldn't remember. Auntie would rush to my room, and to calm me down, sing Latvian folk songs I'd never heard before or tell me another fairy tale until I eventually nodded off again.'

When I was a child my father had spoken of his time at Carnikava as one of happy and peaceful days spent in a rural idyll. He had even shown us photographs taken there. However, something unsettled me about these ostensibly innocent photographs in which my father seemed withdrawn and somehow damaged. His arms were folded guardedly across his chest. It was the expression on his face that had most disturbed me. He looked as if he had just woken from a nightmare at the moment the photograph was taken.

This impression hadn't made sense to me as a child because he'd never given us the slightest intimation of the violent and bloody world he had belonged to before Carnikava. Hearing his words now, I understood that expression on his face – truly he had just woken from the nightmare of his experiences with the soldiers.

At that moment, I felt an inexpressible gratitude to Auntie. I was moved to know that my father had had someone to comfort him and look out for him. In fact my childhood memories of Auntie were of a kindly person, who although capable of little English, communicated to us through her warmth, often planting kisses on our foreheads unexpectedly, much as I imagine she'd done to my father as a boy. But I couldn't escape the thought that my father did not wake up from his nightmares into the love of his own family; he was an orphan thrust amongst strangers. There had not been a soul who could reassure him that the world was as it should be, because he knew instinctively and through experience that it was not.

I turned my attention back to my father's words.

'In the week following our return from Carnikava, I overheard a conversation between Auntie and Uncle about whether I should return to school. Uncle's opinion was that it wouldn't be possible, because I'd become even more unruly after being at the front. He'd decided that, instead, I should go to the Laima chocolate factory with him every day and be tutored there.

'I was confused. "Lessons in a chocolate factory?" I thought to myself. "What could they teach me there?" But I also looked forward to it – I pictured myself gobbling chocolate all day long, as much as I desired. But I'd got it all wrong. Uncle had my day, particularly the mornings, mapped out for me.

'Our limousine would pull up outside the factory at 7.45. I still wore my uniform – I refused to wear civilian clothes and I would give a curt salute to the receptionist. Then I'd trail into the factory behind Uncle as he went about his daily inspection of the workers, who stood to attention by their machines and packing tables.

'The workers would greet Uncle and then me. "Good morning, Private Kurzemnieks," they'd say, and I'd salute in response.

'When we reached his office, Uncle always gave me the same order: "To your duty, young soldier!" he'd say, and I'd head over to a child's desk – stacked with books which he'd organised for me – by the window. Then we would both settle down to our work. Obviously Uncle was very busy with the running of the factory. People would be coming and going all morning – his secretary, section managers, and other people.

'He'd arranged for me to have a tutor – Miss Novackis, she was called – to teach me how to read and write in Latvian, as well as give me lessons in Latvian history. We'd always begin the day's classes with Latvian language. I'd read in halting Latvian from books. I was never any good at reading. I was never any good with books for that matter. I couldn't even handle them properly – I'd fumble with them.

'I was a quick learner, but I couldn't settle. I'd get bored and easily distracted. I couldn't concentrate. It was hard going for a boy of my age, with all I'd been through, to sit diligently at my desk all morning long. As soon as Uncle was out of the office on some business, I'd jump out of my chair and head for the window. I'd gaze down at the street below. I longed to be outside and free, especially if I saw somebody in uniform passing by. It reminded me of my comrades who were still at the front.

'The afternoons were best of all.' My father smiled nostalgically. 'I was the king of Laima. I had the run of the factory and was free to do as I wished, as long as I stayed out of trouble. I'd become a popular figure amongst the workers on the factory floor and would wander among them chatting. I was a greedy little thing as well and I'd stuff both pockets of my jacket with chocolates. Later, I'd find a deserted corner of the storeroom where I'd devour them until I was nearly sick.

'I loved to watch the engineer, too, as he maintained the factory's machinery. I'd question him endlessly, and absorb every detail of how he fixed the plant equipment. Sometimes he'd pass me a small piece of equipment that I'd spend hours on, dismantling it and then putting it together again. I had an aptitude, it seemed, for mending things, which kept me out of mischief,' my father joked, 'but not away from the chocolates.'

I was curious about Uncle and tried to steer our discussion in that direction.

'Tell me, Dad, did Uncle ever wear a uniform?' I interrupted my father.

'No. I never saw him in a uniform. He was a civilian.'

'Did he mix with soldiers and officers?'

My father nodded. 'Occasionally officers would appear at Laima.'

'I wonder what they were doing in a chocolate factory?'

'To be honest I never thought about it.'

'Did you recognise any of them?'

'Only Commander Lobe. Quite a number of weeks had elapsed since my return to Riga when one day, without any notice, he reappeared in Uncle's office. After that he turned up regularly at Laima, so that I started to see more of him. His headquarters were just around the corner from Laima and from the window near my desk I could see him striding towards the factory.'

'Why was Lobe there so frequently?'

'The commander and Uncle were old friends. They'd been in the Bolshevik revolution together years before. They fought against the Bolsheviks for Latvian independence. They belonged to a group called Lacplesis.'

'Lacplesis?'

'That's right,' my father said. 'The Society of the Bear. It was the association of freedom fighters for Latvia. On the rare occasions the commander and Uncle spoke about Lacplesis, it was only in glowing terms of the bravery of Lacplesis members and its noble cause. In fact, I believe Uncle had been given the house in Carnikava as a reward for bravery and services to Lacplesis.'

I made a mental note to try to discover more about this group. (Later I was to learn that in reality Lacplesis were closer to an organisation of Latvian fascists.)

'Uncle also told me many years later that Commander Lobe had worked for him in Laima for a while, early on during the war. Uncle had helped him out with a job and a place to stay. According to Uncle, the commander had been on duty in Ventspils on the north-west coast of Latvia, but for some unknown reason, he'd been relieved of his command, and had left the army. All I know is it had something to do with not obeying a German order.'

My father looked ill-at-ease and shifted in his seat.

'But the commander's visits often had something to do with me as well. I hadn't seen him since he'd ordered me back from the front. At first things were uneasy between us: inside I was rigid with fear as I couldn't forget the threat that he'd made to kill me, but he was determined to break the ice.

'He'd sit down next to me as I studied at my desk and draw in his chair close to mine – so close that I could smell his uniform and the soap he used to wash himself – and check my work over my shoulder. He was less formal than Uncle, very hearty and cheerful, but he had sharp eyes. He watched everything like a hawk.

'One day, he and Uncle had a conversation in which my name was mentioned several times. I kept my head down, but in fact, I was eavesdropping.

'It seemed that he was keen to organise something to do with me. Uncle appeared resistant to whatever it was, but Commander Lobe spoke forcefully back to him. After that Uncle seemed to give in to the commander. In reality, I suppose that Uncle didn't have much choice. Being a member of the SS, the commander usually got his way.

'The following morning, the commander reappeared. He took me away from Miss Novackis. He stood me in the centre of the room and announced that I was reinstated as a corporal. He presented me with a new military jacket displaying the rank of corporal on the lower sleeve and the collar.

'I was over the moon. I'd no sooner put the jacket on – it fitted perfectly – than he ordered me to make ready. I was to go out to lunch with him immediately, even though it was still early. I had a feast of lampreys and strawberry ice cream, while he sat back in his chair and examined me as if I were under a microscope. Then finally he spoke. "Do you want to be a good patriot?" he asked. I didn't know what patriot meant, but I nodded my head gravely, my mouth still full of ice cream.

' "Do you want to help Latvia?" he went on. I nodded my head again, this time more enthusiastically. I would have done anything to redeem myself in his eyes. He tousled my hair. "Good soldier," he said.

'That day changed everything. I spent more time with Commander Lobe, several times a week in fact.

'There was another incident in particular that changed the nature of our relationship. The commander had taken me to a park, and while he sat on a bench, smoking, I wandered off to a merry-go-round to play. At one point an elderly gentleman approached me, curious about how I'd become a soldier. I was lost for an answer – nobody had asked me this before. I ran back to the commander and asked him. I thought the commander would give me an answer. Instead he rose abruptly and, taking me by the hand, hurried back to headquarters.

'The commander was on edge. He sat me down in an armchair and stood towering above me. Then he started talking to himself in a low agitated voice about how the soldiers had found me those many months ago. As Kulis had told him, I had appeared from behind a tree on the outskirts of a deserted village. He was obsessed with the story and repeated it slowly as he paced up and down. Then he stopped and turned to look at me. He began to repeat the story again, but this time he'd embellished it so that it became different from the one Kulis had made up.

'In the commander's version, I was a Russian pigherd who'd been found wandering through a deserted village with a herd of pigs that I was tending. I'd appeared from behind a tree and I'd told the soldiers that I'd become separated from my father and mother and asked if I could join them.

'It was not the last version to appear either. From time to time in newspaper articles, the story was printed with variations. I remember one time, Uncle read aloud an article that said that the soldiers had found me in a village where I was being looked after by two elderly peasant women who'd found me wandering alone in the forest.'

My father laughed.

'It was confusing to say the least,' he said. 'I myself would occasionally get the details messed up.'

'Why did Lobe change the details?' I asked.

My father shrugged.

'You don't think it was to make the soldiers look even more innocent and heroic in their encounter with you?'

My father shrugged again.

'What did you think about this story?'

'Nothing really,' my father replied. 'As I said before I let people say what they wanted to. I wasn't going to make any trouble about it. Only one thing was certain: these stories were very far removed from the truth that I have told you.

'The afternoon wore on and I remained seated in the armchair. The commander was reading through documents at his desk. Suddenly he shouted my name, and I jumped to attention. He leant back and pushed his chair away from his desk and called me over to sit on his knee. Yet again he went over the story, only this time, he made me repeat it after him, word for word. He made it clear that I was to keep to it as much as possible. For the next few days, he didn't take me out in public.

'Then one day I was sitting quietly in his office, colouring in my book, when he suddenly quizzed me on his version of events to make sure I'd remembered it. I recited it verbatim. "Perfect!" he exclaimed, clapping his hands together.

'After that, he began to take me out to cafes again to see how well I performed in public. Unsurprisingly, a child in an SS uniform attracted a lot of attention and people would approach us, curious to know more about me. I'd ignore them and go on eating my ice cream or eels, until the commander gave me a nudge or a pinch under the table and I'd then swing into action like a puppet. I'd put my spoon down and stand and recite as naturally as I could what I'd been taught. If I was in the mood, I'd sing a few notes of one of the songs the soldiers had taught me.'

'Do you think Lobe knew the true story of your capture?'

'I don't think so. I know that when he brought me to base camp for the first time, Sergeant Kulis told the commander that the soldiers had found me wandering alone in a forest on the perimeter of a village. Kulis had made up this story when he first took me out of the firing line and decided to let me live. If he'd told the commander the truth, then the commander would have suspected I was Jewish, and my fate would've been sealed. Even though none of the other soldiers knew I was Jewish or had any reason to want to protect me from Lobe, inexplicably, they all stuck to Kulis's story as well.'

'This story covered up their deeds,' I said contemptuously. 'They portrayed themselves as kindly rescuers, instead of the barbaric murderers of innocent people they truly were.'

These last words shocked my father. His face reddened.

'But Sergeant Kulis wasn't like that,' he offered. 'Despite everything he'd done that I despised, there can't be any doubt that he tried to protect me. He warned me to hide my Jewishness or I would be killed. If he hadn't wanted to protect me he could've returned me to face the firing squad. And

I believe that he never told a soul about my true identity. And the other soldiers, even though they didn't know I was Jewish, they were still kind to me. They protected me because I was a child.'

'The question is, Dad, would they have been quite so kind if they'd known you were a Jewish child?'

My father's face visibly tensed.

After several moments I pressed on.

'What about the Dzenis family? Did any of them ever ask you about how you came to be with the soldiers?'

'Not directly. They'd been told the first version that Kulis had created and whenever anybody was curious about me, Uncle always stuck to that story.'

'So they had no idea what your true identity might have been?'

My father shook his head.

'And they never learnt anything from you?'

'Not a single word from me.'

'You must have had a very strong and determined character to have kept it hidden while living under the same roof with them.'

'I don't think strength had anything to do with it,' my father answered. 'It was fear, son – pure fear! Fear of discovery. Fear of saying the wrong thing. I'd made that mistake once; after the party at the Dzenis' on my first night with them when I said that I wanted my own brother and sister. I had to be certain never to do that again.'

I immediately regretted the way I had almost cross-examined my father. He had suffered awfully under this conspiracy of silence about his identity.

'Terrible,' I said in a sympathetic tone.

Perhaps buoyed by this, my father appeared to relax and was suddenly eager to continue.

'Where was I?' he said, thinking aloud. 'That's right. Commander Lobe was satisfied that I had mastered my routine. He then started to take me on visits to hospitals and clinics to boost the morale of sick and wounded soldiers. I'd tour the wards with him. He trained me to commend the patients, saying "Father Latvia thanks you for your courage and wishes you a speedy recovery." '

My father gave an ironic laugh.

'I was a child, but even I could see how empty those words were. I remember one time saying that nonsense to a soldier who was bandaged from head to toe. I could only see his eyes staring out at me. He wasn't going to recover, and even if he did, I wondered what condition he'd be in for the remainder of his life. There were many sad cases like him. I felt ashamed of my words.'

My father rummaged in his case again.

He passed me a small scrap of tattered paper.

I drew it close to my eyes. It was an article that had been torn roughly from a newspaper. The print was too faded to read, but the photograph above it was distinct enough for me to discern an image of my father in full military uniform, sitting on Lobe's knee and posing among bandaged soldiers and other dignitaries and officials. Standing to one side was the figure of Uncle, who seemed to be watching over the boy.

'Amazing,' I said. 'Where did you get this?'

'The commander tore it out of the newspaper for me. You can see, it says 1943 at the bottom of it.'

'You have had it all this time?'

'Yes. Here in my case.'

My father patted the lid of the case tenderly as if stroking a pet. Doing so, it was almost as if he was taunting me. The case's persona had irrevocably changed for me by this stage. So magical to me when I was a child, the case now had a rather malign presence.

I had a sudden and almost uncontrollable urge to make a lunge for the case and snatch it from my father. I wanted to bury it somewhere and forget that it had ever existed. But I knew that that was not to be. The impulse to destroy the case died away as quickly as it had come and, in its place, I found a question forming in my mind.

'In your case for all this time and you've never breathed a word of it?'

My father's face reddened.

'Why?'

'Just look at it,' my father said, genuinely troubled. 'Worse was to come. One particular day when we had no tours planned, the commander had sent me back to Uncle's office at Laima. I was glad to be back with Uncle. I was tired of being the commander's little wind-up doll. With Uncle, it was exactly as it had been before: I sat quietly at my desk.

'Suddenly the door flew open and in marched the commander. He never bothered to knock. He saluted quite casually and flopped himself down on the edge of Uncle's desk. Then he helped himself to a cigarette from Uncle's tobacco box. The commander was in an excited state, telling Uncle that a group of military officers would be arriving shortly that same day and that arrangements needed to be made for an experiment. Uncle seemed flabbergasted.

'Then the commander began to explain and I could tell that Uncle was not pleased with what he was hearing. But the commander's voice conveyed that he would not countenance any objections.

'Their exchange was interrupted when a group of officers strode confidently into the room, about four of them Latvian, as well as a German in command. One of the Latvians was called Osis and the German had a name that sounded something like Jackal or Jekyll. They had a strong air of authority about them in their fine uniforms decorated with colourful medals.

'These men were only in Uncle's office for a short time, before they headed off into the factory. I must have had some curiosity because I decided to follow them. They went into one of the storerooms upstairs at the rear of the factory. I managed to watch them through the crack in the doorway. One of the officers was pointing at a diagram of what seemed to be a truck or tank. I soon got bored of spying on them. I had no idea what was up.

'A few days later, the same officers reappeared with Commander Lobe. They were immersed in serious conversation, and didn't even bother to greet me. All of a sudden the commander stopped speaking in mid-sentence. The room went quiet. I went on pretending to study, but I couldn't resist my curiosity and raised my head a fraction to see what had happened.

'The commander was standing, as if frozen to the spot, in the centre of the room, staring intently at me. In the next instant he became animated. He clapped his hands together and gave a little jump, like an excited child. He sprang across the room and, in a single movement, he lifted me up out of my chair and high into the air, shaking me like a trophy he'd just won. He planted me on top of Uncle's desk, and began to speak excitedly to the other soldiers.

Almost immediately, upon hearing what the commander had said, the others began to nod their heads enthusiastically. All except Uncle who became angry, almost apoplectic! I'd never seen him like that before.

'The commander simply raised his hand to silence Uncle. Then he turned to me again and, with his face only inches from mine, said: "Do you want to help me on a very special project?" His tone was dramatic and heavy, so of course, I nodded vigorously, eager to make myself useful. I hesitated to look directly at Uncle since I was going against his wish. Suddenly, the commander grabbed me by the waist and lifted me off the desk. Then he turned and strode towards the door with the officers following behind. I managed a brief and furtive glance back at Uncle who looked deeply troubled.

'When we reached the rear steps of the factory that overlooked the yard, Commander Lobe put me down. I had a good view of the entire space. I was surprised because the courtyard was overflowing with people of all ages – old people, babies, women, children, anybody you could imagine. They stood quietly with their bags and cases as if waiting for a bus to take them on a journey. Only the babies were restless and crying. I tugged at the commander's jacket. I wondered what they were here for. I didn't like the atmosphere. I wanted to go back to Uncle.

'He glanced down at me and gave me a broad smile. He put his arm around my shoulder, and led me down the steps. We joined the other officers who'd dispersed amongst the crowd, inspecting them. Once we were in the thick of it, I was too tiny to see much at all so I simply followed the commander, imitating the sharp and stern look on his face.

'Suddenly the gates into the yard clanked open with a screeching sound and two gigantic transport trucks rumbled in and came to a halt. Soldiers guarding the crowd started to bark orders for everybody to get into the trucks as quickly as possible. Chaos broke out. People pushed and shoved to climb on, while trying to drag their belongings with them. I was disoriented and a little frightened by the mayhem and I drew away to the perimeter of the crowd.

'It was then that I noticed a little boy – he must have been only a year or two younger than me – standing nearby. He was crying. He must have become separated from his mother or whoever he was with. I wanted to do something for him so I reached into my pocket and pulled out one of my chocolates from the secret stash. I held it out to the boy. He seemed very surprised and his crying faded to a whimper. Then I could see how thin he was; his eyes protruded desperately from his gaunt face. Tentatively he put out his hand and then he snatched the chocolate greedily like a starving animal. "He's just like me," I thought, "when Sergeant Kulis offered me a scrap of bread in the schoolroom."

'I felt so sorry for him. I knew what it was like, the pit in your belly that gnawed away at you. I passed him another chocolate, which he accepted more graciously this time. Then I passed him another chocolate and yet another one, pacing them, so that his stomach would accept the chocolates and he didn't become sick. Then I noticed something that had escaped my attention up until then – the boy was wearing a yellow star on his jacket. By then I knew what that meant: he was Jewish. He was even more like me than I had imagined. He could have been my little brother. I was tormented. "Should I feed him more?" I said to myself. "Or should I ignore him?" If I showed him any kindness, the soldiers might become suspicious of me.

'Or should I help him to escape? I turned away from him in anguish. Instinctively, I looked towards the fence to see if there was a gap in it. For a moment, I imagined that we could both escape together, through the gap in the fence, as I had done by myself, in my village. But I knew that this time it would be impossible. I remained with my back to the boy.

'That moment has overshadowed my entire life,' my father said in a low voice. 'I don't want to sound dramatic, but I carry his image with me, like it's been imprinted on my retina. Frequently I wonder if he survived, if he grew into a man. I wonder if he remembers that day when I turned my back on him. It was as if I had turned my back on my own reflection at that moment. The questions always come down to that in the end.'

My father was subdued. I felt helpless to console him.

'I noticed that one of the German officers was looking at me. He'd observed what had gone on between the boy and me. He flashed a big smile at me, and at the same time, he began to speak with the other officers, who all nodded.

'They too stared across at me, confronting me with their smiles. At that moment I noticed Uncle standing at the rear door of the factory. He looked worried and disapproving.

'Then I heard the German officer call out my name loudly above the din. Snapping his fingers at me, he ordered me to join him. I pretended that I couldn't hear him and stayed where I was.

'Instead, I glanced across at Uncle. He, too, had seen the officer summon me. I hoped that he would rescue me from this situation, but he only indicated with his eyes that I shouldn't resist the soldiers.

'I went over to the German officer. I still had no idea what he wanted. He snapped his fingers yet again and this time, one of the soldiers stepped forward with a big paper bag. The chief officer thrust it into my hand. It was full of Laima chocolates. I was surprised. I thought that I'd been mistaken about his intentions and that the chocolates were a gift for me. I began to bite into one of them, but he gave me such a slap that it shot out of my mouth.

' "Not for you, idiot," he said harshly. Then he led me over to the rear of one of the trucks and had me stand to attention there.

'He gave an order for the crowd to form a line leading to the truck. Immediately I grasped what was required of me: I was to hand out a chocolate to each person in the queue as they climbed on to the truck. Commander Lobe joined us and he told me that I should make sure to give every person a big smile as I presented their chocolate. It seemed that my job was to pacify them before their journey, especially the children, who loved the chocolates.

'So that's what I did – on and on throughout the afternoon. My jaw ached from smiling.

'I didn't notice Uncle's presence again until the end of the afternoon when he reappeared on the steps. He still seemed very disturbed, not only by what was happening generally, but at what I was doing. He signalled angrily for me to join him. He took my hand firmly and, without a word to anybody, we walked back into the factory.

'However, as we climbed the stairs to Uncle's office, the commander's voice boomed out from behind us, ordering us to stop. He was seething with anger and told Uncle to release me. Uncle refused and I felt his grip tighten on my hand. Commander Lobe tried to break Uncle's grip, but Uncle pushed me behind him. Both men were keyed up and there was a tense exchange of words. It was a terrifying stand-off. Then Uncle uttered something – I didn't hear what – to the commander, who drew back visibly shocked. The commander retreated back down the stairs and Uncle strode to his office dragging me in his wake. For the moment at least, Uncle had won.

'When we reached his office, he told me sharply to get back to my books and to keep my head down, even if the officers and Commander Lobe returned.

'Before long, the sound of the trucks leaving reached my ears and shortly after that, Commander Lobe and the other officers came in. They made themselves comfortable wherever they could find a place. The commander ordered Uncle to get beer and schnapps for everybody. Uncle ordered it but refused to join them in their celebrations. As the men became drunk, their attitude toward Uncle harshened. They criticised him for protecting me. The German officer warned Uncle in no uncertain terms that his behaviour wouldn't be tolerated a second time. With that, the party came to an abrupt end. As he was about to leave, the German officer turned to me and said "Morgens" ("tomorrow"). I realised that my job was not yet over.

'Uncle was subdued that evening as we headed home. He remained silent and preoccupied over dinner, too. Later, I lay awake all night, worried about my terrible duty, although I hadn't any idea of what lay in store for those people.

'The next morning, I was bleary-eyed. My senses were dull from lack of sleep. It was probably better that way. One of the officers came to collect me from Uncle's office. But I had no choice. I knew what was in store for me and I wanted nothing at all to do with it.'

'How many times did this take place?' I asked.

'Three times perhaps. There were no more trucks after that.'

My father paused. He appeared relieved to have finally spoken of the incident. The tightness around his mouth loosened slightly.

'That must have been the idea that Lobe hit upon in Uncle's office – the presence of a child would calm the crowd – and then the chocolates became an added touch after I'd been noticed with the boy.'

My father looked guilt-ridden.

'At least the chocolates seemed to make it easier for them.'

My father was speaking through the eyes of the boy he had once been. In the next breath he suddenly turned against himself.

'A chocolate for their journey!' he exclaimed. 'What idiocy am I talking? I did sense that something dark was going on but Commander Lobe had told me that they were being relocated to another part of the country. But they killed them, didn't they?'

He struggled to control his hysteria.

'Little children. Younger even than me or my brother and sister. They took them away to concentration camps or to forests – to isolated forests – to be massacred – to be robbed of their lives – their dignity – that was their final destination!'

My father flinched involuntarily, as if trying to dodge a blow. He took several deep breaths, trying to calm himself.

'The women and children and old people at Laima were innocent. Their only crime was to be born Jewish. Somewhere inside me I must have registered what their fate, as Jews, would be. After all, Sergeant Kulis had warned me to hide my Jewishness because it meant death. That was my only crime too.'

My father was ashen-faced and drawn.

'Or am I guilty?' he asked. 'Am I responsible, like the soldiers, for what went on? I don't know what to think. Those people in the yard at Laima were murdered and I eased them on their way, not with a gun but with those damned chocolates.'

My father withdrew further into himself. He seemed beaten. Not a shred of his usual animation remained.

'Even though I was only a child, I should have known. I must have blocked it out. It was only later over time that I understood what I had been party to.'

My father bowed his head so that I could no longer see his face.

'But at that time I didn't understand,' my father pleaded meekly in his own defence. 'I was shell-shocked. Frozen,' he said in a weak voice. 'I didn't understand the adults around me, or the world I was living in. I just went from moment to moment – what child doesn't? – grateful for food and shelter and warmth. Even more than that, I was so terrified that my true identity would be discovered. I just kept my antennae up and my head down.'

After several moments of silence, unexpectedly a gasp of grief came from him as he struggled to gain control of his emotions.

He looked up at me. 'Let's stop, son,' he pleaded.

I was thankful to do so. I didn't know how much more I could endure. But I was more worried about my father's emotional state. It seemed as if he were driving himself to the gallows to be hanged by his past. I was overwhelmed at the thought of the toll – the inner terror – his silence must have taken on him. It was not only his physical survival that had been at stake.

I sighed, suddenly exhausted by all I had just learnt and all that was still likely to come.

'It's almost five o'clock,' my father said. 'You get some sleep, son.'

'What about you, Dad?' I asked. I found myself fretting too about my father's current physical state. He suffered at times from high blood pressure and I prayed that it would remain stable under the burden of this night.

'I'll be fine,' he replied. 'I'll just wash the tea cups and then get some rest myself.'

I left him to it, suddenly embarrassed by our intimacy. I sensed my father felt the same way, as he rose without another word, crossed to the sink and turned his back on me.

I dropped off to sleep just before dawn but not before scrawling a few notes on a scrap of paper. The rest I had was fitful, and in the few moments that I was able to doze off I was dominated by dreams whose contents I could only remember in disturbing fragments. At one point I was standing knee-deep in a swamp, paralysed by blood-red, glutinous mud. I struggled to raise myself out of it but was hopelessly trapped in the quagmire. My inner life had been churned up in ways that I was not yet able to fully understand.

I was soon wide-awake again. I lay in bed feeling drained. Outside I could hear the dawn chorus and the sound of my mother rising and moving through the house to the kitchen.

Alex in the second of his uniforms, that of the *Wehrmacht*, circa 1943.

The Latvian commander, Colonel Karlis Lobe.

Left: Alex as a little boy, with Wilma Kulis.

Below: Alex with his rifle slung over his shoulder, in the company of officers including Captain Erzum. The photo may have been taken on the day the synagogue was burnt. It was sent to Alex anonymously in Melbourne.

Alex and officers standing next to the flowers arranged to depict the emblem of the Latvian SS.

Alex sitting on his 'rescuer' Sergeant Kulis's knee, next to the floral insignia of the Latvian SS at Volhov, near the Russian Front. It must have been early autumn in 1943, just before Alex was sent back to Riga by Lobe for trying to escape the frontline.

Alex standing next to the finished insignia.

The newspaper cutting showing Alex in full military uniform, sitting on Lobe's knee and posing among bandaged soldiers and other dignitaries and officials during a hospital tour. Mr Dzenis stands to the right in a black suit.

A film still showing Alex playing with Aryan children at either Carnikava or Dzintari, the other location where the film was shot.

Alex and Auntie in the garden at Carnikava.

The Dzenis' holiday home at Carnikava, near Riga.

Alex, about nine years old, dressed in a cap, quasi-military jacket and trousers, standing by the steps of Moritzburg Castle outside Dresden.

A newspaper cutting showing a still from the Latvian propaganda newsreel in which Alex appeared in 1943.

An article about Alex, with a still from the same propaganda film in which he featured.

ULDIS KURZEMNIEKS RĪGAS JŪRMALĀ

ULDIS KURZEMNIEKS AR MAZO TAUTAS MEITU VASARAS SAULĒ

4 DAUGAVAS VANAGI 34. (74.) num.

9

JUDGEMENT

THE sound of the front door slamming woke me. I drew my arm from under the blankets and looked at my watch. It was nearly 11 a.m. I'd slept about five hours but I was not at all tired. I was instantly alert.

I sprang out of bed and drew back the curtain and was immediately blinded by the light. It was a bright winter's day in Melbourne. The sky was a thin cloudless blue.

The house seemed deserted as I headed for the kitchen. There was no sign of life. Then I remembered that it was Friday. This time every week my mother met her close friend Maria in town for lunch, a film and some window-shopping, returning at about six in the evening.

I went to the kitchen window to get a view of my father's workshop. There was no sign of him there. Just at that moment, I heard the sound of his car pulling up in the drive. A few moments later I heard the rear gate click open and saw him cross to his bolthole.

I opened the window slightly and called out to him: 'Dad! Coffee?'

He gave a slight start and turned to face me.

I'd expected him to be tired and subdued. I was mistaken. He seemed to have regained his composure completely. There was no sign of what had taken place a matter of only hours ago. In fact he looked positively robust. His face had regained its usual animated expression. His cheeks had colour in them – they were almost rosy – and his eyes were so bright that their intense blueness was emphasised. He headed toward the house, warning me in advance not to forget his three sugars.

I took his coffee over to the table where he'd just sat down.

'It's after eleven,' he chided me playfully, 'you should've been up hours ago. I've been working since nine . . .'

'You're superhuman, aren't you,' I tossed back, before it occurred to me that my choice of words might have been an unconscious response to what I had learnt earlier that morning.

I joined my father at the table. In the harsh light of day the kitchen had resumed its normal appearance. It no longer seemed like the confessional from the night before.

My father sipped his coffee in silence. Then I heard him clear his throat nervously and unexpectedly he began to speak in a lively and confident voice.

'I never finished telling you what happened,' he said, searching my face for a response, 'are you still interested?'

His naivety stunned me.

'I've thought of nothing else,' I answered.

His face registered relief and shyness in equal measures. I could tell that he was pleased.

'After the incident with the chocolates at Laima,' he began, 'Commander Lobe had partly surrendered me back to Uncle. I've no idea why this had happened. On occasion I still visited hospitals and other institutions with the commander, but these were interspersed with days in Uncle's office when I simply got on with my old routine of study.

'Until one particular day,' my father said, 'when the commander arrived in an exuberant mood. He didn't bother to greet Uncle and before I could even stand to attention, he'd snatched me up and then sat down on the sofa with his arms around my waist so that I couldn't escape him. "How is my little corporal today?" he asked. "Have you been working hard at your lessons?" I nodded and he looked at Uncle. "Has he, Mr Dzenis?" It was no longer Jekabs, as he used to call Uncle. Uncle nodded but remained silent.

' "In that case I think you deserve a treat," Commander Lobe said, squeezing me so tightly I could barely breathe. My ears pricked up at the mention of "treat". I thought that with a bit of luck he might take me out to a fancy cafe for ice cream the way he used to do. But it was even better than I'd hoped for. He offered me a break in Carnikava. "It's a special holiday, only for important children of the Reich," he said. "You'll have a wonderful time. A whole week there with boys and girls of your own age. Playing on the beach, dancing, exercises every day."

'I nodded, excited by the prospect. Commander Lobe explained that I'd have to leave almost immediately and Uncle insisted that he and Auntie accompany me. Uncle had been wary of the commander's attitude toward me ever since the chocolates' affair.

'The commander shrugged as if he didn't care either way. Then he sprang an even bigger surprise on me. "And you, Corporal," he said slowly and with gravity, "will have a special part to play at Carnikava. Berlin is sending a crew to film you."

'He lifted me off his knee and began to pace up and down, smoking his cigar.

' "Every single person throughout the German empire, even the Führer himself, will learn about the life of Latvia's great mascot," he said waving his hand in the air extravagantly. "It is a great honour for you to be chosen. You must make all Latvians proud of you." '

My father went on to recount his patchy memories of the actual filming. It had taken place in two locations – sections were filmed at Carnikava and also at Dzintari, a town on the Riga coast whose scenery was more appealing than that of Carnikava. He remembered clearly one scene in which he was filmed doing handstands and running on the beach with the other children. In a second scene he recalled what may have been a kind of maypole dancing with a few of the young girls who were dressed in traditional Latvian folk costume. But my father had stated that his other memories were too vague. 'They are like shadows moving across a screen,' he complained, screwing up his face in frustration.

One thing he knew for certain was that the material had been included in a German newsreel, which the commander later told him had been shown in movie theatres across the German Reich. He himself had seen it played in a cinema in Riga.

I was intrigued by talk of the newsreel. Even these scant memories were more than I'd heard during my childhood when my father had mentioned the film. He would boast that he'd become such a celebrity in Latvia that they'd – we never asked who 'they' were – made a film about him. But whenever my brothers and I would pester him about the film's content, he'd always claim to be unable to recall any details.

My father told me now that he didn't know what had become of the film. It had occurred to him when he was younger to find it, but he'd had no idea how to locate it. As time passed, he'd gone on to raise a family, and he'd put it to the back of his mind.

'I decided that he film belonged to a previous life,' he'd said. In any case, he suspected that the footage hadn't survived the war.

I suggested that we contact various film archives in Russia, Latvia and Germany. My father seemed genuinely excited by this. His mood was buoyant now and he perched on the edge of his seat, apparently eager to talk more.

Before he began, however, I was compelled to ask him something we had not yet touched on directly. My father and I had never discussed our emotions with each other, but I decided to take the plunge.

'How did you feel about all of this, Dad? I asked. Mere mention of the word 'feel' made me awkward and self-conscious.

My father was taken aback by my question and seemed perplexed.

'What do you mean *feel*?' He put stress on the word.

'Well . . . did you feel close to the Latvians?' I blustered, not quite able to say what I meant after all. 'Did you feel like one of them when you made this film?'

The vehemence of his response surprised me.

'Don't be absurd,' he said. 'I never felt part of them. They were strangers to me. I had to cooperate that's all.'

My father shrunk back into his seat. He seemed both annoyed and dis-mayed by my question and began to shake his head.

'You don't understand the way it was,' he murmured. 'I just made the best of my situation. I stayed as silent as possible, all my time with them. I was never one of them. Ever! Deep down I knew they were not my people. They were strangers to me. All the time, strangers. They loved me, cared for me, treated me as one of their own.

'But I always knew what I was, even if I didn't know who I was. I was a Jewish boy. That meant I had to be on guard every moment I was with them. I couldn't risk being discovered. I would have been killed. I feared for my life all the time. The fear was ingrained in me. Can you imagine how it would be for a child to live like that every waking moment? And even when sleeping – I never slept well – I had nightmares about it. I always worried that I would talk in my sleep and somehow someone would overhear me.'

My father's features tensed and he stared bleakly in front of him.

'I realise now, speaking for the first time,' he said, 'that I have been frightened all my life.'

This seemed to be an explanation for my father's silence – his persistent fear of discovery.

'It's not like I could've run away or something. Besides, where would I have run to? Back to my village? I didn't know where my village was. I couldn't even remember its name. I still can't. And even if I had, what would I have found there? The pit where my family was buried, the soil still freshly turned?

'There was nobody else to care for me,' my father said with grim finality. 'This was the card that fate had dealt me.'

My father seemed lost for words. Then he leant forward in his seat, staring intently at me.

'Absurd!' he muttered under his breath.

It was the first time in my life that my father had reacted so intensely to something I had said. I tried to steer him on to another topic: 'Why didn't you speak of your experiences when the war had ended?' I asked.

My father shrugged, evasively.

'I wasn't protecting the Latvians if that is what you are getting at,' he said defensively.

Our discussion had taken a turn for the worse, and I worried my father felt that trusting me had been a mistake.

My father took a deep breath. 'Who wanted to hear of the horrors I had witnessed? In those days everybody in Australia just wanted to get on with their lives, forget their past, and I learnt to want the same thing. I just focused on Mum and you boys and the future. I wanted to protect you from my past. Just think of the shadow that would have cast over your lives.'

I knew that that was true, but it was also the case that my father's past now threatened to damage us, perhaps irreparably, not only through our knowledge of his tragedy but with the disturbing enigma of his silence towards us.

'Do you think Mum even suspected anything?' I asked.

My father shook his head.

'I hope not. And that's how I wanted it to be. I didn't want to burden your mother. You know how she is. She'd grown up here, shielded from the war and things like that. She has a kind nature, and she doesn't understand cruelty at all. To expose her to what I'd been through, I feared that it would be too much for her.'

'That's terrible, Dad,' I said. 'To live alone with this. Nobody you could confide in.'

My father gave a nervous cough. Then he spoke again.

'I did tell somebody once,' he said, 'completely on the spur of the moment, in early 1960. I was in the centre of Melbourne. I saw a nameplate on the door of a lawyer's office. I could tell the name was Jewish. I thought to myself, "This man might be able to steer me in the right direction." I don't know what came over me – I went in. It was a small office – a oneman show. The lawyer himself was sitting there behind a desk.

'I asked if I could talk to him. He invited me to sit down and I began to tell him what had happened to me. He was spellbound. He let me talk on and on. When I'd finished, he asked what I wanted to do, and I told him then what I have told you now – I want to know who I am, who my family was, and where I come from.

'The lawyer was silent for some time. I wasn't sure if he believed me. Finally, he spoke: "Forget it, young man!" he said. "If what you say is true, there is nobody left for you. And even if someone did survive, then they would believe that you had died with your family. Nobody would come looking for you, and in any case, how would they know where to find you?" He said that the best thing was to look to the future. "You have a family, build a life with them. Your past is a lost cause!" I was dejected, but there was nothing else for it. I resolved to follow his advice. "He's an educated man," I said to myself. "He knows about these things." I thanked him and left. That was that – I buried my past.'

'Do you regret that, Dad?' I ventured.

My father seemed momentarily thrown by the question. He moved uncomfortably in his seat.

'To be honest,' he replied, 'I feel guilty now about keeping my secret from all of you. Perhaps it seems to you now that I didn't trust any of you. That I betrayed you somehow.'

My father's words struck a raw nerve in me. As I had sat with him through the early hours that morning, I had occasionally felt toward him an anger that I'd only gradually been able to acknowledge. He was correct: I felt that he'd betrayed me and the entire family. Though he may have protected us from the horrors of his secret, I could not escape my growing sense that his secretiveness would, in the long term, make him a stranger to us all.

My father shook his head, ashamed of himself. There was a momentary silence between us.

'I've lied to you all, haven't I?' my father said. 'People outside the family assumed that I was Latvian and I didn't bother to correct them either.'

His regret was palpable and I wanted to spare him any further self-accusation.

'No you didn't,' I replied, 'you didn't lie.'

I hesitated, struggling to find the right way to describe what had gone on. 'You simply didn't tell us everything,' I said. 'It was a sort of half-truth.'

'A half-truth?' my father observed wryly. 'How can anything be a half-truth?'

He understood all too well what I was trying to do – make excuses for what he'd done.

'It's like a truth not fully revealed,' I offered.

'There's no such thing,' he perversely challenged me.

But he was wrong. An image of his brown case, firmly locked, came to mind. I recalled the careful control he'd exercised over whatever was removed from it, in order to maintain the carefully constructed narrative of his life. I reflected on all those years growing up under the same roof as my father, and how we, his family, had let him get away with this narrative. None of us had ever stopped to reflect seriously on the mystery of his origins and existence, and we were content to let him deflect any mild curiosity we did show.

What if we had pushed him harder? Would he have given in and told us more? I wondered whether it was us – our family – who had failed our father by not asking questions, and that his decision not to offer us anything was a terrible indictment of us all. Had we been unwittingly complicit in his silence? Had he seen something in us that disappointed him? I was left with a sense that somehow he had not deemed any of us worthy of his secret.

I had been so absorbed in my reflections, that it was only the sound of my father's voice that brought me back to the present.

'Marky?' he said.

'Sorry,' I said. 'I drifted off for a moment.'

I met my father's eyes.

'You will tell Mum and the boys, won't you?' I said, gently.

My father nodded, grim-faced.

'I don't know how I'll go about it,' he said, 'but I know that I must speak now.'

In an unselfconscious gesture, he raised the brown case which had been on the floor beside him and hugged it to his chest, as if it was both his protector and his most precious possession.

I looked at my watch.

'I'd better get dressed. Mum will be back before too long. She'll be wondering what's up if she finds me like this.'

'You'll tell her soon, Dad?'

'Yes, yes,' he said, brushing aside my question. My father took the cups over to the sink. 'I've got some repairs to do,' he said, and headed out to his workshop.

10

THE GROUND SHIFTS

I REMAINED in Melbourne for another fortnight, rising late and lingering about home in a state of nervous tension. My father went about his business, spending more and more of the day tinkering in his workshop, and I suspect deliberately avoiding me. In a way I was relieved. Already overwhelmed by what I had learnt of my father's childhood, I was struggling to come to terms with it.

I should have been in Tokyo by then but I'd stayed on in order to be there for my mother when she finally learnt about her husband's past. I was frustrated. I wanted the truth to be out in the open. I no longer wanted to collaborate in my father's silence.

When I woke early one morning, feeling unwell, I made a decision: rather than remain in Melbourne any longer, I would head to Tokyo as soon as possible to begin my research. My departure might give my father the time and space he clearly needed to talk to the family.

Three days later, my mother on the front seat beside him, my father backed the car out of the drive on the start of our journey to the airport. From the back seat I kept my eye out for traffic. At one end of our street, I caught sight of the oil refinery. As it came into view this time any nostalgic sentiments evaporated. The corporate signs affixed to the refinery fence were those of powerful German industrial conglomerates. Though these signs had been there all my life, I now began to see them in an entirely new light: Germany, with one of its most forbidding emblems – the belching chimney – surrounded our neighbourhood.

This was what I had grown up with – the inextinguishable German flame at one end of the street and a slaughterhouse, owned as it happened by a Jewish family, at the other. I'd never given much thought to either, but now there seemed to have been a coded message buried in the very landscape of my childhood that I had failed to detect.

*

The flight to Tokyo went smoothly enough, punctuated only by mild turbulence. The same could not be said of my mood. While I felt a deepened sense of companionship with my father there was also an odd sense of foreboding. I felt dislocated, cast adrift and facing an open, possibly hostile sea.

Nonetheless I settled in quickly to a familiar routine in Tokyo. It was a city I enjoyed more than most, and I knew my way about. I had favourite places to eat: tiny family-run soba shops that could seat no more than half a dozen patrons at a time. I enjoyed the anonymous companionship of sitting at the counter, slurping noodles, passing the time in casual conversation with the cook or *mama-san* on the other side of the counter or with the customers on either side of me. In my current state of mind this type of obligation-free chitchat suited me.

When I caught up with friends and neighbours from my earlier days as a student there, they welcomed me back as a long-lost son returning to the home village or *furusato*, and over sake-fuelled suppers that stretched late into the night they filled me in on changes to the neighbourhood and their lives. But when they asked after my life, my family, I would flounder. I could only smile, thank them for their kind enquiries, tell them that my parents were fine and that life was ambling along at a comfortable pace.

The heat and humidity of Tokyo in the summer of 1997 was so stifling that it was always a relief to get back to my *manshon*, as the Japanese called the tiny studios in downtown Tokyo. It was a light-hearted linguistic play on the English word 'mansion' since most of them, mine included, were no more than ten or fifteen square metres. Yet as I opened the front door of my *manshon* a wall of heat hit me. The room was suffocating, like an oven or sauna. Before I had even closed it behind me the door and the window-panes began to rattle, almost imperceptibly at first. I held my breath, waiting to see if the gentle shaking developed into an earth tremor, turning mere inconvenience into real danger. My *manshon* and my nerves continued to rattle, until abruptly, with one slight jolt, the room settled. I switched on the air-conditioner and waited for its effect to kick in.

I flopped down on the tatami floor and began to sink into a heat-induced torpor when there was a loud knock on my door. For an instant I thought it was my father, but I checked the thought.

'Stupid!' I muttered to myself. 'It must be one of the neighbours.'

But I was mistaken.

'*Moshi moshi, yubin desu!*' a voice called out. It was the postman with a special delivery.

The book-sized package he handed to me bore few details on its exterior, apart from a customs declaration and my address inscribed in my father's unusually thick black lettering, as if this would somehow guarantee its delivery. I tore off the outer wrapping and found an unlabelled videocassette encased in bubble-wrap.

I headed back across the darkened room and slipped the cassette into the VCR and pushed 'play'. After several moments the screen came to life: a head and shoulders close-up shot of my father suddenly appeared. Below his image, as if imprinted on his upper chest like a prison ID number, a running time-code and the date of the recording had been superimposed. It appeared to have been made three weeks earlier, in fact on the very day I had departed Australia. But what shocked me was my father's appearance.

I pressed the pause button immediately to take a closer look at him. I recognised the features of the person on-screen as my father's of course, but they were grey and washed out and his eyes were drawn and without any of their usual curiosity. His face was quite immobile and so different from his usually quite animated expression.

After several moments I pressed the play button and my father's image came to life again. He stared directly into the camera. Suddenly from off-screen a man's voice addressed him. 'Would you state your full name please?' The voice had a northern European accent, clipped and precise and was politely solicitous.

My father's head turned towards it. 'Alex Kurzem,' he mumbled in response.

I sat on my futon, spellbound, as my father repeated the story of his wartime childhood to what was apparently a Jewish Holocaust organisation. Only this time he did not speak in any great detail as he had with me in Melbourne. Rather he skimmed across incidents as the interviewer, unnamed and unseen, tried to get a broad picture of what had happened to my father. My father answered the interviewer's questions as best he could, but the harsh lighting and unforgiving angle of the camera positioned slightly above him and off to the left seemed to have made him shy. The scene had none of the intimacy afforded him by the confessional-like atmosphere of the darkened kitchen at home. It was a disconcerting experience for me as well, to observe my father somewhat clinically in this mediated fashion rather than sit close to him at home.

Yet at the same time there was no denying that, regardless of how it took place, simply hearing details of my father's past again brought back the experiences of my time in Melbourne and greatly unsettled me. Just as had been the case in Melbourne, it was as if once again I had begun to inhabit my father's body, and point of view. Only on this occasion it was as if I'd been transported from my room in Tokyo, with its earth tremors and stifling heat to the cold autumnal landscape of Russia, more than fifty years ago.

While there had not been much to be gleaned from the tape that I didn't already know, at one point the voice of an unidentified woman with a heavy northern European accent joined the interview. When my father mentioned Commander Lobe as a person who took an extraordinary and somewhat sinister interest in creating his identity as a mascot she came to life.

I shifted my position onto the tatami floor closer to the television so that I could hear their exchange more clearly. She was shocked that my father had been acquainted with the commander and seemed to know a great deal about his wartime activities. She spoke of Lobe's reputation as a war criminal: according to many historians, he was responsible for the murder of tens of thousands of Jews. She told my father that unwittingly he had kept company with the highest echelons of the Latvian Nazi elite. Even though my father must have been aware of Lobe's wartime activities, he appeared genuinely shocked by the extent of these revelations, so much so that he was left speechless for several moments.

Even this brief reference to Lobe suggested that there was much more not only about him but the other men who had controlled my father's life. While there was little I could do in Tokyo, I resolved to move forward in my investigations once I was back in Oxford.

Shortly after that the interview came to a close. An instant before the camera was turned off I caught a final glimpse of my father rising from his chair and noticed that he had been nursing his case the whole time. Then the screen turned to static.

For a moment I wondered what had driven my father to go almost directly from the airport – he must have dropped my mother home first – to wherever this tape had been made. Perhaps, having begun to speak for the first time, the pressure of his emerging memories was too much for him. He had to find somebody apart from me who would listen to him, and help him make sense of them.

I pushed the eject button on the VCR and the tape sprang out of the machine. I put it back in the envelope. I looked at my watch. It was after 11 p.m. I'd been watching the tape for almost two hours.

I calculated that it must have been midnight in Melbourne. I considered calling my father, who was likely to be awake with insomnia, but not wanting to alarm my mother I decided to wait until the next morning when it would be evening in Australia.

Later that night I unrolled the futon and made ready for bed but the tape had triggered in me another night of fitful sleep. At one point I must have drifted off, only to be woken by the clatter of a can of soft drink as it was delivered by the automatic drink machine in the alleyway below my window. After that I lay awake for some time listening to the sound of others coming and going to the drinks machine, seeking relief from the stifling humidity. I was not alone in my sleeplessness.

I stood up, sweating profusely, feeling dizzy and nauseous. I went to fetch some ice from the freezer, and as I did so nearly tripped on the remote control lying on the floor. In the darkness I stared at it. It seemed to have a malevolent presence about it so that suddenly I surprised myself by kicking it halfway across the room, as if it were responsible for my insomnia and what had happened to my father.

I filled a glass with ice from the freezer and placed it against my forehead; the coolness penetrated my skull and gave me some relief. I walked over to the window and slid it open. Leaning against the sill I gulped down the warm night air. Gradually the pounding in my ears diminished and I remained where I was, gazing up at the night sky. Listening to the sounds of late-night traffic on the Sotobori-dori brought me slowly to my senses and reassured and comforted me. I was grateful for the anonymity of the city.

The usual drop in overnight temperature – a welcome relief in a Tokyo summer – had not come and there didn't seem to be much point in trying to sleep. Instead I prepared myself some strong black coffee, and opened the window.

I was anxious to call my father, even though I was unsure how to broach the topic of the tape with him. He had told me that he didn't feel particularly Jewish. Why had he given his testimony to a Jewish Holocaust organisation? He'd clearly been hoping for information they might have about Koidanov and Panok, but they hadn't heard of these words. Or was there a deeper purpose to his visit? Was he looking to know more about his Jewishness? If so, there were no answers in the tape, which focused mainly on his time with the Latvians. Was he simply hoping to find a community that shared his earliest history? Or was he searching for some sort of absolution from these people, simply because they were Jewish? It was impossible to know.

I looked at my watch. It was now 7 a.m. There was ample time to call Melbourne where it was now mid-afternoon, before I had to go to my research institute.

I dialled my parents' number, and almost immediately my father answered. If I'd thought that he'd want to discuss his past, I couldn't have been more wrong. I was pleased to hear him in high spirits: I imagined that the pressure of the horrific memories that had been building up inside him for more than five decades was for the time being alleviated. Perhaps he even felt safe. I couldn't help but wonder how long this Indian summer would last.

He told me excitedly about a trip he was planning with my mother. They were going to drive from Melbourne to Rockhampton in the sub-tropical north of Australia to visit some old friends who had retired there. We talked for some time about the route he had mapped out for the journey and I could picture them in their car as they sped silently across the dry inhospitable terrain. They had grown so comfortable with each other in more than forty years of marriage and seemed often to communicate almost by telepathy.

'Then,' my father said, waking me from my thoughts, 'your mum and I will continue along Highway One, all the way to Rockie.' He used the shorthand commonplace among Australians, 'Rockie' or 'The Rock', as I had also heard Rockhampton called.

'You should drop in and see Ilse,' I suggested. Ilse was the only daughter of Mirdza. She lived just north of Brisbane on Queensland's coast. I hoped that the mention of Ilse would provide a pretext for discussing the video-tape. But my father shot this down.

'No,' he said, 'can't see Ilse this time. Have to get to Dirk's as quickly as possible.'

'What's the rush?' I asked.

'No rush,' he replied. 'I just don't want to dally-dilly.'

'You mean dilly-dally, Dad,' I corrected him and again made ready to ask him about the tape.

I should have known better. My father had finely tuned antennae, and must have sensed what was coming. He seized the opportunity provided by his linguistic blunder.

'Why not dally-dilly?' he said, exaggerating his Russian accent to dramatise the fact that he was not a native speaker. 'It sounds as good as dilly-dally. Even dilly-dilly sounds good. Dally-dally does too for that matter.'

I couldn't help but laugh. My father knew how to disarm me. But it was also a laugh of nervous relief. I felt like I had resurfaced to a familiar reality. To hear him be as quick-witted as usual reassured me that he was fine, even if he was keeping the demons at bay.

Then, without warning, he changed the topic again, this time declaring loudly into the mouthpiece, 'Mum's just come in from the back garden.'

Before I could utter a single word, he said, 'Here, say hello.'

I heard my mother's voice at the other end of the line.

'Hello, luv,' she said. Her tone was relaxed and she too began to tell me of the journey north that they were planning. She was excited about it – rarely were they able to afford a proper break. I did want to engage with her enthusiasm about the holiday but at the same time I was anxious to speak again with my father.

'That's great, Mum,' I said. 'Can you put Dad back on?'

'Oh,' my mother said. 'Hang on, luv. I'll just get him for you.'

I could tell she was a bit taken aback by my abruptness. I heard her put down the phone, and then call out my father's name. I waited and, after a moment, I heard her summon him a second time. Then I detected footsteps heading towards the phone, which sat in the entrance hall to our home in Mills Street.

Somebody picked up the receiver. It was my mother again. 'I don't know where he's got to,' she said, sounding baffled. 'It's like he's disappeared off the planet. He's not even in his workshop.'

'No matter then,' I said.

'Is it anything important?' my mother asked.

'Just wondered how he's doing,' I said. 'I didn't have a chance to ask him before.'

'You know, same as always,' she answered with a sigh. 'Getting under my feet and making a nuisance of himself.'

It seemed that she still knew nothing about my father's visit to the Holocaust Centre or his clandestine visit to Oxford. I wondered whether I should say something to her.

'Do you think something's bothering him?' she asked.

I detected suspicion and slight worry in her voice.

'Nah,' I said casually, trying to allay her concern. 'Nothing that I know of. He just didn't seem to have time to talk to me.'

I hated myself for lying to her in this way.

'You should know by now what your father's like,' she said, sounding relieved. 'He's always got a bee in his bonnet about something. Dashing here and there like there's no tomorrow.'

I signed off, promising to call again within the week. Though I was frustrated by my father's evasiveness. I knew the lid on my father's past was finally ajar. I just needed to persist.

In the weeks that followed I made regular telephone calls to Melbourne but never successfully broached the subject of the videotape with my father. Whenever he answered the phone and heard my voice, he would tell me that he could speak for only a moment, that he was busy.

'Too busy to speak with your son?' I responded testily on more than one occasion. But he would brush aside my accusation and tell me that he was doing a favour for a neighbour, or about to collect spare parts for his beloved VCRs and broken televisions or even, preposterously, feeding his cat, Princess, who couldn't be kept waiting. Then he would hand the phone over to my mother.

Eventually I was vexed. Why on earth had he chosen to speak of his past and send me that tape, and then been so reluctant to discuss it further?

As the weeks passed I lost the urge to socialise with friends and colleagues in Tokyo. Perhaps as a way of filling my father's silence, I became increasingly preoccupied with the contents of the videotape. In truth, I had time for little else. I developed a ritual around it. I would draw the curtains to block out the skyscrapers of Shinjuku. Then I'd switch on the air-conditioning, which not only sucked the summer damp out of the room but shut out the sound of the street below.

Then I'd remove the tape gingerly from its cover and stick it into the video machine. All the while I'd castigate myself for watching it again. I would play the tape repeatedly and pause at moments that struck me as somehow critical to his story. I found I was able to observe my father in a way I would never have been able to do in real life. I became a clinician of his body language and facial expressions, so that eventually the image on the screen became more real than my father himself. I clung to his words too and jotted them down in a notebook I'd begun in Melbourne. It was a macabre obsession. If anybody had called upon me to recite the words on the tape I am convinced that I would have been able to do so without difficulty.

I did finally manage to complete my research obligations in Tokyo. But although I spent my days immersed in the captivating depths of Japanese kanji the nights were a different matter. I would struggle against my overwhelming compulsion to turn on the machine telling myself that I was in need of an early night, and unroll my futon on to the tatami floor. But my sleep was always highly restless: troubling dreams that I could not decipher were punctuated by periods of bleak insomnia.

When I awoke from such nights, I felt trapped somewhere in a waking-dream – what the Japanese call *yume utsutsu* – from which I would not be fully released until lunchtime. And then it was as if I was surfacing from the subterranean chamber of my father's past into the blinding sunlight.

Then one night while I was replaying the video the nightmarish spell was broken unexpectedly. Though I would have been incapable of making such a gesture in real life I reached out to the image of my father on the screen and, as if it would allay his troubles, touched his cheek.

Two floors below my *manshon* tremors continued deep below the earth's crust, and it seemed that Tokyo was still waiting to see if the vibrations above ground would end in a jolt or develop into something much more terrible. My own foundations were already irretrievably shaken. My centre of gravity was shifting.

I decided it was time to make the journey back to Oxford.

11

CAST ADRIFT

Y flight was the last in a long queue waiting at the end of the runway at Narita airport on the outskirts of Tokyo. I closed the shade and curled up in my seat, covering myself in a blanket. Almost immediately I began to feel anxious, as if everything I had gone through in Tokyo had been lying in wait.

I wanted to know more about the triumvirate of men – Commander Lobe, Jekabs Dzenis and Sergeant Kulis – who had played a critical role in my father's fate during the war years, and whose influence had extended into his new life in Australia. The shadow that loomed most heavily over me at that moment was that of Commander Lobe. I'd grown up believing him to be a kind and heroic person who had figured strongly in what I now knew to be the false version of my father's rescue. The female interviewer on the tape had stated with absolute certainty that Lobe had been not only a very high-ranking Latvian Nazi, but also a war criminal notorious for his cruelty. He had never been punished for his crimes. She had made particular mention of two mass exterminations at places called Slonim and Rumbula. I had never heard of them, and of course, in his fictionalised version of life with Lobe, my father had made no mention of either extermination.

It was still not clear to me why my father hadn't come clean about Commander Lobe after the war had ended when he was free to do so. Why had my father maintained the fiction that he was a pigherd discovered by soldiers? I wondered whether the coercion my father had referred to in London had been more widespread than he'd suggested. Clearly, there was much to discover.

I had gone in search of Lobe in Stockholm in the early 1980s to thank him for his kindness to my father. From London, I'd excitedly phoned my father in Melbourne to tell him of my plan. He'd been hesitant rather than pleased, claiming that I'd disrupt the peaceful life of an elderly couple who did not enjoy good health. As I continued to express my determination to visit the Lobes, he protested more vehemently against my plan. I chose to ignore what I saw as an irrational objection.

It was my first visit to northern Europe in the winter. Stockholm was blanketed in snow and, even though it was the middle of the day, it was almost pitch-dark on the streets. As a student I didn't have much money, but I managed to find a room in a fleabag hotel near the main station. That first night I had to sleep in my overcoat, and when I woke in the morning, my blankets had a thin layer of ice on them.

When I left the hotel the next morning, I found a public telephone in the park opposite. I dialled Lobe's number, but there was no reply. During that day, in between sightseeing, I must have dialled the number at least a dozen times.

The following morning I tried again, but again nobody picked up. I wondered if Lobe had moved house or, even worse, had recently died. I was very disappointed because I wanted to express my gratitude to the hero who'd rescued my father from the terrors of the forest.

Therefore I resolved to make my way to Lobe's address on the off-chance that he might still be there. I got directions from the receptionist in the hotel and boarded a tram that would take me directly to Handen, the suburb where he lived. I got off the tram and headed in the direction of what turned out to be a council estate.

I located Lobe's building and finally found my way to the right floor in a dingy, barely lit elevator. The smell of human urine in the rear corner was so overpowering that I had to cover my nose and mouth with my hand.

I knocked on the front door of what I thought was the right flat. There was no answer.

I waited several moments and then knocked again more loudly. There was still no answer, but this time I was convinced that I'd heard a shuffling sound inside. I placed my ear to the door and just at that moment it sprang open violently, still on its chain. I got the shock of my life. Through the gap I could see part of an elderly man's face. His rheumy eye examined me.

'Yes?' he asked me in Swedish.

'Herr Lobe?' I replied in German.

At first he didn't answer me. His one eye continued to evaluate me. Then he spoke.

'What do you want?' he asked me in perfect formal German.

'You are Mr Lobe, aren't you?' I asked.

'Who are you?' he said.

'I am Mark, the son of Uldis Kurzemnieks,' I replied, using my father's Latvian name.

I'd expected the expression in his eye to change upon hearing this, and for him to welcome me with open arms. The eye looked startled and darted about.

'Go away!' he hissed.

I was greatly shocked.

'Sir, you remember Alex Kurzem, don't you?'

'I told you, go away from here.' He spat out the words.

'The little corporal!' I pleaded with him. 'Remember?'

'Go away or I will call the police!' he warned me. Then he slammed the door shut in my face.

I was completely mystified by his attitude. Surely he couldn't have forgotten, I thought.

I rapped loudly on the door, calling out 'Commander Lobe' and pleading with him to open up, when suddenly, still on its chain, the door flew open again. The long blade of a carving knife came violently through the opening, waving about.

I jumped backwards. Without uttering a word, Lobe continued to brandish the knife. I backed further away, totally bewildered. Why hadn't the mention of my father's name allayed his fears? I wondered. Was he sick? Suffering from some sort of dementia? I could only conjecture. I left.

As I boarded the lift, I was shaking from head to toe. When it stopped during its descent, and the doors opened to two elderly women, they took an abrupt step backwards, eyeing me suspiciously: I must have looked shattered. One of them waved her hand at me indicating that they'd wait for the next ride.

I hurried out of the building, without looking back. There was nothing else to do but return to the hotel. And on the way back I hatched a plan.

The next morning when I got up, I wrote a note. In it I apologised to Lobe for frightening him and explained again who I was. I wrote that I knew how he had saved my father's life and that I wanted to thank him for that.

I folded the letter, put it in an envelope and sealed it. Then I headed back to Handen. I slipped the envelope under Lobe's door and stepped away, waiting at a safe distance. From where I stood, I could nonetheless hear movement inside. Several moments passed.

Then I heard the lock click. The door opened, this time more gently although still on its chain. Lobe's partly hidden face again appeared in the gap. His eye still appraised me, but it was less wary. He must have been satisfied by my submissive demeanour because when the door then closed for a moment I heard the sound of the chain being removed. Finally the door opened to reveal the full figure of Commander Lobe. He was short and fairly rotund; no longer the fit and dashing commandant he'd once been. He looked like any other man in his seventies, apart from the fiery expression etched into his face over the years.

'Please come in,' he said, shaking my hand rather formally.

I stepped inside. The interior was cosy. What the Germans call *gemütlich*. But also quite shabby. It was clear that he was not well off. An elderly woman was standing rather awkwardly behind him. He introduced her as Mrs Lobe. She seemed kindly, smiling warmly at me, and then, as Auntie used to do, she stepped forward, took my face in her hands and kissed me on both cheeks.

'Little Uldis!' she exclaimed. 'A perfect angel.'

Lobe gave a chuckle. 'A little rascal, that's what I remember,' he said.

'He looks like his father, doesn't he, Kārlis?' Mrs Lobe continued.

I felt Lobe appraising me more closely. Then he grunted in response to his wife's words.

Mrs Lobe ushered me further into the room. 'You must be freezing,' she said. 'Come and sit by the heater.'

I sat down on the shabby sofa and Lobe sat down next to me. Suddenly he was full of bonhomie.

'May I offer you coffee?' he said. 'Or something stronger? Schnapps! That'll warm us. Dearest! Glasses!'

Mrs Lobe brought the drinks and the commander proposed a toast to my father.

After that we chatted about him. The curious thing was that Lobe seemed to know so much about my father's life in Australia: his job, the fact that he had three sons and that I was the oldest.

What followed was mystifying at the time and has stayed with me all these years.

'My father has spoken of how you found him,' I told Lobe.

Immediately he went on the alert; I could sense his tension. 'Did he?' Lobe said. 'What did the Corporal say?'

I told him only what I knew at that time: that soldiers on patrol had heard a noise behind a tree on the outskirts of a village. They'd called out 'Come out! Surrender!' and suddenly before their eyes there was a small boy, dressed in rags. None of them could believe their eyes!, and so on.

You could almost see the tension leave Lobe's body. He laughed loudly at what I'd recounted and poured himself another schnapps. But there was one tiny part of him that was still on guard, and coolly observing my movements.

Then Lobe started to add to what I'd just told him, describing how my father couldn't remember his name, not even his first name, or where he was from. All the boy knew was that he was a pigherd who'd lost his animals. He told me how his soldiers chose the boy's name and birthday.

'What was I to do?' he said. 'I couldn't let this child wander alone in the forest. He would surely have died: if he didn't starve to death, the wolves would have devoured him, and if not that, then the partisans would have captured him. They were ruthless – they would have cut his throat on the spot, the partisans. Make no mistake about it!'

By that stage, Lobe was drunk and he became slightly aggressive for a moment.

'Nowadays,' he grumbled, 'those partisans are looked back upon as heroes. Not us though! After the war the Soviets portrayed us as devils.' He paused for another swig of schnapps.

'Tell me,' he said, 'if we were villains, then why did we worry about a little boy in the forest? Who cared whether he lived or died? We did! Nobody else! We, the devils, took him with us.' Lobe laughed harshly.

He rambled on, incoherently, about the war, so that I thought he'd forgotten that I was sitting beside him. I let him talk on. I'd begun to nod off in the stultifying heat of the room when suddenly he gripped my forearm tightly. I snapped awake. For a second I wondered where I was, and what he was talking about when I heard him say, 'He was a brave little boy and what a soldier!'

I laughed out loud because I was a little unnerved. I'd never thought of my father as a soldier. He'd always made it sound as if he were a boy scout.

'No!' Lobe exclaimed. 'He was! He looked magnificent in his uniform. We called him our mascot.'

The heat and the alcohol must have got to him, because he, too, then drifted off to sleep. I sat silently on the sofa listening to his snores and waiting for him to come round.

Finally his wife, who'd been quietly listening to our conversation, left and returned with coffee. She woke him. The doze seemed to have reinvigorated him and he took up where he had left off.

'I am still considered a hero in Latvia,' he said. 'There were so many requests from patriotic Latvians all over the world, even old members of the 18th Battalion – "Why don't you write about your life?" "We want to hear of your feats in the struggle for independence" – those sorts of things – that I decided to write my memoirs.'

At that, he got up heavily from the sofa and disappeared into another room. He returned moments later with a box. I noticed his laboured breathing as he sat down beside me and gently placed the box on the coffee table in front of us. It appeared to be nothing more than an old cardboard grocery container.

'My box of memories,' he said, patting it lovingly, as if it were a loyal old dog. He lifted off its lid and delicately removed a book. Then he passed it across to me. It was a copy of the memoirs he'd just spoken of. I opened it and the frontispiece carried a photograph of him, taken perhaps when he was in his fifties. I wouldn't have said that he was a handsome man – his expression was far too austere – but he did have a commanding presence, even on the page.

He reached across for the book and flicked through it until he found what he was searching for. He cleared his throat in between his ponderous intake of air and began to read a passage aloud, translating into German about how my father was found by the soldiers.

When he'd finished, Lobe poured himself yet another schnapps. 'That's what we did for your father,' he said proudly.

Lobe had had so much to drink that I worried he'd drop off to sleep again. But instead the schnapps fuelled his ire and he began to rail a second time against those who had tarnished his reputation. As he gesticulated somewhat wildly with one hand, with the other he pulled a folded sheet of paper from his box. He gripped the paper tightly and rubbed it repeatedly, almost neurotically, with his thumb. It struck me as a rather childish gesture.

'After the war they called us Nazis,' he said, outraged. 'They said that we Latvians welcomed the Nazis when they entered our country. Absurd! We didn't follow their philosophy. We hoped the Germans would be a means to an end; to free us from Soviet oppression. That's all! They said that we turned on our own people. But they were not our people! They were partisans. Bolsheviks! Traitors!'

I remember thinking to myself 'and Jews as well', completely unaware at that time of Lobe's vicious past.

Lobe claimed to me that he had had one wish his entire life, to see Latvia free, and that was not a crime. At the time I knew little about Latvia's role in the war, but I recalled enough to see that he was trying to justify Latvia's collaboration with the Nazis. There was little I could do to stem the tide of his mounting hysteria as he began to rave, running his words together into an indecipherable mixture of Latvian, Swedish and German. His rant was reaching a crescendo and he'd become quite disturbed, almost apoplectic.

Mrs Lobe must have been listening from the kitchen, because suddenly she rushed in with a tablet and a glass of water, anxiously reminding him about his high blood pressure.

He swallowed it and then sank back on the sofa. I waited beside him in silence, until he had calmed himself, and after several minutes his wheezing subsided.

All through his tirade, and even now, as he rested, Lobe had continued to wave the paper around in his fist. When I asked him what it was, he was startled. He appeared to have forgotten that it was still in his hand and looked at it curiously, but ignored my question. He returned the paper to the box.

Then shifting awkwardly in his seat so that he was almost facing me, he said with finality, 'War is a nasty business. And I have paid the price.'

I was young, with no experience of war. I didn't know how to respond so I nodded, putting on a grave expression that I hoped was appropriate. And the truth was that I did sincerely feel for him, and was indignant on his behalf.

By this time it was getting late and I thought it best that I leave. Besides, I'd grown increasingly uncomfortable about Lobe's words and mood. Intuitively, I knew something was amiss, but I couldn't put my finger on it.

Before I departed I took a photograph of them together on the sofa. For an instant, they both seemed so vulnerable as they sat there, looking up into the camera lens as I focused it. Poor Mrs Lobe gave a weak, tired smile, while beside her Lobe's face regained its sharp, bullish expression. The abruptness of the transformation unnerved me.

But still he wasn't well enough to see me to the door. He couldn't even rise to shake my hand. Instead he gave me a smile from where he was seated and told me that he was sad to see me go. He promised to stay in touch.

Mrs Lobe unbolted the door to let me out and when she shut it I heard her fasten the locks again. It struck me as quite pathetic and I had to pause outside for a moment; I felt quite moved by their circumstances. I sensed that I would never meet them again.

I departed Stockholm, aware that much lay beneath the bonhomie of my father's relationship with the Lobes, but perplexed as to what it could be. I never told my father the truth about what had taken place in Sweden; I'd merely described it as pleasant and that it was good to have met Lobe. He never asked me more about it. Now I was certain that it was the key to something very significant.

I also had questions about the other men in my father's life. Uncle – Jekabs Dzenis – had been a central part of my own life as I grew up in Melbourne. To me he was an austere and formidable figure but I had never sensed any malevolence in his character; rather I thought of him and his wife, Emily, as my grandparents. I fondly remembered driving with him to his holiday cottage in the countryside outside Melbourne. En route, to try to engage him, I'd recited poetry by Goethe, Schiller, and Heine in German. As the car wound its way through the narrow hilly lanes, he gently corrected my mistakes in memorisation and pronunciation.

As a child I had felt sorry for the Dzenis' whom I saw as being buffeted by fate, pawns in the theatre of war. Now my sympathy had evaporated: Uncle had deceived me about who he was – and their exodus from the fatherland seemed less a cruelty and more an attempt to cover their tracks.

Jekabs and Emily Dzenis were dead, but I hoped that I could turn to surviving relatives for more information about the role they had played in my father's past. I knew I'd have to tread cautiously while ferreting out their wartime sympathies and associations.

Then there was Jekabs Kulis, the soldier who had actually saved my father from the firing squad. He would be in his late seventies or early eighties by now. Was he still living in New York City, or, if not, where?

I resolved to begin my investigations when I reached Oxford.

I drifted into a light doze, only to wake with a start as heavy turbulence hit the plane, causing it to shudder violently. I gave up trying to sleep. During the seemingly interminable hours that followed I couldn't help but reflect on my father even though I had tried deliberately to avoid doing so. My image of him had been turned upside down.

On the one hand he was still my father, the person I thought I knew and we had what many would see as a good relationship: we would banter and joke easily with each other, but as is common with fathers and sons, there was also a suffocating silence between us whenever our emotions were exposed. We never confronted each other and, as I matured into adulthood, I understood that we could both live comfortably with that tacit agreement. But it was also true that my father had lived a double life, and I didn't really know who he was.

Why had my father kept the truth from us? While I could accept what he had said to me about protecting his family from the shadows of his past, I didn't believe that this was the full story. Were there threats from other sources that he was still unwilling to discuss? Was he frightened of himself and of his own memories? To never speak of one's memories did not mean that one had escaped them. I could not imagine what it would be like to live with the imminent danger of the revelation of one's self.

When my father looked at my brothers and me, did he see what had been cruelly taken from him? Did he long to utter the words 'my brother' or 'my sister', words that my brothers and I used without a second thought?

Above all, I wondered how my father had managed to keep his past 'unspoken' all these years. Had his enduring silence been a form of survival he was as unwilling to relinquish as his life? Questions like these plagued me during the flight and I realised I would have to let my father fill in the details of his story at his own pace.

I decided to walk to the rear of the plane to stretch my limbs. I had paid little attention to the other passengers, so I was surprised when I entered the rear cabin and found myself in the midst of what appeared to be a religious jamboree. On the side of the plane where I stood, four orthodox Jews draped in their traditional prayer shawls and wearing yarmulke, had gathered in the space around the emergency exit. They were chanting in unison in low voices while davening towards the wall of the cabin. I felt inexplicably confronted by their behaviour and turned away only to notice that on the far side of the cabin a much larger prayer meeting was going on. It seemed that most of the rear cabin had been occupied by a group of Japanese Christians, perhaps en route to a pilgrimage in Europe. Standing at the front of the group, a man in a priest's collar was leading row upon row of followers in slightly fevered prayer.

I moved unsteadily back towards my seat feeling light-headed and disconcerted.

Half an hour later the plane entered its holding pattern, circling to the west of the airport and waiting for permission to land. But I felt anchorless and directionless, cast adrift on a sea between past and present. Filled with an inchoate fear that the mysteries of my father's past would be the harbinger of a dangerous storm for our whole family, I had no idea when and where I would reach safe harbour again.

12

OXFORD (1)

Eventually I settled back into my routine in Oxford, but my academic research quickly took a backseat to my father's story, which now dominated my thoughts.

In the weeks that followed my return, I made numerous phone calls to my father; the little dance that had begun over the telephone in Tokyo continued. Whenever I tried to broach what had happened to him, let alone the tape and its contents, my father would lapse into an unshakeable silence before either abruptly changing the topic or, more often, rapidly handing the telephone to my unsuspecting mother.

I soon grew tired of pursuing my elusive father. In the meantime, I would gather what scraps of his past were available to me and see where they would lead. I retrieved the videotape from where I'd secreted it in the bottom drawer of the desk in my study, perhaps in an unconscious emulation of the way my father had hidden his case.

Then I found myself repeating the ritual I'd developed in Tokyo. I spent an entire weekend with the curtains drawn against the late summer light, playing the tape repeatedly. Only this time, I coolly jotted down further details of his story. By Sunday evening, I had filled a small notebook with observations and queries and, after I had returned the video to its hiding place, I settled into an armchair and began to review my notes.

Ultimately my father's recollections were impressionistic. With few exceptions, they lacked objective markers that could pinpoint a precise moment or place. I had a handful of names of places and people from which to begin my research: Laima chocolate factory, Valdemara Street, Riga, Carnikava, the Volhov swamps, Lobe, Dzenis and Kulis, and the mysterious words, Koidanov and Panok. It wasn't much to go on. My father's vivid account of the burning of people in the synagogue was unaccompanied by a place or a time.

While I did not hold my father responsible for the nature of his memories – one would expect little more from a terrified child's point of view – I felt thwarted by them.

By the time I'd reached the last page of my notes, I realised that my frustration had boiled over unconsciously. In the margin, I had jotted down words such as 'silence', 'memory' and 'truth' which I had then underlined once or twice for further emphasis.

I lay on my bed mulling over the information that I did have. Foremost in my mind were Koidanov and Panok, the words my father had revealed to me at the Cafe Daquise in London. Where did they come from? Were they the names of people or places? Did they have any connection with his family? My father claimed that he'd held these names inside him for as long as he could remember. Had the extermination itself imprinted them on his soul?

I was intrigued, too, by my father's cryptic recollections of his early family life. He had said that he had a younger brother and a baby sister. What were their names? How old were they when they were killed?

His memories of his own father were baffling: some time after being told that his father was dead, Alex saw him. He had lowered himself from a hole in the ceiling of the family home to gently whisper 'Goodbye' to Alex. Finally, my father was adamant that on the night prior to the extermination of his village his mother had taken him on to her lap and told him that they were all to die in the morning.

Without the name of my father's family or village to go on, how would I ever uncover the truth of these memories, or give him back his original identity?

I lived in a university town populated with some of the world's finest scholars. It was natural then, that I begin my search for the meaning of Koidanov and Panok in Oxford. Through academic contacts, I was put in touch with a number of experts in the history of the Holocaust.

Their responses disappointed me. Most of the experts were unwilling to listen to my father's story with an open mind. Their reservations stemmed from the fact that my father's recollections were too vague and anecdotal. I was surprised by this: I thought my father's recollections had been quite sharp for a young child. And I considered anecdotes important to our understanding of the Holocaust. Because most survivors had been significantly older than my father at the time of the Holocaust, their stories contained more objective signposts, most notably the central symbol of the

Holocaust: the concentration camp. My father's story had no such icon; I didn't think this would matter, but soon enough my naivety would be evident.

In the end, however, three professors were intrigued enough to fit me into their busy schedules, and I set up appointments to meet one of them in London and the other two in Oxford. In advance of our meetings, I sent them each an outline of my father's story.

As it turned out, all three took a sceptical stance towards my father's story. Professor M., a distinguished historian in Oxford, delivered the most vehement critique. Our meeting took place in his office in his college. He welcomed me warmly. Within moments of shaking my hand, he told me that he had conducted more than three decades of extensive research into the Holocaust, adding that he was a man who had heard many incredible stories of survival. My father's story, he said, was the most incredible.

I noted some reticence in his voice, but put it out of my mind as he ushered me graciously into his room. He poured me a cup of coffee and offered me a comfortable armchair, while he sat behind his desk.

I began to describe my father's story in closer detail. He did not interrupt me, but occasionally nodded his head or smiled thinly in response to something I said.

When I had finished speaking, he began to cross-examine me about details of the story. At the end of our lengthy exchange, he took a gulp of his cold coffee and then offered me his opinion. He had heard of neither Koidanov or Panok and was unable to place them as the names of persons or locations.

I was prepared at that moment to let the matter rest. He had not been able to help me. However, before I could even thank him, he raised a finger to interrupt me.

'I cannot deny the story outright,' he said. 'The broad canvas of your father's story may be true, but not in all of its details. Some of them are so fantastic as to be improbable.'

I was flabbergasted. 'Which ones exactly?' I asked.

It seemed that he had prepared for our discussion. He rested his elbows on the desk and began to tap his fingertips gently together. He consulted a sheet of paper.

'What bothers me most of all,' he said, 'is your father's claims about the manner in which he survived. No child of five could have survived under such conditions – alone in a forest during a northern European winter. Even soldiers and partisans found it hard to withstand the freezing conditions and depredations of the situation.

'And over and above that,' he continued, 'why would these Nazis – any Nazis keep a Jewish boy alive? What possible advantage would it have had for them?'

I explained to him again, that as far as I knew only Jekabs Kulis, and nobody else, had known my father was Jewish and he alone had instructed my father to keep his Jewish identity hidden. It had involved no great conspiracy of silence among a number of men.

But the professor found this explanation hard to accept.

'There was no way that your father would've been able to keep it secret,' he said irritably. 'Somebody would have caught your father out at some stage. And apart from that, no child of that age could be capable of such vigilance in protecting himself. It would have required a superhuman effort, not only physically. The mental strain would've been unbearable.

'What also creates doubt in my mind is your father's account of his escape from his village. To be frank with you, it would have been absolutely impossible for his mother to have known what was going to happen to her family the following morning,' he said. 'From the chronology you have conveyed to me, I am certain that the extermination must have happened some time in perhaps autumn or early winter 1941. Given my knowledge of history, it is likely to have taken place somewhere in Russia.

'Now here is the difficulty I have with the incident. You have heard of the Wannsee Conference, I take it?'

I nodded.

'The Wannsee Conference took place in January 1942 and is held to be the time when the programme and methods for the mass extermination of the Jews became systematised. Prior to that was a period that I call the proto-Holocaust, when the Nazis experimented with a variety of methods of extermination. At that time they began to clear out the Jewish communities in the villages of Eastern Europe. They did this to make way for the deportation and temporary resettlement of Western European Jews there. The Nazis moved swiftly from village to village in units known as *Einsatzgruppen*, or extermination squads, German-led but manned mainly by Baltic volunteer forces, police brigades and the like carrying out *Aktionen*, as they called their ruthless work.

'The Jewish population in the villages would have been largely unsuspecting about their imminent fate. There are two key things here. Firstly, the communication between villages for the most part would have been poor, so it was highly unlikely that the Jews in these villages knew about the presence of *Einsatzgruppen* until they were literally upon them. The second thing is that the Jews from these villages had a long history of being subject to pogroms, in which the men and boys may have been killed, but not the women and children. There was no way they, including your father's mother – a simple peasant woman according to your father – would have had any inkling that a new imperative for extermination that required the liquidation of all the Jewish men, women and children in her village had come into existence.'

I didn't know how to respond to his assertion. Professor M. was a world-renowned expert in the field. Yet I could not believe that my father was lying about what he remembered. Certainly my father was a great storyteller. The tales of his adventures in the Australian outback and elsewhere had always been slightly embellished – I'd sensed this even as a child – but the raw pain and grief I had witnessed on my father's face were another matter. Unlike the voluble and masterful raconteur I knew, he had struggled with every syllable, as he endeavoured to give life to his experiences.

I'd been absorbed in my reflections and was brought back to the present by a tapping sound. The professor was impatiently drumming his fingers on his blotting pad. It occurred to me then that he'd grown bored with the discussion, or, even worse, he didn't believe my father's version of events at all.

He looked at his watch.

'I am sorry to have to say this to you, young man,' he said, waving his hand in a dismissive gesture, 'but it's altogether too implausible.'

My suspicions had been correct.

'Are you saying that my father is lying?' I blurted out. For a moment, he was taken aback, and looked worried. Then he regained his composure.

Perhaps he thought better of what he'd just said, because suddenly he adopted a more conciliatory tone, and suggested that we move to one of the college's common rooms. I agreed readily. I wanted to be on more neutral ground.

It was late afternoon and the darkened common room was deserted. The professor discreetly closed the heavy wooden door behind us as we entered, softening the sounds of the outside world. We made ourselves comfortable on deep leather armchairs facing each other. A mood of calm and civility prevailed. I waited for the professor to speak.

'Please let me give you some advice,' he said. This time there was a note of sympathy in his tone. 'I do not necessarily deny that an extermination took place,' the professor continued from where he had left off. 'But I cannot accept that events unfolded as your father has described them. In essence, that is my problem with the entire story. He must have embellished it.'

'It's not clear to me why he, or anybody, would embellish such a litany of horror,' I said, trying to remain even-tempered. 'What purpose would it serve? What do you think actually happened then?'

'Only your father knows. It is highly likely that somewhere inside himself, your father feels guilty about his own survival however it may have occurred, so he has dramatised it to make it seem more out of his own control. For example, what child would have the wherewithal to escape in the way that he claims he did – and the personal resources to survive in the forest for such a long time? The wolves at night, the corpses in the forest, tying himself in the trees, caught by the woodsman! It has all the trappings of a fairy tale told to exaggerate his own innocence.'

'You're not serious!' I said angrily.

The professor held up his hand to indicate that he had not finished what he wanted to say.

'And this question of how he was found,' he said. 'Perhaps he volunteered to go with the soldiers in order to save himself . . .'

My sense of outrage was almost palpable. My heart was beating so loudly in my ears that I could barely hear my own response.

'Of course he wanted to live. Who wouldn't?' I raised my voice. 'But that didn't mean that he made a conscious free choice to join the soldiers. What child of five volunteers for anything? He was taken by them. Kidnapped!'

The professor indicated with both hands that I should quieten down. I looked around me and noticed a member of the staff tidying newspapers in the far corner of the room.

'Yes, perhaps volunteer is too strong a word,' the professor said, trying to sound reasonable, but I had no time for his semantics.

'You are wrong,' I said. 'Nobody in their right mind could concoct even a single moment of what my father has been through.'

The professor remained silent for several moments, perhaps to let my anger settle.

'Perhaps you've hit the nail on the head,' he said slowly as if testing the water.

. I gave him a look of incomprehension.

'Perhaps your father is not in his right mind,' he said choosing his words carefully. 'I believe that your father may be suffering from a form of false-memory syndrome that causes him to exaggerate the story that he has thus far told. I'm not saying that he's lying intentionally. It's more complicated than that. Your father has chosen to speak for whatever reason, and he is driven by an urge to make sense of the story as he tells anybody who will listen. I've seen this with other survivors. They have to find a way to describe the indescribable.

'Especially child survivors have to make sense of an arbitrary adult world in which they had no grasp of why they survived. And, as I said before, because they feel guilt about their survival, they believe there is an incriminating truth about themselves that they cannot see, but which, nonetheless, they feel that they must hide. They exaggerate the details of their story, because they cannot face the truth about themselves even when no such truth exists. So it is with your father. Have you noticed,' the professor continued, 'how your father describes himself in the story? He is the cute mascot at the centre of the Latvians' world . . .'

'I don't think he has concocted that,' I cut in. 'They protected him and showered him with love and attention. And I assume you have looked at the photographs and newspaper articles I sent you in which he was featured. And what about the film he remembers starring in? He was a hero to them. My father did not overestimate his importance to the Latvians.'

'True,' the professor agreed. 'But guilt causes complex contradictions in the survivor. Your father also portrays himself, and wants others to see him as, the hapless victim of all the attention showered on him in that crazed adult world. He wants us all to believe that everything that happened to him was fate and beyond his control. Nothing of his survival was down to his own cunning or wits.'

'No!' I protested, 'my father would be the very first to admit that he used all his cunning to survive – in the forest and to conceal his Jewishness from his captors and adopted family. He had to in order to survive!'

And then, dishearteningly, the discussion took a turn in the same direction as it had with the interviewers.

'It's a complicated matter, this survivor business,' the professor reiterated. 'It's rife with contradictions. This denial of involvement in one's own fate is a retrospective survival tactic by the survivor, but this time not to save his body but rather his moral conscience. The fantastical elements of his story distract us from the most important question . . .'

The professor paused mid-sentence. His eyes would not meet mine. Then he spoke.

'Complicity,' he said in a matter-of-fact voice.

'My father was complicit in nothing,' I responded firmly. 'What on earth can a child of that age be complicit in?'

The professor pursed his lips, but remained silent, staring at me intently.

The implication was that as a young boy my father had somehow been a willing participant in his own fate, and was capable of conscious moral decisions. Now he was now trying to cover up his part in the war by manipulating the truth about his role. He was refusing to face up to his complicity.

I needed time to digest this. In a half-absent state, I repeated to the professor that he was wrong.

In response he removed a piece of paper from the pocket of his jacket and offered it to me. He had jotted down a number.

I raised an eyebrow.

'Don't be offended,' he said. 'It's the telephone number of a friend of mine. Your father should speak with her. She's a psychiatrist, an expert in victims of war crimes and violence.'

'And how might she help him?' I asked with some sarcasm. 'Therapy? Analysis?'

'You must not blame your father, Mark,' he insisted, misreading the look of irritation on my face. 'Your father is sick and he's not responsible for that,' he said, with deliberation. 'He was made sick, traumatised by what happened to him, and is now trapped by the workings of the subconscious of a terrified child. This has been the only way for him to handle what happened to him.'

He paused briefly to gather momentum.

'Ultimately, your father is trying to distract us from the most important question,' he said gravely.

I didn't believe that there was much point in continuing the discussion. I had come in search of basic information and felt I'd been subjected to a barrage of criticism and doubt about my father's story. I knew that I would not be able to convince him otherwise.

I rose to leave, hoping that that would indicate to him that I'd had enough, but the professor was determined to have the final word.

'Did your father . . .' he said from his comfortable armchair '. . . kill Jews?' For just a moment, an almost indiscernible smile of satisfaction crossed his face.

I froze to the spot, not because of the professor's question, but because this thought had crossed my mind when I'd watched the taped interview. But my father had denied this at the time and I trusted him. I knew him to be honest and direct, someone who once he spoke about his past, wouldn't skirt around unpalatable truths.

'No,' I answered firmly.

Our goodbyes were terse. I thanked the professor and he told me to take care of myself, as if warning me further against my father.

I made my way along a maze of passageways until I finally reached the main quadrangle of the college. From there, I easily found my way out through the gates and on to Oxford's bustling High Street. Stunned, I hunched my shoulders, feeling diminished somehow by the buildings towering above me as I began to weave my way back to my digs on the other side of the town.

As I walked I recalled that the professor had mentioned a man known as Benjamin Wilkomirski, the key figure in a recent literary scandal. I had only followed the Wilkomirski fraud vaguely. When *Fragments*, the memoir of his childhood during the Holocaust, had first been published, one couldn't help but notice the lavish praise heaped upon it from all quarters. It was considered nothing short of a masterpiece of Holocaust literature. Wilkomirski was proclaimed as the iconic survivor – the innocent child who had miraculously survived the concentration camps.

When the memoir was exposed as a fraud – Wilkomirski was not Jewish and he had no experience of the Holocaust, having grown up in Switzerland – the establishment conceded that they had been deceived by the unsign-posted memories and impressions described in *Fragments*. It made them wary of future impostors.

In our discussion, the professor had gone on to state that my father suffered from a surfeit of such memories. 'Your father's story is highly dramatic and fantastical in nature,' he had said, 'but we cannot verify it. Children's memories are unreliable. They often distort things.'

He made a connection between Wilkomirski and my father.

'With Wilkomirski the world made the error of accepting his story without any anchors, and Wilkomirski has turned out to be an impostor. You should be wary . . .'

He had not bothered to complete his sentence, but his insinuation was clear: he had put my father in the same boat as Wilkomirski. But this was unjust. Despite what he'd endured, my father did have verifiable memories, especially after he was taken to Riga by Sergeant Kulis. In particular there were the newspaper cuttings and other documents that he had removed from their hiding place inside his case. And my father had mentioned a propaganda film about himself made by the Nazis.

The professor's words challenged me to verify my father's story. I knew that I would have to find this film, even a scrap of its footage, if it still existed. Its discovery would put the veracity of my father's story on firmer ground.

Eventually I came to my front door. But I didn't reach for my key. I decided instead to head for Port Meadow, an expanse of common land near my home. As I made my way there along the narrow canal path, I sensed more than ever that my father and I were on our own. Another door had closed in our faces.

I walked across the meadow towards the River Thames, feeling even more dispirited since meeting with the professor. Despite my earlier objections, I had to be honest with myself and admit that the professor's words had planted in me seeds of confusion and doubt.

Were my father's revelations too fantastical or, even worse, a Wilkomirski-like deception?

However, my father had not spent most of his lifetime telling people 'embellished' stories about his wartime past; rather, he'd spent his adult years trying to prevent them from being discovered. And then there was my father's behaviour when giving evidence on the videotape. Surely this was proof, I thought, that my father had not 'softened' his story in order to protect himself. Although I knew my father to be a resilient man I had seen how painful it had been for him to speak for the first time of his terrible past.

Though he had risked condemnation from the interviewers, he hadn't skirted around their questions or compromised his story in any way. He'd stated what he could remember and what he could not and, in particular, much to the annoyance of the interviewers, he had refused to condemn his Latvian 'kidnappers' out of hand.

It seemed to me that having begun the painful task of dragging his wartime past into the open my father would remain adamant about the truth, even when I suspected that this would not be the last time he would face pressure to tailor it to the agenda of the audience.

Doubtless there would be other individuals who would question my father's integrity especially in the light of his fifty-year silence. He'd told me that he'd maintained his silence to protect his wife and sons from the trauma of his past. I'd accepted that but also suspected that he may have faced pressure from Dzenis and Lobe. Did he feel shy or even ashamed about his original identity?

The question that loomed largest was how my father had maintained his silence all this time. I began to reflect on a childhood spent in his company, wondering whether there was anything, in retrospect, that might provide a clue. I reached the riverbank and sat down opposite the wooden footbridge that traversed the river.

I started to nod off in the warm afternoon sun, and as I did, remembered a favourite family anecdote. My father loved 'two-up' – the illegal game of chance and mateship that he'd first learnt to play while on the road in the Australian outback. Two or three times a year he would suddenly announce that he was gripped by the urge to 'play the pennies'. My mother would never let us wait up for him because he rarely returned before midnight. However, one night my father failed to return at the expected hour. At around 2 a.m. I was roused by the sound of my parents' voices in the kitchen. My father had only just come in, and my mother was making him a cup of tea.

As I tiptoed past my brothers to the kitchen they fell in behind me. I put my ear to the door.

'That was a close escape,' I heard my mother say. 'You were lucky this time.'

Upon hearing those words, my youngest brother Andrew became overexcited.

'What happened, Daddy?' he cried out. At the same moment my other brother, Martin, pushed me forward so that I stumbled into the kitchen and almost fell on the floor.

My parents jumped in surprise. 'In God's name, what are you boys doing up at this hour?' my mother exclaimed. 'Back to bed this instant. The lot of you.'

'No!' Andrew protested loudly, ignoring our mother. 'Tell us about your lucky escape, Daddy.'

'Well it was like this,' he said looking slowly at each of us in turn. 'We were all gathered in a circle around the spinner,' my father said. 'He had the coins on the paddle and was holding it in the air. The toss was about to begin so we were all as quiet as mice. You could have heard a pin drop, when suddenly there was a noise, like the whistle of a bird. Only it was the middle of the night. It was the warning signal from Bert, the "cockie" or watch who was on lookout upstairs. The police were on their way to raid us. Before we'd even fully taken that in, Bert called out "Crikey, the coppers are already at the door."

'Everybody panicked. All hell broke loose! Mayhem. Somebody gave the order "Out through the back door", so all of us made a charge in that direction. There must've been more than a hundred of us and we were all desperately trying to squeeze through the door at the same time. Somehow I made it through and into the backyard. It was almost pitch-black so that I could just make out the figures of men hoisting each other up over the fence. You see, we're all mates there and we look after each other.

'Behind us,' my father whispered excitedly, 'we could hear the police breaking down the doors of the warehouse and I thought, "This is it. My number's up", when somebody yelled out: "Over here. There's a loose plank. We can get through the fence here."

'With that we all charged over like a swarm of ants.'

My father's eyes moved slowly across each of our faces with such dramatic intensity that we all held our breath.

'But it was just my luck,' he said, his voice unexpectedly dropping a register. 'Just as I reached the gap, a fat man jumped in ahead of me. And wouldn't you believe it, boys, Fatty was stuck.'

We all squealed with pleasure.

'Alex,' my mother interrupted him, 'don't talk about the poor chap like that. He can't help it if he's overweight.'

My brothers and I shifted irritably on our stools. Our mother had broken the spell.

'But that was his nickname,' my father protested. 'We all called him that. He didn't mind in the least. Anyway, where was I?'

'Fatty's stuck, Dad,' I said.

'That's right. His head and shoulders were on one side of the fence and his enormous bottom and legs were on our side. We were trapped.'

'What did you do?' Martin asked, solemnly.

'What could we do?' my father answered. 'We pushed! We got a good grip on his cheeks and shoved him as hard as we could. But he didn't budge. He was wedged in so tightly that he began to squeal like a little piggy.'

'By this time,' he said, 'I could hear the cops making their way across the warehouse, and heading towards the yard. In the next moment they were at the back door.'

We were all wide-eyed with terror.

'I called out one final desperate time,' my father said. "Everyone together . . . one . . . two . . . three", and we gave Fatty one last big push. Lo and behold we heard a pop, like a bottle of champagne being opened, and Fatty was flat on his face on the other side of the fence.

'With that I jumped through. I was free.'

We all sprang to our feet, cheering. I recalled with clarity how my father then switched to the present tense, heightening the drama of the moment.

'I make my way in the darkness along the back laneways, careful to avoid being caught by the police. There is nobody else around, not a soul. I am totally alone. I have no idea where the other men have gone.

'Then suddenly I come to a clearing and beyond that is a small park. I am sure that my car is in the street on the other side of the park. It is deadly quiet and through the trees I can see my car, its surface glistening in the rain.

'I make a dash for the park. I sneak through the trees. I only have to cross the street and put the key in the lock. It's now or never. I take a deep breath and run for the car. I do it. I escape . . .

'Hey presto! Here I am!' My father snapped his fingers and smiled.

My brothers and I leant back in our chairs, exhausted and relieved.

The room was silent and it took several seconds before any of us could rouse ourselves.

Finally it was my mother who made a move.

'Come on, Alex,' she said. 'Let's get the littlies back to bed.'

The sound of a jogger crossing the rickety bridge brought me back to the present and I suddenly had a revelation. I was certain that my father's silence had some connection with his storytelling. It was not only our family who saw him as a great storyteller. Everyone my father told a story to appreciated his talents. He had embellished his various tales, usually about his early years in Australia, transforming them into wondrous adventures. If my mother was around at the time, she would castigate my father playfully, saying ,'You've put the enlarger on again, luv.'

I sat bolt upright. I had a flash of clarity about my father's two-up story: as he told us about his getaway, my father might have been reliving another event whose memory exerted itself so powerfully in him that he spoke of it as if it had only just happened. Even though the surface details were different my father had been reliving the extremity of his escape from his village. His climb through the fence at the back of his house and his journey past the open graves of his neighbours. I shuddered.

He had found a way to tell us what had happened to him without telling us. Somehow, incredibly, he'd woven a cataclysmic event of his childhood – the separation from his family – into a recent humorous incident. Perhaps the story had denatured his terror and alleviated the pressure of keeping his secret.

I could see already that without the safety valve of his stories, my father was having more trouble suppressing the truth of his childhood than he had perhaps imagined. But this did not in any way compromise the veracity of his words now that he had finally found the courage to speak. To tell his most amazing story the consummate storyteller would have to abandon the tools of his trade, although I could not as yet say unequivocally that I was relieved that the truth was coming out.

The flurry and squawking of ducks on the river brought me back to the present in a flash. It was twilight and the meadow was now nearly deserted apart from the occasional solitary cyclist taking a short cut across the field. I got up and dusted myself off.

13

ELLI

I COULD no longer keep my father's story to myself. When I was a student I'd become friendly with an Israeli woman at my college. We'd first met one evening in college when she'd been seated across from me in the dining-hall.

She'd overheard a conversation I was having with a colleague and had detected my slight Aussie accent. Later over coffee in the common room she'd approached me and introduced herself. Her name was Elli. She was an historian keenly interested in issues related to Judaism.

She mimicked my Australian accent while telling me that she'd spent some of her teenage years in Sydney – her father had been posted there as an executive for an Israeli import/export business. She told me no more than that, and even as our acquaintanceship grew, I could not get her to open up about her years in Australia.

I sought out Elli now, thinking that she might understand my predicament. Although the new academic term had not yet commenced I called Elli on the off chance that she'd already returned from her home in Jerusalem.

She answered immediately. 'Dearie, you're back!'

We exchanged news about our respective travels and then I suggested that we meet for coffee later in the week. Elli must have sensed something in the tone of my voice.

'You sound worried,' she said, becoming serious. 'Is everything OK?'

'I'll tell you more when we meet,' I said.

'As you wish . . .' she replied.

We made arrangements to meet at a tearoom on the High Street.

Two days later I waited for her at the appointed time at the rear of the shop.

I heard the bell above the door ring, and looked up to see Elli struggle into the shop with a carrier full, I was sure, of academic books and journals.

She was something of a cross between a bag lady, and the stereotypical absent-minded professor. In a film she might have been played by a younger slimmed-down Margaret Rutherford. She had the same shrewdly appraising expression.

I spent the rest of the afternoon with Elli doing my best to describe in a coherent manner what my father had told me and all that followed: the question of who Lobe really was and my father's fragmented memories of exterminations, and my inability to unearth the significance of Koidanov and Panok.

I was impressed and grateful for the extraordinary care Elli took to understand the details of my case. When I had exhausted myself she was silent for some time. She was clearly mulling something over. Then she reached across the table and took my hand in both of hers. Her grip was firm.

'Don't worry, dearie,' she said. I could sense the compassion in her voice. 'We'll get this sorted out. First of all, if your father is Jewish then these names that he's held inside him probably have Jewish or perhaps even Eastern European Yiddish associations. And I know just the person to help you with that,' she declared decisively. 'Frank. A genealogist who specialises in Judaic culture.'

I jumped at the opportunity to meet Frank, and there and then Elli called him and arranged for me to meet him the following morning.

I waited for Frank at the Jericho Cafe. I'd barely had time to seat myself at an empty table by the window when I saw a motor scooter pull up outside and, somewhat incongruously, a man in his late forties dismount. He was perilously thin and had a sparrow-like demeanour. His dark hair, dark brooding eyes and beard gave him a rabbinical aura.

Somehow he must have surmised that I was the individual he was to meet. He waved from the other side of the window, giving me a broad and intelligent smile and entered with a vital nervous energy. Over coffee I described my father's story and it was clear that Frank observed the effect it was having on me.

'Both my parents lost their families in the war,' he said. 'It had a terrible effect on me as well. But you've got to learn to live in the light, Mark. Not be consumed by the darkness of the past as some are. You are going to meet some bitter individuals on this journey. My advice is to steer clear of them.'

Frank told me more about his interests in the genealogy and dialects of

Eastern European Jewry, and I learnt of his especial interest in life in the *shtetls* before the war. Eventually we got down to the question of Panok and Koidanov. Frank was immediately dismissive of my suggestion that either of these words might be my father's family name.

He must have noticed how disheartened I was by his opinion, because he quickly promised that he would investigate these words further and get back to me.

Early the next morning I was woken by the telephone. I was groggy and at first didn't recognise the man's voice at the other end of the line.

'I was wrong! There was a family of Panoks!' It was Frank. He was so excited that he hadn't bothered with the formality of a greeting. I was instantly alert.

'It's a very uncommon name for Jews,' he continued, without pausing for breath, 'but there was one extended family of Jews who went by that name. They lived mainly on the outskirts of Minsk, the capital of Belarus.'

I started to shiver uncontrollably. I was shocked and greedy for more good news.

'Anything on Koidanov?' I asked, my teeth slightly chattering.

'Not a scrap,' he replied, 'but I'm working on it. I'll get back to you as soon as I know more.'

I thanked Frank profusely and hung up.

I lay back on my bed. For the first time in quite a while I felt optimistic. 'Was my father a Panok?' I asked aloud. Perhaps he was from Minsk. A Belarussian. I knew nothing about the country. But what was Koidanov?

My thoughts were racing. I was far too restless to return to sleep so I decided that I would head to the Bodleian Library in town where I would look for a detailed map of Belarus.

I was climbing the stairs to the bathroom in order to take a shower when suddenly the telephone rang again. It was just eight o'clock, and was far too early for a regular caller. 'It must be Frank again,' I told myself, 'already back with another clue.'

I picked up the receiver and held it to my ear. At first I thought that there was nobody at the other end of the line. Then I heard a familiar voice.

It was my mother. Immediately I knew that something was wrong. It was the first time that she had ever telephoned me in Oxford.

'Is that you, Mark?' I heard her ask for a second time.

'Mum?'

'It's your father, luv,' she whispered, sounding worried.

'What's up?' I snapped, fearing the worst from a call such as this.

She hesitated. I could hear the sound of her breathing as she struggled to say something.

'He won't stop crying.' She choked on her words for a moment. 'Your father's been crying for two days. Every time I ask him what's wrong he just shakes his head, and says "All the memories are coming back to me now. I can't stop them." That's all he says, over and over. Nothing else. He's been unsettled for months now. Ever since his visit to Sydney to see his friend Otto. Something must have happened up there.'

My mother began to sob gently. 'I don't understand what's going on,' she murmured.

Then she regained her composure. 'You don't know what this is about, do you, luv?'

'No, Mum,' I said, quietly, 'I don't.'

It was clear that my father had not told my mother anything. I wanted to tell her what I knew if only to allay her fears, but I worried that the truth would devastate her. My father had put me in an untenable position.

My mother spoke again. 'Your father said he wants to talk to you in person,' she said. 'You should be here.'

I didn't go to the Bodleian that day. Maps would have to wait. Instead, that evening, I headed back to Heathrow airport to begin my long journey home.

PART II

14

HOME AGAIN

MY father was waiting for me in the Arrivals hall at Melbourne airport as he had some months ago. He was less buoyant than he'd been, and was silent during the entire journey home. This time it was the tape that had become the lodestone of our relationship and until it was broached, we wouldn't have much to say to each other.

I had a strong sense of déjà vu as the car turned into our driveway. My mother waited on the porch and ushered me into the kitchen to give me breakfast. It was as if I'd never been away, as if nothing had changed. In one respect at least, this turned out to be true: my father had still not revealed his past either to my mother or to anyone we knew. Instead, he had video-taped a testimony at a Holocaust centre.

I'd slept well on the flight and didn't feel the slightest bit jet-lagged. Indeed, the bright sunshine of the spring morning energised me. I chatted with my mother before heading out to my father's workshop with a cup of tea.

I crossed the yard, calling out in advance: 'Tea's up!'

My father turned to face me, about to say something.

'Yes,' I said, anticipating him, 'it's got three sugars in it.'

'As if I'm not sweet enough,' he joked in response.

I leant on the doorjamb and watched him as he tinkered inside the open back of a television set. Occasionally he surfaced to sip at his tea and at one such moment I caught his eye.

'So what's going on, Dad?' I asked.

'What do you mean?' he replied, not looking at me.

'Mum's worried about you. She called me . . .'

'I'll be fine,' he said, and buried his head in the television.

'Dad,' I insisted, 'talk to me. You avoid me over the phone and I came all the way back here because of you. What's bothering you?'

My father raised his head. He shrugged and I could now see how tense and coiled up inside he was.

'That videotape I sent you . . .' he murmured.

I nodded.

'I wish I'd never made it.'

'Why?'

'It just didn't work out . . .'

'Why'd you go there, Dad?' I challenged him.

My father scratched the back of his head. 'To be honest I'm not quite sure. I don't know what I was thinking.'

'You *must* have some idea,' I said edgily.

He grimaced.

'I was looking for answers.'

He gave a deep sigh.

'To what?'

'To questions that I don't even know,' he said laughing bitterly, before continuing, 'What happened to me is part of what is called the Holocaust.' He stared at me intently. 'So I thought that Jewish people, more than anyone else, would understand what had happened to me. More than that, I thought that somebody at the centre might recognise the words Koidanov and Panok.'

I considered telling him I had Frank on the case back in Oxford, but for the moment I wanted to stick to the topic of the interview.

'So did they come up with anything?' I asked.

He shook his head despondently.

'I'd hoped they would, being Jewish,' he said.

'To be honest, I think they were more interested in how I felt about being Jewish. They asked me what I knew about being Jewish and if I considered myself to be Jewish.'

'Do you?' I asked.

'I don't know what I am!' My father gave a wry smile. 'I was born Jewish, but the Latvians had me baptised as a Lutheran. I used to go to church with them. I was a Jewish boy raised among Latvian Nazis as a Lutheran. What a mix-up!'

My father attempted to make light of his situation and raised his eyes dramatically to the ceiling in mock confusion.

Then abruptly he changed his tone. 'Seriously, son,' he said, 'I was born Jewish. What happened to me happened because I was Jewish so I think that makes me Jewish, don't you agree?'

My father shrugged and looked slightly bewildered.

'You know how I feel,' he said.

'Anyway, after the man there heard some of my story he told me I should give my testimony. He explained to me what that meant, and I agreed to do it.'

'So how did it go?' I asked.

'I was frustrated by the vagueness of my memories at times. I have the feeling that the interviewers were as well. But I couldn't help that. I was only a child after all. Some things were vivid, others weren't.'

My father was about to say something else, but then stopped himself.

'What?' I asked, giving him a questioning look.

He faltered for an instant.

'Recently things have changed,' he said slowly and with deliberation. He nestled his head in his folded arms, atop the television set.

'It's as if there are two men inside me, and one of them has been asleep for more than fifty years. Now he's waking up, and the two are not getting on so well.'

'How are they not getting on, Dad?'

'The one that is waking up, well, he won't be pacified. It's as if he's whispering in my ear over and over: 'Find out who you are. Now!' So I'm taking his advice. It's a simple wish – I want to know who I am. Doesn't every person have that right?'

I remained silent, staring at the floor but felt the intensity of my father's eyes upon me.

Suddenly my father snapped. He stood bolt upright and rigid as he burst into a torrent of words while still keeping his voice low and controlled. 'It's a cruel fate. Every day, I ask myself why this happened to me. Why did I decide that I wanted to live? Sometimes I think that it would have been better if I hadn't woken up. That it would've been better to have gone to the grave with my family. What does it mean that I survived?'

There was no note of self-pity in my father's words, and his face conveyed only bewilderment as he continued, 'My identity was snatched away as a child, and now I feel that I'm denied one as an adult. There must be some place I belong. Am I Jewish? Am I Russian? Am I a Latvian? Am I guilty or innocent for what happened to me? The more I talk about my past the more confused I am.'

The flow of words stopped as abruptly as they had begun, leaving my father desolate in their wake. I understood better now what had driven my father towards the Jewish community. It was not simply his burning desire to find the meaning of Koidanov and Panok. These questions had worried him for most of his life. I sensed that my father had been clutching desperately at this old Jewish identity in an effort to stay afloat amid the wreckage of his long-manufactured self. He had gone seeking something from the Holocaust centre, but for whatever reason, had not found what he was looking for.

15

ESCAPE FROM RIGA

I RESOLVED to put everything aside in order to help my father solve the riddle of his identity.

Later on that first night back, in the safety of the dark kitchen, my father began to talk to me again.

'I'll tell you about the end of the war,' he began, 'when we fled Riga and took refuge in Germany.'

During my childhood I had never heard my father use such words – fled and refuge – in relation to his time in Europe during the war. In fact, the period from the war's end until his arrival in Australia, was another black box for us all. He had offered us only the scantest of details about what had gone on, as if by magic he had, firstly, resurfaced after the war in a displaced persons camp outside Hamburg and then, in a second sleight of hand, emerged into the bright Australian sunshine.

And bizarre as it may sound none of us ever pushed him to reveal more about that period of his life. We gratefully accepted whatever morsel he fed us, never pausing to digest what we'd been given.

'Here they are,' he said brightly.

'Why are you looking for them?' I asked.

'I wanted to check the date when I arrived in Germany. It should be printed on the papers. Let me see . . .'

My father adjusted his reading glasses, and I seized the moment.

'Here, let me do it,' I said, snatching the piece of paper from him before he could protest or shove it back in the case.

I looked down at the yellowed document. It simply stated my father's name, his nationality – Latvian – his date of birth, and his place of birth, which was given as Riga. At the bottom of the sheet, there was the imprint of an official border entry stamp dated 21 October 1944. My father would have been about nine years old by then.

My father stared at me intently. After a pause I asked, 'Why did you flee Riga?'

'We had to escape the Russians before they entered Riga.' He warmed to his story right away. 'I tell you it was chaos. Suitcases were piled up all over the place in Valdemara Street. Uncle was pacing up and down the room staring at his watch. I sat quietly on the couch. I didn't want to get in anyone's way. You see, I was worried that if I did, one of them would stop and think to themselves "Why are we taking him with us? Why do we need another person to worry about, another mouth to feed?"

'So I sat there in my new navy suit and cap that Auntie had brought to my room the night before. She told me that I would no longer be a soldier, that it would be too dangerous to be one from then on. I loved being a corporal, so I was very annoyed. But I could sense the tension in the apartment and knew better than to create a fuss. Later I learnt that Auntie had stoked the stove in the kitchen one last time for the purpose of burning every single one of my uniforms.'

My father seemed wistful for a moment. 'See this, my case,' he said. 'I had it with me as well. It was brand new then – Uncle had presented it to me as a gift for my belongings – it looked much better than it does these days.' He flashed a grin at me and said: 'Like me, you could say.'

'Uncle became impatient,' my father continued. 'Auntie and Mirdza were fussing in the next room: Mirdza was having a tantrum about being forced to leave behind so many clothes and shoes. Uncle peered out of the window to see if our driver had arrived.

'Mirdza slumped down next to me on the sofa, pouting sullenly. Then she noticed me and reached over and gave me a pinch on my arm for good measure.'

'Where was Zirdra?' I asked my father.

'She wasn't coming with us,' he answered. 'I don't know the exact details but I seem to recall that she had been sent to work with a Latvian medical brigade.'

My father continued with his story. 'The car arrived eventually, and it was mayhem as it was loaded up with our luggage. There was so much of it that there wasn't room for us all. Uncle lost patience again, and returned some of the cases to the foyer of the apartment building. He chose Mirdza's ones, which angered her.

'I tried to stay out of her line of vision, but to no avail.

She saw me standing on the path, waiting to get into the car. "Why can't we leave him behind instead?" she complained. "He's not one of us." Of course, Auntie and Uncle would have none of it.

'As we headed towards the main railway station in Riga, I noticed that the streets seemed to have changed dramatically: like people's faces they looked grimmer and grubbier. Suddenly I remembered that I had not said good-bye to the sergeant nor to Commander Lobe. I turned to Uncle and begged him to take me to them. He said that it was impossible but I would see them soon in Germany, which pacified me.

' "Germany," I thought, "the place that everybody talked about all the time, as if it were heaven, or a pot of gold at the end of the rainbow." It was only natural that the commander and Sergeant Kulis would be there too. It seemed that all the Latvians around me were going there.

'It was a scramble at Riga station. People were milling about every-where, and trying to find any vacant seats on the train was nightmarish. Although Uncle had reservations, people had occupied our seats and refused to budge, even when he waved our tickets authoritatively in front of them.

'Uncle and I moved further down the train toward the front carriages. We found free seats there, which I guarded until he came back with Auntie and Mirdza.

'I must have fallen asleep on Auntie's lap. At one point, I opened my eyes briefly and saw Uncle sitting opposite me. I could see his reflection in the carriage window as he stared into the darkness beyond it. His face was tired and worried – I'd never seen him like that before. Then I must have nodded off again.

'The next thing I remember, was being gently shaken by Auntie trying to wake me. I sat up bleary-eyed and she began to smooth my hair.

' "We're here," she said.

' "Germany!" I exclaimed.

' "No silly, the ship that will take us there."

'I peered through the dirty train window, and saw that we had indeed reached a port. The ship was more like a ferry. "Steuben" it was called. It was going to take us to Gotenhafen, a German port near Danzig.

'We made our way up the gangplank and on to the deck, which was loaded with cargo boxes and cases. There were people who'd boarded before us and were already sleeping in the corridors and even on the floor of the dining-cabin, as we passed through it.

'Uncle must have been a person of some status, because a steward led us to a cabin that was spacious enough to accommodate us all. It was a lot more than most people seemed to get.

'I don't remember much after that. I'd been only half-awake, and I quickly nodded off to sleep in my narrow top bunk.

'Over breakfast, Uncle told us that we would be in Germany by that evening. I was excited by the news, but suddenly I began to worry about what would happen to me. "Would my secret be discovered by these Germans?" I asked myself. I'd met quite a few German officers in Riga, and they'd always terrified me. They were arrogant and behaved as if they could do anything, even read your mind. They'd have no difficulty discovering that I was Jewish.

'I went back on deck and stayed there all day, staring at the murky waters through the swirls of mist. At one stage, I started to hatch a plan of escape for when we'd docked. But I felt muddle-headed and told myself to wait until I saw the lay of the land before trying anything.

'The fog thickened gradually during the afternoon.

' "At least the Germans won't see me," I reassured myself.

'By early evening the lights of a harbour pierced the mist. Uncle joined me on deck. He leaned over the rail, quietly contemplating the vista of the town that was slowly crystallising before us.

' "Gotenhafen," he said.'

My father smiled wryly.

'Gotenhafen,' he said. 'God's harbour.'

'In the months that followed we took refuge wherever we could, as if we were on the run. Families, contacts of Uncle's I presume, took us in for various periods. I don't know who arranged this for us or how.

'We slept wherever we could – on living-room floors, huddled by brick ovens, sharing whatever food our hosts could provide. At one stage we stayed with a family – I think they were called Siegel but my memories of names are confused because we moved so frequently. But we were there for perhaps a month or so, and for the first time, we had a room to ourselves.

'I didn't see much of Uncle in that period. He was away from the house for days on end. I suspect that he may have been seeing officials, trying to get a place of our own or arranging passage further on. When he wasn't away on business, he'd usually arrive home in time for dinner, when we'd all crowd around the table together. There'd be Mr and Mrs Siegel and their two sons about my age who'd always want me to join in their games and other antics.

'But I wasn't interested in that sort of thing. I had more important things to do. I'd quickly found my way about town. I hung around the railway station. Nobody paid any attention to a kid. But I paid a lot of attention to what was going on and I soon worked out how the black market operated.

'Before long, the Dzenis' and the Siegels had me out bartering for them on a regular basis. I traded clothes and valuables for food and medicine. Once, Uncle ordered me to barter the silk stockings that Mirdza had smuggled with her from Riga. Uncle had confiscated them when he'd discovered them. I remember the way he scolded her: "God knows who you think you are or where you think you are going," he'd said. "To a fancy ball or something!"

'Seeing me roll the stockings into a ball and stuff them into my jacket was the last straw for Mirdza. She glowered at me. I think she has hated me ever since – especially when I came back with horsemeat, bread and pickled cucumbers in place of her precious stockings.

'Mr Siegel was a hearty type who loved his food, and when he saw my booty, he slapped me on the back and tousled my hair. Everybody was pleased except for Mirdza, who glowered at me from the opposite side of the table, even though she, too, feasted on the gains from my black marketeering.

'It was crazy when you think of it – a child having the knowledge and skills to do this. They would've starved without me. I was more resourceful than all of them put together. They were like the children and I was the father.'

For an instant I had an image of my father as an Oliver Twist type character – a street urchin with a smeared face – not dressed in rags admittedly, but in a navy suit, darting in and out among the crowds.

'Then one night over dinner, Uncle made an announcement that our departure from the Siegels was imminent. We would be leaving for an unknown destination where the authorities had promised us an apartment of our own.

'Two days later, we were told that we had an hour to gather our belongings, and by mid-morning, we found ourselves waiting in the freezing cold at the railway station. There were long queues of other refugees who were in the same situation as us. We ended up waiting there all day without food, wondering what was going to become of us.

'Finally, an official told us we were going to Essen.

'That night we departed for Essen, hoping that we would end up in our own quarters, no matter how tiny. We were in Essen for only a matter of hours before boarding another train headed for Dresden. We'd barely reached Dresden when it came under siege from intensive fire-bombing. That would make it February 1945.

'The authorities thought that we'd be safer elsewhere so we were evacuated to the grounds of a castle in a place called Moritzburg on the outskirts of Dresden. When we got there, the place was overflowing with people wrapped in blankets huddled together in groups. To my child's eyes, it seemed like there were thousands of people assembled there. We found a spot on the ground as well, and wrapped ourselves as warmly as possible.

'Auntie warned me to stay by her side, but, of course, I didn't. I wandered amongst the throng. They were different nationalities, too – as well as Latvians, there were Lithuanians, Estonians, and Germans. I heard other languages I didn't recognise being spoken. They must've all been on the run from the Allied forces.

'The bombing of Dresden intensified during the night. The noise was tremendous, even from where we were, and the sky was lit up almost as if it were daytime. Everybody was fearful – you could see it on their faces – and some appeared on the verge of panic.'

My father stared intently at me.

'You know what I did next, son?' he said then, without waiting for a response.

'I climbed up the steps overlooking the grounds and shouted for everybody to remain calm. I told them to trust me, that we would be safe. What's even more amazing is that they listened to me. They were like a frightened flock of sheep, but somehow the sight of me, a mere child, speaking confidently, calmed them.'

My father shook his head in disbelief.

'But the truth is that inside I hoped that they would all be bombed. I wanted us all to disappear into oblivion. That's what I really felt.'

'Even you, Dad?'

He nodded.

'I'd had enough. The war, the fighting, the criss-crossing of Germany without any idea where I was being taken . . .'

My father rummaged in his case again.

'Look!' he exclaimed, removing another photograph.

'Here I am at Moritzburg Castle.'

He held the photo out for me to see. Although the image was slightly unclear, one could indeed tell that it was my father, now about nine years old, dressed in a cap, a quasi-sailor's jacket, and trousers. In it, he smiles shyly at the camera, just as he was doing at this moment, a man in his sixties, as he waited for my response.

I could only stare at it in amazement.

'After another day, we were moved on again, this time to Schwerin in the northern part of Germany, where finally we did get a place of our own. But it was a dump! There was no other word for it: a dark damp single room with a single gas ring in the corner for cooking, and heating that didn't work. There was no bathroom – we had to share with at least a half-dozen other refugees on the same floor.

'Still Auntie did her best to make it cosy, so that it felt like a home. I remember the night that the war ended. Everybody from our floor had crammed into the room of one family who had a radio set. We listened in silence to a broadcast from the American military, who announced that the town was now in the hands of Allied forces. The atmosphere was solemn. I glanced at Uncle, but his face was immobile. Everybody was like that – their expressions were frozen. God knows what was going on in their heads at that moment. I guess they thought that their number was up, as they say.

'Suddenly Uncle left. Auntie told us to go back to our room and then followed Uncle out. We waited silently in the darkness of our room. Even Mirdza was quiet, for a change – but not for long!

' "Uldis," she whispered, "what will happen to us?"

' "We're all going to die!" I exclaimed in a terrifying voice.

'I wanted to frighten Mirdza as revenge for all the trouble she caused me.

'She jumped up in a panic. Then, suddenly, she weakened because I saw her silhouette stumble and reach for the wall for support.

'I rushed to her, regretting what I had just said, and tried to comfort her.

' "We will be fine," I said. "Uncle won't let anything happen to us."

'Despite her fear, Mirdza dropped off to sleep. But I couldn't. I sat there in the darkness, listening to her breathing. I was petrified and I worried about what would happen to me. After all, if we were captured by the Allies, then there was the chance that they'd find out the truth about my past and then see me as the worst traitor of all. This time it'd be the Allies who'd put me up against a wall and shoot me for what I was – a Jewish boy among Nazis.

'I didn't know where Auntie and Uncle had gone, but they didn't return till just before dawn. I suppose that they must've been with other Latvians discussing what was going to happen in the immediate future. They woke us up. Uncle wanted to talk. It was as if he'd read my mind. He put his arm around my shoulders, and sat me down on the side of my bed. Then he crouched down to my level and stared into my eyes.

'"From now on," he said, "if any person, no matter who they are, asks who you are, you say that you are the son of my cousin. You must remember this!" Then he turned to the others in the room and warned them, too. "Young Uldis is the son of my cousin whom we care for because his parents died in the war. Remember that."

'Uncle had heard that the Americans were going to hand Schwerin over to the Soviets. He said that this was the worst thing that could happen to us. No Latvian could live under the oppression of the Soviet Union again.

'Among the other Latvian refugees he'd met, it'd been agreed that we needed to head further west to Hamburg, which was in the British zone. We'd be safer there. We had to leave immediately, before the sun came up, and to pack only the bare minimum.

'There was a truck waiting for us in a nearby alleyway. Families were crammed on to the back of it, so that we had to squash in as best we could. I was wedged into a corner but at least I could get some air and see through the slats. The truck soon picked up speed and we got some way out of Schwerin, when it came to a sudden halt. We were transferred to an old bus, so quickly that it was all I could do to hold on to my case. Still it was wonderful, finally, to be able to sit down and breathe properly.

'I nodded off with my head on Auntie's shoulder, and didn't wake until the bus came to a halt in the middle of nowhere. It had broken down and nobody had any idea what we should do. We simply sat there quietly on the bus, while the driver examined the engine.

'A short time later, two soldiers – American – appeared in a jeep and took over. They ordered everybody off the bus. It was quite warm, so everybody headed for the shade of some trees by the side of the road. They lounged there passively, making occasional complaints about their discomfort and the heat of the afternoon. I was embarrassed by their complaints and laziness. I returned to the bus where two soldiers and the driver were working on the bus's engine.

Soon another jeep pulled up. For a second, I froze to the spot when I noticed that there was a black soldier amongst them. I had never seen a black man before. Full of bravado, I resolved to tell him that it was about time for a wash. I walked over to the jeep, but when I got close enough, I got an enormous shock! I realised that he wasn't dirty – it was the colour of his skin! I just stood there, transfixed.

'At a certain moment, he looked across and noticed me. I don't know what expression I had on my face, but he laughed out loud and flashed me a big smile. His teeth were brilliant white, not yellowed and decayed like the Europeans'. I imagined that he must've come from some sort of para-dise. That's where I want to go, this place called America, I said to myself.

'The soldier reached into his pocket and pulled something out, beckon-ing me over the way Sergeant Kulis had done all those years earlier in the schoolhouse. This time I was not tentative. I knew that I'd be safe. I went over to him. Then I saw that it was a chocolate bar. I was so pleased. In Riga, I'd almost lived on the stuff.

'He leant back against the side of the jeep, watching me as I gulped down the chocolate. It was richer and creamier and so much better than Laima's.

'I could tell that he was a kind person and I wanted to communicate with him, despite the – to me – still disturbing colour of his skin. I tried to say thank-you but he didn't understand a word of what I was saying. But some-thing about me must have moved him because he tousled my hair and smiled warmly at me. He passed me more chocolate and some chewing gum as well. He even gave me a puff on his cigarette. I almost choked. I'd never had one before: the Latvian soldiers had never let me smoke because it wasn't good for my lungs they said.'

My father raised his eyebrows.

'I witnessed atrocities but they wouldn't let me smoke.'

'Then the soldier pulled out a scrap of paper and wrote something on it. He pointed at the words and at his chest. Then he kept repeating "America!" and "Illinois!"

I didn't get it.

'"Illinois. What a strange sound!" I remember thinking to myself. "American won't be easy to learn." It's obvious now that he'd written down his name and address in America.'

My father's mood became sombre.

'In all the mayhem,' he said, 'I lost that scrap of paper.'

He shifted in his seat.

'It's a deep regret to me,' he murmured. 'I'll go to my grave without meeting this man who showed me kindness. Who knows how life would have turned out for me if I'd gone to America and found him?'

I wondered the same thing. Australia was a land of refuge from the war in the 1950s, but it would be fair to say that it lacked then the entrepreneur-ial spirit that prevailed in the US. Even though my father loved Australia, I believe that America would have better suited his temperament and sense of adventure.

'Where was I?' I heard my father say.

'The bus . . .' I prompted him.

'That's right,' he said. 'It was eventually repaired and everybody climbed back on board. I hid behind the jeep. I didn't want to rejoin the Latvians. I wanted to stay with my new friend, the soldier. I decided that somehow I would be able to tell him what had happened to me, and that he wouldn't let the Allies punish me.

' "Who knows," I thought, "he might even be able to find out who I had once been."

'At that moment I heard Uncle calling out my name. He'd noticed that I hadn't taken my seat on the bus. The soldiers began a search for me and in a matter of only moments, they'd uncovered my hiding place. The black soldier nudged me out into the open. I tried to convey to him that I wanted to stay with him and that I knew all about soldiering – I even marched about, while miming shooting a rifle – but he only laughed out loud, thinking I was playing the fool. He offered me his hand to shake and then grabbed me around the waist and carried me over to the bus. Uncle was waiting for me on its steps and I knew that he had witnessed my feeble effort to be rescued, even as the war was ending.

'He deposited me, roughly, I might add, on a spare seat next to Mirdza, who gave me a disgusted look.

'I waved a final goodbye to the soldier from where I was seated and then the bus took off in the direction of Hamburg.

'The journey seemed to take for ever. The roads were blocked with cars, and tanks and convoys of soldiers. People were fleeing in both directions. I even saw German soldiers in their *Wehrmacht* uniforms, standing with their hands in the air, having just surrendered.

'It was bitter-sweet. I was glad that the Germans had been defeated, but I also tasted bitterness for the first time. I don't know whether it was hate or not, but my anger for what they'd put me through suddenly overwhelmed me. I thought my head was going to burst. And all around me the Latvians were deadly quiet and staring straight ahead. They seemed too frightened to even glance at what was happening outside the bus windows. They must have feared being caught. Part of me hoped they would be.

'The bus moved on slowly and was eventually stopped by British soldiers on the outskirts of Hamburg. They directed us to Geesthacht. There was a camp there, an officer told us. When they heard this, some of the Latvians panicked and tried to scramble off the bus.

'The word "camp" must've triggered the worst possible associations in their mind. The soldiers had to draw their rifles to calm the potential stampede. Then through an interpreter, the officer explained that the camp was administered by the British. We'd all be fed, clothed, given a bed and looked after by the Red Cross. What's more, the soldiers told us that they had named the camp Saules – that was Latvian for sunshine – and that stopped people in their tracks.

'Most remained standing in the aisle of the bus and many turned to look at Uncle who was still seated towards the rear. He'd already become a sort of de facto leader amongst us, having dealt with several difficult situations en route to Hamburg. He nodded without speaking. That calmed people's nerves and they returned to their seats. Then the bus moved on towards Geesthacht.

'That's where we ended up finally. Our escape from Latvia was over.'

16

TO FREEDOM

IT was now almost 3 a.m. The house was silent apart from the ticking of the clock on the kitchen wall.

But my father showed no signs of flagging. Now that the floodgates had opened it seemed that the flow of memories could not be stemmed.

'Over the next days more people arrived at the camp,' he said. 'It turned out that the camp had been designated especially for Latvian displaced persons, or DPs as they called us. The camp must have held over a thousand people – and there were about seventy in our barracks, number 41.

'There was a long queue on the first day we arrived. Hundreds were milling about, waiting to be assigned to huts and receive their provisions. When we reached the head of the queue we were met by a British officer and a Red Cross worker, who wanted to check our papers. The soldier looked down at me and asked Uncle if I was his son. Uncle hesitated and then thought better of it.

' "No sir," he said. "His father was my cousin. Both his father and mother died in the war, and I am the boy's guardian, sir."

'The soldier did not seem suspicious or even particularly interested in Uncle's explanation, but he did ask for my papers, and to my surprise, Uncle pulled out a wallet full of documentation. "Here are documents from the Riga Orphan's Court in 1943," he said, "where I was awarded custody of the boy. His name is Uldis. My family want to continue to look after him." Uncle passed the papers over to the officer.

'The official looked over the documents. Uncle gripped my hand firmly and waited nervously for a response.

'He complained about the lack of a birth certificate, but Uncle made an excuse about officialdom in Riga, and pointed out that the details of my birth were noted on the orphan's certificate. He told the man that I was born in Riga on the 18th of November 1935. This seemed to satisfy the officer who gave my papers a final cursory glance. He gave a nod to the Red Cross official who handed Uncle bedding and other essentials for me.'

My father lifted the lid of his case and fished out a piece of paper.

'Here is the certificate,' he said, passing it across.

I looked down at the paper. It was dated in 1943 and written in Latvian, so I could only make sense of a small portion of it. What stood out most sinisterly was the address of the court – Hermann Göring Street.

'I didn't know that Uncle had adopted you formally.'

'He didn't. It's more like a guardian's certificate – though he did try to adopt me on a number of occasions. He really wanted me to be his son.'

'Why didn't it happen then?'

'I don't know, to be honest. Uncle could have done it without my consent, but for some reason he was determined that I agree to it. But I wouldn't. He asked me at least three times and each time I refused. He was shocked and disgruntled, but he never insisted that I cooperate nor asked me my reasons. Eventually he let the matter drop.

'I wouldn't have been able to explain myself in any case,' my father said.

'Do you understand now?' I asked.

He grimaced. 'They were not my people,' he said, 'and inside me I felt that if I let myself be adopted then, I would have surrendered completely to them.'

'How long were you in the camp?'

'Over four years. We had to wait for a country to accept us. It wasn't so bad. Except that they tried to get me to attend school. I did go on occasion, but mostly I played truant. I was still too restless after my life with the soldiers to sit at a desk.'

I was not surprised to hear my father speak of his restlessness, since he had been that way for as long as I could remember. And he loved the little adventures he cooked up for us, sometimes enjoying them more than we did. Perhaps it was a way for him to create some of his missing childhood, or what he imagined a childhood should be.

He was great fun to be with, precisely because he side-stepped the difficult times of our childhood. He was rarely ill-tempered, and not the type of father to scold, forbid or punish us. He had always put pleasure and enjoyment above the practicalities of money, and many people, including my brothers, understandably came to judge my father harshly for what they saw as his financial profligacy.

One day, on trust, he had handed over his life-savings – our security – to a Frenchman known only as Michel, with whom he'd become acquainted.

Michel had tempted my father with a business proposal and had convinced him that it would be a sure-fire winner. The money had barely touched Michel's palm, when he vanished. Incredibly, my father had demanded neither contract nor guarantees of any sort from the Frenchman. We lived hand to mouth for many years after that.

There was a time when I too found it difficult to forgive my father for this mistake. I worried especially on behalf of my mother, who found our financial insecurity extremely difficult. Living in a constant state of exasperation with my father, she made an almost saintly effort to cope with his recklessness and to protect us from its consequences. If we turned to our father for fun, we turned to our mother in times of trouble, looking for love and affection. This, more than anything, was a testament of her love both for him and for her sons.

Learning about my father's early life was akin to looking through a kaleidoscope: its shifting colours and shapes kept me enchanted for hours on end, but my eyes ached from searching for patterns. I now saw his attitude towards money especially as symptomatic of a 'madness' that had infected him. Money, like life itself, was a gamble which came and went easily.

But it was not the madness of a poor soul, lost to himself: my father's madness somehow tempered the coexistence of child and man within one being. I realised now that part of my father was still a child of five, frozen in time at the split second before he had witnessed the extermination of his family.

He removed two photographs and laid them both on the table. I reached for the one nearer to me. It was a group photograph of the Latvians who lived in Barrack 41 at Saules. In the photograph, my father sits at the very end of the front row with all the other children, while the adults stand behind.

My immediate impression of the picture is that my father seemed to be a stranger or 'outsider' among these people. It is not simply because he is positioned at the edge of the frame. Rather it is his demeanour, and most notably his clothes. It is easy to discern from the others in the photograph, dressed as they are in thick woollen overcoats with pallid, drawn features, that it is winter. My father wears short trousers and his feet are bare. His body language indicates that he is freezing: he is hunched in on himself, trying to keep warm. Nonetheless his small face grins determinedly out of the photograph.

I wanted to ask my father directly about how he saw himself in this photograph. But it seemed such an intimate question and I was too shy. I returned the photograph to its resting place and picked up the other one. This one, too, told a story different from the idyllic depiction of camp life my father had offered us as children. I'd seen the photograph just once before, during one of my father's storytelling sessions years earlier. It was stuck to the back of another photo he wished to show us and he had inadvertently drawn it from his case. As it had fluttered to the floor, I made a grab for it ahead of my father. I caught a glimpse of it for an instant, before he snatched it back from me with an unexpected force.

Even though I was only a child, what I had seen in that moment filled me with unease. Free to examine it at length, now I understood why the photograph had disturbed me. It is an ostensibly innocent looking snap of my father, around nine or ten years old. He is sitting alone at a table decorated with flowers. But if one looks closely, the boy appears deeply unhappy, as if, despite his own best efforts to maintain his composure, the mask has slipped from his small face to reveal terrible damage. His expression was so raw, that it pained me to look.

I wanted to ask my father about this photograph as well, but again I held back, not wanting to further intrude upon his suffering.

I suddenly remembered that Auntie had told us that, during his time at Saules, my father would frequently wake up screaming in the middle of the night. It now occurred to me that in both the photographs I had just seen, the after-effects of his nightmares were still visible on my father's face.

Was he oblivious to his own suffering? Whatever effect he'd imagined these photographs would have upon me, I could only feel anger against all the Latvians in the camp, including Auntie and Uncle.

My father spoke again.

'The living conditions in the hut were cramped,' he said. 'All the families created their own space by hanging blankets to create rooms of sorts. In our place, we'd crammed in the bunkbeds and a small table that we sat around for hours on end.

'Uncle worked in the camp's office, and sometimes Auntie would get me to take something over to him. He was never busy when I dropped by. He usually sat behind a large desk, chatting with other Latvian men who were also in the office.'

My father paused and looked at me excitedly.

'Do you know who one of them was?' he asked, and without waiting for an answer, went on, 'apparently it was Konrad Kalejs. The war criminal who's been in the news recently.'

I had heard of Kalejs, who'd been a member of Latvia's notorious Arajs Kommando, an extermination squad that even unreconstructed Latvians had difficulty explaining away. Kalejs had lived freely in the United States and later in Australia, before his true identity had been uncovered. Shamefully, the Australian government had vacillated over his prosecution for war crimes, and Kalejs had died before being brought to justice.

'Whenever I played hookey from school, I'd go to deal on the black market. When I'd return home with the day's booty, I'd make a grand show of it. Uncle and Auntie would look up, smiling, as I flung down my bag – the same one that Kulis had given me to collect wood – and laid out what I had bartered for that day: chocolates, tobacco and the occasional note or coin. I'd sit on the edge of my bunk while Uncle counted the coins. He kept a small box hidden under the floorboards. He would get it out, untie it, and add the day's takings to the coins and notes that were already in it.

'Auntie would be responsible for the food. She had her own secret box, and would store the chocolates and sugar in it. But before re-tying the box and hiding it, she always passed me a chocolate as a reward. Sometimes I'd forget that I was meant to be civilised, as Uncle demanded, and I'd revert to my time in the forest. I'd snatch the chocolate from Auntie's hand, and retreat to my bunk, like an animal returning to the lair with its catch. Auntie would shake her head despondently. Those days in the forest have left their imprint on me.

'But they were always pleased with my work. Uncle would compliment me, saying such things as, "You are truly, what do these English say, a wheeler and dealer!"

'Once, when Mirdza was still living with us, and she heard Uncle praise me she harrumphed indignantly, saying, "He must have a touch of the Jew in him!"

At the mention of that word, I headed for my bunk – I half-expected to hear the sound of Mirdza receiving a slap like the one Ausma had once got for making a similar accusation. But nothing happened. It was no longer a crime to be Jewish, though obviously still an insult.'

'Did you ever think of telling the Dzenis family that you were Jewish?' I asked. 'After all, as you said, it wasn't a crime to be Jewish by then.'

'What would've been the point?' he answered.

'Would they have accepted you?' I pressed him.

My father didn't answer. His body language made it clear that he didn't wish to dwell on the issue of his Jewishness, which even now seemed to make him nervous. I wondered what it was that made him want to skirt around the issue?

When he spoke again, it was to change the topic.

'I spent four years in Geesthacht.'

'You've said that, Dad,' I replied. 'What other things did you get up to?'

'This and that,' he answered, shrugging and rubbing the back of his neck.

His reluctance slightly annoyed me though. I assumed that it was due to the almost instinctive caution that he had lived with for so long.

'Weren't you ever tempted to tell anyone about the kind of people who were in the camp?' I asked.

'To be honest, it never crossed my mind.'

My father paused.

'I was still in another world. Looking back, I know I had no idea what had happened to me and who these people really were. I was shell-shocked and vulnerable and disturbed by what I had gone through. I can tell you that I wasn't the only one like that. There were individuals in that camp who died under mysterious circumstances. In other words, they committed suicide.

'In the early years after the war, Europe was in chaos and I clung to the Dzenis family who'd promised to take me with them wherever they ended up. They were my anchor. How could I inform on their compatriots?

'I should have been old enough to take care of myself,' he said. 'After all, I was nine.'

'No way!' I exclaimed. 'Think of children today at the age of nine.'

'There was another reason I kept quiet about the past,' he said. 'The British who ran the camp seemed to really like the Latvians. I didn't understand that. One minute we were at war with them, the next they were looking after us!'

'Do you think that they knew who these Latvians were?' I asked.

'They might've chosen simply to turn a blind eye to things. It was strange that there were no questions asked about these people, that they were given some sort of special status and priority, when the Allies knew that they'd not been occupied by the Nazis, but had cooperated with them.'

'It seems that the Latvians have done a good job of whitewashing their past, and many of them got away with it,' I said.

'They investigated Commander Lobe, you know. For war crimes.'

'When was this?'

'The early 1960s.'

'Who was it?'

'The Swedes. I think on request from the Soviets who claimed that Lobe had ordered massacres. They were interested in what I had to say then about my memories. I signed a statement . . .'

'Against Lobe?'

'No, the opposite! For Lobe . . . in his defence.'

'Is this what you meant that day in London when you said they made you do it? Uncle and Lobe?'

My father nodded.

'Did you lie?'

My father was taken aback by my directness.

'I don't know if I did or did not,' he answered. The expression on his face tightened. 'I have memories of exterminations – the ones I mentioned to you – but I don't remember specifically if Commander Lobe himself was there. I do know that he was in charge of the 18th along with another soldier, Captain Rubenis. I didn't have much to do with him though.'

'Do you want to tell me about this statement?' I asked my father, who gave a deep sigh and shifted in his seat. He nodded.

17

THE AFFIDAVIT

WHILE I did want to learn as much as I could about whatever my father volunteered about his past, at certain moments I found myself resisting my father's words. I had begun to sense that he hoped for redemption or absolution in exchange for his confessions. I didn't know in what shape or form he hoped to find this, nor whom he hoped would deliver it, but I prayed it was not from me. I felt that I had little wisdom regarding his situation and that I too was now struggling to keep from drowning in the horrors of his past.

'It must have been sometime late in 1963,' my father began. 'By then I was living in Melbourne.'

He shifted in his chair again, trying to make himself more comfortable.

'One day I heard from Uncle. He wanted to see me as soon as possible.

'I found my way to their home in Elsternwick. It was in an ordinary suburban street, one in a row of small white cottages. Theirs was partly hidden behind a picket fence and a front garden dominated by a beautiful silver birch that always reminded me of the forests I'd patrolled with the soldiers in Latvia. Uncle and Auntie had created a little bit of their homeland.

'I went through the gate and started to make my way up to the front door when suddenly I stopped and looked down at my crumpled suit and brown case. I was overcome with shame. I felt that I didn't have much to show for ten or so years of life in Australia. I'd spent most of my life here as a vagabond, which suited me down to the ground at the time, but somehow I still couldn't shed that shabby aura.

'I tried to smooth out the creases in my suit, and then went up to the front door. I had to knock only once before the door was opened by Auntie. It had been quite a while since I'd seen her but the expression of kindness in her light-blue eyes was always the same. Before I knew what was happening she was hugging me and then kissing both of my cheeks.

' "Come in, Uldis, come in!" she exclaimed warmly, ushering me into the living room.

'Inside I was reminded even more of the past. The furnishings and decorations were as if they'd been transported from the flat in Riga. The curtains had been closed to keep out the strong Australian light so that the room was in semi-darkness apart from the soft light coming from a lamp on a side table. One wall was covered with shelves of books. Only the muted ticking of a grandfather clock in one corner could be heard.

'What I most remembered was the sweet scent – a mixture of flowers, ripened apples and furniture polish – identical to that in the flat in Valdemara Street.

' "Please sit, my boy," Auntie said. "I'll tell Uncle you're here." She always referred to her husband as Uncle in my company.

'Auntie tapped lightly on a door on the opposite side of the room. It was then that I heard Uncle's voice, telling her to enter. She flashed me a nervous smile before disappearing inside and closing the door tightly behind her.

'After several moments the door opened again, and when I looked up Uncle was standing in the doorway. From where I was seated, he towered above everything in the room. He'd not lost his aura of formality even in Australia, the most easygoing of places. He stepped forward with his arm outstretched, and I rose to shake his hand. Then he told me to be seated again.

'Auntie hovered nervously behind him. She seemed concerned that Uncle and I should be pleased to see each other. I had no idea why as there'd rarely been any tension between Uncle and me.

'He told Auntie to prepare coffee for us, and she disappeared into the kitchen.

'Uncle and I sat quietly for several minutes. He seemed to be coolly appraising me. I could sense his unease but I hadn't the slightest idea what was bothering him.

' "You look well!" he said finally. "Strong! And you've put on some weight too."

' "It's the good Australian food," I answered.

'Uncle gave a little smile, before lapsing into silence again.

'I began to feel on edge when suddenly he spoke again.

' "Why have you come here?" he asked.

'I was taken aback.

' "Sir?" was all I could manage to say. I thought of this visit as my responding to his summons.

' "What do you want?" he insisted.

' "To see you and Auntie," I blustered, feeling even more confused about why I was there.

' "I have always believed that we would never see you again," he said slowly.

'Then it must have registered with Uncle how startled I was by his comment.

' "After all that happened . . ." he added without completing the sentence.

' "But you were kind to me, Uncle. You cared for me. Auntie loved me like I was her own," I answered.

'Immediately I felt that I'd said too much, been too emotional, as I saw Uncle stiffen.

' "Were we?" he said, somewhat distantly, while still sitting formally and staring straight ahead.

'Fortunately Auntie returned just at that moment.

' "It is so good to see Uldis, isn't it, Jekabs?" she said, while pouring coffee for the three of us. "You do look well."

' "It's all the good tucker and hard yakka," I replied.

' "Yakka? Tucker?" Auntie laughed. "What are these yakka and tucker?"

' "Yakka is Aussie for work and tucker's food," I declared, proud of my mastery of the Australian lingo.

' "It's a strange place, this Australia!" she said, clapping her hands together in amusement.

' "Fair dinkum!" I exclaimed, spurred on by her delight.

'I'd picked up this term as well and was keen to show off in front of them. They were at a loss and both stared at me as if I was mad.

'That's Aussie for "certainly"!' I explained this time.

'Auntie chuckled at my authoritative tone, and repeated the term out loud, and we both burst into hysterics at her mispronunciation.

'Opposite us, Uncle remained stony silent. In fact he seemed to be so uncomfortable with my presence that I decided there and then that I should leave, even if I'd only just arrived.

'But as soon as Auntie saw me make a move to depart, she jumped to her feet, insisting that I stay for dinner. I didn't want to cause any fuss but she was adamant.

'That evening she prepared a feast of all the Latvian dishes that I loved as a boy, especially the eels and lampreys. Over the meal Auntie was very talkative, telling me about their life in Australia, and how perplexing the customs were. They found it hard to adjust to the new world at their age.

But despite that Auntie obviously liked it here. I regaled her with one of my stories about my life in Australia. Her eyes lit up with pleasure and amazement at some of my tales: she loved especially the story of my escape from the job on the railways in the outback when I'd climbed on board a passing trolley and headed off into the night, destination unknown.

'Later Uncle invited me to join him in the living room while Auntie cleared away the remains of the meal. He told me to be seated and then sat down himself. He lit a thin cigar without offering me one, and smoked it quietly. I felt like a naughty pupil before a headmaster, waiting for him to speak. I still had no idea what I had done wrong.

'After several minutes Auntie rejoined us. I thought that it was time to go, and again reached for my jacket. Immediately she stopped me.

' "You've had a lot to drink," she said. "Why don't you stay here tonight?"

'It was true. Uncle had been offering me vodka all evening.

'I muttered something about work the next day, but Auntie dismissed this, turning to Uncle.

' "He must stay with us, mustn't he, Father?"

'Uncle merely grunted his assent.

'Auntie made up a bed on the sofa in the living room while Uncle and I sat in silence. Finally it was Uncle and I, alone and without any risk of interruption.

'He poured us each a brandy, his favourite, and raised his glass. "To the men of the Kurzeme Battalion!" he said.

'Then he looked me directly in the face, and said, "You must have many memories of your time with them?"

'I was surprised by his question because after the war he'd given me the impression that he wanted never to speak of the past again.

' "Yes," I mumbled. "A few."

' "They were better times for us, weren't they?" he said. "How did we end up here, in this wasteland on the other side of the world?"

'I laughed, out of politeness, but I didn't share his opinion at all. I loved the life here. Europe with its landscape of destruction was the wasteland as far as I was concerned. I never wanted to go back there.

' "Good memories are they?" Uncle probed. But before I could answer, he continued, "Do you remember when you first came to Riga? What trouble you were. I took you to our apartment on Valdemara Street. Everyone was there to welcome you. But you didn't want to stay! 'I am a soldier,' you insisted. 'I must stay with my troop.' And the difficulty we had in getting you to sleep in a bed. The only place you really loved was in Carnikava."

'I nodded, and began to tell Uncle of my happy memories there, mostly with Auntie. However, he didn't want to dwell on my recollections and instead shifted the conversation on, asking me if I remembered Commander Lobe.

'I thought it was a strange question because, apart from Uncle and Kulis, the commander was the man with whom I had the most contact. How on earth could I ever forget him?

' "He was a good soldier," Uncle said, "and a good man!"

' "He was kind to me," I commented, wondering what else I could add.

' "Not only you," he said. "He was generous to all of us."

'Then he fell silent for several moments before he spoke again.

' "I am sure you haven't heard of his recent problem?"

' "No," I said, "I haven't seen Commander Lobe since the war."

'Uncle knew this so I wondered why he had raised the topic of the commander in this manner.

' "All I know is that he went to Sweden."

' "Stockholm in fact," Uncle said. "With his wife."

' "Are they well?" I asked.

'He ignored my question, saying instead, "Like us, he was fortunate to have escaped the tyranny of the Soviet Union. We exchange letters now and then, and always on Latvian National Day. Your birthday, remember?"

'I nodded.

' "However, some time ago the letters stopped coming. Only a matter of weeks ago I learnt the reason. There has been a claim that the 18th Kurzeme battalion, when it was still in the form of the Police Brigade, was involved in a massacre of Jews in Belarus in the winter of 1941. The Slonim massacre they call it. Some former members of the 18th – the ones who didn't get out of Latvia – have already been arrested and tried by the Soviets. They were found guilty and have been executed. Have you heard of this catastrophe?"

'I was shocked. It was the first I'd heard of this and I told Uncle so.'

'Did Uncle mention the names of any of the men executed, Dad?' I asked.

My father nodded grimly. 'Tillers, Upe. I knew Upe better. He was with the band of soldiers that captured me.'

Even now my father seemed in a state of disbelief.

'Uncle said that the Soviets were liars. The whole thing had been a show trial and that historical records could not place the 18th anywhere near Slonim at that time. In fact, the 18th did not arrive in Belarus until March 1942 so it was absurd to hold them accountable for an incident that had occurred months earlier.

'According to Uncle, the Soviets wanted to punish the Latvians, especially the high-ranking ones, for their collaboration with the Nazis. What they didn't understand, Uncle claimed, was that the Latvians were driven purely by patriotism. They didn't share the ideology of the Nazis. They hoped only for independence.

' "Now the Swedish have become interested in Lobe's background," Uncle said, "because he'd been the commander of the 18th. If there were even the slightest possibility that he could be extradited to Latvia there is no doubt he would be executed. It doesn't seem to matter to the Soviets at all that Lobe was never permanently and totally in command of the 18th. Throughout the battalion's tour of duty in Belarus, Lobe occasionally shared command with Captain Rubenis whenever he was recalled to Riga on other duties. You might not remember him."

'I was surprised when I heard this,' my father said, 'but it also cleared something up in my mind. I've always been a bit confused about who was in command of the 18th. I've nearly always recalled Commander Lobe in that position, but I also remember another officer who occasionally appeared as top dog. I'd heard him addressed as "Captain" but that was all I knew about him. He showed no interest in me at all, so I rarely saw him.

' "Perhaps they should be investigating Rubenis rather than Commander Lobe," I heard Uncle say. I couldn't believe my ears. There seemed to be no loyalty amongst the desperate. Uncle was clutching at straws to defend the commander and it struck me as odd that on the one hand Uncle denied that the 18th was in Belarus while at the same time claiming that another member of the same battalion could be responsible for the crime. Either the battalion was there, or it was not. I thought to myself then that Uncle knew more about the movements of the 18th than he was prepared to let on.

'But I said nothing, allowing him to press on.

' "How on earth could the 18th have been responsible?" he repeated.

'I nodded absently because at that moment while Uncle was speaking something much more significant struck me: what if the 18th had been in Belarus sooner than claimed? To me, Uncle's insistence that the Soviets were lying didn't seem entirely plausible. What if it was the Latvians who were lying about when the 18th had arrived in Belarus? It was in their interest to cover their tracks since they'd participated in atrocities. It wouldn't take much to create false documents to support their claims. This led me to a new train of thought: what if I had been picked up sooner, before the Slonim massacre, by the 18th? After all, if Commander Lobe had lied so easily about the circumstances in which I was saved, then surely he wouldn't have hesitated to alter the date the troops had found me. What if I had been with the troops at Slonim?'

My father paused.

'But what about official records of the 18th?' I asked him.

'They may have been altered too in order to protect the reputation of the 18th,' my father conjectured.

Then, after several pensive moments he continued.

'Of course, I was only a child and had no sense of the passing of time, but what bothers me is even I find it hard to completely accept that I survived alone in the freezing forests for that length of time.'

'The six to nine months before you were picked up?'

My father nodded.

'A few weeks – that I can imagine – but six months? That would explain my impression that there was snow on the ground when Kulis took me out of the firing line. It may have been in the winter of 1941, and not as they said, in May of 1942. Thinking about it now, I wonder whether the murder of the people in the synagogue at the time I was with Sergeant Kulis – you remember don't you, son? – the incident I told you about . . . What if that was Slonim?'

'And there's one more thing,' my father said, and then hesitated.

'The extermination in my village . . .' he said, slowly. 'My memory is that it took place in the early winter in 1941.'

'That sounds right,' I agreed, recalling that the professor from Oxford had made a similar estimation.

'If only we knew the village's name,' he said. 'Then we could know for certain if any extermination did actually occur there in late 1941 and before the Slonim massacre. That would at least make it possible that I could have witnessed Slonim.'

'And we could also confirm if it was physically possible for the 18th to be able to make it to Slonim from where they took you,' I added.

'My village,' my father said with finality, 'is the starting point for unravelling my past.'

Now animated and red-faced, my father continued to recount his meeting with Uncle.

'After what had occurred to me about the massacre at the synagogue and the presence there of the 18th, including me,' he said, 'I knew that I had to be honest with Uncle and with myself. I was torn. I wondered how best to broach what I suspected. I began by telling Uncle that I did have memories of a massacre in a town. He was immediately alert.

' "What do you remember?" he asked.

'I was straightforward with him, telling him that I was able only to recall some details.

'He listened intently to my description of events, and I'd barely uttered my final word when he waved his hand dismissively. "Nothing more than impressions," he said. "Your memories have to be clearer than that and you need to be sure that your memories are true."

'I was surprised and confused by Uncle's comments. Even though my memories were incomplete I knew that I had not imagined the incident.'

My father's voice rose even now, as he insisted that he had not been lying. He put his head in his hands.

'I did witness that atrocity,' he said, 'even if Sergeant Kulis usually tried to keep me from seeing the worst of things.

'And I told Uncle what I later realised about those people – that they must have been Jewish. Much later, I also remembered one man with long strands of hair hanging down either side of his head. And also his large black hat. He must've been a rabbi.

'Uncle didn't seem to believe me. "How could you tell such a thing about these people?" he asked, sounding outraged.'

My father wiped his fists across his eyes, as if clearing his vision.

'I know I was right,' he said to me. 'You've heard my description, haven't you? I'm more convinced than ever that the building was a synagogue.

'Uncle glowered at me.

' "Do you remember if Mr Lobe was with you?" he snapped. "Did you see him commit violence against these people or not?"

'I had to be honest with Uncle. I didn't recall seeing the commander there.'

' "So what do you know for certain?" Uncle said gravely. "You don't know if you were in Slonim. You don't know if Lobe was there. What do you know?"

'In one respect Uncle was correct. I saw so much violence when I was with the brigade that there was sometimes a confusion of faces and locations. The only soldier I remembered for certain on the day of the killings was Sergeant Kulis because he shot at the burning people. So the 18th was there that day, wherever *there* turns out to be.

'So, I felt compelled to answer "no" to Uncle's earlier question: I did not see Commander Lobe himself.

'Uncle jumped at the chance to warn me. "If you're confused then I would be very cautious about speaking about the past," he said. "After all, you were only a child. What can a child remember?"

'Uncle seemed to relax for the first time since I'd arrived. But I felt beaten down by him.

'You know, thinking about it now,' my father said to me, 'I wonder if Uncle, in fact, knew more than he'd let on about Slonim – that he knew Commander Lobe was implicated in Slonim.'

'It's possible,' I agreed, 'that Uncle knew the true chronology of when you'd been picked up – assuming there is another truth – and was testing the waters about what you actually remembered. He'd have to reassure both himself and the commander that you had no objective details that would jeopardise the commander's defence.'

My father nodded.

'Perhaps he and the commander had wrongly assumed that I would have no memories or at best only highly confused ones. The strength of some of my impressions did unnerve him. Talking with you about it now, it occurs to me that Uncle's behaviour was intentional. He had been manipulating me, playing some sort of power game with me. His distant and unfriendly attitude had been a ploy to baffle me so that when he finally chose to relate properly to me, I would be eager to listen to him.

'I have to admit that his strategy worked. He knew my sense of obligation to the Latvians had been deeply ingrained in me.'

My father was silent for a moment.

'If only I'd stood up to Uncle,' he said, anguished.

'But you couldn't remember, Dad,' I replied. 'You still can't.'

'But why can't I, when I remembered other faces, other details?'

He began to castigate himself.

'What if somehow I've chosen to forget? That I've blocked things out because deep down I am loyal to Lobe and the Latvians?'

'Dad,' I argued, 'you feared Lobe and the other soldiers. You may have blocked memories out of terror, rather than loyalty.'

My father nodded his head slowly but I could tell he was not convinced. He returned to the incident at Uncle's.

' "You know, young man," Uncle said, "you can do Mr and Mrs Lobe as well as Auntie and me a great favour."

'Without waiting for a response from me, Uncle went on. "You'd never want to harm them," he said, and then gave a thin smile.

I waited for him to continue.

' "Commander Lobe is preparing a written defence that he wants to present to the Swedish authorities. It would be a fine thing if you showed Mr Lobe your support," he said slowly. "Let the authorities know Mr Lobe didn't do anything."

'I knew then where this talk was leading.

' "Some of us have already submitted statements testifying to Mr Lobe's good character," Uncle said.

' "Mr Lobe needs your help. A simple statement from you, nothing more than an innocent child at the time, would do much to support his defence."

'I didn't want to anger Uncle again, but I tried to be frank. "It's difficult for me to say anything either way," I said.

' "Tell the investigators how good Mr Lobe was to you, how he rescued you," Uncle insisted. "That you cannot remember any wrongdoing on his part. That should suffice. Everybody will believe you in this situation because you were a child of only five or six years. Why would you lie?"

' "Precisely because I was a child in your power, and still am," I thought to myself. It seemed to me that Uncle had it all worked out in advance and was determined that I cooperate.

' "Let me be direct," he said, as if he was being perfectly reasonable. "You owe Mr Lobe your life. Now is your opportunity to pay him back. He didn't have to keep you alive."

'I was shocked,' my father said. 'I was grateful to be alive but I didn't ever imagine that a price tag would be put on my life. And I didn't think it would be put to me so bluntly.

' "You just said Commander Lobe wasn't a violent man," I blurted without thinking, "but now you say he could have killed me, a child, because I was an inconvenience?"

'Even though I thought it made sense, it had been stupid to make such a comment. Uncle became irate, no doubt believing that I was trying to be clever.

' "I know for a fact that the Lobes have very little," he said sharply. "Think of poor Mrs Lobe. She's old now. How could she manage by herself if anything happened to her husband? It would be cruel to deny your help. And very dishonest to condemn a man based on a few vague impressions."

'I faltered. The truth was that I'd witnessed other things when I was with the soldiers and even though I knew no dates and places my impressions were not vague. They were so vivid. I will never escape them.

'But another part of me wanted to end this struggle. Uncle must have thought my silence was resistance because he rose impatiently and moved towards the window. He peered out into the darkness through a gap in the curtains as if he was expecting someone, then suddenly he turned back to me, his face contorted with barely suppressed anger.

' "Do it for me!" he barked. "You owe me your life!"

'I was dumbfounded by his vehemence.

' "I wouldn't know what to write," I tried to excuse myself.

' "Let me take care of that," he said, firmly. "We'll deal with this in the morning, before Mother wakes."

'Uncle was calmer by then. He rose and put out his hand to shake mine and I accepted it. With that he wished me goodnight and disappeared to his room.

'I tried to make myself comfortable on the sofa with the blankets and pillow Auntie had left for me but it took a long time before I finally nodded off. I was torn by what Uncle wanted but already I sensed his victory over me.'

As he had been on the Underground in London, my father was clearly anguished over what had happened so many years before.

'I woke early the next morning. It was still dark. Then I noticed a thin line of light coming from the partly opened door to Uncle's study. I remained as I was with my head on the pillow but through the crack I could see that Uncle was already up and dressed. He was at his desk scrutinising something.

'I got up and went over. He hadn't heard me stir so I tapped lightly on the door. The instant he saw me he stood up and beckoned me in.

'Before I could even wish him "good morning" he thrust a sheet of paper into my hand, saying, "It needs to be signed and witnessed before I send it off." I was still sleepy-headed and for a moment I didn't understand what he was referring to. Then I remembered.

'I read what Uncle had prepared for me. It stated unequivocally that I had no knowledge of Slonim, or of any other incident, adding that I had spent some years in close company with the commander during the war. I viewed Mr Lobe as a man of good character, it continued, and that I remembered nothing of Mr Lobe as a violent man. I had never seen him kill anyone.'

My father was subdued.

'Do you have a copy of it?' I asked, hoping that there'd be one in his case.

My father shook his head.

'Uncle didn't offer me one,' he said, 'and I never thought to ask. I was uneasy and wanted the matter to be dealt with as quickly as possible. Uncle told me that he was going to deliver it to a lawyer in Melbourne personally, a Latvian man, who would then forward it as evidence in support of Commander Lobe's appeal.'

'Who was this lawyer?'

My father leant back in his seat, squinting as he tried to recall the man's name.

'Eglits,' he said. 'That's it. Mr Eglits.'

'I wonder if he's still alive.'

'If he is, then he must be in his nineties,' my father said.

'I'll see if I can track him down,' I said.

'Why?' My father was surprised.

'To see the statement of course,' I answered. 'It is a piece of evidence.'

My father seemed uneasy.

'Evidence against who? Why do you want evidence?' he asked.

'I don't exactly want it as evidence against anybody in particular,' I said, trying to calm my father's growing anxiety. 'But it is part of the jigsaw of your story.'

He appeared to accept my explanation and returned to the events surrounding the affidavit.

' "We could get it witnessed now," Uncle said. "There's a police station nearby."

'So I agreed to do it there and then. What choice did I have? Was I complicit? I looked up to Uncle. I always obeyed him, and now he wanted me to repay a debt. The Latvians did save me and I didn't want to bite the hand that had fed me. To this day, I feel guilty about what I did.'

My father shot me a despairing, almost pleading look.

'Uncle coerced you that day. He made you feel guilty for being alive,' I said, trying to console him.

My father's hands rested on the kitchen table, but were gripped together so tightly that his knuckles had turned white. He stared at me intently.

'They forced you to keep silent throughout the war,' I said. 'They erased your identity and turned you into their little mascot.

'Lobe did save you,' I continued. 'From what you are saying I'm starting to think he did so for his own reasons. After the war the Latvians kept you as an alibi in case things went wrong in the future. If the Latvian soldiers were called to account for their collaboration, what better way to bargain against their own guilt than with an innocent child?'

My father seemed shocked by both my analysis and by my vitriol towards the Latvians. He was silent for a moment. Then he said, 'You know, worst of all, Uncle couldn't get me out of the house quickly enough. He didn't even give me a chance to say goodbye to Auntie. "We won't be long at the police station," he said. "You may as well continue on from there. Gather your things. I'll tell Mother that you wanted to get an early start. She'll understand."

'When we left the police station, Uncle was anxious to be rid of me. He looked at his watch pointedly and told me that he'd other urgent business at home. He didn't even offer to shake my hand. Perhaps he felt as uncomfortable about the affidavit as I did.

'He walked away from me, briskly. Without thinking, I called out to him, so that he stopped and turned to look back at me.

' "Every day I put the past behind me. Over and over," I said. "I never talk about it with anybody, not even Patricia. I hope I never have to again. To you or to anybody. You should know that."

'Uncle didn't say a word. He stared at me for several moments as if registering something about me. Then he raised his hand and gave me a brief wave. I watched him until he disappeared around the corner, and then I picked up my case and headed in the opposite direction, towards the train station. The streets were deserted and there were only a handful of early morning commuters on the platform. I waited with them. I had no idea where to go.'

I could see that the question of his presence at the Slonim massacre had cast a shadow over my father. He felt guilty for having signed a statement exonerating Lobe when he might have committed a crime, and yet it had been the only thing he could do in the circumstances. Had his faulty memory prevented justice being done? Though he could not be certain that Lobe had been at Slonim, or indeed whether the massacre he himself had witnessed was at Slonim, the affidavit raised for him the question of his own complicity.

I knew that we must find the truth about Slonim, if only to help my father come to terms with his decision to sign the affidavit. But I feared my father would not forgive himself easily.

18

NO ESCAPE

'I'D reached rock bottom. For the greatest part of my life I had followed every order the Latvians had given me. Now they wanted more. I couldn't betray them. Perhaps what Uncle had said was true. I owed them my life. I thought that I'd never be free of them. They'd find me wherever I went. The past would rear up to draw me down and suffocate me.'

'Did the affidavit reach Sweden?' I asked.

'I assume it did. I did hear later that Commander Lobe was cleared.'

'Did Uncle ever mention this incident to you in later years?' I asked.

My father shook his head. 'Never.'

He was quiet.

'So you think it highly likely that the 18th was involved in Slonim?' I continued.

'Why would the Soviets pursue this otherwise?' he replied. 'And as I said earlier, my instinct tells me that on the night I visited him, Uncle knew more than he let on, that the 18th and Commander Lobe were there . . .'

'Lobe could be fairly certain that his own soldiers would not betray him after the war. They were as guilty as he was,' I said. 'But who might if he remembered enough in the future?'

We both went quiet since we knew the answer: my father.

My father mulled this over.

'But the question remains,' he said finally, 'did the extermination of my family occur before late 1941?'

'And where the soldiers captured me. Was it anywhere near Slonim?' my father said, suddenly becoming more alert.

'There's an atlas in my room,' I said, rising to fetch it. 'Let's find Slonim.'

We hunched over the atlas, our heads close together, scanning the maps of Eastern Europe. We finally located Slonim in the central south-west of Belarus.

'This would mean the 18th would need to have been somewhere in the vicinity of Slonim at the end of 1941 if it took part in the massacre,' I said. 'And if you were taken shortly before that, your village must have been not too far away.'

'That's right,' my father said. 'I couldn't have travelled very far in a matter of weeks. I do remember going in circles as well.'

My father pulled the atlas closer. Suddenly he stopped and pointed his finger at the map.

'Look at this town,' he said excitedly. 'Stol'btsi. To the north-east of Slonim.'

I didn't understand what had roused his interest so pointedly.

'Don't you remember?' he said. 'I mentioned that the 18th was positioned at a place known as "S" when they picked me up. That was where I first met the commander. "S" was about a day's march from the schoolyard where Sergeant Kulis took me out of the firing-line.'

My father continued to hold his finger on the spot but was staring at me intently. Then his finger began to move across the page again, as his eyes scanned the area surrounding Stol'btsi.

'The commander and the soldiers were careful to only ever refer to "S" and not its proper name. Why on earth did they do this unless they were deliberately obscuring their movements for some reason . . .

'What if S was Stol'btsi, Marky?' he said, barely able to contain himself. 'What if my village was somewhere nearby as well?'

'We've got to find out the significance of Koidanov,' I said. 'Give me the atlas. My eyes are better than yours.'

I drew the map closer, and examined it. There was no Koidanov in the vicinity of Stol'btsi.

'Perhaps it's too small a place to be recorded in an atlas, no more than a hamlet or tiny *shtetl*,' I said, trying to be optimistic.

'We need to get hold of a more detailed map,' I added, recalling that I had been about to do so in Oxford when I'd been abruptly summoned back to Australia. I leaned back in my chair and noticed my father was doing the same. We laughed.

My father raised his glasses and rubbed his eyes.

'You're tired, Dad.'

'No,' he protested, 'not in the slightest.'

He returned his glasses to the end of his nose and stared down at his hands.

'So the affidavit was the end of your association with the Latvians, apart from the Dzenis family . . .' I said.

My father screwed up his face as if tasting something sour. 'It wasn't quite as simple as that,' he said. 'Of course I didn't want anything to do with Mr Lobe after what had taken place.

'But word had obviously got around the Latvian community and there was a sort of pressure put on me. The commander was a national hero to all Latvians. You couldn't have said a word against the man in the Latvian community in Australia.

'Most of the threats were low-key: veiled references to my duty to Commander Lobe and how good he and the other soldiers had been to me. That would happen when I came into contact with some of the old soldiers at social functions at the Latvian Community House. They'd reminisce about their time in the army and then they'd turn to me and say: "Isn't that so, Uldis?" '

'They weren't just being nostalgic with you?'

'Don't be absurd!' my father snapped. 'I understood the nuance. They were reminding me that I was one of them, and had been there with them, through it all.

'Some threats were more direct – anonymous letters sent in the post, warning me to remain silent about Commander Lobe and the battalion's wartime past.'

I was shocked. This was the stuff of spy novels and films, not my father's life.

'Have you kept any of them?' I asked.

My father shook his head. 'I burnt them as soon as I received them. I didn't want your mother to come across them. Even my case didn't seem secure enough. They must have come from old soldiers who'd emigrated to Australia. Or other Latvians who knew of my exploits with the army.

'It didn't end there either. It got worse after I married your mother and we settled together in Melbourne. There was one man in particular who was more blatant than the rest – Arnold Smits. I'd first encountered Smits in Riga during the war. Even though I was only a child, I could tell that he was a deeply nasty person. He was a sports journalist on a newspaper in Riga but he collaborated with Commander Lobe on some special projects as well. He was heavily involved in Nazi propaganda to incite hatred against Jews, demanding that Jewish vermin – that's the term he used – be barred from Latvian sports and other rubbish like that.

'Smits emigrated to Melbourne after the war and wrote for a

Latvian newspaper in Melbourne. One day – it must have been around 1958 or 1959 when Mum and I were living in Pascoe Vale on the other side of the city – Smits appeared on our doorstep. I was immediately suspicious. I didn't want him in my home – I didn't want your mother to be exposed to this man – so I stood out the front with him, out of earshot of Mum.

'He told me that he wanted to write a series of articles about my life in Latvia for the Latvian newspapers in Australia. I made it clear to him from the outset that I wouldn't cooperate. At first he tried to cajole me into it, telling me what an honour it would be. "Don't you want your story to be read by everybody who doesn't yet know it?" he said. Of course, it was the official version he wanted to write about and not the truth.

'I didn't want anything to do with his plan but he was like a dog with a bone. In the end I was frank with him. I told him that the story was a pack of lies and Lobe was not the hero Latvians believed him to be. He laughed directly in my face telling me that he was going to write the articles no matter what my objections were.

'He did exactly as he said he would. The articles were published in 1959. I have a copy here if you want to see it.'

Once again he dug deeply into his case. The articles were written in Latvian. He offered to translate them for me there and then, but at that moment, in the middle of the night, I felt too weary to listen to more of these men's lies.

'Tomorrow,' I replied. I could see that my response had disappointed him but he didn't push me. Instead, as he returned the article to his case, he removed another tatty and yellowed newspaper cutting.

'See,' he said. 'Smits and I.'

He passed the scrap of paper across to me. It was a grainy photograph with a caption, printed decades ago. In it, my father, barely distinguishable, and another man were hunched over a chessboard, absorbed in a game, and surrounded by a crowd of onlookers. As I examined it more closely to see if I recognised any of the faces in the crowd, he told me that he and Smits had belonged to the same chess club in Melbourne.

'I don't know whether or not Smits joined just to keep an eye on me,' he said, 'but whenever I ran into him there, he would insist on partnering me. I beat him every time just as I'd beaten every soldier in the 18th once they'd taught me to play.

'He always demanded that we sit in the far corner of the clubrooms, as far as possible from the other players, saying that he needed silence in order to concentrate on his strategy.

'As we entered into the depth of our game, he would make it very clear to me, smiling his death's head smile, that nobody would believe my word against that of real Latvians, and I would make certain people very unhappy and risk dire consequences if I tried to discredit Latvia or any of its people in any way. I would sit there with my head down and try to focus on the game in front of me, though more than once I came very close to sweeping the pieces off the board and denouncing him. But I never did. Who'd have listened? Nobody would have been interested. In those days Australia was a sleepy backwater, full of immigrants who'd come to forget the past not dig it up.

'After the war Australia welcomed thousands of people from the Baltic States. "Balts" we were called. We were seen as refugees from Stalinism and thus on the Aussies' side. The authorities weren't suddenly going to have a change of heart and stir up a hornets' nest by hunting for war criminals.'

My father was right. It was not until the 1990s that the Australian government examined with any vigour how many Baltic war criminals had come to its shores.

'Once Smits's articles were published,' I heard my father say, 'I felt more locked into the official version of my story than ever. Having made it all the way to the freedom of Australia, I felt the right to be left in peace had been taken from me. As I'd feared, these men kept in touch with each other, and each in his own way was set against me.'

'It doesn't go on these days, surely?'

'The last threat I received was almost two decades ago. I guess they thought that if I hadn't said anything by then, I wasn't going to talk at all. And many of the old soldiers were starting to die off.'

My father paused for one moment and then continued.

'God knows what will happen if my story gets out,' he mused, trying to make light of the situation. 'They'll all turn over in their graves and come back to haunt me.'

For a moment I felt a surge of anger not only towards the Latvians, but towards my father as well. I felt that his choice to remain silent about these threats had somehow added to his betrayal. He appeared to sense this, and he opened his case and began to fumble absently with its contents, obviously keen to avoid my ire. It was a cunning theatrical move but it also struck me as rather desperate, and my anger turned to pity.

I imagined myself subtly tormented as he had been for most of his adult life. During those early years in Australia he had looked to the future and resolved to make a new life for himself. But the tentacles of this Latvian nationalists network, unable either to leave its past behind or to face it honestly, had stretched out and ensnared him.

As if he had followed my train of thought, I heard my father say, 'I was to blame too.'

He shifted uncomfortably in his seat.

'Even though I looked to my new life here I held back from breaking those bonds completely. These men were the only link to the past, for better or worse. I used to have fantasies that one of them somehow knew my real name – don't ask me how – and that one day he would take pity on me and tell me.

'I let them behave as if they owned me because I didn't want to alienate them. For years that tore me in two inside. That's the truth of it.'

'Dad, you've never said a single word to any of us,' I said. 'Not even Mum.'

My father ignored my words and instead gave a deep sigh.

'Even though the old soldiers are all gone now, the idea that they might have been able to tell me who I was taunts me from their graves.'

My father looked at me searchingly. 'I've been naive, haven't I?' he said.

19

STOCKHOLM

MY father seemed oblivious to the passing hours. I cast a furtive glance at the clock on the kitchen wall and saw that it was almost four in the morning. I was exhausted but, now that my father had finally broken his silence, I was reluctant to stop our conversation.

'Hearing all of this makes everything fall into place,' I said. 'Even though Lobe avoided a trial and extradition he must have lived in constant fear of some sort of retribution. That would explain his behaviour when I visited him in Stockholm.'

My father gave me a questioning look.

'What did happen?' he asked. 'You simply said that the visit was fine.'

'I decided not to say anything, because you'd seemed so set against me going there at the time.'

My father simply nodded.

Then I began to tell him in detail what had gone on in the Lobes' flat that day. My father listened intently without interrupting me.

'After I left the Lobes,' I said, 'I hurried along the path that led away from the flats. I was excited and wanted to get back to the city so I could call you in Melbourne. But as I waited for a tram, a number of things began to nag at me once my euphoria gradually evaporated.

'Above all, I was alarmed by Lobe's first reaction to me when I'd knocked on his door the previous day. I realise now that after I'd slipped the note under the door, he must have been fairly sure that I knew nothing of the truth. No wonder he was so suspicious initially, and so exaggerated in his welcome later. Added to that was his semi-deranged tirade about his association with Nazism. I began to wonder how close this association was, and more to the point, how close yours had been. I was unsettled as well by something in Lobe's and your description of your discovery by the soldiers . . .'

My father became alert, and sat upright in his chair.

'What was that then, son?' he asked.

'It was eerie,' I answered. 'The words you both used were almost identical. And there was another thing that occurred to me as I stood there in the freezing wind – the perspective of your description. It was as if you had been one of the soldiers who witnessed the boy step from behind the tree. From the outside looking in, rather than from the point of view of the frightened child stepping out to be confronted by a band of soldiers brandishing rifles and bayonets.'

'As I told you,' my father said, 'Commander Lobe had drummed that version into me, and the only way I could believe it was to memorise his every word and repeat it exactly. Still, it's amazing that you picked up on that.'

'Yes, but I was stumped at the time and could find no explanation for it. As I journeyed back into the centre of Stockholm, I decided to put this unnerving observation to the back of my mind. In fact, I hadn't thought about that day until you spoke to me in London. I realised then that there might be something complex in your association with Lobe and Uncle.'

'Of course, it's only now that I've got some inkling of why you seemed so apprehensive when I called to tell you that I intended to visit Lobe,' I ventured. 'You must have been petrified that I'd learnt the truth about your past life with the 18th Battalion. And what sort of men they were.'

My father was silent. My last comment must have seemed accusatory to him and I sensed his reluctance to engage with me.

I returned to the affidavit.

'The thing is, Dad, would Lobe have known or even worried about whether you'd witnessed things?'

'I don't know,' he answered. 'At the time I was with him I don't think he even gave it a second thought. That's how it was with the soldiers. I was like a puppy to them. Half the time they heaped attention on me, and then at other times they just ignored me. None of them worried about what I might see, apart from Sergeant Kulis, who was usually protective of me.

'But when Lobe decided to get me to make a statement on his behalf, he must have wondered what I had witnessed and whether it was incriminating.

'And certainly after my visit to him in Melbourne, Uncle must have conveyed to the commander that I did have recollections that could incriminate him. That must have played on Commander Lobe's mind for all those years, along with the chance that even more of my memory might return.

Perhaps in his mind the question of my loyalty was never really settled with the signing of the affidavit . . .'

I nodded. 'So when I appeared on his doorstep, identifying myself as your son, he must have feared the worst. He must've thought that you'd told me, your son, the truth and that I'd come seeking something. Revenge, perhaps? Why else would Uldis's son visit him?'

My father agreed.

'It looks that way. How else to explain his response? One thing is clear, even though Commander Lobe had been able to fight off his extradition years earlier, he'd probably spent the remainder of his life in fear that some-body would eventually come after him.'

'He promised to stay in touch, but I never heard from him,' I said.

My father looked sheepish.

'Shortly after your visit,' he said, 'a letter came from out of the blue. I was surprised when I saw the envelope and realised it was from Commander Lobe. He'd never written to me before.'

He raised the lid of his case slightly and with his usual adroitness produced an envelope. He removed a sheet of paper and smoothed it out on the table. He lowered his eyes and began to read, translating as he did so.

' "My dear Uldis Kurzemnieks.

' "It is a long time since we last saw each other. I hope that you are in good health. From time to time, I hear news of your life in Australia from Mr Dzenis. I am happy that you are successful and have your own family." '

My father paused.

'I'll skip the pleasantries,' he said, 'and go to the nitty gritty.'

I watched him as he scanned the page.

'Here we are,' he said, and began to read again.

' "Recently I was pleased to meet your son Mark. A fine boy! We spoke a lot about the war, and I told him of the special bond between us. I am sure that there is no need to remind you of it, my little Corporal . . ." '

My father raised his head and looked at me.

'Can you believe that?' he said, slightly astonished. 'He called me Corporal, as if to remind me that I still belonged to the battalion and that he was my commanding officer.'

My father didn't seem to need any reminder. I had noticed that even though Lobe had been a civilian for many decades, my father still called him Commander.

He took up where he had left off.

' "We were all very fond of you. Mr Dzenis loved you – you were the son he'd always wanted. His wife, Emily, adored you. Mrs Lobe and I did, too. When I said farewell to you in Riga, we agreed to bury the past. But I am worried that one day before too long, you, Corporal, will forget your promise to me. It would break my lifelong trust in you if you spoke of your memories now. Besides, memory is a strange thing. It can play tricks on all of us, so that we are unsure of what we remember and what we do not. Do you really want to destroy our reputations? You cannot betray all that many of us have done for you. Your debt can only be repaid by loyalty – nothing else!" '

My father ceased reading.

'That's it, more or less.'

He folded the letter slowly and returned it to its envelope.

In the ensuing silence, my mother's faint snoring could be heard from their room on the far side of the house.

Suddenly the kitchen clock on the wall caught my father's attention.

'Crikey, Mark,' he exclaimed. 'It's 6 a.m. The world is going topsy-turvy. We should both get some sleep.'

He got up from the table.

'One thing, Dad . . .' I stopped him.

My father looked at me expectantly.

'Was I right?' I said.

He looked confused. 'Right about what?'

'Would you have wanted revenge?'

My father did not hesitate. He shook his head in dismay.

'Revenge?' he said, 'what's that worth? Nothing! It only makes you bitter and sick inside – and as bad as them! I never started out by wanting to point the finger at anybody.'

'What about justice then?' I asked.

'Justice? I don't even know what justice would mean for these sick, elderly men. Better to let them face their own consciences, if they have them.'

I rose to join my father.

Just then the kitchen door opened and my mother peered in. She must have woken and heard our voices in the kitchen.

'You're both up early,' she said.

20

FEAR

At times during my stay in Melbourne my father appeared willing to reveal more about his past to me. Then abruptly he would turn in on himself. Sometimes he seemed so worn down by the burden of his secrets that, irresistibly, the flotsam of his memory would float to the surface of his consciousness like debris from a submarine disaster.

He still hadn't told my mother anything. Nonetheless she seemed to tire very easily, and frequently went to her room in the early evening. My father and I often found the night stretching out awkwardly before just the two of us.

After saying goodnight to my mother, my father would turn the television off and quietly retrieve his case from where he had placed it, outside their bedroom door, so he wouldn't disturb my mother's sleep.

Case in hand, he would pass me in the living room and head for the kitchen. I would listen as he seated himself at the kitchen table and switched on the reading lamp as if to announce that he was ready to speak and I should jump to attention and join him.

Perversely I would remain seated, vainly attempting to assert my independence. The moment I heard the familiar clicking of his case unlocking I would waiver, and then rise to join him.

Later that week, as I entered the kitchen, I noticed that he had opened a thick volume on the table before him. He furrowed his brow and squinted at the book. He concentrated so intently on one page that he didn't even bother to acknowledge my presence with his usual grunt.

I sat down beside him at the table.

'Dad?' I whispered.

He gave a slight start.

'What's the book?' I nodded towards it.

He looked at the cover as if he too was noticing it for the first time.

'An atlas,' he mumbled.

'Koidanov and Panok?'

He regarded me silently for several moments.

'The most important thing is I've got to find out what these words mean,' he said grim-faced. He sat isolated and discouraged in the small circle of light thrown by his reading lamp.

'Dad,' I said, 'I promised you in London that I would help you.'

He nodded but continued to scan the book in front of him.

I hadn't yet told him that I had begun my own investigations in Oxford. I kept silent principally because I felt I'd dug around without his permission.

'Any luck?' I asked.

'Nah,' he said, rubbing his fists over his eyes liked an overtired child. 'It's like looking for a needle in a haystack.'

He sighed heavily.

Then without looking up at me, he pushed the atlas across the table in my direction.

'Pages twenty-three and twenty-four,' he said in a matter-of-fact tone. 'Eastern Europe. See if you can spot Koidanov or Panok.'

I turned to the pages in question. They were densely inscribed with a vast array of foreign words tumbling over each other higgledy-piggledy.

'The first thing we'll need is a magnifying glass!' I exclaimed, trying to make light of the situation.

My father didn't laugh.

Sobered by his response I buried my head in the book once again before concluding aloud, 'We're going to need far more detailed maps than this for starters.'

I decided that it was time to tell my father what Frank had discovered in Oxford.

'In any case,' I said, 'we won't find Panok anywhere on these pages.'

My father gave me a questioning look.

I hesitated for a moment. I felt cautious about Frank's revelation – I had heard nothing further from Frank since my arrival in Melbourne and there was nothing to confirm that my father was a Panok.

I feared that my father would jump at even the simple likelihood that he was a Panok and that he would be bitterly disappointed if we couldn't prove it.

'Come on,' he urged, becoming impatient.

Cautiously I told my father about what Frank had unearthed, that there was a family of Jews known as Panok who had lived in the vicinity of Minsk in the pre-war period.

And, just as I had feared, my father's face reddened with excitement.

'I told you, son,' he said, rising from his chair, and moving around the room, 'I remembered these words for a reason. I bet it's my name. I must be a Panok.'

My father repeated the word several times, savouring it, while he paced back and forth. Then he sat down again, and I saw that he was so moved by the news that his entire body was trembling slightly. Without thinking about the usual physical reserve between us, I reached across and gripped his forearm to steady him and to get him to look at me directly.

At that exact moment my father jerked backwards and removed a handkerchief from his pocket. He threw back his head and held the cloth against his nose, which had suddenly, as if under pressure from the news, begun to bleed profusely.

'Some tissues,' came his muffled order.

I fetched some and then waited in silence, watching him. The bleeding was so strong and voluminous that it took several minutes to subside. But when it did, my father immediately picked up where he'd left off, still gripping his bloodied handkerchief.

'I must be a Panok,' he said emphatically. 'Why else would I remember this word?'

I smiled at him, but my father must have sensed my inner reserve. He stared at me shrewdly.

'What's bothering you?' he asked.

'I don't want us to jump the gun,' I said. 'That's all. We should take it one step at a time. Find a way to confirm whether you are a Panok or not.'

He looked at me, as if to dismiss my caution, and then reached across for the atlas.

'Minsk, you said?' he asked, without waiting for confirmation from me. 'Where the hell is that?' He stared at the open page in front of him.

'Belarus,' I answered, deciding instead to feign enthusiasm, rather than dampen his spirits. I pointed to a spot on the map.

'Here it is.'

After Frank's discovery, and prior to my sudden departure for Australia, I had crammed in a small amount of reading about the country. I now recounted it to my father who sat attentively opposite me.

'The country is falling apart at the seams,' I began. 'A former satellite state of the Soviet Union, Belarus is now ruled with an iron fist by a despotic communist dictator, Alexander Lukashenko. Lukashenko has chosen to align the country, economically and culturally, with its Russian master. It seems to be one of the countries in Eastern Europe not to have benefited from the collapse of the Soviet empire. It is still impoverished and largely underdeveloped.'

My father's attention began to waiver and he interrupted me.

'Let's get back to this Koidanov,' he said. 'It could be where I'm from and, if so, it must be somewhere here if I am a Panok . . .'

My father hunched over the atlas like a diamond merchant hunched over a jewel. After several minutes, he leant back.

'No luck,' he said.

He looked tired and drawn and his optimism seemed suddenly to have faded.

'We'll crack this, Dad,' I said feebly trying to reassure him despite my own feeling of discouragement.

'I've already waited a lifetime,' my father said ironically and then fell silent.

I took advantage of the hiatus to change the topic to one I'd been dying to raise.

'Now that there's even the slightest chance of a name,' I said, 'you must tell Mum and the boys. Now.'

I was shocked by my challenge.

My father shrugged and stared straight ahead, avoiding my gaze. In the odd flat silence between us I waited for him to say something.

In the end all he said was, 'I'll tell them sometime soon.'

'What's wrong with now?' I demanded.

My father pretended not to have heard me, and instead turned the pages of the atlas as if searching for something.

'This can't go on,' I insisted. 'They deserve to know.'

His eyes began to move slowly from one object to another in the room, as if he was keenly interested in each.

'You're avoiding even listening to me?'

'I didn't hear you,' my father blustered. But I knew that he had.

Annoyed, I said, 'I can't keep covering for you.'

Then I changed tack. 'What's bothering you, Dad?' I asked, trying to sound conciliatory.

My father shifted in his seat. He closed the atlas, and reached for his case, snapping it shut and placing it between us on the table. His head dropped forward as if he were being forced to own up to a felony.

'It's that I am . . .' he said, 'you know . . .'

I waited for him to finish the sentence. But he didn't.

'You're what?'

'Jewish.'

He winced at being forced to say the word.

I didn't understand.

'Will they accept it?' he asked, as if ashamed. 'Your mother didn't know she was marrying a Jew.'

'I don't think that it will make a scrap of difference to Mum,' I said. 'What will disturb her is that you kept your past from her for so long.'

My father gave me a sharp look.

'I'm worried that it'll be too much for her,' he said. 'She's not strong at the moment.'

I'd noticed this myself. I had never seen my mother so low-spirited.

'Still no idea what's wrong?' I asked.

My father shook his head.

'She feels weak and unable to breathe,' he replied. 'She's been to the doctor but he can't find anything wrong with her.'

I wondered whether it was her intuition that something was wrong with my father that was causing her symptoms. My mother had a keen loyalty to my father and rather than confront him and bring a matter to light – she was awkward with emotional language and mistrusted it – she would choose to internalise her doubts.

'Martin and Andrew will be fine about it,' I said. 'When will you tell them?'

My father held his hands together as if praying and then rested them on his case.

'This week,' he said with finality. 'The same time as I tell Mum. God knows how Martin will react . . .'

My father noticed my puzzled look.

'Think about it,' he said. 'Martin's married to a German girl.' I could see that he was uneasy about the possibility of her discomfort.

My father screwed up his face.

'It's not your problem,' I said tersely.

'I don't want to make him feel awkward. Or anybody for that matter. Think of Uncle's family. Mirdza, Edgars and their children. All the other Latvians who've helped me. They'll say that I've betrayed all their kindness. And what about other Latvian nationalists – you know some of the old soldiers have threatened me before.'

I did understand my father's reluctance. I feared too that their oft-expressed patriotism for the mother country would blind some of the Latvians to the truth, and provoke their condemnation. My father would risk losing the last remnants of the only family he had known as a boy.

But my intensifying desire that the truth come out fuelled in me a new bravado. 'You've done nothing wrong,' I snapped. 'If they can't accept you, then sod them!'

My father rubbed the back of his neck.

'There's more to this, isn't there?' I said.

'What?'

'About being Jewish . . .'

He nodded. 'I can't explain it,' he said in a low voice. My father gripped his head in his hands, with his elbows resting on the table.

'Are you afraid of being Jewish?'

My father raised his head and looked at me sharply. I had hit a raw nerve. 'I don't know, son,' he said.

'All the time I was with the soldiers they spoke of Jews as vermin. Jews were evil, they said. I had to listen to this day in and day out – and remain silent – until it was drummed into my soul, until I felt ashamed of being Jewish.'

With their insults against Jews and, more frighteningly, in '*Aktionen*' against them the soldiers and other Latvians had terrified the little boy in their midst. Worse perhaps, they had shamed this child to his very essence. Not only did my father have to hide his identity from others, he'd had to hide away from himself all these years. It was a terrible self-obliteration.

My father hesitated, struggling to describe something else.

'When I summoned the courage or stupidity – I don't know what you'd call it – and went to the Holocaust Centre I'd imagined that the shame would lift.

'But it didn't: somehow within myself I didn't feel comfortable there as if I'd betrayed my Jewishness. I was somehow unworthy of being Jewish, even though I'd been born Jewish, and had no right to speak about who I was. By the time I'd left the centre I realised that I was completely and utterly trapped by who I was. I felt doubly cursed by my fate.'

I felt almost uncontrollable anger rising at what a child living with a kidnapped and hidden identity must have gone through. Over fifty years on, it seemed that he was still struggling with himself to reclaim it.

'What about the interviewers?' I asked. 'Did they understand what you'd been through?'

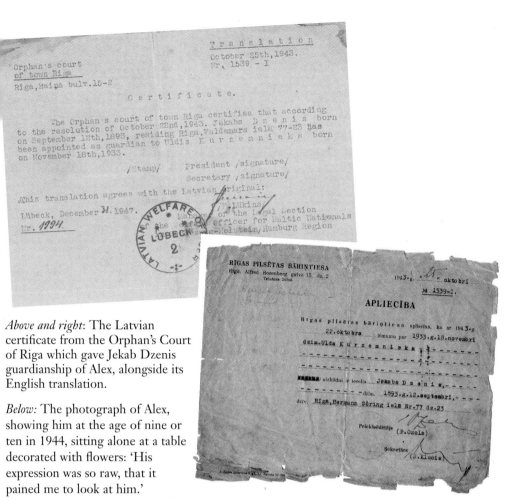

Above and right: The Latvian
certificate from the Orphan's Court
of Riga which gave Jekab Dzenis
guardianship of Alex, alongside its
English translation.

Below: The photograph of Alex,
showing him at the age of nine or
ten in 1944, sitting alone at a table
decorated with flowers: 'His
expression was so raw, that it
pained me to look at him.'

Latvian SS grenadiers in a dugout in Russia, circa 1944.

Alex with a friend at Saules Displaced Persons Camp, outside Hamburg, circa 1947.

The *Nelly*, the ship that ferried Alex away from war-torn Europe to Australia in late 1949.

The house in which the author grew up in Altona, Australia, Alex's home for over forty years.

Above: Alex as a young man in his twenties in Australia.

Right: Alex and Patricia in the early 1960s, a few years after they first met.

Below: Alex and Patricia in 1996.

Above: Solomon Galperin and his best friend Volodya Katz, with whom he escaped from Koidanov in 1941.

Above right: The photograph of Solomon Galperin, possibly Alex's father, which was taken in 1961 and which arrived unexpectedly in the post in 1997.

Right: A possible portrait of Hana Gildenberg, who became Solomon's wife and Alex's mother. It was found in the dusty bag of photographs in the old family home in Koidanov.

Left: Colonel and Mrs Lobe in their flat in Stockholm, where the author visited them in the early 1980s.

Below: Alex, Patricia and Mark with the newly discovered family in Minsk.

Above: Father and son outside the family home at Koidanov in 1997.

Right: The memorial to the martyrs of the Koidanov massacre.

Below: The Galperin house today.

МІНСКАЕ ДАБРАЧЫННАЕ
ТАВАРЫСТВА «ГІЛФ»

220012 г. Мінск
ул. Крапоткіна, 22
тэлефон 234-22-73

МИНСКОЕ БЛАГОТВОРИТЕЛЬНОЕ
ОБЩЕСТВО «ГИЛФ»

220012 г. Минск
ул. Крапоткина, 22
телефон 234-22-73

Left: The Certificate from the 'Gilf' Society, certifying that Solomon Galperin survived Auschwitz, remarried and had a son, Eric Galperin.

Out № 164

From 10/ 07/ 1998

CERTIFICATE

'Gilf' - the benevolent society of Minsk Jews former prisoners of Nazi Concentration Camps and Ghettos certifies that Uldis Kurzemnieks (real name Elia Solomonovich Galperin) was interned in the Ghetto of Kojdanov (now Dzerszinsk) Minsk region, Byelorussian Republic together with his family, from July 1941 till October 1941 when the Ghetto was liquidated, and all the Jews of Kojdanovo exterminated. In this Ghetto, in October of 1941 perished Aldis's (Eli's) mother Chana Galperina, his brother and his sister. Aldis, miraculously saved himself.

Aldis's father - Solomon Eljevich Galperin /1901-1974/ was not shot, but was taken to the Auschwitz Concentration Camp. He survived and after the liberation, returned to Kojdanovo, where he got married for the second time. Currently in Minsk lives Aldis's (Elia Galperin) brother - Eric Solomonovich Galperin, who was born in 1947, from the second marriage of Aldis's father

Chaireperson for the "Gilf" Siciety

(Frida Rejzman)

Below: The official rejection of Alex's application for assistance from the Claims Conference in New York in 1999. This was later rescinded after much contention.

CLAIMS CONFERENCE ARTICLE 2 FUND
15 EAST 26 STREET • SUITE 906
NEW YORK, NY 10010
TEL: (212) 213-4034

Mr. Uldis Kurzeminieks
178 Miles Street
North Altona, Vic 3025
Australia

January 27, 1999

Re: Art-2 claim Nr: 9 21988 9

Dear Mr. Kurzeminieks,

This is to confirm with thanks the receipt of your certificate from the "Gilf" society of Minsk and income documentation.

Regretfully, I have to advise you that your claim does not fit into the presently effective eligibility criteria of the Fund (please, see attached the explanation letter), since as you stated in your account of events, you joined the 18th Latvian Police Battalion which in the Summer of 1943 was transformed into an SS Legion.

I am really sorry not to be able to answer you in a more favorable manner.

Sincerely,
Vladimir Kharlamenko
Vladimir KHarlamenko

CASEWORKER
V. KHARLAMENKO

'They had their questions to ask,' my father said.

'Perhaps after all,' he said, 'it's been wise to have stayed silent all these years . . .'

'I understand, Dad. At quite a few moments my instinct was to tell you to get up and leave the interview.'

'You felt that, son?' My father's face became more animated. He seemed relieved that I'd wanted to support him. My father looked down at his hands.

'I couldn't bear it,' he said. 'I felt like I couldn't breathe. I just fled. I can't remember clearly what happened after that. I didn't black out, but it is a blur.

'The next thing I *do* remember clearly was being on the street. I had enough sense to make it to my car parked on the other side. I got in and locked the doors, but I wasn't capable of driving anywhere. And that's when somebody knocked on the car window. A woman. She introduced herself as Alice Prosser.

'Will you meet her?' I heard my father ask.

'Who?' I replied. I'd been so immersed in the scene he'd just described that I had only half taken in what my father was now saying.

'Alice Prosser,' he repeated, slightly irritated. 'I was just telling you about her. I met her at the Holocaust Centre. She understands my situation. She's a Ukrainian Jew from Odessa. She came to Australia in the early 1970s as a political refugee. She won't go into much about what happened to her. All that she was willing to tell me was that she'd been arrested there, declared an undesirable and quickly deported. After being shunted from country to country, she finally found asylum here.'

My father paused.

'I'm sure they tortured her,' he said quietly. 'Anyway, Alice is a volunteer at the Holocaust Centre and that's where I met her. You know what she told me?' he asked, and didn't wait for my response, 'that I have the "true spirit of a survivor".

'Those were her exact words. I've never thought of myself in that way. Imagine her saying that to me after all that she'd been through herself!'

'Too bad those interviewers didn't seem more sympathetic,' I couldn't restrain myself from commenting.

'They had their questions to ask,' my father repeated.

I remained unconvinced.

'You have to understand what they've been through in their own lives. They've been made bitter and sick by their suffering,' my father said, gently. 'You can't blame them.'

I found his generosity of spirit hard to accept, even though I was not surprised by it. It typified the man. I only wished that he was more forgiving to himself.

'I told her about you,' my father said. 'She wants to meet you.'

I sensed that my father had already set the wheels in motion for a meeting with Alice and I was annoyed.

'Go on,' he cajoled me, 'you won't regret it.'

I felt cautious about meeting Alice. Since his brief visit to Oxford months earlier, I'd been slowly drawn into a world dominated solely by my father's quest. I had a brief vision of this Alice as an usher, checking my ticket before escorting me to the seat where I would watch the rest of my father's story play out.

'Make the arrangements,' I sighed.

'I'll call her in the morning,' he said, pleased.

My father glanced at the clock on the kitchen wall.

'Look! It's almost two in the morning. Get to bed you rascal,' he whispered with affection. 'Keeping me up this late!'

21

ALICE

I GOT up late the next morning. My father was in the kitchen drinking coffee. He looked up when he heard me come in.

'Get dressed, Mark,' he said. 'Alice wants to meet you this afternoon.'

He told me that she'd wait for me in Acland Street in St Kilda, a beach-side inner suburb of Melbourne and his old stomping ground.

'Two o'clock at Cafe Sheherazade,' my father said. 'I usually meet her there. She loves it. "It's very kosher," she says.'

The Sheherazade was renowned both for its Jewish food – members of the Jewish community would congregate there for coffee and cake – and its atmosphere, which was redolent of pre-war Eastern Europe. When I was a small child, Sheherazade's front window attracted me more than any other on Acland Street. We would pass by it on the way to the Monarch cake shop to buy what my father maintained was the best cheesecake he had ever eaten. Invariably I would dawdle in front of Sheherazade's window and stare in, instantly hypnotised by the sight of the well-dressed Jewish ladies, their eyes sparkling as they chatted vivaciously with one another.

It was just before two when I stepped into Sheherazade whose interior had been modernised since I was a child, but which somehow seemed shabbier than I had remembered. The last of the lunchtime crowd was beginning to clear. I found a table at the rear of the main room, and ordered coffee with the inevitable piece of cheesecake.

A few moments later, a stocky woman in her late sixties entered. She was tiny, almost dwarfish, and used a walking stick to steady her lopsided gait. On one arm, she nursed a shopping bag which appeared to be stuffed with clothing, books, newspapers and tins of soup, as if she carried all her belongings with her.

'God, no!' was my initial, uncharitable, reaction. 'Another one of my father's crackpot friends.'

She headed directly across the room towards me, with a broad smile and her hand outstretched.

'I'm Alice Prosser,' she said. 'You're Mark. I recognise you from your photo.'

I must have looked surprised.

'Oh yes,' she said. 'Your father carries a photo of you with him. He's so proud. His son who studied at Oxford.'

I laughed, embarrassed. Oxford seemed far removed from my life at this moment.

I exchanged a few pleasantries with Alice about the weather and the like, in an effort to break the ice, but she didn't seem to have much time for idle chit-chat, so I jumped right in. 'So you know my father from the Holocaust Centre?'

Alice nodded. 'But sadly not the best of circumstances,' she said heavily.

I stared at her, waiting for her to continue.

'Your father's told you about what went on there?'

I shrugged.

'What did happen, Alice?'

Our coffees arrived at that moment. Alice took a long sip, and rummaged in her bag for something. She pulled out a small leather pouch, plucked out some tobacco and papers, rolled a cigarette and lit it.

The waitress who had just served us approached tentatively. She looked down at Alice, giving an apologetic smile. Alice looked up at her.

'Is something the matter?' she asked.

'The cigarette, madam. I'm sorry,' the young woman said. 'This is a no-smoking cafe.'

Alice nodded, contorting her lips into a tight-lipped grimace. She stubbed out the cigarette on my empty cheesecake plate.

The waitress removed the plate and, holding it at a distance as if it still gave off noxious fumes, disappeared.

Alice remained slightly hunched over her part of the table.

'You know,' she said, shaking her head in disgust, 'every time I come here they say the same thing to me – no smoking. It's worse than the old Soviet Union. At least there you could smoke wherever you wanted.'

I watched her as she returned her tobacco pouch to her bag, and wondered at her stubbornness.

'It just wasn't a place that suited your father's character,' she said cryptically, finally responding to my question.

She fell silent for a few moments, and then continued much more quietly. 'I was working in the back near the interview room when I saw your father come in with one of the interviewers,' she said. 'I couldn't help but notice him because of his face. You must know what I mean . . . he looks like a sad clown, and those expressive blue eyes.'

I knew exactly what Alice meant. It was not the first time I had heard my father described in this way. I recalled as a child, when my father would take us to visit his old friends at the travelling circus he'd also worked in, how fond he was of the clown act – the Zakkini Brothers. To me they were the saddest people I'd ever laid eyes on – four Italian Jewish émigrés from the war – such were their glum expressions. My brothers and I would always tease my father, telling him that he should quit his job and become Zakkini Number Five. He would always laugh in response, and nod in agreement. 'That's me, boys,' he'd say, 'a sad clown too.'

'I guessed that he'd come to give his testimony. That's where they usually did them. Anyway, because I was a volunteer at the centre, I do all sorts of jobs around the place. That day, I couldn't help but overhear parts of your father's testimony. And the parts I heard astonished me. An amazing story, one of the most remarkable I have ever heard. Imagine! A child could survive like that. As I listened I could hear him struggling to explain things clearly to the interviewer. I felt terribly sorry for your father.'

At that moment Alice set down her coffee cup with such a clatter that some of the other customers in Sheherazade stopped what they were doing and stared in our direction. She however was oblivious to them.

'But it was your father's destiny to live to tell the story,' she declared, opening her eyes wide to reveal her yellowish eyeballs. Despite the seriousness of what Alice was describing, I didn't know how long I could suppress a smile at her theatrics.

'Tell me,' I said, 'why wasn't the visit to the centre . . .' I searched for the right word, '. . . successful?'

'Put it this way,' Alice replied, 'in my opinion I think your father felt uncomfortable at the centre, that he believed that somehow he didn't fit in. Perhaps he felt that because he was not after all raised a Jew that he didn't belong there. Who knows? Even though I am a volunteer there I don't think it was the most appropriate place for him. I'm not saying more than that.'

I reflected on how Alice's words resonated with my father's. I heard her voice again.

'In the short time I've known your father,' she said, 'I can see that he is an exceptional man. He embraces life, I could tell that immediately. But it doesn't mean that he hasn't suffered – he's been exposed to things that a child should never be – or isn't still suffering. But your father isn't the type of man who wants or needs to dwell on it. He simply wants to tell his story, and even then not just for his own benefit. He told me later that his story was a lesson for everybody, Jewish or not, about human cruelty to each other.'

Alice lit another cigarette, taking a long draw on it, and then quickly put it out.

'At one point I noticed that the interview room was empty. The testimony had come to an end only a few minutes earlier, according to the interviewer whom I came across in the corridor. I felt very sorry for your father after hearing his story. I wanted to say something to him – give him some encouragement. I decided to look for him. With a bit of luck, I thought, he might not have left the premises.

'I was right. I found him in the museum. He was wandering among the exhibits, taking in their horror. They must have reminded him of things he'd seen as a boy. Even the images of life in the pre-war *shtetl* must have upset him – what a terrible sense of loss he must have felt looking at the world denied him by fate – because as I approached him I could see that he was shaking slightly.

'I touched him gently on the shoulder. I didn't want to alarm him. "Do you remember me?" I asked. "I was working back there."

'Your father nodded. I extended my hand to him.

'There was an awkward silence. Your father was lost for words but it didn't matter. I knew what he was going through. Then, before I knew it, he gave a weak smile and turned away from me, blank-eyed, as if in a daze.'

Alice became agitated and breathless as she related this to me.

'Alice, are you OK?' I asked.

'Of course I'm not,' she answered heavily.

Alice was then silent for several moments as she gathered her breath. Then she continued. 'I watched your father slip out the exit. I decided to follow him. He was on the doorstep outside the museum entrance. Then he walked back to his car, parked on the opposite side of the road. It was just to make sure that he was OK. He climbed in, and started the car. But after several minutes, it had still not moved so I decided to check on him.'

I pictured Alice hobbling across the street, her walking stick in one hand and gladbag in the other.

'I reached the driver's side. Your father seemed to be in a state of shock. He stared straight ahead, oblivious to the world around him. Your father didn't even seem aware of me. I tapped lightly on the window. He snapped out of his state and wound down the window, giving me a questioning look as if he didn't recognise me. "I'm Alice Prosser," I introduced myself again, "can I join you?" After a moment's hesitation he simply nodded.

'I climbed into the car, and we sat there together in silence, your father still unable to drive off.

'In the end I had to tap on his arm a number of times before he turned towards me. I sensed that your father wanted to talk and suggested we move on to somewhere else. Within minutes we pulled into a car park that looked out at the sea. It was a bleak afternoon, and the place was deserted. We sat in silence, watching the waves. I had to say something to break their spell so I told your father that I'd overheard some of his story. It was unavoidable: the walls at the centre are paper-thin.

'I believe your father's story and I told him so. He was so taken aback that he asked me two or three times, "You believe me?" and then added, "even though my memories are patchy?"

' "Memory is a strange thing, Alex," I said.

' "I know," he said. "Something important, like my mother's face, I cannot remember at all, but I can still taste the *kes* my mother would make for the family, as if it was yesterday."

'Your father had used a Yiddish word and when I told him, he was surprised and baffled.

' "I don't know where the word came from," he said. "Maybe I heard it as a child." Your father repeated the word over and over – "*kes kes kes*", he said, as if he was relishing the cheese itself.

' "Do you remember the taste too?" he asked me excitedly. His eyes were moist with nostalgia for its taste.

'I nodded. Your father was overwhelmed that I shared an experience from his past. Perhaps he realised that he was no longer alone, as he had been in his silence.'

Alice shifted slightly in her seat, taking the weight off her bad hip.

'At that moment,' she said, 'I trusted that your father was telling the truth about his past. The task was to uncover it.

'I've met your father here a couple of times since then. I tell him little things about being Jewish, life in the *shtetl* and Jewish ceremonies, and he is always fascinated. Who knows, we might make a good Jew out of him yet, and turn you into a good Jewish boy as well!'

I laughed.

She seemed disconcerted, as if she'd misunderstood my response.

I leant forward. 'My father and I,' I joked, 'we're a couple of old dogs. Too old for any new tricks!'

For a moment I feared that she was going to pinch my cheek.

'We'll see about that.' She smiled, as if she knew me better than I knew myself.

Alice took a sip of her coffee, and made a sour face because it had gone cold.

We sat in silence for several minutes.

Finally Alice rose and gathered her bags, suggesting that we meet again soon.

'I'd like to come to the house,' she said, 'and meet your mother.'

I said nothing.

'Your father's still not told her then?'

I shook my head.

Alice made a tutting sound.

'I must go,' she said.

I watched Alice as she hobbled across the cafe, and out through the door.

I remained in Sheherazade for some time, drinking another coffee and reflecting on my meeting with Alice. I felt that I'd been in the presence of a magical dwarf who'd appeared from somewhere deep in the forests of Eastern Europe. I tried to make sense of what she had told me, what she had been alluding to about the Holocaust Centre, but to no avail.

Through the window I could see that Acland Street was busy with the early evening crowds. I could understand my father's lifelong attraction to the area with its vibrant street life – it must have been reminiscent for him of the mood and communality of the *shtetl* in which he dwelled for the early years of his life. It contrasted starkly with the atmosphere of the suburb where he now lived.

It struck me then that my position in Acland Street had diametrically shifted. I was no longer a little boy peering into Sheherazade. Now I was a man, still my father's son, but I was inside looking out.

22

THE LETTER

WHEN I turned into the driveway I saw that our house was in darkness. I wondered where my parents were as it was unusual for them to be out at this hour of the evening on a weekday. I parked the car and went inside.

I made my way to the living room, not bothering to turn on any lights and called out their names but there was no reply. I sat down in one of the armchairs. Outside I could see the headlights of cars as they passed by, and expected that at any moment I would see the headlights of my parents' car coming up the drive.

Sitting alone in the dark I had an image of Martin, Andrew and me waiting expectantly for my father to return from work when, suddenly, I saw the headlights of my parents' car. They were home from wherever they'd been.

My mother seemed subdued when she came in.

'I'll get some dinner for us,' she said quietly, going straight through to the kitchen.

My father turned on the television – it was time for the evening news – and sat down in the chair opposite me.

'Where have you been?' I asked.

'Just dropped by Mirdza's,' he replied.

'How are they?'

'They're getting along fine . . . nothing new.'

After dinner the three of us watched television but none of us seemed very interested. Nor was there any of the usual banter that accompanied our evenings at home. My mother remained as dejected as she had been earlier in the evening, and my father seemed unable to settle. He got up constantly to fetch small electronic gadgets, which he repaired on the floor in the centre of the room. Eventually my mother rose, pleading tiredness, said, 'Goodnight', and went to her room.

My father tinkered with an old camera on the floor while I stared at the television, half-heartedly trying to follow the plot of a police drama.

I looked away from the screen.

'So what did you talk about with Mirdza and Edgars?' I asked.

He was evasive. 'This and that,' was all he said. He continued to tinker with the camera.

'What did you think of Alice?' he asked without looking up.

'She's a nice lady, isn't she?'

'She is.'

'What did you talk about?'

'This and that,' I answered, imitating my father's response.

I could tell that I'd irritated him but I couldn't help myself. If he was going to keep things to himself then I would do the same, I thought stubbornly.

We both lapsed into silence once again, and before very much longer, we bade each other goodnight and went to our respective rooms.

It was the middle of the same night. I'd always been a light sleeper and the sound of somebody moving in the hall had woken me. I thought that it must be my father, troubled by another nightmare about his past. These nightmares were becoming a frequent occurrence: I would hear him stir and then make his way to the kitchen for a cup of tea. On these occasions I would get up and follow him, pretending that I needed a glass of water, then feign surprise at finding him there. In this way, he slowly began to confide in me more of the memories that seemed to be triggered by his nightmares.

This night, too, I got up and headed towards the kitchen expecting to find my father. I was surprised to find the kitchen in darkness.

'Dad?' I whispered. There was no response. Then I heard an indistinct noise coming from the adjacent utility room.

I approached the closed door; there was no light coming from under it but the muffled sound became stronger. I put my ear against the door. It was my mother, weeping quietly.

I was suddenly certain that my father had told her his story. I reached for the door handle.

But then I stopped, unable to open the door. I was petrified by my mother's grief. I had had the same feeling when I had first seen my father's tape. As I stood there, frozen to the spot, I knew that I should have done something, made even a single gesture to console my own mother. But much to my enduring shame, I did not. I didn't know how and I feared too that she was beyond comforting. Instead I left her alone: bewildered and frightened.

I lay awake for some time until I heard the sounds of my mother's footsteps returning to her room.

The next morning dawned sunny and unusually mild for early spring in Melbourne.

Over breakfast my mother was perky but her features were drawn. My father seemed to be avoiding both her company and mine. No sooner had he gulped down the last of his cereal than he got up and headed off to his workshop. My mother and I were left alone to face each other.

'It's a lovely day, Mum,' I said, enthusiastically. 'Let's go down to Williamstown beach.'

We lived a couple of miles from the bay at Williamstown, one of the oldest parts of Melbourne.

I parked on the front close to where my mother had spotted a vacant bench. We made our way to it and sat down. We were silent, listening to the sounds of the waves lapping gently against the small boats moored just offshore.

Suddenly, out of the blue, my mother spoke.

'I've seen the tape,' she said. 'I know now what was bothering your father. All those years, he never said a word.'

She told me that after I had left the house to meet Alice my father had simply left the tape on the kitchen table, telling her that he was off on an errand and that she should watch the tape while he was out.

'Your father didn't return until nearly four o'clock,' she said. 'He went straight to his workshop. I tried to speak with him but he refused to say a single word about it. There was no choice, I left him to it. You know how obstinate he is – he'll only talk when he's ready to.

'Moments later the phone rang. It was Martin, and I'd no sooner hung up with him than Andrew called,' my mother said.

Both my brothers had been at home when my father had appeared on their doorsteps. Without even exchanging pleasantries, he had passed over copies of the tape. As with me, he had given neither of them a clue about the tape's contents.

Certainly my father was a shy man and he must have known that its content would be traumatic for us, but nonetheless it struck me as perversely reticent the way he had gone about revealing his past to us by videotape.

'How did Martin and Andrew react?' I asked my mother.

She turned away from the view of the bay so that I could see her full expression. It was clear that she was disturbed.

'Andrew was too upset to talk about it very much,' she said quietly. 'It's really shocked him.'

'And Martin?' I asked.

'Martin hardly said a word about it,' my mother said. 'He told me about the tape and then changed the topic. But that's Martin's way. He keeps things to himself.

'Your father was like a man possessed yesterday,' my mother continued. 'Not long after he returned home, he announced that he was going to visit Mirdza and Edgars.

' "Now?" I asked him. "Are you going to tell them?"

'He was desperate to have it all out in the open.

' "Will you come with me?" he asked.

'Of course, I couldn't let him go by himself. Edgars is a reasonable man, but I worried about how Mirdza would react. This would be difficult for her to accept. He was so impatient to get over there that he jumped in the car and waited for me there – beeping the horn several times to hurry me up.

'Mirdza answered our knock. She was startled to see us standing on her doorstep, she welcomed us inside. Edgars was home as well, reading the newspaper in the kitchen. Your father didn't even wait for Mirdza to prepare coffee. We'd barely sat down when he started telling them his story.

'Mirdza and Edgars sat in silence staring at him the entire time. I'm not even sure how much they absorbed of what he was saying; he was speaking so quickly and jumping from event to event. When he'd finally finished they looked shell-shocked. They didn't say a word.

'Then after several moments your father looked at his watch. "We'd better be going," he said. "It's almost seven. Mark might be home by now." Your father got up and as he did so he produced a copy of the videotape from his case.

' "Let me leave this with you," he said, putting it on the table.

'With that, we were out the front door and on our way home. I felt sorry for Mirdza and Edgars as they waved us off from their front gate. Your father had swept in like a whirlwind and then disappeared as quickly.

'What I don't understand,' my mother said, turning to look at me, 'is that I saw on the tape that it'd been recorded over two months ago. Why didn't he show me sooner? He's kept it from me all these years we've known each other, and even after he'd told those characters on the tape.'

I had no answer to her question.

'How long have you known, Mark?' she asked.

I'd been put in an awkward position once again. I did not want to tell my mother about my father's visit to Oxford. Somehow his odd muteness about the past was one thing but its offence would be worsened by the revelation of a secret journey to the other side of the world.

'Just this week too,' I answered instead.

'Still, for better or worse, we all know now,' she said. 'But he owes people more of an explanation than simply thrusting a tape at them, don't you think?'

I nodded.

'It's funny,' my mother said pensively, on the way home from Williamstown. 'You know how your father's been about chocolate all his life? He wouldn't share it with anybody, or if he did, he had to be in charge, handing out a piece at a time.'

My father had always been a 'chocoholic'. He would hoard supplies of chocolate, hiding little stashes all over the house. His addiction to it had become a family joke.

'A few weeks ago,' my mother said, 'he gave it up completely. In one go. I came home one day and found him clearing out his various stashes. Bars and slabs and boxes of the stuff were piled up high like a treasure. I thought he'd lost his mind.

' "In God's name what are you doing?" I asked.

' "Disposing of it," he said. "You can have it. Or give it to the grandkids, if you want."

' "But why on earth?" I asked, but your father only shrugged. "Lost my taste for it," he said.'

We turned into the driveway.

'You OK, Mum?' I asked. I didn't know what else to say.

'I'll be OK,' she said. 'I'll be as right as rain. Just need time to take it all in.'

I admired her attitude but I wondered if she would be 'as right as rain'. Her mood was sombre and she shook her head resignedly.

'This world . . .' she said.

I don't believe that she ever really recovered, despite her best efforts to put on a brave face. I still wonder if it would have been easier for her to deal with my father's revelations if I'd not been so fearful of her emotions during those days.

Now that my mother and the rest of the family knew about my father's past, it was as if a brief Indian summer had descended on our house: the curtains had been drawn back and the windows thrown open to let in the fresh mild air. My father's decision to speak gave me the tacit go-ahead to begin a more concerted search. Two mornings after he had made his disclosures, I was reading the newspaper in the living room when I heard what sounded like a minor explosion in front of our house.

'What on earth?' I heard my mother exclaim as she came into the room and hurried to the front window to peer through the curtains.

When I joined her there I saw a dilapidated car shudder and stop.

The driver's door opened and Alice Prosser got out, collected her bag from the passenger's side and struggled up the driveway. She was carrying a rolled-up map, and a number of books under her arm.

'Poor thing,' my mother said sympathetically. 'She looks like she's in constant pain with that leg of hers. I wonder who she is . . . she must want your father to repair something for her.'

Evidently my mother had no idea who Alice was.

'Come away from the window or she'll see us staring at her,' my mother said, giving me a nudge. 'I'll get your father. You look after the lady.'

'Alice!' I exclaimed as I opened the door. 'This is a surprise. Come in.'

At that moment I heard my father enter the kitchen. It was an awkward moment. I could see my mother wondering about this goblin-like woman whom we'd befriended.

'This is my wife, Patricia,' my father said. Alice reached out for my mother's hand.

My mother seemed momentarily nonplussed.

'Alice has been helping me with my story,' my father added, noticing the question in my mother's eyes.

'Oh . . .' she said, before collecting herself and offering Alice a chair.

Alice put down the books and map.

My father and I joined her.

'Fine to smoke?' she asked, and receiving a nod from my mother, she got out her tobacco pouch and rolled a cigarette.

'Coffee, Alice?' my mother asked.

'Please, Patricia. May I call you Pat?'

'Yes, you go ahead, dear.' My mother seemed to have shed her suspicious attitude.

Alice placed her hand on top of the pile of books. 'I haven't had a chance to look at these yet,' she said. 'The target is "Koidanov". We've all got to put our minds to it.'

'I'm not clever enough for that,' my mother said from where she was preparing coffee. 'I'll make the drinks and sandwiches instead.' After she brought our coffees to the table she retreated to her territory on the other side of the kitchen bench, near to the stove and sink.

In the end the discovery of Koidanov was surprisingly easy if not quite straightforward. Once we had finished our coffee, Alice reached for one of her many books, all of which were written in either Yiddish or Russian. She popped her reading glasses on the end of her nose, put a pen behind her ear and got down to business. Hunched over the table and squinting at the pages of the book in front of her she reminded me of a Damon Runyon character, perhaps a bookie taking bets on my father's past and future.

'Let me see . . .' she said, going through various possible spellings, 'Koidanov . . . Kuidnov . . . Koydanev.'

Within about ten minutes she had found mention of Koidanov in a list of the various *samulbuch* that had been published.

'A *samulbuch*,' she explained, 'is a collection of historical information – photos, anecdotes, essays and memoirs – that were kept by the Jewish communities of many towns and villages in Eastern Europe.

'Here,' she said, pointing at a word on the list. 'There's one for a village called Koidanov in the Minsk region in Belarus. Aaah . . . I know why you couldn't find it on any map. It states that just before the Second World War the name of the village was changed to Dzerzhinsk. Named after the ignominious founder of the *Cheka*. Stalin must have been keen to give the place a more Soviet flavour.'

In the atlas I'd scoured with my father nights earlier I had in fact come across the name Dzerzhinsk. Alice shifted her attention to another book among the stack on the table. This one contained maps of pre-war Europe and she consulted one in particular. She had no difficulty in pinpointing Koidanov and we gathered around her, staring at the spot where she had placed her finger. I was unsure. Koidanov lay some distance to the north-east of Stol'btsi – the town that my father thought might have been referred to as 'S' by the soldiers and the site of their base camp, and not far from where they claimed to have 'discovered' him.

Map 2: Belarus

But it was possible, especially if my father had wandered for months on end in a wide circle before being picked up by the Latvian police brigade in the vicinity of Stol'btsi. Taken there by Kulis, who received permission from Lobe to adopt the boy as the troop's mascot, he was tidied up, given a uniform and could easily have been dispatched to Slonim, where the massacre had occurred. Of course it was only feasible if my father had been picked up by the soldiers earlier than they claimed. Professor M. at Oxford had conjectured that any extermination in my father's village would have to have occurred before December 1941 if my father was also to have witnessed the Slonim massacre at the end of 1941. That is, of course, assuming that the Soviet accusation against Commander Lobe and the Latvian police brigade was justified. Or perhaps my father had been picked up in May 1942, as Lobe and others claimed, and was not a witness to the massacre at Slonim but to another, unnamed, incident.

I scanned the map further to reconfirm what my father and I had already discovered: that to the south-west of Stol'btsi lay Slonim. Was this distance also too far for the 18th to have ventured on duty?

I cast a quick glance at my father who was already staring at me. He must have had a similar train of thought. I was on the verge of commenting on this when he indicated with his eyes and an almost imperceptible shake of his head that I should say nothing.

Fortunately Alice hadn't noticed our exchange. She continued to stare at the name on the map as if it would somehow magically transform into a window through which we could see Koidanov, past and present. We were all buoyed by the discovery that Koidanov was an actual place. Alice rifled enthusiastically through her books trying to learn more about it, while we hovered expectantly around her.

My mother placed another cup of strong black coffee on the table for Alice, who sipped it gratefully. She then reached across for another of her tomes, this one written in Russian. In it she found a brief reference to Dzerzhinsk and a massacre that had occurred there on 21 October 1941. It spoke of the killing of sixteen hundred patriots by fascists during the Great Patriotic War.

Alice grunted in annoyance. 'In other words,' she said, 'translating from Soviet speak, sixteen hundred Jews were murdered in the Holocaust.'

'What do you mean?' my father asked.

'The Soviets didn't acknowledge the Holocaust,' Alice explained. 'Exterminations of this sort were just called crimes against patriotic citizens. And the Second World War was referred to as the Great Patriotic War.'

She leant back in her chair and took another sip of coffee. 'The next thing we need to do, is to establish contact with Koidanov. I have one contact in Minsk. A Mrs Reizman. A historian who works at a Holocaust research centre there. We've exchanged letters a couple of times.'

She plucked her address book out of her shopping bag.

'Here it is,' she said. 'If anyone has access to information about Koidanov, then Frida Reizman will be the one.'

Alice rolled another cigarette and took a long drag.

'Why don't we write to her now?' she suggested.

'This minute?' My father seemed shaken by the immediacy of it.

'What do they say in English?' Alice asked, looking at me cheekily. 'Strike something while it's hot . . .'

'Strike while the iron is hot,' I corrected her.

'OK . . . OK,' she said.

'We need to get all the details of your story written down,' Alice said, 'and then send it off to her.'

My father's face started to brighten at the possibility opening before him. He nodded in agreement.

I felt my mother looking at me from across the kitchen. She gave a smile when our eyes met, excited in her own cautious way. She reached into one of the drawers under the kitchen bench and pulled out a pad of paper and envelopes.

I sat alone in the living room, listening to the soft murmur of the voices of my father and Alice as they composed the letter. I began to plan the logistics of the journey to Minsk. My thoughts were interrupted when I heard Alice call my name. I went through to the kitchen where my father sat anxiously by her side.

'It's finished,' she said, looking up at me. 'Tell me what you think. You're the young man with the good education.'

I laughed and returned to the living room to proofread the letter. It was fine, describing as much as it could of the details we had to go on – the words Koidanov and Panok, and a description of the massacre my father had witnessed in his village.

I heard the sound of Alice's walking stick on the polished kitchen floor as she hobbled around, stretching her legs. Her face appeared around the doorway, followed by my father's.

'You approve?' she asked.

'Of course,' I replied.

'It's great, Alice,' my father added.

Alice smiled shyly, pleased with our praise.

'You must post it yourself,' Alice said to my father. 'It will be symbolic.'

'Do you think something will come of it?' my father asked.

His words had a hopeful tone, but Alice only shrugged.

'Time will tell,' she said.

My father stood up. 'I'll take it to the post office straight away,' he said, already heading for the front door. 'Be back soon.'

'I'll come with you,' I called after him, grabbing my jacket.

I tried to keep up with his stride; shamefully, he was in better shape than me.

'Why didn't you want me to mention Slonim to Alice?' I asked, already slightly breathless.

'I don't want Alice to think that I was associated with something like that,' my father answered, maintaining his speedy pace.

'You mean you suspect that you might've killed people yourself?'

My father nodded.

'You didn't, did you, Dad?'

It was a question I had always dreaded asking him. I was relieved that we were both facing ahead, and I didn't have to look him in the face.

'Never,' he said.

I saw him shake his head.

'Never,' he repeated.

'Not once did I lay a hand on another person, even though the soldiers tried to get me to do so. Much to their amusement I would always run away, petrified.'

We continued to walk side by side.

'There was one incident, the worst of all,' he said quietly, as if he feared the neighbourhood would hear him.

'We were on patrol in a forest. I'm not sure where. The soldiers captured a Jewish lad – he must have been with the partisans. He was no more than sixteen or seventeen, a teenager really. They bound his hands together and led him back to our camp. When we got there they tied him to a tree with a long piece of rope. Then they started firing their pistols on the ground around his feet to make him jump and dance around the tree. They were laughing as if it were a game.

'I couldn't bear to look. I'd caught a glimpse of the terror in the boy's face. Just as I was trying to slip away, one of the soldiers thrust a pistol into my hand. "Shoot!" he shouted at me. "Shoot!"

'They all began clapping their hands together, chanting "Shoot" over and over.

'I was almost as terrified as the boy. I was trapped. There was no way out. The only thing that came into my head was to aim badly at the boy's feet, so that's what I did. The bullet struck halfway up the tree instead. The soldiers let out a groan of disappointment and one of them demonstrated how I should aim the pistol. I nodded my head confidently as if I'd now grasped what I should do.

'I took aim again – and mind you I was already an excellent shot from target practice with the soldiers – and this time I deliberately fired just over the head of one of the soldiers standing on the opposite side of the tree.

'He ducked but I knew I wouldn't have hit him anyway. A few of the soldiers began to hurl abuse at me, but I believe that Sergeant Kulis realised that I'd mis-aimed deliberately. He gave me a furtive warning glance and then strode quickly over to me and gave me a clip around the ear.

' "He's a fool," he called to the other soldiers. "He needs more pistol training." With that he began to push me towards the barracks and out of harm's way. He'd defused the episode but I knew that he viewed what had gone on as a test of my willingness and loyalty to the squad. And I'd failed. I wasn't capable of killing anybody, Jewish or not. I must have had something in me that resisted that.'

We reached the post office and stood outside the entrance.

'The soldiers killed everything they could lay their hands on. Incidents like that made me feel that I was a killer just because of what I witnessed. Just because I was with them. Perhaps those interviewers are right. I am a killer of Jews, not literally, but because I stood by and did nothing.'

'Dad, you were only five or six then,' I tried to reassure him. 'What could you have done to stop them? You would have been powerless against grown men. They would have turned their guns on you and killed you.'

My father nodded.

'But,' he said, 'perhaps that would have been a better solution to my fate. To have died as a child, forgotten unknown martyr, rather than face their hate and accusations now.'

My father was quiet.

'What happened to the boy?' I asked.

He shook his head. 'When I returned later in the day, the rope was still tied around the tree but there was no sign of the boy.'

23

NIGHTMARES

AFTER his initial enthusiasm at sending the letter my father's spirits began to flag. One morning I found him alone in the kitchen, staring bleakly into space.

'Even if Koidanov turns out to be my village,' he said, 'what will be there for me but a handful of memories? And they are here with me.' He tapped his chest.

'So what do you hope for from the letter?' I asked.

'To be honest, son,' my father replied, 'I don't know. Are we clutching at straws? Who would remain there to miss me, or remember me? My entire family perished.' And then he added, 'Though I still cannot place my father at the extermination . . .'

I had no answer for that.

I also suspected that working from the scant clues that we had provided would stymie Frida Reizman's efforts, no matter how enterprising.

The question of Panok remained especially oblique and intriguing for us all. Frank had finally contacted me with the news that his search had failed to establish any definite connect between Panok and the village of Koidanov. Yet why were the two words so strongly associated in my father's memory?

Frank also told me that the Panoks who had lived near Minsk in pre-war times had all perished in the Holocaust. It seemed that there would be no Panoks to find.

Yet my father would not let go of the mystery of the Panoks. On several occasions he insisted that Panok must be his name, only to retreat moments later into a state of stoic resignation, claiming to have no interest whatso-ever in who he might have been.

I began to worry about his mental and emotional fragility.

Despite the sombre mood that had descended over the household as we waited for a reply, by day at least we maintained a semblance of normality. My parents tried to return to the routine of their daily lives. My father spent his days in his workshop tinkering. On Sundays he and my mother went out for lunch or visited friends. Often they were drawn to the secular synagogue of Cafe Sheherazade. My mother would browse through her women's magazines over coffee and cheesecake, while my father sat on the edge of his chair, restlessly observing the comings and goings of other customers. He seemed eager, almost desperate, my mother said, to talk to the ones with sympathetic faces, to tell them his story.

I was somewhat buoyed by the hours I spent in research in the library, trying to get a picture of the historical context of my father's fate. At times, rather frustratingly, the research itself threw up different versions of the same event. In the end I could construct only the very broadest of canvases, based on indisputable historical evidence.

For example, records revealed that in July 1941 Heinrich Himmler had visited Minsk. The purpose of the visit was ostensibly to facilitate 'living space' for Western European Jews deported to the east. Himmler was keen to see the eradication of Jews in Belarus for that reason, and during that period he ordered *Aktionen* to begin in the region. (This was prior to the Wannsee Conference of January 1942. The Final Solution, the systemised efficiency of the gas chambers and death camps, had yet to be implemented. In the pre-Wannsee period shooting the Jews one by one and leaving them in mass graves had been the predominant means of clearing the Jewish population out of the villages and towns of Eastern Europe.)

The killings were carried out by *Einsatzgruppen*, composed variously of Baltic police brigades and other military units. These groups were ultimately under the command of the German SS but had an internal hierarchy of local commanders. I learnt that *Einsatzgruppen* had entered parts of White Russia, especially the area surrounding Minsk, and begun their *Aktionen* in the late summer and early autumn of 1941.

During subsequent days I learned also about the Latvians in the region. A police battalion, commanded jointly by Commander Lobe and a Captain Rubenis, had been dispatched to the region in November/December of 1941 to assist in 'mopping up duties' and hunting 'partisans', an umbrella term used along with Bolsheviks as a euphemism for the Jewish population. These facts coincided exactly with my father's confused memory of the presence of both Lobe and Rubenis when he was with the soldiers. It also accounted for the fact that my father had insisted initially to me that his battalion had hunted only for 'partisans' and not Jews. As a boy of five he would have accepted at face value what the soldiers had told him. What was most significant was that according to one version (though this was contradicted by other versions) the Latvian brigade would have been there in time for the Slonim massacre.

In mid-1942 the brigade was incorporated into the *Wehrmacht* as the 18th Battalion. It was eventually recalled to Riga in the late spring of 1943 where after a brief period it was again transformed, this time into an SS unit, the Kurzeme battalion, under the command of Kārlis Lobe. In July 1943, the Kurzeme battalion was sent to the Russian front south of Leningrad to a place called the Volhov swamps, north of Velikiye Luki, exactly as my father had remembered. Crucially the transformations of the Kurzeme battalion had involved at least two changes of uniform which again resonated with my father's explanation to me and to the interviewers at the Holocaust Centre. I verified that there had been an extermination in the town of Koidanov and that indeed it occurred on 21 October 1941.

Each night after dinner my mother would wash the dishes or do the ironing whilst my father sat at the kitchen table in silence as I, much like a private detective reporting to a client, related the grisly details that had come to light that day.

On one such occasion, after learning of the Koidanov massacre and recounting it to my father, something very sinister occurred to me.

'Perhaps . . .' I began, and then stopped myself.

'Perhaps what?' my father was suddenly alert.

'Oh nothing.' I didn't want to let my father into my train of thought.

It had suddenly crossed my mind – what if it had been the Latvian police brigade who had committed the Koidanov massacre? In other words, what if he had been adopted and cared for by the very men who had murdered his mother, brother and sister and his extended family? The thought sent a shiver through me. I didn't want my father to have to even contemplate the terrible possibility that Lobe and Kulis may have murdered his family.

I was glad that I'd held this suspicion back from him. I learnt later that the Koidanov extermination had been perpetrated by a Lithuanian brigade, also operating during October 1941 in a number of villages south-west of Minsk.[1]

During my research, I came across a controversy about the actions of the Latvian police battalion that directly touched upon my father's memories. It pertained to the massacre in Slonim, which may have been within striking distance from 'S', where the brigade had set up temporary camp.

According to the records, in the post-war period the Kurzeme battalion had been held responsible by the Soviet authorities for a massacre that had taken place there in late 1941 (though again I found a number of conflicting dates for the incident). A war crimes trial had resulted in the execution of several members of the brigade who had not managed to escape Latvia. Others, including Lobe, claimed that the brigade hadn't been involved and had never been in the vicinity of Slonim. Judging by what I read, their involvement was still a matter of controversy among historians and Latvian patriots alike.

What attracted my attention above all, and most troubled me, were several eyewitness accounts of the massacre. Witnesses stated that they saw Jews – the elderly, women and children – herded into a synagogue and burnt alive. This account perfectly reflected the memory my father had recounted to me. That horrific incident had taken place on the day he'd been tied to the roof of a train and transported with the battalion to an unidentified location. It was also the day when many soldiers had jostled and queued for a chance to be photographed with the unusual boy soldier in his uniform.

Had my father in fact been taken to Slonim where he witnessed the massacre? When I put it to him, my father had prevaricated.

'I saw no massacres,' he said. 'It could've been another time and place.'

---

[1] I also learnt much later that the Lithuania troop had been led by one Anton Gecavicius who, now known as Anthony Gecas, had been found in 2001 alive and well in Edinburgh, under the auspices of the British government. There is a story to tell of our subsequent involvement in the intricacies of the Gecavicius affair that would bring us into contact with the Lithuanian government. But here is not the place for it, or many other incidents in connection to this story. These incidents (many of them to do with the whitewashing of Latvia's past) in one sense were peripheral to our concern to find my father's identity. But, paradoxically, they were central to our efforts to validate my father's search, as often they attempted to discredit it. It was these sorts of incidents, where accusations against my father were put in the public arena, and damage done without later retraction, that on the one hand distracted us from the immediate concerns of my father's story. On the other hand, these incidents also speak of the significance of a small boy's story to contemporary political and national self-interest and the ends to which my father and I had to fight for the truth of his memory.

'That may be the case,' I replied. 'Certainly many synagogues would have been set alight as the troops went about their dirty business.'

But then he had a change of heart.

'The soldiers claim to have picked me up in late May 1942, but what if it had been sooner, much sooner, even before Slomin? The key question is how long I was in the freezing Russian forest, and you know I still find it hard to believe that I was alone there throughout the entire winter. How could a child survive such deprivation?

'It was Commander Lobe who told me about how they picked me up, even that it was the summer season. Perhaps with time I've grown confused. I remember clearly that Kulis rescued me from the firing squad but in my mind I've pictured that it was summer because that was what the frightening Lobe had insisted. But, you know, I am sometimes troubled by a sense that there was snow on the ground when I was going to be shot. That's my problem, my memories blend together between what I actually remember and what I was instructed to remember.'

My father paused.

'Why would they have lied about such a thing?' he asked. 'Lobe even insisted in his memoir that it was early summer . . .'

'To cover their tracks,' I reminded him. 'You could have been a witness against any of the men who were there.'

'I wonder what happened to the photographs that were taken of you on the day of the massacre you recall. I wonder if any of the soldiers kept them.'

My father shrugged. 'It seemed unlikely. Who would be crazy enough to keep something that implicated them as a war criminal?'

The fragile silence of our household was disturbed almost nightly by the wails and shouts that emanated from the spare room where my father had taken to sleeping to avoid disturbing my mother. I would lie half-awake in fear and anticipation of what that night's dreams would bring to my father. My mother and I often found ourselves together outside his room, our ears pressed against the closed door, eavesdropping on the tormented man.

Sometimes, we would hear him stir and begin to move about the room. At that point my mother would tap lightly on the door.

'Alex?' she would whisper, as if unsure it was her husband on the other side. 'Alex? Are you OK?'

We would hear his muffled and drowsy-sounding voice answer, 'I'm fine. Just a bad dream. Go back to bed.'

'I'll talk to him,' I would say to my mother. 'You get some sleep.'

'Tea?' I would say to my father through the closed door.

His usual response would be: 'OK, son, I'll join you shortly,' though on a few occasions he ordered me to go back to bed. He needed his privacy, and I wondered what he had seen in his dreams that he couldn't share.

On most occasions, however, I would prepare tea in the kitchen. My father would enter some minutes later after what I imagined to be a process of recovering himself, literally, from his dreams. Sometimes he sat silently, as if in shock, sipping from his cup. I would sit opposite him, waiting for him to speak. These moments were both ghoulish and titillating because I didn't know if he would be able to recall what he had just dreamt and if it might somehow be another clue to unlocking his past.

But that past was beginning to overwhelm him.

One night I woke with a start. For a moment, as I lay in my bed, the house was quiet. I got up and tiptoed down the hallway. The door to my father's bedroom lay open. The room was dark. I softly called his name but there was no reply. I continued towards the kitchen where I could see light coming from under the closed door. I gently opened it, just a fraction. My father was sitting at the table with his head in his hands. He was utterly still and was so absorbed in his thoughts that he had not heard me.

I opened the door further.

'Dad?' I whispered.

He gave a slight jump, and turned toward me.

'Another nightmare?' I asked.

He nodded.

'Recall any of it?'

He shook his head.

'But a memory came to me the instant that I woke up. In fact I wasn't sure if I was awake or not.' He laughed darkly.

My mother suddenly appeared in the doorway and stayed, listening.

'For a moment I was back in the town where the synagogue had been set on fire with all those poor people inside. But this time everything was more vivid.'

He stopped speaking and screwed up his eyes as if to avoid seeing what was in his memory.

'I could see the expressions on people's faces, the little children. And the cries as people burned. I can hear the screams even now as they clawed at the burning doors trying to get out. And then the silence that followed, apart from the sound of the wood crackling, I can still hear that, if that makes sense.'

For an instant he seemed to struggle for breath, as if he too were being immolated inside the synagogue, deprived of oxygen.

'And there were other flashes of images. Men and women stripped naked and shot in the back of the head. I think that happened on that same day. I thought that it had gone from me, as you said, that I'd blocked it out, but there's no escape from them this time. It's like a film that plays itself over and over and I cannot control it. Now that I remember I will never forget it . . .'

My father was silent for several minutes and then he seemed visibly to gather his spirit together.

'You still don't know where and when this was?' I ventured.

He shook his head despondently.

'I want to remember,' he said reflectively, 'but not this. This is madness.'

I turned to my mother who was still standing in the doorway. She was weeping quietly.

The strain of nights such as these eventually made it difficult to maintain even good spirits. But the dreams were not always alarming. Ever since we'd found Koidanov, my father had gone through phases of excitability that opened up more pleasant and nostalgic memories and dreams of life in his village. Yet even then he sometimes found himself traumatised by a growing sense of what he had lost, and a growing bewilderment over why he alone had survived.

One night I made my way to the kitchen where I found my father standing by the sink, waiting for the kettle to boil. He was staring at his own reflection in the kitchen window and he must have heard me enter because he wasn't startled as I came up behind him.

As I came closer I realised that he was not staring at himself but outside. 'Dad?' I whispered.

He raised his hand in the air, indicating that I should be quiet.

I waited expectantly and suddenly he spoke, or rather exclaimed.

'An apple tree! I've just had a dream about one. It's jolted my memory. There was an apple tree in our back garden. I'd always be climbing it, playing in it, picking apples for my mother.'

He was elated.

'I can see my hands in front of me,' he continued, 'trying to get a grip on the trunk as I climb it. Then suddenly I am in a fork of the tree and looking down through the branches and leaves to the earth which seems miles below me.

'My mother is down there, looking up at me. I'm reaching out and plucking apples and then tossing them down to her. She catches some in her apron, but she misses others which roll on the ground.'

I noticed that he was recounting his dream to me in the present tense as if he had returned to a past more vivid and real to him than the moment I shared with him.

'I can see her lips breaking into a smile and then she laughs as her apron begins to overflow with apples. She is calling out to me "Enough! Enough!" But the eerie thing is that I can't hear her voice. I've no idea of how it sounds. Then she calls out my name, but again I cannot hear her. And worst of all I am looking at her face but I can't see her features. They will not crystallise for me.

'I look away for a moment. Something has distracted me.'

He gripped my forearm tightly.

'It's below me and slightly to the left,' he said.

'It's a shed and a man is moving about inside. I can't get a clear view of what he's doing.'

My father moved his head to one side as if trying to get a clearer view into the shed.

'Wait!' he exclaimed, raising his hand to silence me before I had even uttered a word. 'The man has heard my mother's and my laughter and he's come to the doorway. He's looking up at me. It's my father, Mark,' my father said excitedly. 'My father!'

'Can you see his face?'

'No.

'He's gone. He's turned away. But I can see inside the shed now. Skins! Skins of animals. They are hanging behind him. These are what he works with. He makes things out of them. People come to the shed to buy things from him. He must be a shoemaker or tanner of some sort.

'The dream didn't end there,' he said. 'Suddenly I was flying. I soared high into the sky so that I could see all the houses in my street. I caught sight of the house with the apple tree and the shed. It was wooden and there was a drive running alongside it, wide enough for a cart. I know that this house is where I lived.

'I descended like an angel so that I hovered just above the height of the roofs. I could see people – ordinary-looking village people, not dressed fancily or anything – walking, chatting with each other and going about their business. But again it is deadly quiet.

'I wanted to look at their faces but I couldn't. I could only see the tops of their heads. But I'm certain I knew them. I had no control over my flight and suddenly I was back in the tree . . .'

My father rubbed his eyes as if he had only just now roused himself from his dream. His sadness was palpable.

I began to question him, hoping that he would remember more, even if only a single signpost that might help us both.

My concern frustrated him.

'No,' he sighed wearily, 'I didn't see the name of the street I was on.' He gripped his head in his hands. 'Or the town or what country it was,' he added.

'It was a town?'

'I don't know,' he said tetchily.

'I don't even know if the place was large or small. It seemed small but that was because I was high in the sky.'

He paused for an instant.

'But I'm absolutely certain that I would recognise the house and the area if I ever came across it.'

I was concerned. Was this simply a dream in which he had imagined how his life might have been? Or had sleep itself triggered a real memory of his past?

'I wonder if we'll find it in Koidanov . . .' I ventured.

My father didn't respond at first. He was lost in thought.

'I associate the tree with happiness. I climbed it all the time. That's where I played with my friends as well.'

My father smiled.

I was grateful for his expression. I wanted him to recapture some sense of happiness, however tenuous.

'We'll have to wait and see what comes of the letter to Minsk,' my father said soberly, 'before we can solve the mystery of this dream.'

He was right. Hard footwork alone would help us uncover the enigma of Koidanov.

Whenever Alice visited us during these weeks she too would quickly succumb to the solemnity that pervaded the house. She would sit slightly hunched and frowning at the kitchen table, rolling herself cigarette after cigarette as my father recounted each and every fragment of memory that had come to him the night before. She was galvanised by even the slightest of his recollections. She would fix him with her shrewdly observant gaze and pat his hand gently as he spoke.

My father told her about the dream of his home.

'We must send these details off to Frida Reizman immediately,' she said. 'Who knows? With some luck . . .'

I voiced my concern: 'Those little bits won't give an investigator much to go on. It could be any apple tree in any village anywhere. How many houses in Russia have apple trees in their back gardens?'

'You stay the pessimist,' she replied. 'I'm sending a telegram to Frida Reizman with news of the apple tree and the man who might have been a tanner.' Alice stubbed out the cigarette she'd been enjoying and placed its remains back in her tobacco pouch.

24

A TELEGRAM

IT had been more than six weeks since the letter and the follow-up telegram had been sent to Frida Reizman in Minsk.

One Saturday afternoon my parents and I were in Sheherazade when my father's mobile phone rang.

He pushed the answer button with his stubby arthritic fingers. 'Yes?' he said.

His face reddened suddenly.

'Truly?' he said, excitedly.

'We're in your neighbourhood now. The usual spot.'

'OK, see you soon.' My father signed off.

'Alice,' he said. 'She sounded breathless. She wants us to stay put. News from Minsk.'

Suddenly he seemed more apprehensive than excited. We sat in silence waiting for Alice. My father fidgeted with his phone while opposite me my mother tapped her fingers lightly on the table, staring into space.

Finally Alice appeared at the glass door, grinning. She hobbled across to us and, before she'd even sat down, slapped a piece of paper down on the table.

'A telegram,' she announced with finality. 'From Minsk.'

We each read it, slowly, absorbing its few words. 'Regarding the man from Koidanov with the unusual fate. A possible family member living in Minsk. A letter to Alex Kurzem will follow.'

'Who have they found?' I exclaimed. 'Who exactly? A cousin? An aunt? Who?'

My mother was slightly vexed too. 'She should've included more information rather than leave us on tenterhooks like this.'

Alice nodded in agreement.

Typically my father was the most pragmatic amongst us. 'We'll just have to be patient,' he said stoically. 'One step at a time.'

'Good God, Alex!' my mother said. 'Don't you want to know as soon as possible?'

'It says possible family member,' he replied, reaching for the telegram. 'As I said, all in good time.'

My mother and I rolled our eyes in frustration but we both knew that my father was grateful for any delay allowing him to brace himself for whatever came to light.

A week later, just after my father had left the house on a repair job, the postman delivered a letter from Minsk.

'Should we open it?' I asked.

'Keep your shirt on,' my mother said, gripping the letter tightly. 'Your father will be back shortly.'

But I could tell that she was as anxious and excited as I was.

We were in the kitchen when we heard my father come in.

'The post's on the coffee table, luv,' my mother called out.

There was silence in the next room for several moments before my father joined us.

He held the envelope aloft. 'From Minsk,' he said. 'I guess you know that already.'

My mother and I waited with bated breath, like excited schoolchildren, as my father fumbled with the envelope for several seconds before giving up.

'Here,' he said, thrusting it at me. 'Read it to Mum and me.'

I objected. I thought he should be the very first to lay eyes on its contents.

'But I can't find my reading glasses,' he protested, pretending to look for them. 'Where did I put them?'

I was sure that he was simply stalling.

'I need a cup of tea,' he said, turning to my mother.

My mother hastily prepared tea and brought it over to him.

'Are you ready now?' I asked reaching into the envelope.

'No,' he said. 'One more thing. I must let Alice know at once.'

He reached for the phone.

'Just a message for you, Alice,' he said. 'Come over as soon as you can. A letter has come from Belarus.'

'We may as well get on with it,' I said, growing impatient.

When I tore open the envelope, something fluttered to the floor. It appeared to be a photograph.

Before I could react my father bent down and snapped it up, looked at it, and went deadly pale. He stuffed it into his shirt pocket without a word.

'What have you got there, luv?' my mother asked.

'Nothing important. I'll show you later.'

My father sat down and sipped his tea while my mother stood behind him, gripping the top of his chair, eager to hear the news.

I pulled out the letter and saw that it was written in Russian. We would have to wait for Alice to arrive.

This time I called Alice's mobile number, and she picked up immediately.

'Yes,' she said. 'I've heard your father's message. I'm already crossing the Westgate bridge. I'll be with you soon.'

I hung up and relayed news of Alice's imminent arrival.

My father looked drained and decided to go to his room to rest.

'But Alice'll be here any moment,' I protested.

'Don't worry,' he replied. 'I'll listen out for her old bomb.'

My mother and I waited for Alice in the kitchen. Soon we heard the tell-tale rattle and bang of her car as it turned into our drive.

Moments later I heard my father greet Alice as he let her in.

'What's up?' I heard her reply as she hobbled into the kitchen. For an instant I was startled by her appearance: she could have easily passed for an eccentric private detective. She looked slightly dishevelled in her raincoat and carried an oversized tote bag; a lit cigarette drooped from the corner of her mouth. For an added touch of eccentricity – deliberate or not I don't know – she wore a large black fedora with a yellow feather tucked into its silk band.

Taking a long drag on her cigarette, Alice began to translate in a quiet voice.

' "Dear Alex Kurzem. It is an act of God that has brought you to us in Minsk. My name is Frida Reizman. I am an historian at a Holocaust research centre here. One morning, three weeks ago, I was at my desk at the centre, reading through the manuscript of my book when there was a knock at the door. It was a letter for me." '

'Only three weeks ago?' my father interrupted. 'That took some time to reach her.'

Alice shushed him and then continued.

' "I opened the letter and soon I couldn't believe what I was reading with my own eyes. When I had finished learning your remarkable story, I had to sit and think about it for some time. Suddenly there was another knock at the door. It was my printer-publisher Mr Erick Galperin with a printout of my book. Erick and I got down to business. After a while we took a break. I had only recently become acquainted with Erick but had to tell somebody about your extraordinary letter."

' "I told him that a man from Australia was searching for his identity. He remembered two words which might be clues, Koidanov and . . . before I could say another word Erick interrupted me. 'Koidanov?' he said, surprised. 'I was born there! My family was from there.' We were both truly amazed by this coincidence."

' "Erick's father's family all perished in the liquidation in Koidanov and he was moved by your terrible fate and the fact that your family may have died alongside his own father's original family, and worst of all, may share the same grave. Before the war Koidanov was not much bigger than a village. So if you were from Koidanov, Erick believes that your family may have known his father's first family. They might have been neighbours or visitors to each others' homes."

' "According to Erick, if you were about five when the massacre happened, then you may have even known Erick's father's three children who died that day. His father's eldest was a boy about the same age. Ilya Solomonovich Galperin was his name. Who knows, perhaps you and Ilya played together when you were young. You may even have been best friends."

' "I told Erick not to be too hopeful. But still you never know do you? Then I told Erick about the second word, Panok. Erick thought he had heard this word, but he could not remember where."

' "Erick wanted to know more about your family, and the only other thing I could tell him was that your father might have been a tanner. It was good fortune that Alice sent the telegram with the extra details . . ." '

Alice gave me a look of vindication. 'See,' she said. 'I told you every little bit helps.'

I raised my hands in surrender.

Alice adjusted the reading glasses on the end of her long nose.

'Now where was I?' she said. She began to read once again.

' "Again Erick interrupted me. He was surprised because his father, Solomon, was a tanner, too, who repaired shoes. Koidanov was a small place. It barely needed two tanners. Your fathers must have known each other even if they were in competition."'

'True,' my father interrupted. 'Surely they knew each other.'

'Listen to this!' Alice said. 'According to Erick, Solomon had a workshop next to his home where he worked on the skins.'

Alice peered over the rim of her glasses.

'Just like the little shed next to your house . . .' she commented.

'That's right!'

Alice put the letter down. My father's expression was a mixture of shock and pleasure.

'Shall I go on?' Alice asked.

'Please.'

Alice brought the letter closer to her eyes.

'Erick had the idea of sending a photo of his father to you,' Alice read. 'He hoped you might recognise his father from when you were a child.'

Alice examined the envelope. 'It's not here,' she said, shaking it vigorously.

'I have it,' my father said, removing it from his pocket. After glancing at it briefly, he passed it to my mother.

She was startled by what she saw and, with shaking hands, she passed it to me.

I looked down at the picture of a man. I was stunned and passed it quickly on to Alice who held it at arm's length and then drew it closer to her. She too was transfixed by the image in the photograph.

She pulled out a tiny magnifying glass, and held it up to the photograph, scanned it thoroughly, and finally looked up.

'I have never seen such a likeness before,' she declared.

The room was quiet for several moments.

'Does Frida give any more details about the photo?' I asked, breaking the silence.

Alice perused the letter.

' "The man is Solomon Galperin, Erick's father." We know that,' she said. 'The photo was taken in 1961. Apparently he lived all his life in Koidanov, apart from the war. Although you were only a small boy,' Alice read. 'Do you remember his face?'

My father examined the photo closely for several moments, but then shook his head.

'What about the name Galperin?' Alice asked. 'Does it ring a bell?'

My father shook his head.

I blurted out what was surely on all our minds: 'I think the man in the photograph is your father.'

'Look at the resemblance,' my mother said. 'You could be identical twins.'

My father nodded without hesitation.

'But I can't remember my father's face at all,' he said. 'Nor my mother's. It bothers me that I can't when I do remember the faces of so many of the soldiers and scenes from the war. Why can't I remember my own family?'

Unexpectedly my father had a change of heart.

'How on earth could this be my father?' he snapped. 'If the picture was taken in 1961, my father would have been long dead by then. My mother told me that he'd died long before even she and the rest of my family had perished.'

Suddenly Alice raised her hand to quieten us. 'Listen to this,' she said. 'Erick states that his father, Solomon, survived the war. Solomon fled Koidanov to join the partisans but was caught and taken to Auschwitz and later Dachau. He survived because he was a good shoemaker. After the war, when he made it home, he learnt that his entire family had perished. He remarried and he and his new wife had a son, Erick.'

'So Erick could be your half-brother,' my mother concluded. 'You might have the same father – Solomon.'

'Could your father have survived the war?' I asked my father.

He buried his face in his hands. He was completely bewildered. 'But why would my mother tell me my father was dead?'

Alice's attention shifted back to the letter which she still held in her hand. Her eyes scanned quickly down the two pages.

'Amazing,' she said.

Her eyes shifted from my father to my mother and then to me.

'Who'd have expected Erick to be in Frida's office the same day the letter sat on her desk? You'd have a greater chance of winning the lottery.'

'I think we all need a brandy,' my mother suggested and rushed to put out glasses.

While my mother poured the drinks, Alice put down the letter and slowly rolled herself a cigarette, gazing at the letter.

'Frida's included Erick's number,' she said. 'Shall we try to call him?'

'Now?'

Alice nodded.

My father appeared thrown by the suggestion.

'Strike while the iron is . . . what do they say?'

'Hot,' I offered.

Alice smirked at me.

'It's probably too late there,' my father said, hopefully.

'Not at all,' Alice said firmly, looking at her watch.

*

The call did not go smoothly. Alice had to shout down the line in an effort to make herself heard and in less than ten minutes the call had ended.

'There were such crackling noises on the line,' she complained.

'What was Erick like?' my father asked enthusiastically.

'Hard to say,' Alice replied. 'He seemed sane.'

'I told him about your resemblance to Solomon and he was baffled. Then it was strange – he had the same idea that we have. What if you are Solomon's son? That you are Ilya Solomonovich, the eldest of the Galperin children whom everyone believed had died. Ilya would have been about five years old at the time of the extermination – the same as you. Solomon had often spoken of Ilya and had laid flowers on the mass grave in memory of the boy, his wife and his other children.

'Erick got carried away with the idea and pleaded for you to come to Belarus immediately. He said that there are many things that he can do for you, Alex. He can take you to Koidanov and introduce you to people who knew your father and who probably knew you as a little boy. People who know even more than he does about the past.

'After that the line was bad. The last thing I heard him say was "Tell him to come. All will be revealed." '

We sat in silence, taking in the significance of the letter and now the call. Had we made direct contact with my father's past for the first time?

I glanced furtively at my father. He looked excited but grim.

'I'm not convinced I'm a Galperin.'

There was a note of hysteria in his voice as he continued, 'I don't know who I am. Will I ever know?'

Then he wavered again. 'Imagine if it were true,' he said, looking hopefully at each of us. 'I would have a brother. Erick would be my brother.'

We listened as he repeated the word 'brother', relishing it.

Then his caution overcame him again. 'No, it can't be,' he said. 'Perhaps Panok is my name . . .'

Finally, Alice spoke. 'There's only one thing to do,' she said. 'We have to get Alex to Koidanov.'

Then she turned to look at me. 'Any ideas, Mr Oxford?'

My mother and father both looked at me expectantly.

'Let me think about it . . .' I faltered, secretly feeling daunted by the task.

'Well, don't take too long,' Alice said with determination. 'We need action on this. Now.'

*

The letter and the phone call seemed to have ignited my father's psyche. No longer confined to his dreams, incidents and impressions of the past now flashed before him at all hours. One night in particular, my parents and I were at home watching television and he was lying on the floor in front of the fire.

Suddenly he sat upright. His face was almost apoplectic. His eyes bulged wide.

'Alex!' my mother exclaimed. 'What's wrong?'

The sound of my mother's voice calmed him.

He got up to sit on an armchair, shaking his head to rouse himself.

'I'd been asleep in a bed. Something has woken me. There's another child next to me. He must be my little brother. Then I hear a sound, this time coming from the ceiling.'

My father's eyes were feverish and, again, he spoke in the present tense.

' "Mama," I call out and my mother comes into the room. It's not really a room, it's . . . it's how do you say? – it's partitioned off from the next room by a curtain. "I can hear something," I tell her. "No," she whispers, "you must have been dreaming. Go back to sleep." She kisses me. I watch as she leaves the room.

'I hear the sound above me again. Something is moving up there. I can just make out a shadow through a gap in the curtain.'

Involuntarily my father moved his head to one side as if trying to peer through the gap from a different angle.

'Legs!' he exclaimed. 'Somebody's legs . . . a man's. They're coming out of the ceiling. They're wearing trousers and boots. I recognise them – they are my father's boots. Why are they hanging from the ceiling?

'I can hear something else now – the whispers of men's voices and my mother's but I can't see from where I am. I get up and tiptoe to the curtain. My mother's there. And a man with a beard. And my father. I am confused. I haven't seen my father for ages. My mother has told me that he is dead. But he's not. He's not! He is here in front of me. Or is he a ghost? Am I dreaming? I am frightened and return to my bed. I feel safer there.

'Now I hear the sound of footsteps coming towards me. I open my eyes. Even in the darkness I know that it's my father. He's hovering above me but he's not a ghost.

'He strokes my hair.

' "Papa?" I cannot resist saying his name.

'He doesn't answer me.

'He touches my cheek.

'He kisses my forehead.

' "Goodbye," he whispers.

'My father is turning away from me. I watch him leave the room. What is happening? I get up and cross the room to the curtain. I peep through the gap. I cannot see clearly so I rub my eyes.

'The man with a beard is still here. I know him but I can't remember who he is.

'My mother is now at the door. She is waving goodbye to somebody!

'Wait! It's father and the man with the beard. Where are they going in the middle of the night?

'My mother is closing the door.

' "Mama?" I call out from where I am standing, partly hidden by the curtain.

'She turns.

' "Papa, I saw Papa."

' "Papa is not here."

'She takes me back to my bed. She hugs me.'

My mother and I sat in stunned silence while my father, exhausted, stared blankly into space, seemingly trapped between the past and the present.

My mother, ever practical, rose silently and went into the kitchen. After several moments she returned with a mug of tea for my father. My father gulped at it greedily as if it were a magic potion that would deliver him with speed and finality to the present.

'I've got to get to Koidanov,' my father said.

'As soon as possible,' added my mother.

PART III

25

OXFORD (2)

T WO weeks after the letter arrived I found myself waiting with my parents at Melbourne airport for my flight to Oxford to be called. The plan was for me to organise the journey to Belarus, and Latvia as well, which my father was keen to visit – he had not seen Riga since he'd fled with the Dzenis family in late 1944. My parents would join me in Oxford and then we would make the journey together.

Even though I'd returned to Oxford on numerous occasions it was torturous to sit opposite them in the airport coffee shop, laughing and joking in spite of the difficulty I had leaving them. I worried that it was the worst possible moment for me to abandon them – for that is how it felt to me – to the ravages of my father's memories.

Nearly thirty hours later I turned the key in the door to my digs in Oxford. Exhausted, I dumped my bags in the hall, collected my post off the mat, and went through to the kitchen where I poured myself a glass of water. Then I sprawled out on the sofa where I began to open the letters. I had been gone for nearly three months and there were cards from friends and notices from the bank and from the dentist reminding me of an appointment I'd forgotten in my rushed departure for Australia. Nothing of any importance.

It was then that I noticed the message light flashing on the answermachine. I reached across and pressed the button. The machine replayed a dozen or so messages. On the final one I heard my father's voice.

'Mark?' he said. 'You're not back yet? Call me when you get in.'

My heart skipped a beat.

I looked at my watch. It was now 10 p.m. in Melbourne. My parents would still be awake. I sighed, picked up the phone, and dialled my parents' number.

My mother answered. I could tell instantly that something was up. Her voice lacked its usual melodic tone.

'You got home all right, luv?' she asked.

'No worries, Mum,' I replied, and then said slightly impatiently: 'Dad's called already. Can I speak to him?'

'He's sleeping,' she said.

'OK, I won't disturb him,' I said.

'He was so shaken that I had to give him a sedative.'

'What's happened?' I said, panicking.

'I shouldn't have said anything. He's fine. You're not to worry yourself. Call him tomorrow, luv.'

'Will do. Take care.'

I heard her voice trail off, subdued and tentative as she said, 'Goodbye.'

But I did worry. All afternoon as I dozed and slowly unpacked I counted the minutes until it was morning in Melbourne and I could call my father again. I pictured my mother alone in the house with my sleeping father. There was nobody there to support her. It would not be the last time that I would have a sudden, almost inexpressible realisation of how hard all this was for her, and how frequently friends and family would overlook the burden that had been placed on her – the man she had been married to for over forty years was in one sense now a stranger to her.

At eight in the morning, Melbourne time, I called again. The phone had barely rung before my father picked it up. He sounded groggy. He coughed and then began.

'Somebody called,' he said. 'We'd barely come in the front door after seeing you off when the phone rang. I picked it up and at the same time, I don't know why, my intuition perhaps, I switched on the speaker-phone so that your mother could listen in. It was a man's voice. I didn't know who he was but I did recognise the accent – it was Latvian.

' "You were the little boy who was helped by the Latvian soldiers, weren't you?" he asked, without introducing himself.

' "Yes. So the story goes. Who's speaking please?"

'There was silence at the other end of the line. Then he spoke again.

' "You can call me Daugavas."

' "How do you know about me?"

' "Many Latvians know about you," he laughed wryly. "Recently it's all we talk about. Some say you are destroying the good reputation of our community."

' "For telling the truth about what happened to me?"

' "I don't wish to argue with you. Before I go any further with this I need your word – this conversation will be confidential."

' "I cannot give guarantees. I will try, that's all. What does this concern?"

'Suddenly the man seemed nervous and hesitant, I thought he would hang up. I waited patiently, put no pressure on him. My strategy worked. He began to speak of his own volition.

' "Recently I was back in Riga. One night at dinner I began to tell people about a man living in Melbourne, you, and your association with Latvia. They were kind to you, weren't they?" he asked. "The ones who looked after you."

'I was embarrassed. "I guess so," I replied. "I have always said that."

' "When I finished your story," he said, "one woman there told me that she'd seen a photo of a young boy soldier standing among Latvian and German soldiers. The photo was in the house of her husband's grand-mother in Munich. This woman is the widow of a high-ranking German soldier during the war. Once when he came back from active duty, he brought this photo. He told her, 'This boy, he's a good luck charm!' "

' "It could be me," I said to the caller. "So many people wanted to take my photo."

' "Can I see the photograph?" I asked. "When can I meet you?"

'With that, his mood changed. I sensed his reluctance. I shouldn't have pushed him.

' "I must go," he said, and abruptly hung up.

'My mind was restless all night. I had to find this man. Then first thing yesterday morning the telephone rang again.

'I recognised his voice immediately.

' "Mr Daugavas," I said. I decided to confront him on the spot.

'I knew that he must've been torn about letting me see the photograph, otherwise why would he have called back. I adopted a reasonable tone. "Please don't hang up, sir," I said. "I understand your predicament and I think you understand mine. I want to see the photo. I have a right to see it."

'Then there was a long silence at the other end of the line. At first I thought he'd hung up again, but then I heard him sigh heavily.

' "Look. Can't you understand? This is difficult for me. I want to help you, but I don't want to be involved in any trouble."

' "Why? It's only a photo."

' "It's a shocking photograph."

' "I don't understand."

' "The image is a violent one of you laden with weapons. If people see it they'll start asking questions. Who are these men with this little boy? What are they doing? What are they thinking? Why is this child in their midst? Are they members of an extermination troop? Now do you see?"

' "This can be just between us."

'The man seemed to be thinking.

'Then he spoke. "I can't take the risk," he said. "I'm sorry."

' "Please sir, hear me out," I pleaded. "It's my past, that photo. Please. I have so few photos, so few things from anyone who cared for me at that time. And the soldiers they did care for me so well you know, they loved me like their own. They always protected me. Fed me first. Gave me water. You know what I would do for them? In the summer, on patrol, I would pick strawberries for them. From among the bodies of dead soldiers rotting in the fields. And such delicious strawberries. So big. I always came back with handfuls and I passed them out. One for each soldier. That was one of my jobs. You see I was one of them. Why would I betray them? I would be betraying myself if I did." I went on like this, I can't remember every word exactly, trying to convince him.

' "Let me think about this. I promise I will call you back."

' "When?"

' "Today. Before three. You have my word."

'He did keep his word. He called back after lunch. He agreed to meet me but only on one condition. I could see the photograph but I could not keep it. Why let me see it, but not have it? I decided to agree and argue my case when I came face to face with him. Amazingly he wanted to meet that night as if we were secret agents or something. I was flabbergasted. He suggested that I wait outside Luna Park, knowing that an amusement park would be closed on a mid-week evening and that the area around it would be deserted.

'I went there at the appointed time, and just as I suspected there wasn't a soul around. It was a humid summer's evening, but with rain pouring down so heavily that I could barely see a thing. I had to keep the wipers on.

'I saw a car pull slowly into the kerb; its headlights blinded me for a moment. Then I saw a tall man get out and head towards the entrance. You remember it, don't you? The giant open mouth, illuminated with enormous white teeth.'

My father was describing the gateway to the Park.

'I waited to make sure it was him. In my rear-view mirror I watched the man pace up and down. Then I got out and went over. I'd never met him before. He didn't say a word to me. He simply removed an envelope from inside his coat and pulled out a photo. Immediately I reached for it but he stepped back.

'He shook his head. "I can't let you have it," he said.

'He held the photo aloft for me to see it. There was enough light from the entrance for me to tell instantly that it was me. I wanted to examine it more closely but the man kept a firm grip on it. He wouldn't let me touch it at all.

'I don't know – something came over me – I felt the photo belonged to me. It was of me – and this stranger had decided I shouldn't have it.

'I snatched the photo from him. He was shocked. He hadn't expected that kind of response from me. I was too fast for him. I made for the car as quickly as possible, got in, and locked the door.

'He appeared at the window, breathless with anger. He stood by my car for a while, trying to bargain with me, but I refused point-blank to hand back the photo. Eventually he gave up.

'I watched the tail lights of his car disappear into the distance, and then headed off in the opposite direction.

'Mum was waiting up for me. I got out the photo to show her. It's terrible.' My father described the image to me as best he could.

I could barely believe what I heard, and raged inwardly at these men – both at those who posed for the photograph, and the man who took it.

'Do you recognise any of the men?'

'The man standing beside me with his arm around me. His name, if I remember him correctly, was Erzum. Captain Erzum.'

I grabbed a pen and made a note of the name.

'Anybody else? Sergeant Kulis?'

'No.'

'Lobe?'

'No . . . but that doesn't mean they weren't around. Who knows?'

My father paused.

'You know, I think that this is one of the photos taken on that day I saw the synagogue burnt.'

'Is there anything visible in the background?' I asked, hoping that there would be something that could identify where it was taken.

'Nothing,' my father replied. 'Only the side of a train carriage. It's a terrible photo but I suppose it's better than nothing. A remnant from my past.' He laughed bitterly.

For a moment a terrible chill passed through me. But I didn't dare ask my father any more. I would see the photograph in good time.

'One thing is certain, Dad,' I said. 'You've got to be careful who you show this photo to.'

He nodded. 'There'd be some who'd use it against me,' he said soberly, 'no matter what the truth behind the image.'

In the weeks following my return to Oxford I set about organising my parents' journey. I had no idea how long it would take to put everything in order. It was winter now, and that would make travelling difficult. I hoped to be in Belarus and Latvia by April or May, when the better weather had arrived.

It was during this period that I arranged to catch up with my acquaintance, Elli. I'd kept in touch with her while I was in Australia. I suggested the coffee shop in Blackwell's.

I arrived before her and found a small table by the window overlooking Broad Street.

Suddenly a shadow crossed my table. I looked up to find Elli.

'Dearie,' she said. 'It's good to see you back.'

She touched my arm warmly. 'I've been worried about you. All the pressure you're under.'

'A relief to be in a quieter place for a while,' I mumbled, then smiled.

'How are your parents these days?'

'They're surviving.'

'That sounds grim.'

I nodded, playing with my coffee cup.

'If there is anything I can do?'

'There is . . .'

I decided to tell her about the photograph.

Elli, as usual, proved to be a good listener. When I had finished, she was quiet for several moments.

'You don't have a copy of it?' she asked.

'No. My parents will be here in the spring though. If my father agrees I'll show it to you then.'

'Your father should guard it closely. If anybody got their hands on it . . .' she said. She didn't finish her thought.

She looked at her watch. 'I must go, dearie,' she announced. 'Things to do. Let me know if there are any more developments with the photograph.'

She bent forward and pecked me on the cheek.

I watched Elli as she made her way through the now crowded cafe and towards the exit.

Moments later I gazed down at the street and noticed Elli as she hurried across Broad Street. It hadn't been my intention to spy on her, yet I couldn't help but observe her as she stopped to greet two men who had clearly been waiting for her on the steps in front of the Bodleian Library. They shook hands and all three then headed off in the direction of the High Street, talking animatedly amongst themselves.

For just an instant Elli turned her head slightly and glanced back in the direction of Blackwell's with a quizzical, slightly suspicious look. I jerked my face away from the window. I didn't want her to know that I didn't trust her.

Some months later, by early spring of the following year, having organised my parents' journey to Oxford in May, I turned my attention to the visit to Belarus and, most importantly, Koidanov. I'd called my father to see if he could cajole Alice into joining us on the trip.

He picked up the phone but he was not his usual bright self. His tone was cautious.

'What's wrong?' I asked.

'Nothing.'

'You sure?'

He hesitated.

'Somebody's been calling . . .'

'Daugavas again?'

'No. They won't identify themselves.'

I took a deep breath.

'Only the one person?' I asked.

'No. Different people.'

'What do they want?'

'Just to warn me to keep quiet about the Latvians. That I shouldn't bite the hand that fed me. One told me that consequences will be bad for us and that the world would judge me as a Nazi. Would I or my family be able to live with that?'

My father sighed wearily. 'It's got to the point where your mum won't answer the phone.'

'Have you told the police?'

'No. What can they do about it?'

'Put a trace on the calls for a start.'

My father coughed nervously. 'It'll be all right . . .'

'You've got to tell them.'

'Nobody will harm us.'

I argued with my father for several minutes, but the more I did so, the more obstinate he became. In the end I gave up.

'Whoever they are,' he said with firmness, 'they'll tire of doing this nonsense.'

I hoped he was right.

The next day, in disturbing synchronicity with events in Melbourne, I too began to receive mysterious telephone calls. Whenever I picked up the receiver, there were no direct threats at the other end of the line, only silence.

This happened about a dozen times; usually I would probably not have given these calls too much thought but now I found them unnerving – I suspected that they might be related to my father's story and the appearance of the photograph. What did these people want from my father and me?

Matters escalated over the following week. The calls had stopped suddenly when I had a strange encounter in the Bodleian Library.

I was standing in a queue to use a photocopier, absorbed in a book and paying no attention to those around me.

Suddenly, I heard a man's voice with an American accent directly behind me. 'The worst time of the day,' he said.

'Sorry?' I looked up from my book.

'The queue.'

The man was probably in his late twenties. I nodded to him in a not unfriendly way and returned to my book. But I had the uncanny sensation that his eyes were staring into my back.

'Reading history?' I heard him ask.

I turned and nodded once again.

He squinted at the cover of the book.

' "Police brigades in the Second World War." That's a specialised topic,' he said.

'Some independent research,' I explained.

'You Belarussian?' He asked, catching sight of the book's subtitle which referred to Belarussia and the Ukraine.

'My father is,' I replied.

'A little family history then?'

'You could say that.'

'My family were Jews from the Ukraine,' he said. 'Many died at the hands of the police brigades in operation there.'

'I'm sorry to hear that,' I said. 'My father's family died under similar conditions in Belarus.'

'Your father is from Minsk?'

'No. Most likely from a town not far from there. Dzerzhinsk.'

'Most likely?'

'It's a long story.'

I excused myself. I was beginning to feel uncomfortable with his intrusiveness.

'No matter,' he answered. 'Another time?'

I nodded and turned once again to where I had left off in my book.

Then I heard his voice again and saw his proffered hand in front of me. 'Samuel Schwartz,' he said.

'Mark Kurzem.'

At that moment a copier became free and I dashed for it, relieved to have broken contact.

About thirty minutes later as I was coming down the stairs in front of the library someone called my name. It was Samuel Schwartz. He caught up with me.

'Hello!' he said, full of cheer. 'We meet again!'

He glanced at his watch.

'You feel like grabbing a bite to eat?'

I didn't want to but he caught me off guard. I couldn't think of an excuse quickly enough. 'That'd be nice,' I replied.

He looked around.

'King's Arms?' he suggested.

We crossed to the pub on the opposite corner.

The King's Arms was crawling with students at this hour but I managed to find a quiet corner while Schwartz fetched drinks.

He put down two pints of beer even though I'd asked for a cola. He sat down closely beside me and raised his glass in a toast.

'To poor old Belarus and the Ukraine!'

'So how's the research?' he enquired.

'So-so.'

'You're not English, are you?'

'Australian.'

'Ah. From down under.'

'It's all a matter of perspective,' I replied.

He laughed.

'And you?'

'The States. New York.'

He took a sip of his beer. 'This topic you're looking at . . .'

'Yes?' I gave him a questioning look.

'The shadow never leaves you, does it? Even if you're from a later generation.'

I nodded.

'So how is the situation in Australia with these war criminals?'

I shrugged.

'Australia seems to be full of them,' he commented. 'Judging by their record to date, the Australian authorities haven't been keen to prosecute. The last wave – the vicious camp guards, the middle-ranking officers, the Balts – were given free entry to Australia and allowed to construct new identities, or blatantly flaunt their old ones. The blessing of Australia, its freedom, bearing a poisonous fruit.'

'You seem to know a lot about it,' I said.

'I follow the news. Besides these criminals are part of my history,' he replied pensively. 'I find myself thinking about what I might be able to do in hunting them down. Become a Mossad agent!' He laughed self mockingly. But I could feel him shrewdly evaluating my reaction.

'Why not try the Wiesenthal Centre?' I suggested, lamely.

'A tough job. A necessary one, don't you agree?' he said, as if seriously considering my suggestion.

'Of course.'

'One is morally obliged to help in any search if one has information to offer.'

He glanced at me meaningfully.

I understood then where his conversation was headed.

I hadn't been able to place this man but was certain that I'd seen him before.

Then it struck me. He was the younger of the two men I'd seen with Elli on the steps outside the Bodleian. I dismissed the thought. I'm becoming paranoid, I told myself. Whether this was the case or not, I felt uncomfortable in his company.

'Thanks for the beer, Samuel,' I said, rising from my seat.

Schwartz was nonplussed but reached out to shake my hand.

'I hope we can meet again soon,' he said.

'Yes,' I responded non-committally.

What I hoped would be my last glimpse of Schwartz was of him seated, his hands clasped and resting on the table, smiling benignly at me.

Three days after this incident, Elli invited me for dinner at her house. I wanted to steer clear of her but she insisted and I accepted reluctantly.

'My father will be here as well,' she said. 'He's just arrived this morning from Israel for the weekend.'

As she led me into her dining room that night I immediately recognised her father as the other man I'd seen with her and Schwartz outside the library days earlier. Over dinner he questioned me vigorously about my father's story, fishing for details, until I felt that I was being interrogated for some hidden purpose. He grew frustrated as I began to resist his probing. We had barely finished the meal when I pleaded off, saying that I had a fierce headache. Rejecting their offers of medication and assistance, I quickly exited and hailed a taxi.

The taxi dropped me in front of my house. I noticed a car parked on the other side of the street, facing into the traffic. This was not unusual, but my senses, already on the alert after dinner, registered that the man – it was too dark to notice anything other than that he appeared youngish – behind the steering wheel was closely watching my house.

I noticed that he sat more upright as I made my way along the path to the front door.

I let myself in, went upstairs and, without turning on any lights, peered through a crack in the curtains of an upstairs window.

He strained to look up at the house and I saw his face at the windscreen. It was Samuel Schwartz.

I decided to confront him and headed downstairs. But by the time I had fumbled with the door's inside lock and dashed out to the street, his car had disappeared.

I never saw Elli's father or Samuel Schwartz again. I never met with Elli again.

In the days that followed I would occasionally spot her on the street in the city centre, but was careful to avoid her. She called me a few times as well; I remained friendly but distant.

Elli gradually disappeared completely from my life.

I was glad to be free of her. I realised how naive I had been. I knew nothing about her background. I was to learn later that her father had been an investigator for the Israeli intelligence service. I wondered how much of the intrigue that had developed and would continue to emerge had been triggered by my revelations to her.

On the same evening of Elli's dinner, long after Schwartz's car had disappeared, my telephone rang.

Before I could even say hello, I heard my father's voice at the other end of the line.

'Mark?' he said. 'Are you there?'

'This is late to call,' I replied.

'The house was broken into last night,' my father blurted out immediately. 'We'd been out and when we got home we noticed from the car that there was a light on in the bedroom. Your mum was sure we hadn't left it on by mistake. I told her to wait in the car while I unlocked the front door quietly. I opened it just a fraction and the cats flew out with their tails on end. I got the fright of my life. I opened the door further and called out. There was no reply. I went into the hallway and I could see immediately that somebody had searched the living room. All our papers and documents were strewn everywhere. The bedroom had been completely ransacked too. The lock on my wardrobe door was shattered and all the contents dragged out. The strange thing is that nothing of value was taken. Not even our camera, television or video or mum's jewellery. Only our papers had been gone through.'

'Did you call the police?'

'Nah . . .'

I'd had this same conversation with my father some time earlier.

'Whoever it was, they were looking for something but not valuables. Probably the photograph . . .'

I agreed. The culprit would not have known that my father kept any item to do with his identity, including his photographs, in his brown case.

'Still, you need to report it,' I insisted.

My father ignored what I had just said.

'Look, don't worry about things here,' he said. 'I'll keep you informed.'

With that, he pleaded fatigue and hung up.

Now it seemed that with the appearance of the photograph my parent's situation had escalated to one of physical danger. Over the last week or so I had come to feel that the task of uncovering my father's past also involved protecting him, and my mother, from something that I wasn't yet able to identify clearly.

Although I had not seen the photograph, its existence unsettled me more than any other of my father's mementoes. How many more images of my father were floating out there in people's wardrobes, cupboards and photo albums, the secret storehouses of their past?

The question was answered sooner than I imagined.

By the time my mother and father arrived late the following week, another surprise was in store for me. A sympathetic letter from an elderly woman had reached my father the day before he and my mother left Melbourne. It was from Ventspils – a regional city in north-western Latvia. She made no mention of how the photos came to be in her possession, only that she felt my father should have them.

He passed me the envelope.

It contained a series of four photographs of my father in his SS uniform in the company of his 'rescuer' Sergeant Jekabs Kulis. The sergeant and my father were pictured tending what initially seemed to be a small garden plot in a camp. My father told me that it had been taken at Volhov, south of Leningrad. It must have been autumn in 1943 before Lobe sent him back to Riga for trying to escape from the front.

'Look,' he said, placing the tip of his index finger closer to the flowers.

They were arranged to depict the emblem of the Latvian SS.

Troubling as these images were, they did not have as disquieting an effect as the photograph I had been waiting to see: my father posing with pistol at his side and rifle slung over his shoulder in the midst of other members of the 18th Battalion.

Despite the physical menace that hovered in the background I felt optimistic for the first time since my father's last visit to Oxford. From nothing at all we'd unearthed a village where my father might have spent the first five years of his life. And we had made contact with a man, Erick Galperin, who might turn out to be his half-brother.

These were joyful discoveries, but they were tinged with sadness – a haunting reminder of what had been lost – brother, sister, mother, aunts, grandparents, uncles, everyone who made little Ilya who he was.

We had learnt later from Erick that his father, Solomon Galperin, had returned to the family home, hoping to find his wife and children, including his son Ilya Galperin, my father. Solomon had stayed in Koidanov until his death in 1975. If my father had spoken sooner of his past then father and son might have been reunited.

There were other painful memories and realities to be confronted.

Alongside the potential rediscovery of a family home there was the topography of the ghetto in which my father's family were incarcerated, and the mass grave where my father had witnessed his family's extermination.

Still, I had learnt something of my father's resilience in the past months. While what was happening to him was extracting a heavy emotional toll, he maintained that this would provide him with ballast for what lay ahead.

I tried to distract myself from my concerns by focusing on the minutiae of our travel plans until our early morning departure for Minsk.

26

BELARUS

OUR plane circled above Minsk airport waiting for permission to land. As we descended we saw a number of planes dotted around the perimeter of the main runway, many of them rusty and dilapidated and all partly dismantled for their spare parts.

Erick Galperin was waiting for us in the Arrivals hall. He was modestly dressed in a suit that matched my father's but had seen better days. He stepped forward shyly to greet my father and then presented my mother with flowers. There were numerous introductions to be made. My father introduced me to Erick and his wife, Sonya, who in turn introduced us to their children, Dimitri and Irena, my cousins.

Matters grew more confusing as we were then presented with a procession of individuals who all claimed to be distantly related to my father. An elderly woman named Luba, an English teacher from a town near Minsk, introduced herself to my father as 'your father's wife's cousin's daughter'. My father smiled politely but there was a glimmer of amusement in his eyes as he leant across and whispered to me, 'God forbid. What have you got me into?'

'No,' I countered, 'this is your family. You got me into this!'

When our entourage finally exited to the forecourt we were faced with our transportation for the visit: an old blue minibus, decorated with polka-dot curtains, plastic flowers and party lights, flashing on and off in what seemed to be a gesture of welcome.

The driver stood proudly next to the rear door and with a wave of his hand beckoned us to climb on board. The interior was also decked out in a vivid blue colour and was smothered in the overpowering scent of air freshener. My mother retched involuntarily.

Seated to the rear of the van was a young woman, in her early twenties, who was chewing gum. She was blonde, courtesy of a bottle, and wore wraparound dark sunglasses.

'Hello,' she said in languorous English. 'I am Natasha, a friend of Erick and your interpreter. I've been waiting for you.' She peered over the rim of her sunglasses and continued to chew gum as she offered us her hand.

With a slight pop from the exhaust, the bus moved forward jauntily on to the highway to Minsk.

The road was deserted for the entire journey apart from the occasional horse and cart moving slowly along its dusty shoulder. Erick, speaking Russian, pointed out sights to us en route as Natasha, acting as sultry as she could, gave desultory and dubious interpretations of Erick's words. My mother held her hand above her face and rolled her eyes at me. This very serious visit was becoming more surreal by the moment.

As we entered downtown Minsk we were rescued from Natasha's commentary by the driver, who turned on the sound system. In an instant, the van was transformed into a mobile disco as Russian pop blared out through loudspeakers as if to announce our arrival to the population of Minsk. Judging from the reactions of people we passed by on the side of the street, Minsk certainly knew we were there – pedestrians turned to see where such a racket was coming from, and when they spotted the bus, they pointed at us and burst out laughing.

We eventually stopped in front of a vast run-down Soviet-era hotel. A flashing neon sign spelt out 'Hotel Planeta and Casino' in bright red letters.

'It looks more like a brothel,' said my mother.

We checked in and with Erick's help found our rooms. Our floor was guarded by a large elderly woman, the perfect *babushka*. She was the first of many such porters we would meet, ensconced on a sofa opposite the lift doors on our floor.

She gave us an appraising look, nodded dourly and returned to her knitting.

The next morning I got up early for our journey to Koidanov, about twenty miles to the south-west of Minsk, and made my way down to the hotel foyer. My father was standing at the hotel's panoramic window, gazing at the view of downtown Minsk in the near distance. There were low-lying buildings, mostly modern but punctuated by the odd piece of Soviet monumentalism and the occasional pre-war construction that had survived the devastation of the German invaders.

Nearby I saw Erick standing with my mother and an attractive, vivacious woman.

'I'm Galina,' she said. 'Your new interpreter.' I was surprised. She explained that she was to replace Natasha, our Mata Hari from the previous evening. Natasha had been 'fired' and, mysteriously, no explanation was forthcoming. (Later I cornered Galina to find out the reason and Galina had merely said the word 'vodka' and mimed swilling from a bottle.) Galina turned out to be an excellent replacement. Quite the opposite of Natasha, she didn't chew gum or wear dark glasses. There was nothing of the vamp about her. She was forthright and spoke flawless and idiomatic English.

As we walked toward the bus, I saw the driver lean into the front cabin and turn on the flashing rooflights. He then looked at us gleefully, giving us a thumbs-up sign and hoping for our approval.

'Tell him to turn off the lights,' my father whispered to me as I jumped into the front seat beside the driver.

I leant across to the driver and pointed upwards to indicate the roof.

'*Da! Da!*' He answered, beaming proudly. 'Beautiful.'

He'd misunderstood me and turned a switch that made the lights flash faster.

'Beautiful,' the driver repeated.

'Off!' I persisted.

My mother leant forward. 'Don't hurt his feelings,' she said, 'or he won't take us anywhere.'

The driver started the engine and for a moment the entire vehicle was blanketed in exhaust fumes.

My mother reached for a handkerchief to cover her mouth. 'We're all going to die,' she said darkly.

The engine rattled loudly and with a few jerks we took off into the traffic.

After ten minutes or so on a narrow highway we came to a turn-off with a battered sign saying 'Dzerzhinsk 14'. At first sight it was difficult to gain any impression of what might make Dzerzhinsk distinct. As we drove through the industrial sprawl on its outskirts it seemed merely to epitomise a drab industrial Soviet town. And with its expanse of grey concrete public housing it was clear that Dzerzhinsk had expanded since the war.

'Not far now,' Erick declared as we wound our way through streets, dodging the odd horse and cart as well as dilapidated cars and trucks. Then without warning we came upon an enclave of old, colourfully paint-ed wooden houses with carved shuttered windows, on half-paved streets. 'This neighbourhood was the village before the war,' Galina translated for Erick.

I cast a furtive glance at my father. He was staring out of the window pensively, his hand held to his cheek. This gesture was to become habitual during the week of our journey. Sometimes he would instantly recognise the material world of his past. At other times, however, he would withdraw into himself, holding his hand to his cheek, only to re-emerge moments later either claiming or rejecting what he had just seen as part of his own history.

'Dad?' I whispered, lightly touching his arm. I didn't want to startle him.

He didn't respond.

My mother gently grasped his elbow so that he snapped out of his dream-like state.

His eyes were intensely blue and alive with curiosity.

'Do you recognise anything?' my mother asked.

My father shook his head.

'Not anything specific but it all seems very familiar.'

Erick leant across to the driver, shouting instructions for him to pull over. He jumped out of the rear of the minibus and beckoned us all to join him on the deserted street. It was mid-morning and the houses presented closed faces to the world. But when I turned around unexpectedly I saw several curtains twitch. Our arrival had not gone unnoticed.

Erick looked at my father.

'This is the street you grew up on,' he said. 'October Street.'

My father turned slowly in a circle again lightly touching his cheek. 'I just don't know,' he said.

Erick grasped my father's hand and led him two houses further down the street. We followed.

'You grew up in this house,' Erick stated emphatically, pointing at the house in front of us. There was little to distinguish this house from any of the others in the row.

'Here?' My father was surprised.

Erick nodded his head several times.

My father was silent as he examined the exterior of the house. He approached the front fence and stared even more intently at the building before him. Erick joined my father.

'Your home!' I heard Erick insist.

My father turned to my mother and me. He gave a shrug, looking bewildered; then he came over to us.

'I don't remember this place,' he said in a dispirited tone.

'Perhaps it's been altered,' my mother suggested.

'That's right,' I added, trying to sound encouraging.

But my father remained doubtful. 'I don't remember,' he repeated.

Erick must have sensed the gist of our exchange because he became slightly agitated and began to repeat 'your house' over and over.

His insistence only confused my father even more, so that he retreated into himself, uttering in a low voice, 'My home was different. It had a drive down one side where my father had a cart and next to that there was a shed where he worked and the apple tree that I used to climb. I remember that clearly.'

His recollection made him more resolute. 'No,' he said. 'This is not the house I grew up in. It's the wrong house.'

'Are you absolutely sure, Dad?' I asked.

'Absolutely,' he said slowly.

I was disappointed for my father, and for all of us, but I admired his faith in his own memories, and his refusal to yield to the incredible pressure we all felt to confirm Erick as his half-brother.

Everybody remained still, waiting for him to make the next move. My father shook his head and looked away from the source of his disappointment. I watched as he crossed to the other side of the street.

With a subtle nod he beckoned me over.

'I must be a Panok after all,' he said with finality. 'Not a Galperin. I hoped for all our sakes that this would work out. We'll have to start all over again.'

I felt grim but my father didn't seem to notice. He was immersed in his own train of thought.

'What can I say to Erick?' he said with compassion in his voice. 'He was so happy to find he had a brother. Did you see his face? This will break his heart.'

And I had seen my father's face. Despite his reservations, I knew that he too had hoped that some of his early childhood might be returned to him. Something had to be done to salvage the immediate situation. We couldn't simply turn around, get back in the car, and with a brief apology about having made a mistake, make a quick exit from Belarus.

I returned to Erick, who was still waiting in front of the house.

'You grew up here after the war?' I asked through Galina.

'Yes,' Erick replied, shifting on the spot and not looking at me. I wondered what the matter was, and then immediately reprimanded myself – he must have been as disheartened as my father.

'Your father didn't change houses when he came back from the war?' I persisted.

'No,' he retorted, now slightly belligerent and pointing at the house. 'He returned to this house where I was born.'

'When did your father sell it?'

'In the early seventies when he got sick. He came to live with us in Minsk until he died.'

'Who lives there now?'

'I don't know,' Erick replied.

The glimmer of a scowl crossed his face. I decided to let the matter drop partly because my father was now moving slowly along the street, looking in all directions. His expression changed, becoming more alert. He stopped. He had seen something that the rest of us could not.

'Over there seems familiar,' he said, pointing further up the street.

My father headed off towards an intersection, where he again came to a halt. He turned to look at us.

'I know this,' he said about the intersecting street. 'It goes down to the village hall, I am certain of it.'

My father smiled broadly.

'I remember the hall,' he said. 'That's where I went to see a film once, when a travelling show came to town. I went with another boy, my friend. We walked down the hill together, hand in hand. I can't see his face or remember his name. But I do remember that my father tossed me a few coins for an ice cream from the man who stood in front of the hall. That was the first time I ever tasted ice cream.'

My father forged ahead.

A few metres further into that street we came to another intersection. My father stopped dead in his tracks.

We waited in silence.

'This is the way the soldiers . . .' he said, staring down the path before him. There was no need to complete the sentence.

He was visibly shaken but after several moments he seemed to gather himself. With a wave of his hand he motioned for us to follow him and set off at speed along the path. We hastened after him.

About two hundred metres further along, the path opened up into a grassy space about the size of a football pitch.

'That's where it happened,' he said in a low voice.

My father led the way forward but he had lost his vigour. He walked with trepidation, almost tiptoeing, as if he was creeping up on the scene from over fifty years ago and he did not want the soldiers to notice him.

He turned at one point and summoned us to keep up as if we were reluctant tourists who had suddenly lost their taste for the journey ahead and begun to dawdle.

But there was no going back.

He came to a halt. His eyes were empty, and he had forgotten that we were standing right beside him. He appeared to recognise a topography from the past, and began to make comments aloud, as if confirming what he saw to another person.

'Yes,' he said. 'This is it . . .'

He looked back up the path he had just taken.

'It's strange,' he said, suddenly becoming aware of us. 'I remember being led down that path towards the soldiers. But it was steeper before so I could see what was happening ahead of us. I was holding my mother's hand and my little brother's as well. But I'm confused. I was with them but I didn't go to my death with them. Something must have happened to have stopped the executions that day, but for the life of me I have no memory of what it was.'

My father turned in all directions.

'Over there,' he said, pointing at a track off to the right. 'That's the direction I came from when I ran away from home. It happened during the night after we'd been led down the hill, after my mother had told me that we were all going to die in the morning.'

He headed over to the path and began to retrace his steps from the night of his escape. He walked tentatively across the open space as if trying to find his way in the dark.

'Up there,' he said, this time pointing off slightly to the left. 'That's where I headed – up the hill and into the trees.'

We all turned our heads in that direction. Indeed there was a hillock with a few trees at its peak.

My father appeared to forget about us once again and strode across to the hill. Though I felt slightly ashamed to do so, I hurried ahead of the others so that I could continue to 'eavesdrop' on his words.

'Not as steep as I remember,' he said. 'It seemed like a mountain at the time. I climbed as fast as my legs could take me.'

My father stopped and stared back down the slope with a frown on his face. But he was unaware of the scene unfolding in front of him: my mother had run out of breath and was now struggling to climb the slope.

Fortunately at that moment I saw Galina and Erick come to my mother's aid and together they made their way slowly in our direction

By this point my father had reached the top of the hillock, and hand to cheek, stood very still looking down over the vista below us.

He nodded grimly. 'Yes,' he said. 'Yes.'

At that moment the others reached us.

'You OK, Mum?' I asked.

She nodded, still quite breathless.

'Trees, Erick,' my father called out. 'Were there more trees here?'

My father hadn't even noticed that my mother had joined him. And even though it was not intentional, for a moment I was annoyed by his lack of regard for her condition.

'Yes,' Erick replied. 'I used to play up here as a child sometimes. They removed many of the trees years ago.'

My father was silent and we waited for him to speak.

'In the morning I saw the people being led from over there. Near that cottage. I was peering between the trees. They were lined up on that hill as the soldiers pushed and prodded them down in groups,' my father said, indicating the path we had taken earlier.

'Then I saw my mother and the children and . . .'

My father gasped as if the air had been violently knocked out of him. 'The rest of my family were among them and they were almost there . . . the pit.'

My father took a deep breath.

'My mother was holding my brother and sister. She looked away from what was going to happen to her and that's when I am sure she saw me up amongst the trees. For a split second I saw her eyes. She recognised me.

'I am sure that she must have been beside herself with worry when she'd woken in the morning and found me gone. At least she knew I was alive, for what that was worth . . .'

I stared at my father who seemed to be in a state of shock.

'I bit my hand not to cry out,' he said in a strangled whisper. I saw him raise his hand and bite it, as if reliving the horrific scene. A trickle of blood dripped down his wrist and on to the cuff of his shirt.

My mother had noticed too at the same instant.

'Alex!' she cried out but he didn't hear her.

Panicked, she dashed forward and began to shake him.

'Alex!' She was alarmed. 'Stop it! Please stop it, Alex!'

My father returned to us. His face was ashen and he seemed fragile and disorientated. He stared down at his bleeding hand.

My mother pulled out her handkerchief and gently bandaged it, while my father stood like a helpless child.

'C'mon, luv, let's get out of here,' my mother said, putting her arm in his and moving him away from the edge of the hill.

My father didn't resist.

As we made our way down the hill Erick pointed us in the direction of a simple monument on the right. It was the memorial to 'the martyrs of the Koidanov massacre', as he described them. It had obviously been neglected for many years and was partly obscured by the bushes and tall grass.

'This way!' Erick ordered, and dashing ahead of us, he began to tear away at the foliage.

By the time we reached him, he had managed to clear the debris from around the dedication plaque.

Reading aloud, Galina translated it for us: ' "Here lie sixteen hundred men, women, and children who suffered at the hands of the fascist invaders." '

My father stepped forward with his head bowed. My mother, who stood close behind, passed him three roses which she'd had the foresight to bring with her from the hotel.

We stood quietly as my father placed the roses at the base of the memorial, his mother's gravestone.

As we made our way slowly back to the site of the mass grave, my father stopped and took me to one side.

'This is my village,' he whispered. 'I'm sure of it. But I'm still not certain that I'm a Galperin.'

Then, leaving me with that thought, he took off in pursuit of the others who had reached the base of the hill.

We had been so absorbed in our search, we hadn't noticed the sun come out. It threw off a warm light, so that its presence alleviated some interior chill.

We'd also been oblivious to the attention our visit had attracted. A few yards away a number of children had gathered by a bench, staring at us with both shyness and frank curiosity. One of the boys waved to us, indicating that we were welcome to make use of the bench. He wore a cheeky grin and as we approached to sit down he called out to us, 'Hello, Mister America.'

'Not America,' Galina explained. 'Australia.'

This provoked a wide-eyed response. We must have seemed very exotic. The children began to gather around chanting 'Kangaroo' at us. My mother burst out laughing with pleasure – she loved being around children – and took a seat on the bench, as did my father and Erick. I remained standing and only half-listening to my mother and father as they tried to tell them more about Australia.

I looked around and only then noticed that a handful of people had come out on to the front porches of their houses and were observing us silently. From where I was standing they all appeared to be quite elderly, and my immediate thought was whether any of them had witnessed the massacre. I wondered whether they had been the ones my father had remembered standing on their balconies, laughing and chatting as women and children were led to their death.

I suggested to Galina that she and I walk past these houses. I was not surprised when an elderly man called out to us from where he was seated on his front porch.

We stopped.

Although he must have been at least seventy years old, his face was alert with curiosity. He spoke and Galina translated.

'What are you doing here?'

'I am trying to find out more about what went on in this square during the war,' I said.

'The massacre by the fascists?' He fixed me, with a shrewd assessing gaze. 'Why?' he asked.

'My father's family perished in it,' I answered.

'Jews, were they?'

I nodded.

The man gave a low grunt and shifted the blanket that covered his knees.

'I saw it,' he said, after a silence of several moments. 'I grew up in this house and from here I could see everything. I remember it better than what I ate for lunch today.' He chuckled to himself.

'What happened that day?' I asked.

'It began in the middle of the night. We were woken by the sound of men in the square. Father and I went out on to the porch, as did some of our neighbours. Soldiers and a group of men – about twenty or thirty of them – were there. We couldn't understand what was going on. The soldiers were guarding the men who were digging.

'One of the officers caught sight of us and ordered us back indoors, telling us that we'd be put to work digging as well if we didn't disappear.

'The sound of the digging went on till first light. That's when I sneaked a look through the window.'

He indicated the window behind him.

'I couldn't believe my eyes – there was an enormous gaping hole in the earth where the square had been.'

The man rose unsteadily to his feet and shuffled to the edge of the veranda and closer to us. Slowly he raised his arm and pointed in the direction of the slope we had descended earlier with my father

'They came from there,' he said. 'Women. Children, babies, old people. Jews, they were. Hundreds of them. The queue led all the way back up the hill as far as the eye could see. The babies were wailing and many of the children were in tears. Their mothers were trying to calm them but the soldiers showed no patience. They prodded at the little ones with their bayonets, screaming at them to shut up.'

His finger shifted in the direction of where my parents were still seated on the bench. 'The soldiers pushed and shoved them down there.

'And over there, near the memorial, that's where the officers stood. You can see that it's higher than the square so it gave them a good view over the crowd. They were German, their uniforms were different to those of the soldiers.'

The man paused for a moment.

'At the base of the hill, the Jews were put into groups of about ten or twelve. Soldiers forced them to undress and then lined them up in front of the pit. Then another group of soldiers – with rifles – stepped forward.

'I knew by then why the earth had been dug up and those Jews knew what was going to happen to them. Not a single one of them made any effort to fight back or run away. True, there was nowhere for them to flee in the face of those men and their weapons. But better that than give up the way they did . . . The soldiers raised their rifles and fired into the line so that the people fell backwards into the hole. Sometimes if it didn't fall in the right way, a soldier would step forward and kick a body the rest of the way in.

'They didn't waste their bullets on the babies or children; they simply used the bayonet. A quick sharp lunge and that was the end of that one.'

Throughout his description the man's voice had remained low-key and the expression on his face blank so that it was impossible to tell how this had affected him.

'This was repeated several times,' he continued. 'Like clockwork. A new group was shot and shoved into the pit. Even though you could see that many of the soldiers were drunk, they were efficient. And all the way up that slope the Jews queued in silence, watching what was happening below – to their friends and neighbours, members of their family – and waiting for their turn.'

The man turned away from the open space before him. If it had once been the village square it was now a derelict place used by children unaware of its poisonous history.

'It was then that the strangest thing happened.'

His hand trembled as he raised his arm to the sky.

'Without any warning at all, I swear, the sky turned black and the heavens opened. Not just rain, but a deluge. A flood of such power. In seconds the square turned into a muddy mess. The soldiers and the Jews were drenched and slipping all over the place. The Jews began to panic. I could understand why – I did too from the safety of my house. It was mayhem. I could see the officers giving orders for the soldiers to control the crowd.

'And then the thunder started, and bolts of lightning began striking so close to the ground. It was as if God himself had descended and was going to destroy us all.'

The man crossed himself before continuing. 'Even the soldiers became spooked. Some of the firing squad had put down their rifles. They didn't want to continue with the killings. The commanding officer must've made the decision to stop because, next thing, the Jews were being forced back up the hill and into their houses. Even the ones who were already naked and about to die were forced to dress – they grabbed at any piece of clothing from the pile that had been dumped by the pit from the previous victims – and then ordered up the hill.

'After that I saw the remaining soldiers gather their weapons and packs and head off. They left the pit just as it was: open and piled with bodies, and filling up with water. The rain didn't cease all day, not for a single moment, until nightfall.'

The man paused. In the background, the sound of children laughing and playing in the square could be heard.

'When it was completely dark,' the man said, 'I crept out on to the porch. I stood there for some time. At first I thought it was silent. But soon I detected the sound of movement coming from the pit.

'I was petrified. I ran back inside and told my father who gave me a clip around the head for disobeying the soldiers by going outside. He told me that it was the sound of the dead bodies as they shifted around on top of each other. I'd heard groans too and told my father that some of the people were still alive. But he only laughed. "It's just the ghosts departing from their bodies," he told me. "Leave them alone or they'll take you with them as well."

'That put the fear of God into me. I went to my room and closed the curtains, not even having the courage to look out of the window any more.

'The next morning I was woken early by the sounds of gunshots. I parted the curtain a fraction and peered through. It was the same scene as the day before – the killing had begun again. It must've been going on for some time because the hill was by then half-emptied of Jews. I crawled back into my bed and covered my head so I wouldn't hear the cries and wails that had begun to reach my ears.

'As I lay there I wondered what the Jews had done the previous night. I'd dropped off to sleep despite my fear of the ghosts, but they must have been awake all through the night knowing what was going to happen to them in the morning.'

The man took another break from what he was saying and this time lit a cigarette.

'Just one more thing,' I said.

He looked at me, innocently.

'What did you think about what you saw?' I asked.

He shrugged and rubbed the back of his head. I couldn't tell whether it was out of embarrassment.

'They say not a single Jew survived,' he said with finality.

But it was not an answer to my question.

With this chance meeting and the clarity of his recollections, this man had unwittingly solved a mystery that had fostered doubt in the Oxford professor. It was possible that my father had begun to make the journey down the slope in the company of his mother, holding his little brother's hand, just as he had remembered, only to be turned back by the eerie storm before he faced his own death. And that explained how his mother knew exactly what was in store for herself and her children when the storm was over. She had gathered her young son on to her knee and told him that they would all die the following day, prompting him to flee during the night.

The man had retired to his seat once again and covered his knees with his rug. I thanked him so profusely for speaking with me that he was taken aback.

'Nothing at all,' he replied, still smoking.

He hadn't the slightest inkling about the burden he had lifted from me. Even though I had trusted the general sweep of my father's story, Professor M. had planted in me a tiny seed of doubt.

Galina and I walked back slowly towards the bench. All around us was silent apart from the playful laughter of my parents and Erick as they chatted with the children.

Although it could never be proved beyond dispute, two days in Belarus had already reinforced the truth of what my father had claimed. Later, after I had returned to Oxford, I wrote to the professor who had been most insistent that my father had concocted the incident with his mother. I explained to him what I had learnt 'on the ground' in Koidanov. He never replied.

27

CONNECTIONS

WE were seated in a cafe not far from the site of the extermination where Erick had brought us for a lunch of *plov*, a Russian speciality akin to pilaf. 'My mother never cooked anything like this,' my father said to me, making a sour face. 'I'd never have forgotten it.'

After lunch my father became immersed in conversation with Erick, telling him further details of his story and of his life in Australia. I'd heard these stories many times now and decided to take a walk around the neighbourhood. Within minutes I was surprised to find myself back where the visit to Koidanov had begun – on October Street.

To my right I recognised the house that Erick had insisted was my father's. Then I began to make my way along October Street in the opposite direction. I had gone only a short distance when, unable to resist a *plov*-induced torpor, I located a patch of grass by the side of the road and sat down. I let my eyelids droop shut.

As they lowered, I could just make out the staring face of a *babushka* at a window in the house opposite. I raised my head slightly to look, but caught spying, she snapped the curtains shut.

I must have drifted into a half-sleep momentarily; a sharp cackle and snorts of laughter close to my ear roused me. Still on the ground, I was surrounded by four elderly women, all of whom were wider than they were tall, dressed in headscarves and colourful skirts over trousers. The one who'd cackled in my ear gave me a broad toothless smile, then she eyed me suspiciously. She stretched herself upright and began to chatter with the other *babushkas* who shuffled around me on their heavy feet.

Then she spoke. I didn't understand a single word she'd said.

She spoke again and I could tell that she was repeating herself. Another joined in, saying the same thing.

Then I recognised one of the half dozen words I understood in Russian. 'Foreigner?' she asked.

I looked up, shading my eyes against the sun, and nodded my head vigorously.

'Yes,' I said. 'Foreigner.'

The women clapped their hands together.

'You speak Russian!' one of them exclaimed with delight.

'No,' I laughed, waving my hand in front of me.

Spurred on by the breakthrough, such as it was, I began to explain in English. 'I'm here with my father.'

They looked at me blankly.

'He's looking for his village,' I went on. 'The home he grew up in.'

They exchanged glances with each other and then burst into roars of laughter, shaking their heads at me.

'Papa,' I said, banging my chest. I was fired up now and tried another strategy.

I jumped to my feet and began to mime that I was searching for a house. I held my hand above my eyes, walked over to the fence of a house, and peered intently into its garden. Then, putting on a sad expression, I shook my head, before moving on to the next house and miming the same actions.

The women continued to stare at me, open-jawed, as if I were an alien who had just descended on October Street. I was on the verge of giving up, when all of a sudden, one of them cottoned on.

'House of father?' she asked.

'Yes.' I was delighted. 'Yes.'

The others nodded and made comprehending noises.

'October Street?' another chimed in.

'Yes, yes,' I repeated.

'Name?' Another Russian word I could understand.

The ringleader looked at me shrewdly.

'Which should I try, Galperin or Panok?' I wondered aloud to myself.

One of them immediately picked up on what I had just said.

'Galperin?' she asked. 'Galperin?'

I nodded. 'Galperin house?' I asked pointing in the direction of the house we had seen that morning.

They shook their heads in unison. One of them pointed in the opposite direction, further down a section of the street I'd not yet seen.

I followed the line of her finger but I couldn't see where she was pointing. Good naturedly, she took my hand and led me along the street with the others in tow until, about a dozen houses down, we came to a stop outside a neglected-looking green building.

'Galperin,' she said, pointing.

'Galperin?' I asked.

She nodded firmly, folding her arms.

It might be the house, I thought. There was a driveway that ran along-side the house that matched my father's description. I wanted to know who, if anybody, lived there now. I needed to get a closer look. I tried to explain this to my companions but failed. Then I remembered Galina.

I made a gesture to the women that they should wait for me, and with-out waiting to check whether they understood or not, dashed off in the direction of the cafe.

Everybody was just as I had left them. My father was still involved in an intense conversation with Erick, gesticulating dramatically to make his childhood Russian clear. Neither of them noticed my breathless arrival, and I didn't want to disturb them. Galina was chatting with my mother.

'Can I borrow you for a moment?' I asked Galina.

'Something the matter?' my mother asked, looking up at me.

'Nothing,' I replied, not wanting to build up anyone's hope at this stage.

Galina questioned the women while I waited beside her anxiously.

'They insist that this was the Galperin house from before the war until sometime in the 1970s,' she said excitedly. In her short time with us, Galina had generously become caught up in our search.

'Are they certain about this?' I asked.

Galina turned to the women and asked them again. In response they nodded their heads resolutely.

'Ask them who owns it now.'

'A woman from a nearby village,' came the reply.

One woman was certain that it was a place called Fanipol, about ten miles from Koidanov. She also knew the woman's name.

'Gildenberg,' she said. 'Dina Gildenberg. She's from one of the old Jewish families of Koidanov. She bought the house in . . . when did old Solomon Galperin die? It must have been 1976 . . . no . . . 1975. The son . . . what was his name? Erick, that's right . . . from Minsk sold it to Dina Gildenberg about ten years ago. The house was deserted for years.'

After a moment's pause she added, 'She's in Koidanov now. I've seen her. She does casual work in the canning factory up the road from here . . .'

'I want to meet her now,' I declared. 'Will she be there?'

'Probably. I don't know her,' the woman answered.

It seemed typical of village life that the women knew all about Dina but didn't actually know her.

'Where is the factory,' I demanded.

The women volunteered to lead me there. As we made our way to the factory, they remained in high spirits and fired questions at me about who I was.

At one point, one of them said, 'You're not a Yid then, are you?' only to be hushed by the others.

I answered their questions as best I could, but all the while I was thinking about Erick. Had he led us to the wrong house? Why?

Galina volunteered to enquire after Dina while I stood in a huddle with the women outside the small factory. As the minutes passed they became restless.

There was a mumbled discussion amongst themselves and suddenly they moved off, giving me a cursory wave. I was startled. I didn't know any of their names. I hadn't even thanked them. But before I could even make a move to go after them, they had disappeared into the next street.

Just at that moment Galina reappeared at the factory door accompanied by a woman whose appearance surprised me even more than the *babushkas'* hasty departure. Her resemblance to my father was uncanny. She was stockier but had his kind and jolly expression, his rosy chubby cheeks, and the same intense, watery blue eyes. In the centre of her face was the same slightly bulbous putty nose and impish smile.

It was her persona though, the same inflexion of shyness in her demeanour, that convinced me she had to be related to him.

Galina introduced her to me, and she took my hand. Dina had been allowed to leave the production line for a short time and had agreed to take us back to the house and let us inspect it.

On the way Dina volunteered as much information as she knew about the family history on her side. She explained that her family and the Galperins had intermarried in the previous generation. Her father was Boris Gildenberg, and Boris's younger sister, Hana, had been married to Solomon Galperin. They had lived together in the house on October Street. Dina's aunt was the Hana Galperin Erick had spoken of as my father's mother. That meant Dina and my father were probably first cousins. Confirming the *babushka*'s account, she told us that she had bought the house from Erick who had made the sale in an effort to raise funds to buy a printing press for his business.

Dina's family had been lucky: they'd escaped the Holocaust. Her father and mother moved to Moscow in the late-1930s and Dina had grown up there. She moved to Belarus in the 1980s, after Solomon had passed away. She'd never met him and knew only that his three children had died along with Hana and other family members in the mass killings. Only Solomon had survived the war but Dina had no idea how.

It appeared that Erick had not even told Dina of our existence, let alone our visit. She was not aware that another of the Galperins, her cousin, if my father was that, had survived under incredible circumstances and that she was about to meet him.

'Erick Galperin could tell you much more about the history of the family and the house,' she said.

I remained silent.

We came to a stop outside the house the *babushkas* had led me to, but I wanted to go no further without my father and mother. Galina set off in a hurry to fetch my parents. I told her to say nothing of our discovery. I wanted my father to reach his own conclusions once he had seen the house.

Meanwhile Dina led me to the door at the side of the house. She pulled out a large key and was about to place it in the lock. I gestured for her to stop.

I was reluctant to enter. If this was his home then my father should be the first to enter.

'Father,' I uttered, hoping that Dina would understand.

She must have as she agreed to wait.

Before very long the blue bus pulled up near the gate and my father sprang from it, followed by my mother, Galina and Erick. My father immediately began to appraise the house, all the while gripping the picket fence. Behind him stood Erick, looking decidedly apprehensive and shifting from foot to foot.

I joined them.

'What do you think, Dad?' I asked.

My father raised his hand to quieten me.

'It looks familiar,' he said in a low voice. 'I remember the door being on the side as it is here and this is like the drive where my father used to put his horse and cart.'

'But there should have been a shed on that spot,' he said, pointing at the neighbouring house adjacent to the driveway.

He held his hand to his cheek.

'Why don't we see if the neighbours are in?' I suggested.

I knocked on the door while my father waited at my side.

Within moments an elderly peasant couple appeared.

'Yes?' The man eyed us suspiciously. Then he suddenly noticed Erick standing quietly in the background.

'Erick, hello!' he called out, becoming more friendly.

Erick nodded sheepishly then looked away.

My father ignored the exchange.

'We are trying to find out about the house next door,' he explained. 'Before the war was there something built here, next to the drive?'

'There was a small shed. After the war old Solomon Galperin sold us this piece of land to build on.'

My father shifted away from the house and pointed at the earth. 'It would have been about here,' he said.

'Yes, exactly there.'

My father became more animated. He turned and gazed down the rear garden.

'The apple tree,' he exclaimed. 'There it is.'

He set off down the yard and we followed behind. He stopped below the tree.

'This could be the tree,' he said, looking at each of us. He wore a look of startled pleasure. 'I remember picking apples for my mother. I'd toss them down to her until her apron was overflowing and she'd cry out, "Enough, no more!" '

It was then that I noticed Dina standing shyly halfway between the house and the apple tree. In all the excitement I had forgotten to explain my father's visit to Dina. They had exchanged polite nods, but remained unaware of exactly who the other was.

'Dad!' I called out, joining Dina.

My father walked back up the yard and stood awkwardly, smiling and clutching his case.

'Have you heard the name Ilya Galperin?' I asked Dina.

'No . . .' she replied slowly. 'Is he a member of Erick's family?'

'He was one of Solomon's and Hana's children,' I said. 'Their eldest boy.'

'One of those who perished . . .' Dina began to say.

'No,' my father interrupted. 'He might be alive. I might be Ilya.'

Dina looked bewildered by my father's declaration and he tried to explain why he had come to Koidanov. She looked from my father to me and then to Erick – who had joined us.

'He is Ilya,' Erick said, raising his arm slightly as if introducing my father on stage.

Dina and Erick exchanged words in a language that was not clearly Russian; perhaps it was a Belarussian dialect but it was obvious that there was tension between them, possibly because Erick had not informed her of any of this beforehand.

I stepped in.

'May we see inside the house?' I asked Dina.

The door squeaked open on its rusting hinges. I followed behind my father and mother as they tentatively entered the run-down kitchen, which appeared not even to have running water.

'When I bought this house it was deserted,' Dina said, self-consciously, 'and in even worse condition than it is now.'

We moved deeper into the house, which consisted of two other rooms. Both were bare of furnishings apart from a solitary chair and a small divan.

My father looked around.

'Do you remember this room?' I asked,

'This might have been where I slept . . .'

My father shifted the chair from its position by the window and stood where it had been.

'The bed would've been here,' he said. 'I was lying with my head at this end on the night my father said goodbye to me. The dividing curtain must have been over there. Later I would've seen him leave that way, over there, through the door.'

My father pointed directly at the main door we'd just entered through, visible in the kitchen on the far side of the house. Then he stared up at the ceiling.

'My father's feet would've been dangling just over there.'

I went over to inspect the ceiling. There was evidence of a trapdoor to the roof space that had been boarded up.

My father joined me to inspect it. He noticed something else. 'Look,' he said, pointing off to the right.

There was a row of about a dozen rusted hooks that had been nailed into a ceiling beam.

'Yes,' my father nodded. 'They could've been used to hang a curtain. And when I came to the curtain to eavesdrop on my parents, they were sitting at a table there.' My father pointed in the direction of the kitchen.

Dina, who had been watching and listening intently to my father added that in fact there had been a table there when she'd moved into the house.

'Isn't that correct?' she said, turning to Erick who'd been strangely silent.

'Yes,' he replied uncomfortably.

It seemed as if the layout of the house coincided with my father's memories of it.

'So *this* was the Galperin house,' he said. As if reading my mind at that moment, I heard my father's voice: 'From before the war.'

'Yes,' Erick said.

'I grew up here?'

'Yes.'

'I have another memory,' my father said, 'of a soldier coming into this room. Not a Nazi. A friendly one.'

My father squinted, trying to remember more.

'He was visiting a lady, not my mother, but another who lived with us, I think.'

'That must have been your Aunt Sonya, Solomon's sister,' Erick replied. 'She did live here. She died with the rest of the family. She was engaged to a Russian soldier who was sent to the front. Nobody knew what became of him. He never came looking for Sonya after the war. He must have perished too.'

'Can you think of anything else about the history of the house or the family?' I asked.

Erick shook his head, as did Dina, but suddenly her expression changed. 'One moment. There is something . . .'

She crossed to the divan and began to rummage underneath it.

'I forgot. Last year, some of the floor had to be replaced. The carpenter found it hidden there. I meant to tell you, Erick. Sorry, I forgot.'

We waited expectantly. What did she have there?

She rose with something in her hand. 'These.'

She dusted off a plastic bag and held it aloft.

'Old photos,' she declared. 'I don't know who the people are. You are welcome to look.'

I reached for the bag and sat down on the one chair in the room, removing a handful of photos. I flipped slowly through faded pictures of individual faces and family group portraits. It was difficult to say when these had been taken but they probably pre-dated the war. Judging by their garb, some of the people were Jewish. One particular photograph of a young woman gave me pause. Smiling confidently at the camera, she was in her early twenties and had an attractive and open face. She was dressed up in her finest and may have been off to a special occasion. I had no idea who she was and passed the photograph to my father.

He shook his head.

I returned the photographs to the bag and removed another handful which I began to go through before passing them on to my father.

Suddenly I stopped, transfixed. The photograph I held before me had been partly torn so that its top right corner was missing, but one side of the face of another young woman was still clearly visible.

'It's Krystal,' I gasped. Whoever this woman, staring intently into the camera, was, she was identical to my niece, my brother Andrew's daughter.

My father reached across for the photograph.

I was still dazed but I heard him say, 'Oh my God', and then pass it to my mother who similarly exclaimed, wanting to know what a photograph of her teenage granddaughter was doing amongst these faces from the past.

We were silent, overwhelmed by what we'd just laid eyes upon.

My mother spoke first, clearing her throat. 'The eyes,' she said. 'And the shape of the face. She's so like Krystal, isn't she?'

'Uncanny,' my father replied.

'She must be related to us somehow,' I said. 'Who is she?'

I passed the photograph to Erick. He examined it closely.

'It might be Hana, your mother,' he replied. 'But I'm not certain. I only saw one photograph of her once.' Erick returned the picture to my father.

'Do you remember this face?' my mother asked gently, looking over her husband's shoulder.

'No,' he answered. 'But it's so like Krystal, it must be someone close to me. My mother? I must be Ilya Galperin. I believe it.'

He shook his head.

We were all infected by his sense of astonishment. How could a man with only those two mysterious words – Panok and Koidanov – have found his way home nearly sixty years later, to the room where he had slept as a child in the company of his baby sister and younger brother, to the place where he had been nurtured by his mother and father, before the Nazis tore them apart.

I followed my father and the others as they made their way back up the driveway toward the blue bus.

I stared at my father's back. He was hunched forward, carrying the bag of photographs that Dina had given to him as a gift. Such a gift. He was still shaking his head in amazement.

28

SOLOMON AND VOLODYA

IT was late afternoon, but the day wasn't over for us. Erick wanted us to meet an old, dear friend of Solomon's. Erick rode up front with the driver. He'd been sullen since we'd discovered Solomon and Hana's house at number 12 October Street.

The bus rattled to a halt outside a run-down cottage. Paint was peeling from its walls and the shutters on the windows swung loosely on their hinges.

Erick turned to look at us.

'We are at the house of Volodya Katz,' he said. 'My father's best friend from before the war up until he died.'

Erick was the first out of the bus and waited for us to join him.

'I'm sorry,' he said, 'but Volodya can only meet Alex and Mark, and, of course, Galina to translate.'

'Why can't Patricia come?' my father protested.

'Volodya is uncomfortable with having too many people in his humble surroundings,' Erick explained.

'Don't worry,' my mother said. 'I can take a nap while you're gone.'

We passed through a gap in the fence where a gate had once been, and made our way along a path to the house. Before we'd even reached the front door it opened, and a very elderly woman appeared on the veranda. Beside her, and holding her hand, was an equally aged man with startling blue eyes that seemed to look through us.

He raised his hand in the air and called out: 'Shalom! Ilya Solomonovich!'

'Shalom!' my father responded.

We climbed the steps up to the veranda, where Volodya stood with his arms outstretched. He embraced my father awkwardly. It was then that I realised he was blind.

'Ilya Solomonovich,' Volodya wept at the words. 'Ilya Solomonovich.'

'Yes, yes, that's me,' my father answered, slightly self-consciously. It would take some time for 'Ilya Galperin' to sit comfortably with him.

'This is my son Mark,' he said quickly.

Volodya beckoned me towards him. He gripped me strongly by my shoulders and appeared to take my measure intuitively.

'My wife, Anya,' Volodya said as the woman behind him stepped forward and greeted each of us. Although she was well into her eighties, one could tell that she was someone of character. She still had piercing and decisive eyes – she must have been handsome and charismatic as a young woman. She took my father by one hand and Volodya by the other and guided them into the house while we followed behind.

The room was dark and sparsely furnished with a few shabby pieces. There didn't seem to be any heating apart from a small brick stove. The floor covering was pitted and buckled linoleum. The couple seemed to live only in this room and in the far corner there were two bunk beds made out of wooden planks with thin blankets strewn over them.

The table had been set for a modest tea which Anya served while Volodya began to speak.

'I could not believe my ears,' he said, shaking his head, 'when Erick told me that Solomon's boy had been found alive. In Australia!'

My father smiled.

'You knew my father well?' he asked.

'Your father and I were good friends all our lives. We were the same age. We grew up together in this village. Even after your father married Hana, and I Anya, we remained close. We were always at their house on October Street.'

Anya nodded.

'Your mother was an excellent cook,' she said. 'She could make a feast out of nothing.'

'What was my mother like?' my father asked.

'She was very gentle,' Anya said, wiping her hands on her apron. 'She was young. She must have married your father when she was about sixteen. That was the custom in those days. Solomon was older than her – he must have been about twenty-one. They were a lovely couple and even though a matchmaker had been involved, they cared for each other. You could see it in the way they were when they were together.'

My father leaned forward, hanging on Anya's every word.

'She showered so much love on you and your brother and sister.'

'Do you remember me?' my father asked.

'Of course I do,' Anya replied. 'I used to nurse you when you were a baby. When you got older you loved to sit on my lap. Not as much as you loved to sit on your Aunt Sonya's. You were the apple of her eye. She was your father's sister. A real beauty. She lived with your family. Your mother and Sonya were great friends. They'd known each other all their brief lives too. She'd been planning to get married to a Russian soldier . . .'

My father interrupted, exclaiming: 'I mentioned that before. I have a memory of a man in a uniform.'

'Sergei was his name,' Anya said. 'He was very quick-witted and charming. He'd make us all laugh when he was there. Do you remember Aunt Sonya?'

My father shook his head.

'You don't remember her singing to you?'

'Not at all.'

Anya paused. She'd noticed my father's mood darken at her last comment.

'As you got older you didn't want to sit on my knee any more. You'd wriggle away from me and stand with your hands on your hips, telling me that you had business in the village. You'd make all of us laugh out loud with your antics. You were quite the man about town. Everybody in the village knew you. You'd talk to anyone – the policeman, the baker, anyone. You'd have a word for them all. You were a good boy. You had a kind nature. You were always considerate. Helping the old people in the village, chatting away to them.'

My father shook his head, laughing. He was both moved and embarrassed.

'I had no idea I was such angel.' He pulled a face of mock surprise.

'Oh, but you weren't,' Anya joked. 'You were a rascal too, especially when you were out and about with one of those boys. What was their name?'

She paused.

'Panok,' she said, clapping her hands together. 'Now those boys were trouble. Always up to mischief and trying to involve you.'

'Panok!' my father exclaimed, almost jumping out of his chair in excitement.

'There was one your age. The pair of you were inseparable. You'd have your arms around each other's shoulders as you walked around the village. You both loved playing in the apple tree behind your house.'

'That's right,' my father said. His face was bright red and his blue eyes shone with pleasure and emotion.

'We used to play "pirates" in the apple tree. One of us would climb up to the top and act as a lookout and report on the pirates about to invade our village.'

My father turned to look at me.

'So that was the answer all along,' he said. 'Panok was my best friend. Tell me, do you know what became of him?' My father touched Volodya's arm.

'He perished that day,' Volodya replied. 'With the rest of his family.'

My father sank back into his seat, defeated.

'None of them survived?' he asked.

Volodya shook his head.

The mystery of Panok had been solved and, although he didn't remember it, I realised that my father had probably witnessed the extermination of his dear friend, also only five, on that day.

We sat in silence. Anya poured more coffee.

After some time my father spoke again. 'Do you remember my birthday?' he asked.

'It may have been late in 1935,' Anya answered. 'But I can't say for certain.'

'What about my little brother and sister, do you remember them?'

'Very little. By that time, I was spending more time in Leningrad with my sister who was unwell. I returned to the village occasionally but there were few chances to meet with Solomon and Hana.'

'Do you remember?' Anya asked her husband.

'The little girl . . . no. But the boy was perhaps called David. You were definitely Ilya. Named after your grandfather who was also Ilya. A tradition among we Jews.'

I looked at Volodya and noticed that there were tears in his eyes.

'I miss our village,' he said. 'It was a true *shtetl*. Of course there were the usual fallings-out and scandals, but people looked after each other. That's all gone now.'

Volodya wiped his cheeks. 'When I finally reached home after the war I was told that every single Jewish soul had perished.'

His large bear-like hand reached for Anya's.

'We didn't even know that each other had survived then,' Anya said.

Volodya nodded grimly. 'I'd made my way through the forests to the north-east of Belarus,' he said, 'and when I got back the village was almost deserted. Fortunately this place was still standing but it was in bad condition. I set about repairing it and, one day, when I was on the roof I saw

Anya coming along the path. I rubbed my eyes to make sure I wasn't dreaming. Anya had survived.'

'You are both survivors,' my father said.

'We were fortunate,' Volodya said.

'Anya was in Leningrad with her sister when Belarus was invaded. She stayed there and later joined the partisans.'

'And what about you?' my father asked Volodya.

'I joined the partisans too. Outside Mogilev in the north-east of Belarus.'

'And my father?'

'Your father was a survivor too.'

'My mother told me that my father was dead. Why would she have done that?'

'So that you wouldn't have given the game away,' Volodya replied.

My father gave him a puzzled look, forgetting that the man was blind.

'We – your father and I – didn't want anybody, including you, to know where we were hiding,' Volodya said.

'I don't understand,' my father said.

'Let me start at the beginning,' Volodya said. 'The fascists invaded our country in 1941. There'd been scraps of news and rumours that the Nazis were rounding up the men and boys from the villages and taking them away. We knew what that meant – it was going to be like the old days of the pogroms. None of the Jews in the village knew what to make of it. But we were sure that the elderly, the women and the children would be safe. We knew that if the Nazis came into Koidanov we'd be done for. Some of the other men in the village were also making plans to get away before the Fascists arrived. There was a lot of talk about joining the partisans that were forming in the forests everywhere throughout Belarus. A few men talked about heading further east away from the invaders.'

'In late summer of 1941,' Volodya recalled, 'I visited your parents to discuss the situation. We sat at the table, drinking coffee – like we are now – tense and anxious. I put it to Solomon that we too should think about escaping. He was reluctant.

' "And my family?" your father said. "My children? What about them?"

'I had to convince him of the danger to both of us. "The Germans aren't coming for the women and children," I told your father. "They'll be safe if they keep to themselves." Your father knew the history of the pogroms, after all.

'But he couldn't be convinced that this was the best course of action.

'I had another idea. Anya was already in Leningrad with her sister. I told

Solomon and Hana that I'd hide in the roof of my house but spread the word that I'd joined the partisans.

' "Ridiculous!" Solomon said. "How will you survive up there?"

' "I'll store food and water with me and anything else, then I'd wait until the middle of the night," I told Solomon.

'Suddenly we heard a noise and jumped up. Somebody had been listening to our plans. Do you know who it was?'

My father shook his head.

'You,' Volodya laughed. 'You'd been eavesdropping from behind the curtain. Your mother ordered you back to bed but you didn't want to sleep. You were stubborn, that's for sure.'

'I remember a scene like that. The talk had woken me up. Wait!'

My father stopped abruptly. 'Did you have a beard?'

'That's right!' Volodya burst out laughing. 'Like this,' he added, indicating its large bushy shape. 'What a memory you have!

'Eventually Solomon came around to the idea on the condition that we hid in the roof of 12 October Street instead. That way he could keep an eye on his family. Hana was keen on that – she could fetch anything we needed and let us know when it was safe to come down.

' "If events do not go to plan," Solomon said, "I'll escape – take the family – in the middle of the night."

'We had to be certain that nobody – not you, not even the neighbours – knew where we were. Hana would tell the neighbours that her husband had fled during the night to join the partisans and she had no idea if and when he'd return.

' "We'll have to keep it from Ilya," Solomon said. "He doesn't know how to keep a secret. We must tell him that I am gone . . ." '

'It hurt your father deeply to have to say that.'

'My mother told me that my father was dead,' my father said. He looked perplexed. 'I'm sure of it.'

'You were only a child. Gone must have seemed like dead in those days,' said Anya.

'We decided we would put the plan into action at the right moment,' Volodya continued. 'It was another two months, October 1941, before we did so. The news had reached us that the Fascists were in the region of Koidanov. The remaining able-bodied men began to flee and the streets became more deserted day by day. By the middle of the month, Solomon and I were living in the roof.

'Less than a week later, late one night, Hana told us she'd heard that the fascists would arrive within the next few hours. Solomon and I had had a lot of time to think up in the roof. We weren't as well protected as we should've been, so we'd decided to escape and hide out deep in the forest for a few days, until the fascists had passed. Your mother and Sonya agreed with us.

'One night, when the children were fast asleep, Solomon and I let ourselves down. Your father wanted to see you before we left. He went quietly to your bed and kissed you. You stirred for a moment, calling out "Papa." '

'I remember,' my father said. 'He said "Goodbye", didn't he?'

'Exactly as you say,' Volodya answered.

'Then we made ready to leave. Hana had organised a bag for each of us – filled with food that she'd prepared. I bid farewell to your dear mother and your Aunt Sonya.

' "Come back to us," Hana whispered.

'We promised we would, but in truth we weren't confident. We opened the door just enough to slip through. The last thing we saw were Hana and Sonya's faces, peering at us with worried expressions. Solomon raised his cap to them and whispered "Farewell" one final time. The door closed.'

'I saw you leave,' my father said sombrely. 'I'd woken again. I called to my mother and told her, but she said that I'd been dreaming. That Papa had died.'

Everybody at the table was silent.

'The night was cloudy, which gave us some cover as we left Koidanov,' Volodya continued. 'But your father was still torn. No sooner were we on the outskirts of the forest than he wanted to return to Koidanov. In the end I talked him out of it.

'Over the two days that followed we trudged on. Each night we took a few hours' sleep while the other kept watch. On the third day disaster struck. We'd been going in circles and had ended up within minutes of Koidanov again. We huddled together for some time and then, when it was safe, we headed back into the forest. We'd only been on the move a short while when we heard the sound of repeated gunshots in the distance. Solomon stood upright, frozen to the spot.

' "Get down!" I shouted at him. "In God's name, what are you doing?"

' "I'm going back!" he cried. "There's something wrong."

'I grabbed your father by the arm but he shook me off. "My family is there!" he said.

'Solomon understood that I loved your family too. But I knew that we could not stop whatever was happening back in Koidanov.

' "What good would it do if we were caught?" I argued with him. "We must move forward, wherever that is."

'Solomon went mad. He gripped his head and wailed for what seemed like an eternity. I didn't know how to help him. Suddenly everything went quiet, and a terrible rain began. We were drenched and had to huddle together. It didn't stop all day. By the evening we had to head off – it was too risky.

' "All right," your father said. "What are we waiting for?" He looked defeated. We headed back into the forest.'

The room was deadly quiet. My father stared at his hands resting on the table.

'You know I was there that day?' he said.

'Where?'

'In the village. I saw what happened.'

Both Volodya and Anya seemed too overcome to speak.

'I saw it all. My own family. The others. The killings went on for two days.'

'I cannot imagine,' Anya said softly. 'Our grandson is nine years old. Even a child of that age could not cope. Not even an adult . . . do you want to tell more of this?'

'I too ended up in the forest outside Koidanov on the day of the exterminations,' my father said. 'What if you and my father had passed within reach of me with no idea I was there?'

Anya touched my father's hand.

'We need brandy,' she said.

The fortifying liquor seemed to revive my father.

'Tell me more about what happened to my father and you,' he said to Volodya.

'We were tired and hungry but kept pushing ourselves in the direction of Mogilev in the north-east,' Volodya said. 'Sometimes a farmer shared his food or gave us shelter, but we never stayed more than a single night. We couldn't put anybody else in danger. Germans, Latvian and Lithuanian police battalions were on patrol everywhere.

'We made it to the outskirts of Mogilev. Solomon knew there was a risk but he wanted to get into the town to find out if there was any word of life back in Koidanov. I tried to stop him, but he wouldn't listen.

'That morning he set off for town. I agreed to wait for him until the next morning. If he didn't return by then, I wasn't to wait any longer. The following day came and there was no sign of him. I decided to wait a further night but as another day dawned, I assumed that he'd been captured, that his fate was sealed. I never thought I would see your father again.

'Eventually I met up with a group of partisans. I fought with them in the forests, attacking trains, until the war ended.

'You're kidding!' my father said. 'I used to guard the supply trains. The soldiers would hoist me up on to the carriage roofs where they'd make me shoot into the air with a rifle to frighten off the partisans.'

Volodya shook his head in disbelief.

'Imagine if I'd been shooting at you,' he said.

'Thankfully you missed.' My father laughed darkly.

'Later I was sent to Riga and, after a few happy days there, it was decided that I should again join the soldiers. This time they took me to the Russian front. It was terrible. The humidity was unbearable. And the mosquitoes at night were the worst. We slept in dugouts that were always full of water.'

'When was this?' Anya asked, sitting up in her chair.

'The summer of 1943.'

'Where exactly were you?' Anya asked.

'The Volhov Swamps,' my father said, 'south of Leningrad.'

'This is beyond belief!' Anya interrupted my father. 'I was in the Volhov swamps with the partisans at the same time as you.'

Anya got up and crossed to a shelf.

'See this,' she said, indicating a framed certificate there.

My father and I joined Anya and examined her award.

'For bravery in the war. From Stalin, no less. Before he decided Jewish partisans needed punishment and not reward.'

My father's eyes then moved to a photograph perched on the shelf.

'That's me,' Anya said. 'Taken during the war.'

He picked it up.

Suddenly he gave a very slight start that nobody else seemed to notice. His face went pale.

'You were beautiful,' he said.

Anya laughed, pleased.

We returned to our seats and my father continued with his story.

Evening approached. My father and Volodya jumped from one topic to another as my father greedily devoured what Volodya knew. But there was still more that my father wanted to hear about his father's survival.

'Early one morning,' Volodya began, 'there was a loud knocking at the door. When I opened it, before me was Solomon, dishevelled, dressed in an SS overcoat, haggard but smiling. I couldn't believe my eyes.

'My long lost friend had come home.

' "You are alive!" That was all I could say at first.

' "Believe it! It is me! Flesh and blood!" Solomon laughed.

' "Come in! Come in!" I said. "Some food? Some drink?"

'He had the hunger of a bear. I let him gulp down the food without inter-ruption until he could eat no more. He told me that after we'd separated he had in fact made it into Mogilev. But almost as soon as he entered the town he was stopped by a policeman wanting to see his papers. He had none of course and was arrested. At first he worked in a number of labour camps, until finally he was delivered to Auschwitz. He survived there for over two years. You know what saved him? His skill with leather. He looked after the guards' boots, and for that they kept him alive.

'Much later he was transported to Dachau. He told me he wouldn't have survived there for long. The conditions were even worse than in Auschwitz – but liberation turned out to be only months away. That must've been around the end of April in 1945. The Allies even gave him the chance to emigrate to America. But he wanted to return to Koidanov to see if his fam-ily was still here. Your father then made a journey back from hell. He walked all the way across Europe from Dachau concentration camp in Germany. When he entered Koidanov he'd found his house deserted. He decided then to find me. I had to confirm the awful truth about his family: that all had perished, even you.

'Solomon was exhausted beyond belief, but still he insisted on seeing the mass grave. He went by himself. It was many hours before he returned. For some days after that he never said a word. And then his silence broke, and Solomon returned to us, changed – we all were – but stronger.

'He began a new life but he never forgot his first family.'

Anya reached across and gently took my father's hand.

'Try not to despair,' she said. 'He never forgot you, his little Ilya. What a happy, friendly and good boy you were. You have the same feeling as Solomon.'

'My only inheritance,' my father said sadly.

'No!' Anya sprang to life. 'You have more than that! Your family were good people. You carry that goodness in you. The Nazis took you, but they never touched your goodness. I can see that. Don't ever forget it – you must always keep it close to you.'

My father shifted in his seat, uncomfortable with the vehemence of Anya's emotion. He signalled to me with his eyes that he wanted to leave.

He sighed loudly and looked at his watch. 'We've been here over three hours,' he said feigning surprise. 'We should make a move. Mum'll be wild.'

We made our farewells. Volodya and Anya remained on the veranda, vulnerable and frail, waving as we passed through the gap in the broken fence. I wondered whether we would ever see either of them again. As it turned out, we did not. They both died within months of each other before we had the chance to visit again.

The following evening, our last in Minsk, we found ourselves in Erick's modest apartment in one of the city's inner suburbs. The room was dominated by a very large table laden with food and drink prepared by Erick's delightful wife, Sonya. At one end of the table, Erick showed my father the few photographs he had of Solomon during the post-war years until his death.

'If only I'd spoken sooner,' my father said. 'We might have found each other.'

'You weren't to know,' Erick replied.

'I thought everyone was dead,' my father continued grimly. 'I had nobody to look for. And nobody was looking for me. I was dead to this world.'

'Even if you had spoken, it would have been impossible to find anybody here,' Erick added. 'Can you imagine what Belarus was like under the Soviet system?'

Later, as the evening drew to a close, my father tapped on the side of his glass and rose. All filled their glasses and then quietened.

My father held his glass high. 'I am not a very good toast-giver,' he joked. 'I just want to say that it's been a long way home, but it has been worth it. We have found each other now.'

We raised our glasses in response.

'To the brothers!'

The following morning we waited in the departure lounge for our flight to Riga.

My father leant forward, his hands clasped together.

'You really believe he led us to the wrong house on purpose?' he asked me.

'He must have,' I said impatiently. 'How could he have been confused about where he grew up?'

'But why on earth . . .?'

'All I can think is that he was torn. He wanted you to be Ilya Galperin but if it turned out to be true, then that would make you the eldest son. The house in Koidanov would be yours to inherit. He must have been worried that you would want to claim it after he'd already sold it to Dina Gildenberg.

'He must have thought that the other evidence – the mass grave, the memories of Volodya and Anya – would be enough to convince you even if he showed you the wrong house.'

Erick had not counted on my father having retained memories of his home and village. I hoped that it was the sheer desperation of life in Belarus that had driven him to be so cruel.

The boarding of the flight to Riga was announced, and the three of us made our way wearily to the departure gate.

I quietly observed the profiles of my mother and father as they rested in their seats across the aisle from me. My father must have sensed my gaze because suddenly he opened one eye and, without looking at me, asked, 'When do we get in, Marky?'

'Not long now!' I replied. 'How're you feeling?'

'Worse than yesterday but not as bad as tomorrow!' he laughed.

I got up.

'Some water, Dad?'

'I'll come with you,' he said, following me to the rear of the plane.

We stood together at the water fountain.

'Will you change your name, Dad?' I ventured.

My father raised his eyes to heaven.

'God forbid,' he chuckled. 'To Ilya Solomonovich Galperin? What a mouthful!'

I had something else on my mind.

'Dad,' I ventured, 'what was it that bothered you when you looked at Anya's photograph on the shelf?'

'What do you mean?'

'I saw your reaction,' I persisted.

My father didn't respond immediately. He sipped his water, reflecting on my question.

Then he spoke. 'Do you remember when I was in Volhov, hiding in the tree, when the partisans passed below me?'

I nodded.

'And I caught a glimpse of one of the women and thought I recognised her. Judging from the photograph I saw of her in Koidanov, I now believe that woman was Anya.'

My father returned to his seat.

Moments later, the voice of a stewardess announced our descent into Riga.

29

RIGA

W E made our way through passport control at Riga's gleaming new
international airport, a stylish edifice of glass, Baltic pine and
concrete. While Belarus had paid a high price for its struggle against
Nazism, Latvia, which had welcomed its Nazi occupiers, had now begun to
prosper.

In the taxi on the way to our hotel in the old quarter of Riga, we saw that
the landscape was dominated by enormous billboards advertising Vodafone,
Mercedes Benz, and Kylie Minogue.

'Unbelievable,' I heard my father say, next to me.

He had always described Latvia as grey and cold – a place for dour
Nordic-looking people, whose forests might be inhabited by elves and trolls
and woodsmen. Latvia, I thought, might prefer it if we were to go away,
leaving its past undisturbed, so it could get on with its bright new future.

I woke at dawn, and decided to go for a walk in the old town. I dressed
quietly and slipped out on to the damp cobbled streets that reeked of
powerful antiseptic. I wandered through the narrow lanes and could see
now that I'd misjudged the affluence of the city. In this quarter there were
fewer signs of gentrification: for every renovated shopfront there was also a
run-down or abandoned building.

It was now daylight and there were more people on the street. I turned
into a broad square that had a fountain in its centre. The sound of the water
drew me over to it, and I perched on its edge, taking in the buildings that
formed the perimeter of the square. Opposite me was a relatively new
building, The Museum of the Occupation of Latvia.

In my research of Latvian wartime history and its post-war dealings
with its past, I had soon come across references to the museum. According
to one report the site of the museum was originally occupied by a museum
of Jewish history in Latvia. The Jewish museum had been evicted from the

site and shunted into a single room in a backstreet of the old town. The author argued that this incident symbolised the way the Latvians handled their wartime history: replacing one of the most savage aspects of their recent past with a 'cleansed' version.

Indeed opinions on Latvia's 'complicity' during its period of so-called occupation remain divided. According to some historians, Latvia was not 'occupied'. Many Latvians had 'welcomed' the Nazi visitors, whom they saw as liberators from Soviet oppression. But there was more than political expediency behind this attitude. Some historians argue that Latvia adopted the Nazis' ethos enthusiastically because of its native, often virulent anti-Semitism.

I looked at my watch. It was almost eight o'clock. I hurried back to the hotel.

My father and I had lots of territory to cover on that first day. He wanted to find the flat on Valdemara Street where he had lived with the Dzenis family, and the Laima chocolate factory.

My mother pleaded off, saying that she was content to rest for a while, but I could detect disappointment in her voice. I knew that she felt her exhaustion was disloyal to my father.

We hailed a taxi outside our hotel.

'*Valdemara iela*,' my father told the driver, without giving a house number.

'Don't you remember the exact address?' I asked.

'No. But I would remember the building instantly. Mirdza said that it was number 99. Wherever it is, I'll find it.'

'It's that one,' he said, nodding at a building diagonally across from where we were standing. We crossed the street and stood before the brick and concrete apartment block.

'It's not number 99,' I said.

'But I'm certain this is the one.'

He lingered in front of the building.

'Number 99 must be around here somewhere,' I said. 'Come on.'

We began to make our way slowly along Valdemara Street. My father seemed perplexed and he dawdled, reluctant to move on.

He had taken no more than a dozen or so steps when he stopped abruptly.

'No,' he said firmly. 'Mirdza must've got it wrong.'

Without waiting for me he strode back towards the building we'd just left. I caught up with him outside its entrance.

'This is it,' he insisted. 'Flags flew on either side of the front doors. On one side there was the Nazi flag, on the other the Latvian flag.'

I walked up to the building's facade and examined it. Indeed, there were two metal cups embedded in the brickwork that might have functioned as flagpole holders.

I called my father over to see.

He only nodded a response, then backed away from the building in order to get a view of its upper storeys.

'We lived up there on the top floor. That was my bedroom window,' he said, pointing.

I walked up to the glass doors on the ground floor and strained to get a look inside but the foyer was in complete darkness.

'Come on,' he said brushing past me and pushing open the door. He stepped in ahead of me. The deserted foyer reeked of cat urine.

'The foyer is exactly as I remember it,' he said quietly. 'Of course it was in better condition back then.'

He pointed to the centre of the room. 'There was a stand there with fresh flowers in a vase. It was changed every day by the elderly caretaker. Mrs Impuls was her name. I used to love coming down in the morning when Uncle and I were off to work. As we went downstairs and got to about there' – he pointed to the last of the steps – 'I'd close my eyes for just a second and breathe in the smell of the flowers.'

He gazed up into the darkened stairwell and began to climb the stairs. I could sense his mounting excitement as we reached the third floor. Before we'd even reached the landing, he turned to me, his face beaming, and pointed up at a door on the left.

He knocked but there was no reply. He knocked again and waited. After several moments he reached for the doorknob and began twisting it frantically. The door was locked. He hammered loudly on the door, abandoning all restraint.

'If only I could get inside,' he said.

He thought for a moment.

'I know,' he said, crossing the landing to another door and knocking loudly.

'Hello!' he called out. 'Anybody home?'

'The building is uninhabited, Dad.'

He ignored me and continued to bang on the door. Eventually he gave up, and in an uncharacteristic gesture of disappointment he remained motionless for some time with his head resting against the door.

*

Later that morning we stood opposite a famous landmark to Latvian independence on *Brivibas iela*.

'I want to show you something,' my father said. 'It's this way.'

Once on the street, he picked up speed. Then abruptly he stopped.

'Look!' he said, indicating with a nod of his head.

In the near distance was a small art deco clocktower. Its face was illuminated, as was the lettering down the side of the tower that spelled out 'Laima'.

My father reached the tower and gazed up at it.

'Laima, Laima,' he said affectionately. 'This was a famous meeting spot for everyone in Riga. "I'll meet you at the Laima clock," they'd say.'

'What does "Laima" mean?' I asked.

'Luck,' he answered wryly.

He looked around in all directions.

'Let's get to Laima chocolates,' he said, taking off up the street.

He stopped at a street corner and waved back at me.

'Quickly!' he called out, attracting the attention of passers-by. 'It's down here. *Miera iela*. Peace Street.' Then he hurried on.

I caught up with him further down *Miera iela* where he'd suddenly stopped. Transfixed by the building opposite him, he didn't appear to notice me. It was a factory, and perched on its rooftop was an enormous sign – 'Laima'. He had found it without a moment's hesitation.

'It's been over fifty years,' he said pensively, 'but it's as if it were yesterday. See over there!'

My father pointed across at the entrance, a wooden door adjacent to a row of dusty display windows.

'That's where Uncle was waiting for me when I met him for the first time. I can see him now stepping out of the shadow of the wall and on to the pavement with his hand extended.'

He continued to reminisce in a hushed tone about his time at Laima. I glanced at him, and saw that he was looking in all directions as he spoke, as if he were frightened about being overheard. He seemed acutely conscious of the fact that he'd been in the company of Dzenis and Lobe.

'OK?' I asked, giving him a curious look.

'Let's go around the back,' he said. In a flash, he disappeared around the corner of the building and I found him in front of a tall steel gate topped with barbed wire.

He placed his hand on the gate then leant with his back against it. I was certain he was remembering the deportations from the yard.

'You know now what was going on in there?' I asked him gently, sure of what his answer would be.

His nod was almost imperceptible, as was his simple 'Yes. Those people were Jews transported to an unknown destination where their fate was more or less sealed.'

'Did you understand at that time what was going on, Dad?'

'No,' he answered firmly. 'I must've been only eight years old when this occurred. I'm not trying to excuse myself. I sensed that something was up but I couldn't put my finger on it. It was only later that night when I was alone in my room that it clicked. But then I told myself that Uncle would not let that sort of thing happen. He was a decent man, a fair man. Even now I cannot accept that. I believe he was forced to cooperate. Like me. Did I do wrong to pass chocolates to those poor people?'

We were both silent now. My father pressed his back against the gate as if he could block the passage of the trucks and their unfortunate passengers.

Then all of a sudden he bolted, fleeing in the direction he had come, without a final glance at Laima. I chased after him, calling out for him to wait, but he was already some way down *Miera iela.*

I called after him again. He did not stop or look back. He maintained his frantic pace, keeping his head down as he passed *Annas iela*, where the former quarters of the Latvian SS had been located. Annas Street, such a sweet name for a street of such poison.

I caught up with my father just as he reached the far end of *Miera iela.*

'What's going on?' I asked.

He fought to regain control of his breathing.

I waited until he was ready to speak.

'It's harder than I thought,' he said looking around and avoiding eye contact with me.

I sensed that he was embarrassed by the intensity of his response to seeing Laima again.

'My past is coming back too quickly,' he said in a low voice. 'It's good to find things, but bad to remember. Maybe that's what it is.'

I guided him back to the hotel for some rest.

30

CARNIKAVA

THE following morning my father and I stood on the concourse at Riga railway station.

'This is where I always arrived when I came to Riga,' my father said, 'and that's where the limousine was waiting for us the time Kulis took me to Uncle.'

He pointed at the entrance that we had just passed through.

'I marched across here ahead of Kulis as if I were in command. People passing by stopped and stared at me, a boy of no more than seven or eight by that time, in my uniform with jodhpurs and knee-high polished boots. Some civilians even applauded me and of course soldiers on the concourse saluted me.'

My father beamed broadly to himself, caught up in his recollection.

Suddenly he snapped out of it. 'Come on,' he said. 'We've got to find the train.'

The train would take us to Carnikava, where we hoped to find the Dzenis' *dacha* or holiday house still standing.

My father had only his memory to go by.

'Once we're on the platform of Carnikava station,' he said confidently, 'I'll know the way like the back of my hand. After all, Auntie and I would make the journey from Riga almost every weekend when I was with the Dzenis family.'

While he went to find out train times and buy our tickets, I waited on the concourse. It was nothing like the gleaming airport, its drabness alleviated only by a solitary flower stall.

He soon reappeared waving two tickets in the air.

'I got them *so* cheap,' he said proudly, as if he'd been involved in bargaining for them.

The express was a series of dilapidated carriages drawn by an ancient engine, which at that moment let out a whistle to indicate its imminent departure.

The train began to groan and move slowly forward.

'Hurry!' my father shouted above the din. He grabbed me by the arm and dragged me onboard.

I had dozed off and, on waking, found myself confused about where I was.

I caught sight of my father's face reflected in the windowpane of the train carriage. Whatever he was looking at, judging by the delicate and considered smile on his face, it seemed to give him much pleasure.

Suddenly the reflection of his eyes met mine and instantly I sensed his shyness at having been observed unawares. He gave me a comical and slightly wry look but it was as if a veil had suddenly descended over his true mood.

The couple of hours spent in the train en route to Carnikava were a welcome respite from the hectic schedule of our journey across Europe thus far. I was exhausted, and must have dozed off a second time, for the next thing I recalled hearing at the edge of my consciousness was 'Carnikava' over and over. It turned out to be the conductor's voice echoing loudly over the loudspeaker. It brought me to with a start.

My father was already preparing to leave the carriage. He climbed across me and began to make his way down the aisle, calling back to me to hurry.

After the train ground to a halt I joined him on the deserted platform. Nobody else had disembarked.

'So what do we do now?' I asked, watching the rear of the train as it pulled away. 'Find somebody who can give us directions to the house?'

'What on earth for?' He was astounded by my suggestion. 'I can remember the way.' With that, he tightened his grip on his case and strode confidently towards the station exit.

I hovered beside my father, and quietly watched as, hand held to cheek, he turned in all directions, getting his bearings. Suddenly a cloud seemed to lift as his face broke into a broad smile.

'This was the short cut we always took,' he declared and strode down a narrow track barely discernible in the tall grass. I hurried after him as he disappeared from sight.

Less than a minute later, on a bend in the path, my father had stopped.

'Lost your way already?' I asked.

'Of course not!' he said dismissively. 'Somewhere around here we should come to a fork in the path which joins up again further on. Auntie and I would each take a different path and race to see who'd get to the other end first. Auntie would take off her shoes and count down "Three, two, one!"

Then she'd make a great show of waiting before whispering "Go!" and off I'd run. I always got there ahead of Auntie, who'd arrive breathless from running and laughing. We'd both sit in the grass, trying to get our breath back. Then Auntie would present me with a sweet or a chocolate, usually from Laima. "To the champion Corporal Uldis Kurzemnieks," she'd declare seriously.'

'So even Auntie thought of you as a soldier?' I asked.

He thought for several moments.

'Yes and no,' he said. 'She was always respectful. She didn't make fun of me being a soldier like some people did. As if I was an oddity like a toy soldier.'

'A small boy in an SS uniform would strike most people as pretty odd,' I said. 'Didn't you feel strange yourself?'

'I knew it was an SS uniform but I didn't understand what that meant, I simply thought of it as a soldier's uniform and I was proud of that. But going back to Auntie, I know she also didn't like me in the uniform. On a couple of occasions I overheard her and Uncle discussing it. Auntie said that it wasn't right for a child to wear such a hideous outfit. She said I should be allowed to be a child. I remember from the sound of Uncle's voice that he seemed to agree with her, but he warned her not to say such things in front of other people.'

My father moved on again. Not fifty metres further on he came to an abrupt stop and turned to look at me.

'I told you it was here,' he called out excitedly.

The main path led directly ahead, but branching off to the left was a narrow trail, overgrown with grass and weeds, and barely visible. It looked as if nobody had used it since my father as a young boy.

'Do you want to race me now, Dad?' I joked. In fact I was half-serious about my suggestion. I sensed within him the exuberance of the young boy as he raced along the path and I was keen to share this happy experience with him.

He laughed gleefully but then gently dismissed my idea, saying, 'Nah. Too old for that now, son.'

We found the point where the two paths rejoined, just as he had predicted. He smiled proudly at me, seeming to want recognition or even approval for the veracity of his memory. I did not hesitate.

'Your memory . . .' I said, shaking my head in amazement. My father had kept this path somewhere in his mind for nearly fifty years.

He strode away into the waist-high grass.

A short distance on, he pointed off to the left.

'Beyond that field,' he said, 'is a stream where Auntie sometimes let me play. The Carnikava house is close now.'

He headed off to the right, with me trailing behind, until finally we came out on to an unpaved road.

'The house is over there,' he said, 'behind those trees.'

We passed several seemingly deserted houses and entered a wood. Through the thin wall of trees, a house, drenched in brilliant sunlight, came into view.

'Carnikava!' my father exclaimed.

It stood in the near distance, a squat two-storey edifice guarded by iron gates.

'Carnikava,' he repeated. He moved forward and rattled the gates.

'Locked!' He looked crestfallen.

He was still gripping the bars when suddenly we were startled by a voice from behind us. We both spun around at the same time. An elderly man in overalls stood before us. He was as tiny as a dwarf, and had neither hair nor teeth, judging by his toothless smile.

'What do you want here?' he demanded, a touch imperiously.

'We've come from Australia . . .' my father replied, in his friendly and casual way.

'Is that so?' The man was unimpressed.

'Did you know the people who lived here during the war?' my father asked.

The old man eyed us both suspiciously for a moment, before deciding to continue to speak to us.

'Only by sight. From Riga, they were. There were three daughters. Didn't see much of them. Then the war came.'

'There were no other children?'

The man shook his head. Then something occurred to him. 'No, I'm wrong,' he said. 'There was a boy who suddenly appeared in their midst during the war.' The old man laughed to himself.

'He was quite a sight, getting about in a soldier's uniform. An SS uniform in fact. The family must have had some important connections because many of their guests too were officers from the SS, coming and going in their fancy cars. I've no idea what became of them though . . .'

'They emigrated to Australia,' my father replied.

'That so?' the man said, warily. 'You knew the family?'

My father nodded and then began to pace up and down in front of the barred gates, like a caged tiger, staring in at the house.

'Who owns the place now?' my father asked.

'No idea. It's been empty for years.'

'How can we get in?' My father looked at the man with a pleading expression.

The man rubbed the back of his neck and then walked away from us, indicating that we should follow him.

About a hundred metres along a stone wall we came to a narrow section of fence that had collapsed.

'Welcome to Carnikava!' the old chap cackled.

We climbed through, gingerly navigating a pile of broken rocks. My father glanced at me, and then called back to the man, 'Thank you, sir!'

'For what?' I frowned.

'Not quite sure yet,' he answered.

The house loomed before us, like an enormous frog.

'How did Uncle get this place?' I asked.

'From Lacplesis. A reward for bravery. For fighting for Latvian independence against the Bolsheviks, the Soviet occupiers.'

But my father wasn't even remotely interested at this moment in the history of Latvia.

I remained at some distance from the house and let my father approach it by himself. He circled it cautiously, as if at any moment it might lash out and snatch him in its jaws. When he finally reached its facade he tentatively stretched out his arm until it came to rest on the wall. He stood there silently for several moments, as if communing with the entire house. Then he began to move, one hand still touching the wall of the house, as if he were somehow placating it so that he could safely close in on his memories.

Further along he came to a window placed high in the wall. He pulled a handkerchief from his trouser pocket and began to rub vigorously at the pane but he was unable to break up the thick encrusted dirt. Annoyed, he turned his back on the house and walked away from it.

As he approached me it was not difficult to see the mixture of anxiety and impatience contorting his features.

'How could they let the place get so run-down!' he exclaimed to himself in a disgusted tone. With an almost child-like directness he added petulantly, 'I want to get inside. Where'd that old guy get to? He might be able to show us a secret way.'

The man had disappeared as suddenly as he had first appeared. My father scratched his head, looking in all directions before giving me a bewildered shrug and joining me where I'd now positioned myself – on the steps in front of the building's entrance.

'They used to lock me inside sometimes,' he reminisced. 'It was my fault. I'd be rebellious and try to run away but I'd never get any further than the beach down that track over there.'

He pointed to a path that ran alongside the property.

'I loved the seashore,' my father said, 'as long as I didn't have to go in the water. As I said before, the first time I ever saw the sea was at Carnikava and I was overawed by its power. I'd practise doing handstands in the sand,' he said, taking a seat beside me on the steps.

'Most of all I loved walking along the beach hunting for amber. It used to wash up on the Baltic shoreline like common seashells. I'd collect it in my pockets and, before I'd head back to Carnikava, I'd divide it up. Half in one pocket for Auntie and the other half I'd wrap in my hankie and hide in my other pocket. That half was for my escape. I figured that if I ever got away from the Latvians, I'd have to bribe people – the police and ships' captains and the like – to get me to another country. I always hoped it was America – even though I didn't know where America was. I just thought of it as paradise – sunny and warm with happy smiling people in nice clothes.'

My father looked around for several moments before he spoke again.

'Remember me telling you about the film they made about me?'

I nodded.

'This is the very spot they filmed me playing blind man's buff with the other children,' he said.

He pulled his brown case on to his lap. He clicked open the lock. This time there was no secretiveness, no holding the lid in a partly opened position so that nobody but himself could see inside. His hands fumbled in the morass of papers and photographs and he drew out a tatty, yellowed scrap of paper. It was not even a full sheet and its edges indicated that it had been roughly torn by hand.

'Look!' my father commanded, passing across the scrap.

It was a newspaper article. I handled it gently: it seemed so fragile that it would disintegrate without warning. In the centre of the sheet was an image I recognised. It was my father in uniform, reading a map.

When telling us stories as children my father had held it up a number of times as a prop to whatever he was recounting. But it had always remained firmly in his grip and only ever briefly revealed. This was the first opportunity I'd ever had to scrutinise the photo at some length and I could now discern that he was actually in military uniform. It occurred to me how deftly he had always handled this picture – he had positioned his thumb or one of his fingers over any telltale sign that would give away the truth about his uniform. I was unsettled by my realisation of the effort he had made to keep the truth from the family. What sort of reaction did he fear from us?

'I am certain that this photo is a still taken on the day the film was made here,' he said.

'What newspaper is this from?' I asked.

'*Vanagi*,' he replied. '*The Eagle*. A paper in Riga. It was taken in 1943.'

My father looked around again.

'Over there,' he said, pointing to a small clump of trees about twenty metres away from us. 'That's where it was taken.

'I recall some things from the day of the filming,' he said, reflectively. 'Various people arrived throughout the afternoon. A group of kids about my age appeared on a bus. Later Lobe arrived with an entourage of officers who inspected the grounds of Carnikava.

'Lobe insisted to Auntie that I get back into my uniform. You see, Carnikava was the only place that I was willing to take off my uniform. In the summer I'd spend all day at the seashore and virtually lived in my swimming trunks.

'We were up at around dawn the next morning. I was still sleepy but Auntie dressed me in my uniform, smoothed my hair, and took me down to a room where a crew-member was making the other children ready for the film.

'One group of girls were already dressed in folk costumes and their hair had been plaited with colourful ribbons. They were being looked after by a lady in a white uniform who was giving them bowls of ice cream. At that hour! When she saw me, she came over and offered me a bowl as well. I couldn't believe it! I thought: "This is going to be a great day."

'Then another woman came up to me and began to straighten my uniform. I wriggled about, trying to enjoy my ice cream.

' "Be still!" she said impatiently. "Don't forget you are a soldier! We must make you handsome for the film."

'Then she tried to apply make-up. I squirmed at that and screwed up my face.

' "Soldiers do not use this!" I stamped my foot. "It's for ladies."

'This only caused everybody in the room to laugh at me.

' "Shush with you," she said, playfully, planting a kiss on my forehead.

'I could feel my face turn hot and red with outrage.

' "You don't like my kisses?" she exclaimed.

'Fortunately for me, somebody interrupted us. They were ready to film me. Outside in the morning sunshine the crew were waiting with a camera. The girls rolled their eyes and began giggling when they saw me.

'Everything had been planned, down to the last detail. The director organised our positions around a maypole, telling us to join hands to rehearse our dance.'

'A maypole dance?' I laughed. I simply could not imagine my father dancing.

'I know,' he said, shaking his head in mock disbelief. 'And those girls I had to dance with. They were real little Aryan maidens with terrible, fierce tempers.'

My father screwed up his face as if he were being asked to dance with them this instant.

'One girl complained that she didn't want to be next to me. "The little nuisance", she called me. "I'm not holding hands with any of these awful girls," I said arrogantly. That started the girls off again. "You're not even a real Latvian!" one of them said to me.

'I pinched her,' my father chuckled loudly, 'and all hell broke loose.

'The commander gave me a harsh warning. I settled down quickly.

'After that, I can only recall bits and pieces, because the fun had gone. It was work and, with Commander Lobe hovering threateningly in the background, I just did what I was told.

'They filmed us eating lunch. The girls tormented me again, this time because I couldn't use a knife and fork properly. I showed them up later though when we had to change into our swimming things and play on the beach. I could run faster than any of them, and I was the only one who could do handstands.

My father and I both laughed, but then his mood altered.

'Imagine if we found the film,' he said pensively.

Without another word, he got up and made his way down the steps. He walked directly towards a small copse that had been planted in a semicircle with the opening facing towards the house.

Before he actually reached it, he stopped and nodded his head as if confirming something to himself. Then he headed to one particular tree. He beckoned me with a wave of his hand.

By the time I reached him he was crouched at the base of the tree and patting the grass all around him.

'I'm looking for treasure,' he said with disarming simplicity.

'Treasure,' I repeated. 'What treasure?'

'Buried treasure that Uncle left behind when we fled Latvia.'

He registered my look of disbelief.

'No,' he protested, 'I'm serious.'

'It was in the summer of 1944. He and Auntie had taken me to Carnikava by car for the weekend. Uncle must have sensed that the writing was on the wall for Germany and Latvia, and he began to make plans for our departure.

' "This might be our last visit here," Uncle explained. "We will have to leave many belongings behind. Collect a few of your things that will fit in your case." That's the case I'm holding now. Uncle bought it for me in Riga.

'That first night in Carnikava I was asleep when something woke me. As I came to, I heard a noise coming from outside my bedroom window. I didn't know what to do. In truth, I'd got used to the good life – being safe from the elements – and I thought it might be wolves. But as I sat there on the edge of my bed, I soon realised that it wasn't wolves, it was a digging sound.

'I went over to the window and peeked from behind the curtain. There was enough moonlight and I could just make out the garden. By these trees – literally where we are standing now – I could see two figures moving about. As my eyes got used to the darkness, I saw that it was Auntie and Uncle. Auntie was holding a small lamp close to Uncle, who was digging up the soil.

'I noticed that Uncle had two small sacks at his feet which he then placed into the hole he'd created. I have no inkling as to why, but at that moment Uncle looked up at my window. I backed away quickly but I was sure that he'd caught a glimpse of me.

'I pressed myself against the wall, worried because I knew that I'd just witnessed something that I shouldn't have. I crept back into bed and drew the covers up so that only my eyes and the top of my head were visible. I couldn't sleep. I lay there worried that Uncle would be fierce with me the next morning.

'Downstairs I heard the sound of a door closing and then footsteps as Auntie and Uncle made their way upstairs. They passed by my door but moments later I heard one set of footsteps return and stop outside. I could tell that they were Uncle's. I held my breath, waiting for the handle to turn but he seemed to think better of it and moved on.

'Early the next morning I woke with a start. There was a shadow over me. I let out an unholy scream and tried to spring out of bed. Whoever it was put his hand over my mouth and held me down on the bed. Then I saw that it was Uncle. He put one finger to his lips indicating that I should be quiet, and then he sat down on the edge of the bed. He spoke in a whisper, explaining what he and Auntie had been doing the night before. That he had some gold and silver that he couldn't take with him.

' "You must promise to keep it our secret," he said solemnly. "It's yours. If Auntie and I never return, it's yours. After all this mess is over, come back and get it." Then he got up wearily from the bed. "Get dressed," he said, "and go down for breakfast."

'At the door he stopped and turned. "Don't forget," he said. "It's our secret."

'With that he was gone.

'I think it's still here.' My father frowned intently at the ground. 'Nothing seems to have been disturbed.'

'Uncle didn't come back for it?'

My father shook his head. 'No, he never returned to Latvia. And he never once mentioned the hidden treasure to me again. Not even after we'd emigrated to Australia.'

'He must have told someone else about it,' I suggested. 'And they've collected it.'

'Who would he tell?' my father responded as if my idea was absurd.

'His daughters or grandchildren perhaps?'

'No.' He shook his head vigorously.

'We would've known about that, one way or another. The loot should still be here, below our feet.'

'What happens now?' I asked. 'Do you want to look for it?'

'What, with our bare hands? Don't be stupid. Perhaps we'll come back another time,' my father added.

'When?'

He tried to shrug me off. He began to walk away from me and towards the hole in the fence we had climbed through.

'When are we going to get another chance to go back for it?' I called after him.

'Look,' he said, turning back to me. 'I don't want their gold and silver. It's not mine.'

'Uncle said you should have it.'

'Leave well enough alone, son,' he replied irritably.

'Why don't you want it?' I persisted.

My father turned to face me. 'Because that would mean they'd bought me,' he spat out incensed.

He looked at his watch. 'If we don't hurry, we'll miss the train back to Riga.'

Without waiting for me, he strode to the gap in the fence and on to the unpaved road, where for one moment, he faltered. He seemed to be torn between continuing on his way and turning for one final glance at the house that had now taken on a malevolent presence: there, my father had been used as a propaganda tool – a little mascot for the Reich and its poisonous ambitions.

He did not turn around. Instead, together we began to retrace our steps back to the train station. He quickened his pace, as if in flight now, from Carnikava.

By the time we reached the station my father's mood was calmer and more pensive.

'Who would have thought we'd find Carnikava again?' I ventured, hoping that he'd confide his feelings to me. 'Quite a jackpot!'

'Carnikava was no prize,' he snapped harshly at me.

I was shocked.

I could tell that my father instantly regretted his tone with me.

'Too many memories there,' he said. 'Memories and ghosts.'

'You don't believe in ghosts!' I joked, hoping to return him to a better mood.

'After seeing Carnikava I do,' he hit back. 'The place is full of them.'

The train to Riga pulled in and soon we were safely ensconced within a carriage heading away from Carnikava. He would likely never see his wartime refuge by the sea again. He seemed relieved.

31

THE FILM

IN the months since my father's astonishing revelations in the Cafe Daquise in London, as one of my tasks I had contacted various film archives in Russia, Germany, Latvia and elsewhere. In my communications I'd described the bare details of the film that my father had given me.

Nothing had come of the search. None of the organisations had the film in their archives. At the time I'd kept it from him because I wanted to surprise him if I found it. I didn't want to get his hopes up unnecessarily.

The Latvia State Archive for Audiovisual Document was among those that had responded in the negative, but now that I was actually in Latvia I decided to approach the Archive again. Having just been to Carnikava I knew how meaningful it would be not just for my father, but for all of us, to see the film.

We returned to the hotel from Carnikava just before three, and went our separate ways. My father was keen to return to his room and check on my mother.

I went to my room and placed the call to the Archive immediately. After a brief reminder, Miss Slavits, my contact there, recalled my unusual request. I described to her the new information I'd got from my father that day. I skirted around the issue of my father's SS uniform. I was still uncertain about the depth of Latvian nationalism, particularly in a government institution, and had no idea whether Miss Slavits would willingly locate a film if she knew its potential for controversy. My parents' experiences in Melbourne had taught me that some Latvians did not take kindly to my father's story.

As it turned out, Miss Slavits was willing to assist me provided I could pay the Archive for its time. She warned me that the closing time was five o'clock and that it was already well past three. We were due to leave Riga for London early the next morning, so this would be my only opportunity. I put on my jacket and left the hotel.

The taxi took me to the outskirts of the city where it stopped outside a building. I hurriedly paid him and made my way to the entrance. I cursed. It was a department store. Apparently my garbled instructions had confused the driver. Anxiously I hailed another taxi, and frantically stabbed at the paper on which the address that Miss Slavits had dictated to me was written.

'Yes, yes.' He took off wildly into the traffic.

I looked at my watch. It was now nearly four. I urged the driver to hurry. He floored the accelerator, and the car surged forward as if about to take off into the air.

Within minutes the taxi screeched to a dramatic stop outside a drab concrete building. A sign on the facade indicated that this was the Archive.

I sprinted up the steps that led to the entrance. I quickly glanced again at my watch: 4.15. I tried the door but it was locked. I pushed my face against the glass of the door, and peered inside. At first glance the dark, vast, cavernous space appeared to be deserted. However, as my eyes grew accustomed to the dim lighting I could just make out a bulky silhouette at a desk. It stirred slightly, giving me a start.

I tried the door again. The creature inside did not react.

I tapped on the glass. No response.

I hammered the glass with my fist and the silhouette rose slowly from behind the desk and moved laboriously towards me. I could see now that the person was extremely squat, as wide as he or she was tall. This impression did not alter as the figure reached the other side of the glass barrier. Now I could see that it was an elderly woman, dressed in a para-military uniform. It was her turn to push her face up against the glass pane and to scrutinise me with her filmy eyes.

'Miss Slavits,' I shouted, my face close to hers.

She showed no immediate sign of letting me in. Her eyes sharpened as she appraised me. After several moments she seemed satisfied and opened the door. She began to shuffle slowly back to her desk indicating that I should follow her, which I did. The guard eased herself back into her chair.

'Miss Slavits,' I repeated.

Without even the slightest glance in my direction she thrust the visitor's book and pen under my nose. After a bored cursory glance at my signature and without looking up, she pointed her finger at a door on the far side of the room.

I entered a darkened corridor where I was greeted by a captivating young woman. 'Mr Kurzem?' she said. Miss Slavits's English was gentle and melodic. 'My office is this way.'

We made our way through a maze of dark corridors. As we did so, Miss Slavits told me about three reels of film she'd unearthed since we spoke.

'They were in a dust-covered shoebox at the back of a filing cabinet,' she explained, slightly embarrassed. 'They may have been there for decades. I'm sorry that I did not find them earlier. I haven't seen them yet and there is no description of the contents except for the words "Latvian country-side". That could mean anything but it may be worth looking.' She gave me a sympathetic smile.

'Can we view the footage now?' I asked. In truth I didn't hold out much hope that I would find my father's film. I imagined that much of Latvia's infrastructure had been destroyed by the Nazis as they retreated.

'Certainly,' she replied, and led me to a neighbouring viewing room.

It took several seconds for my eyes to adjust to the brightness of the fluorescent lights. We both donned bright pink dustcoats in a limp gesture towards film preservation and sat down before an archaic Steenbeck footage machine.

'I should warn you that the condition of the films may be very poor,' she said, while turning the lighting down very low and gingerly removing the first reel from the box. She gently loaded the spool onto the machine and began to pump a pedal so the film jerked along frame by frame. For a moment I stared at a blank screen before black-and-white images appeared. The reel's quality had deteriorated considerably, so that I could barely make out the images of soldiers marching across a field. The commentary in German, which seemed to be describing the experiences of German soldiers in Latvia, was largely drowned out by the crackle of static. She let the reel run to its end to be certain.

I shook my head.

'The next one?' she asked.

I nodded. The second reel, too, contained images of German soldiers on patrol in the Latvian countryside. I watched it through to the end. By then a cloud of disappointment had descended upon me.

I sat in silence as Miss Slavits loaded the final reel.

The first images that appeared on screen seemed to be much the same as those on the previous reels – German soldiers marching. I didn't see the point of sitting through more of the same thing. Filled with gloom, I got up and, without waiting for Miss Slavits to turn off the machine, began to remove my dustcoat.

At that precise moment, with my back to the screen, I heard the words of the German narrator – '. . . and now we are outside Riga . . .' I spun around to face the screen, and snapped at Miss Slavits to let the reel continue.

She was taken aback but managed to reverse the footage several frames to where the commentary had begun. This time I saw the images that had accompanied the words. There was Carnikava, shot from its front gate, where my father and I had stood only hours before. It was in much better condition and bathed in sunshine, not a bit ominous.

The German narration continued, accompanied by happy children's music in the background, and the camera cut to a close-up of the steps leading up to the front door. As the voice began to describe the presence of a young soldier at Carnikava, the doors to the house burst open and a throng of children dashed down the steps and into the sunshine. Among them was a boy, no more than eight or nine years old, in uniform. My breath stopped for an instant. I recognised his face immediately. It was my father. He bore a remarkable resemblance to my nephew James: an identical smile and a double cow-lick of hair framing his face.

'It's him,' I said in a hoarse tone.

Miss Slavits stopped the Steenbeck.

'You must sit down,' she said, sounding concerned.

'I'm fine,' I protested, taking a deep breath and easing myself back into my chair. 'I don't want to see any more. My father should see it first. Can I bring him?'

'Now?'

'Of course.'

'We are closing very soon,' she said, looking at her watch. 'I'm sorry. Tomorrow?'

'We're leaving first thing in the morning,' I explained. 'Back to London.'

Miss Slavits was silent for a moment. 'From what I have just seen,' she said slowly, 'your father was a very special boy.'

Her inflexion puzzled me.

I shrugged. 'Can my father come now?' I asked in a bewildered voice, pleading my case.

Miss Slavits considered my request for several moments. Then she nodded her head sympathetically.

'Can I use your telephone?'

'From my office,' she answered. 'This way please.'

The telephone rang in my parents' hotel room. Before I had even begun to explain, my father started on me.

'I've been knocking on your door for the last hour. We've been worried sick,' he said, alarmed. 'Where are you?'

I cut him off. 'Can Mum hold the fort there?'

'What's up?'

'Listen! I want you to write down this address and get here as soon as you can . . .'

'I'm just relaxing with a cup of tea . . .' my father started to grumble.

'Don't argue, Dad,' I said irritably.

'First tell me what's going on,' he said.

I ignored his demand. 'Get a taxi!' I insisted, and then dictated the address.

'I'm on my way,' he said. The line clicked as my father hung up.

I turned to Miss Slavits. 'My father will be here very soon,' I promised her.

I waited in the dark entrance hall. My footsteps echoed as I paced back and forth near the glass doors. About twenty minutes later a taxi swung into the driveway. I watched as my father got out of the car looking disorientated. As he moved towards the entrance he noticed me on the other side of the glass doors. I held it open for him.

'Where are we? Stalin's tomb?' he joked.

'Just follow me, Dad.'

I led my father to the projection room where Miss Slavits was waiting for us. I introduced them.

'You must be very excited,' Miss Slavits said, unaware that I'd revealed nothing to my father.

Suddenly it dawned on him. 'You've found the film?' he exclaimed, his eyes bright with excitement.

Before I could respond, Miss Slavits cut in. 'One moment. You must wear a jacket,' she remembered, going to the closet. When she reappeared with another pink dustcoat, I led my father over to the Steenbeck and positioned his chair directly in front of the screen. With a nod I indicated that she should restart the machine. As the commentary began, I cast a furtive glance at my father. I could just make out his features in the light cast by the glare of the screen. He was spellbound. I turned my attention back to the footage, and on second viewing I was able to absorb more of the images and the commentary in German that described my father as a waif 'rescued' by the Latvian SS.

As the commentary proceeded I watched my father continue his march across the lawn with the other children now following behind – a Jewish boy soldier with a group of Aryan children under his command. Then the footage jumped abruptly to a new scene. My father was now blindfolded and surrounded by the other children: the stooge in a game of blind man's buff. The boy was spun around and around and then left staggering and groping as he tried to catch the perpetrators. And then I noticed something even more unnerving – on the perimeter of the circle of children, I momentarily caught sight of Jekabs Dzenis, smiling benignly at them.

The scene shifted to the seaside, where all the bright happy Aryan children in their swimming costumes frolicked on the beach as if in some German naturist ritual. Amongst them was my father, bare-chested like the others, doing handstands on the sand.

The screen gave another hiccup and revealed an image of the children at dinnertime. The camera focused on my father who struggled to use his knife and fork properly. But the camera did not linger there for very long. Soon it was bedtime and as lullaby music played in the background, the face of a sleepy kitten appeared on-screen. A nurse then appeared and tucked in the sleepy little children. Just as the narrator informed us that all was well in the world for the children, the footage ended abruptly, and the screen went blank.

'That is all. Just over two minutes of footage,' I heard Miss Slavits say.

I continued to stare ahead, relieved that she'd not yet turned on the lights.

What had just been revealed to me seemed somehow too intimate, and I was reluctant to engage with my father.

Then I heard Miss Slavits ask him if he wanted to view it again.

Out of the corner of my eye I saw my father nod his head vigorously.

She rewound the film, and then suddenly we found ourselves back in Carnikava, my father springing down the stairs with his Aryan playmates. When the footage came to an end again we remained seated in the darkness. Nobody said a word.

Miss Slavits spoke first. 'What do you think?' she asked gently, as she turned up the lights.

My father was overcome with emotion and unable to utter a word. I heard him blow his nose.

Then he said, 'Who would have believed it?' After that he lapsed into silence again.

We took leave of Miss Slavits outside the archives. Once our taxi was on the main road into the centre of Riga, my father leant back in his seat. He was exhausted but his body seemed electrified by what he'd just seen.

'It was as I told you, wasn't it?' he said. 'Only a shame that more footage did not survive. Still there was enough to prove I wasn't lying.' My father closed his eyes. I wondered whether he was sleeping or replaying the footage in his mind's eye.

I let him be. I gazed out the window as the taxi made its way past the Independence Monument on *Brivibas iela*. What a mockery the film made of Latvia's flirtation with Nazism. They'd made a Jewish boy into a symbol of racial purity.

I was roused from my thoughts by the sound of my father shouting frantically to the driver to stop. His eyes were bulbous and panicked, as if he were suffocating.

The car screeched to a halt and my father sprang out and on to the pavement. Shocked, I followed him, tossing money for the fare to the driver. On the pavement I gripped my father by the arm and shook him until he gasped as if breath had been knocked violently into him. He jerked away from me.

Passers-by stared at us.

'Dad! Are you all right?' I cried out. 'Speak to me.'

He gave a weak nod. He looked around but seemed unable to take in his surroundings.

'Let's find somewhere to sit down,' I suggested.

On the opposite corner of an intersection I spied a brightly painted cafe. We crossed over to it. Neither of us could have been more surprised at what we found – it was a Jewish cafe with a large blue Star of David painted on its window.

An eager waiter greeted us and guided us to a table by the window. The cafe was empty and had a forlorn atmosphere that was somehow accentuated rather than diminished by its bright blue and yellow interior and the artificial grapevine suspended from the ceiling. The menu listed my father's favourite foods – blinis, latkes and most loved of all, cabbage rolls.

'Have something to eat,' I suggested. 'It'll give you some strength.'

My father shook his head. 'A cup of tea will be fine.'

The waiter had been hovering expectantly.

'Two teas, please,' my father said.

'Nothing to eat?'

'No.'

The waiter's face dropped.

As he went to fetch our tea he snapped his fingers grandly in the air, and from out of nowhere there appeared a violinist who wouldn't have been out of place in a production of *Fiddler on the Roof*. The man looked embarrassed as he burst into a lively tune.

'That music is giving me a headache,' my father said tetchily.

The waiter returned with our tea and my father greedily snatched at his cup. He quickly stirred in three teaspoons of sugar and then took a sip.

'Not enough sugar!' he exclaimed, making a sour face. My father had always had an exceptionally sweet tooth. I watched him add yet more sugar. He took another sip.

'Better?' I asked.

'So, so,' he replied.

My father now seemed less restless, almost contemplative with his hands loosely clasped in front of him. He looked around him.

'It's harder than I thought,' he said, avoiding eye contact for a while.

'I didn't do anything wrong,' he said, looking at me for reassurance. 'But I feel guilty that I ended up on the wrong side with the people who were doing evil to others.'

'You're not guilty of anything,' I insisted, but my words fell on deaf ears.

'Why did they keep me alive?' he said to himself.

'They used you, Dad,' I said, my anger towards these men growing. 'They exploited you for their own purposes. You were a good luck charm . . .' I searched for other words. '. . . a prisoner of war.'

A knot of confused feelings had began to unravel, and he spoke.

'I *was* a prisoner . . . a frightened child . . . but nobody could see the bars around me, except perhaps Commander Lobe. He must've known what he was putting me through. I was a pet that was being trained. There was nothing I could do to change my situation. All the time everybody reminded me of how lucky I was to be alive, and how grateful I should be to Latvia. I always had to show my gratitude to them. I had to do the right thing for them. I always made sure that everybody was happy and pleased with me. What would have happened if I'd disobeyed them? But inside I didn't accept it. I knew that I was not one of them, and I never would be.'

Exhausted, my father fell silent.

The Latvian soldiers had rescued him, but they had stolen him from himself. I thought back to the film and its background of happy children's music, suggesting the life of a mascot was nothing but an innocent game, while off-screen he was constantly terrorised by the threat of death.

My father rose suddenly, telling me to take care of the bill. It seemed that he'd had enough.

EPILOGUE

FOLLOWING my parents' return to Australia I spoke to them regularly by telephone. As far as I could gather they had slipped back into their normal routine.

On one occasion when I spoke with my father, he told me how pleased he was to be home.

'You don't think of Belarus as home?' I asked.

'Of course not!' he replied somewhat indignantly. 'I'm an Aussie.'

With surprising candour he expressed gratitude for his life in Australia, telling me that his early vagabond days there as an elephant boy and a roustabout in a travelling circus, as well as his itinerant existence in the remote outback, had helped him to bury and forget his past. And in spite of his own intensity, or perhaps because of it, my father enjoyed the laid-back ethos of 'she'll be right mate' prized by so many of Australia's inhabitants.

Back in Oxford, as I absorbed the experiences of the past months, I found I had further questions about my father's story as well as recent events. But while I spent hours in pursuit of answers I became increasingly frustrated by dead-ends.

Not long after his return to Melbourne, my father received a letter from Erick Galperin informing him that Anya had died after a short illness and that Volodya, blind and not able to care fully for himself, had been admitted to a state care facility where he had died some months later.

As far as I knew there were no other witnesses who could cast more light on my father's story, and without the elderly couple's reminiscences my desire to learn more about my father's early life and that of his parents was thwarted. Erick continued to claim he knew little of his family's history.

My research into my father's life in Riga and on patrol with the soldiers proved equally frustrating. Though I had my own intuitions, there was so much I wanted to ask Jekabs Dzenis and the other men who had come into contact with my father. How had they felt about the boy soldier and mascot in their midst? Why had they kept him? Were they trying to convince themselves that they hadn't corrupted their own humanity?

But Uncle and Auntie had died, as had Commander Lobe, many years before. And, recently, just as a 'reconciliation' between my father and his stepsister Mirdza seemed possible, she too passed away.

Trying to know more about Jekabs Kulis, the soldier who had taken my father out of the firing line, I traced a family to New York, from where Kulis had written to my father in the 1950s. I tried to make contact by telephone. An elderly woman with a thick European accent picked up the receiver. When I mentioned who I was and what I was seeking I heard her gasp before hastily denying any knowledge of my father.

'We are Czech Jews! Leave us alone!' she cried, before slamming down the telephone.

When I reported this to my father, he appeared resigned and advised me to leave them in peace.

'What point would it serve?' he said. 'Even if it is them, they are probably too old and sick to want to remember me now.'

'The Kulis' have probably never been able to forget you,' I protested.

But my father was adamant. The trail went cold after that. Although nobody has come forward with information I suspect that there are individuals – descendants of soldiers and perhaps old soldiers themselves – in Europe and elsewhere who know something about the little mascot. For whatever reason they remain tight-lipped.

And what of the enigma of Slonim? In the end I learnt from the work of the historian Andrew Ezergailis that the 18th Battalion was in fact stationed in the town of Stol'btsi in Belarus, as we had suspected. Given its proximity – a day's journey from Slonim – it was feasible that the 18th had been there. But I was confronted with a greater problem – I learnt that the presence of the 18th in Belarus at the time of the Slonim massacre is mired in a yet wider controversy. Some historians have claimed that the battalion was there but suggest variable dates for the massacre itself. Whilst some suggest that it was an isolated incident, others have argued that the massacre persisted as a series of incidents that date from the end of 1941 through most of 1942. According to some, even if the battalion was present, extermination duty was not necessarily one of their official duties typically assigned to them. Whatever the truth behind these controversies, we will never know whether my father actually witnessed what happened at Slonim or whether it was one of the many other unnamed massacres he saw the soldiers commit. What remains indisputable is that my father cannot lay to rest his sense of accountability for what he remembers of that day and for what he does not.

And then there are our discoveries from our journey to Belarus. The mystery of the dusty bag of photographs from my father's original home in Koidanov persists. Who are these people whose framed sepia-toned faces stare out at us? Cousins, uncles, nieces, grandparents? It is as if they are pleading to be recognised and remembered. But we can only identify one half-torn image of a young woman, smiling shyly, who just might be Hana Gildenberg, my father's mother.

Sadly, too, the relationship between my father and Erick, his step-brother, has waned. The exact reasons for this estrangement remain obscure. It may be the language barrier: my father's Russian is that of a child. But it has also proved difficult for the two men, one in his late sixties and one in his forties, to overcome the tyranny of distance, physical and historical, that separates them, in order to forge an easy bond.

The situation is not made any easier by the fact that my father often still returns to the question of 'Panok', and again raises the possibility that he might still have been born a Panok and not a Galperin. He does so despite the correlation of his recollections with Volodya's during our day in Koidanov.

Who was Elli, the woman who befriended me in Oxford? She suddenly disappeared without explanation from the city and without a forwarding address. If her father was an Israeli intelligence agent then was he behind the break-in at my parent's home? No valuables were stolen but my father's papers had been ransacked as if the intruder was searching for something specific. Was it the photograph of my father posing with members of the 18th battalion?

Was either Elli or her father connected to the two men who appeared on my parents' doorstep early one morning, claiming to be war-crime investigators? They too had come seeking the photograph of my father with the soldiers: how had they known about it? And why had they refused to give their names to my father?

Every effort I made to find answers to these mysteries left me stranded with only my own intuitions and suspicions. However, the evidence that I did have was sufficient to support my father's version of his childhood, and I wanted public vindication for him.

Somewhat naively I encouraged my father to return to the Holocaust centre in Melbourne armed with new details from our visit to Belarus and Latvia, in the hope that the experience would be a positive one for him. He would now be able to present himself to his interviewers as legitimately Jewish, whatever that meant in this context, and be embraced by them.

It was not to be. Inexplicably the male interviewer had become determinedly set against my father. In a public interview, he stated that my father was not Jewish, that he was not possessed of a Jewish heart, and that my father had never lost his sense of loyalty to the Latvians above all else, and most disturbing of all, he cast doubt on the veracity of my father's story, despite the plethora of evidence we now had. We decided to leave him to his insinuations. In one final push for recognition I turned to the Claims Conference in New York, the organisation primarily responsible for evaluating claims of Holocaust suffering and awarding appropriate 'compensation'. It too declined to recognise my father's experiences in the Holocaust. 'How has your father suffered?' one of their representatives demanded of me. 'Your father was not even in a concentration camp,' she argued indignantly.

Then came its embittering decision to the effect that my father had volunteered for the SS: '. . . since as you stated in your account of events, you joined the 18th Latvian police battalion which in the Summer of 1943 was transformed into an SS Legion.'

After many months of argument, the Conference was eventually forced to overturn its verdict.

In the midst of this struggle my father remained stoic. But as the months passed, I learnt from my mother that his insomnia had returned, fuelled by nightmares from which he awoke disorientated and in a cold sweat. He had none of his usual appetite for food and had lost weight. It seemed that the past and his more recent experiences had worn him down: he could not be placated by the space and the sunshine, the bright optimism of the 'lucky country'.

My mother's health also continued to worry us. Finally a diagnosis was reached. She was suffering from a rare form of cancer that the medical consultants deemed unresponsive to treatment. Her condition fluctuated; for days and weeks on end she would be fine and a stranger would never guess how unwell she actually was.

Then one day in September 2003 I received a call from my father. My mother's health had suddenly deteriorated and she had been admitted to the hospital. He couldn't bring himself to tell me that the prognosis was extremely poor. My mother's sister called me the following morning to tell me to come home as soon as I could.

That evening I caught a plane to Melbourne.

A month later my mother died.

A darkness, not threatening but sad and bewildering, settled over our home. My father had lost his dearest friend and partner.

One evening, sitting in the blanketing gloom of the unlit kitchen, my father and I both succumbed to a lingering sense of guilt which had until then been too painful to broach: we wondered whether in some way his story had contributed to her death.

'Your mother was a practical woman,' my father said, 'and people mistook this for toughness. She wasn't. Your mother was too soft, too kind. She was exhausted by my story. It was too much for her.'

During the weeks that followed, he gradually lost interest in the unanswered questions about his past, telling me that the search didn't seem worth it any more.

'The pieces we have,' he said, 'we'll make do with them.'

Two months later I decided to return to Oxford: we'd rattled around under the same roof for long enough, usually avoiding each other's company – I had an inexpressible anger and grief towards the world that had taken my mother and sensed I was not a person my father wanted to, or should be, around.

The morning of my departure arrived. I didn't know how long it would be until I saw my father again, and I wanted to make a gesture of conciliation. I found him seated at the kitchen table, browsing the morning paper, as was his habit.

'Dad,' I said.

He looked up.

'Fancy a visit to Williamstown?'

'For what?'

I shrugged awkwardly, shifting from foot to foot as if I was an ungainly teenager. 'Coffee, perhaps,' I said. 'Or lunch, or an ice cream. A strawberry one, even.'

For the first time in a long while he smiled. It was at my mention of strawberry ice cream. He was silent for several moments, thinking over my offer.

'OK, son,' he said finally.

Later that morning we found ourselves sitting on the same bench I'd sat on with my mother six years earlier. It had been the morning after she'd seen the videotape of my father's interview and she finally knew what had been bothering her husband so much.

Once again, the dinghies moored just offshore bobbed in the light breeze, the occasional sound of one of their bells punctuating the silence between me and my father.

For some time I'd wondered whether the search we had undertaken had brought us enough in itself – proof that the past had actually unfolded as my father claimed – and the doubters be damned. Still many questions remained unanswered and a resolution seemed elusive. I worried that I'd been naive about the heavy toll memory had taken on my father.

'Has this been worth it?' I asked.

'What would make it worth it? Who knows? I have a name.' My father shrugged. 'And the film clip as well.'

'Now that your mother's gone,' he added gloomily, 'I ask myself that question every day.' He began to shake his head. 'But the truth is my story is all that I have now . . .

'From that single moment when I opened my eyes, and chose to live – without knowing clearly what that even meant – and stepped outside into the darkness, my life took an unimaginable turn. And look where I've ended up sixty years on. The other side of the world!'

My father got up without warning and headed for the shore where for several minutes he watched a black swan walking on the beach. Then he returned to where I'd remained seated, and stood in front of me, obscuring the sunlight and my view of the bay.

'I don't know what I lost,' he said, without prompting. 'How can you know the life you didn't live? I took the chance to survive and I've never railed against that. This is just the way that life turned out for me. Any number of times I could've been exposed or even let myself be discovered, but I made my survival into a companion, and it has stayed by my side, all throughout my life.'

'Would it have been better if you'd never spoken of the past?' I pressed him.

'I honestly don't know, son,' he said slowly.

'Even after sixty years, it unsettled me in a way that I could never have imagined. I thought I was in charge of my life but it wasn't so. How I survived even now dictates my life and all I can do is follow at a safe distance, chained to it. It's as if there are two persons in my body. There is the Alex everybody knows and there's another Alex who was a secret. They'll have to learn to accommodate each other again.'

I had my answers to the questions I had harboured since that day at the Cafe Daquise in London when my father had suddenly become a stranger to me. I believed that now I was closer to an understanding. There was no resolution, no absolution, no closure, no moving on, no getting over it, no pop psychology solution. Only an accommodation of the past. My father had somehow known this all along.

I realised that I too had to find a way of living, comfortably or not, with this, my legacy.

INDEX